Hindu Rulers, Muslim Subjects

ISLAM, RIGHTS, AND THE HISTORY OF KASHMIR

MRIDU RAI

Princeton University Press
Princeton, New Jersey

Published in North and South America and the Philippine Islands by
Princeton University Press, 41 William Street, Princeton, New Jersey 08540

First published by Permanent Black, Delhi, India

Published in the United Kingdom by C. Hurst & Co. (Publishers) Ltd, London

Library of Congress Control Number 2003106173

ISBNs 0-691-11687-3 *cloth* / 0-691-11688-1 *paperback*

www.pupress.princeton.edu

This book was composed in Adobe Garamond

Printed in England

1 3 5 7 9 10 8 6 4 2

For My Parents

Contents

ILLUSTRATIONS

Acknowledgements

I would like to express my gratitude for the assistance I have received from various people and institutions in researching and writing this book.

Since this work has grown out of a dissertation I wrote at Columbia University, I am grateful first of all to my supervisor there, Professor Ayesha Jalal. I thank her for her unflagging encouragement and inspiration. She taught me the importance of speaking from a position of intellectual honesty, particularly on a subject of sensitivity such as this book addresses. I hope it does some justice to that lesson. I am grateful also to Professor Sugata Bose, who has been unstintingly supportive of the project from its earliest hiccups as a rough grant proposal to its present form. My gratitude is owed also to Professors David Armitage, David Cannadine and Leonard Gordon, each of whom I had the privilege of working with and learning from at Columbia University.

My heartfelt thanks to Professor Barbara N. Ramusack who made it possible for me to start on this endeavour in the first place: she shared with me, a treasure trove of her own notes on Kashmir from the India Office Library while I was still only writing a seminar paper in my first year of the graduate programme.

The research for the book was conducted, in large part, in Jammu and Kashmir, and in years when life was, to put it as euphemistically as a friend once did, 'uneasy'. Therefore I cannot emphasize enough that my work would have been simply impossible without the help of friends in the field. My thanks, first of all, to Parvez Dewan, who literally opened up the Jammu and Kashmir Archives for me, consented to holding interminably probing conversations—educated beyond any enquirer's dreams—and provided the hospitality of his home. I thank him for all this and above all for his friendship. In Jammu, I would like to thank Shri Kirpal Singh, a friend and a prince among archivists.

For making possible my first research trip to Srinagar in 1995, I owe my thanks to Mrs. Farida Khan who introduced me to her mother and brother: Mrs. Mohammed Abdulla and Afzal Abdulla. My gratitude to them not only for the comforts of their beautiful home and for the luxury of coming back to stimulating conversation, but also for divine *kahwa* and delectable Kashmiri food. I am equally indebted to Shujaat Bukhari and to Khursheed-ul-Islam for their friendship, good humour, contacts and safe trips across town.

Writing this book has made me more keenly aware of the many friendships, both within and outside the academy, that I have relied on so heavily over the last few years. My heartfelt thanks to Nausheen Anwar, Vijay Dhawan, Suzanne Globetti, Marc Hetherington, Heige Kim, Fred Lee, Nomi Levy, Lara Merlin, Farina Mir, Sanjay Muttoo, Kirsten Olsen, Patrick Rael, Nerina Rustomji, Aradhana Sharma and Tasneem Suhrawardy. I am truly grateful to them for the many necessary moments of hilarity, for lending me their ears as I 'kvetched', and for the funds of inspiration I derived from each of them.

I also thank most sincerely Mahesh Rangarajan not only for volunteering to read a draft of this book but also for offering his many perspicacious and invaluable comments. Many thanks, of course, to Rukun Advani at Permanent Black for trusting in this book and also for the painstaking editing that makes it easier on the eye than it might otherwise be.

I wish to record my gratitude for the help I received from the staff of the following institutions: the National Archives of India, New Delhi; the Nehru Memorial Museum and Library; the Jammu and Kashmir State Archives; the India Office Library and Records. I am indebted to the British Library for permission to reproduce the images that appear in this book.

I thank Columbia University for giving me a Travelling Fellowship for 1994–5 and the Taraknath Das Foundation for providing me with funding with which to finish up writing. I also thank the Freeman Foundation at Bowdoin College for giving me a Summer Fellowship that allowed me to return to Kashmir and Delhi in 2000.

However, none of this would have been possible without the support of my family. My love and thanks to my parents, Rajendra and Rani Rai, and my brother, Animesh, for their encouragement, understanding, indulgences and confidence in me.

Abbreviations

BL   British Library, London

CRR   Crown Representative's Records, Political Department

IOL   India Office Library and Records, London

JKA   Jammu and Kashmir State Archives

NAI   National Archives of India, New Delhi

OER   Old English Records

Introduction

Who has not heard of the Vale of Cashmere;
With its roses the brightest that earth ever gave,
Its temples and grottos and fountains as clear
As the love lighted eyes that hang over their wave?
Oh! to see it at sunset,—when warm o'er the Lake,
Its splendour at parting a summer eve throws,
Like a bride full of blushes when lingering to take
A last look of her mirror at night ere she goes![1]

—Thomas Moore, 'Lalla Rookh'

The idyllic setting of this poem has not been matched by a felicitous history for its inhabitants. One of the most enduring dilemmas for Kashmiris has been that while 'outsiders' have their breath taken by the splendour of the landscape, they evince little interest in its people. Thomas Moore had never actually set eyes on either Kashmir or Kashmiris, but he was quite right: the fame of the beautiful valley had spread well beyond its mountain walls, evoked in countless travelogues and histories, and in the memoirs of vacationing Europeans. His unobserved account slid easily into becoming a banal stock-in-trade; a convenient substitute for thinking assessment—based on actual observation—characteristic of many accounts of Kashmir produced by non-Kashmiris. As a result, despite all the admiration expressed for the natural beauty of Kashmir, Kashmiris themselves seemed invariably to be wanting in their appraisement. Henry Lawrence, agent to the governor-general in Punjab, visiting

[1] The poem was first published in 1817 and Thomas Moore was offered the princely sum of £3150 as an advance for it. Moore read up on the region availing himself of detailed descriptions from colonial historians such as Alexander Dow and travel writers such as François Bernier and George Forster. *The Complete Poems of Sir Thomas Moore* (New York: A.L. Burt, n.d.), pp. viii, 488.

1: 'View of the City and Jummu Musjedd (in Srinuggur)' by J. Needham, after drawings by Mrs H. Clark, 1858, P2441. By permission of the British Library.

Kashmir in 1846, found it easy to see much merit in the French traveller Victor Jacquemont's description of it as 'an ugly picture in a magnificent frame'.[2] A sense of paradise lost and bestowed on the wrong
people became prevalent in European writing. Most travel accounts
opening with the panoramic perspective eventually zoomed in on the
details; the houses, the culture, the society, in short on what the inhabitants had made of their surroundings. Here, and almost invariably, Kashmir and the Kashmiris seemed absurdly mismatched. The
latter were described as lying, 'despicable creature[s]',[3] prone to 'a
whining and cringing manner',[4] who had generally made a mess of the
paradise they had been blessed with. This, in turn, provided the justification for turning the gaze away from Kashmiris and focusing once
more on the landscape of Kashmir, which was God-given and majes-
tic, and for which its people needed to be given no credit.

European travellers were in this respect continuing an older tradition, prevalent since Mughal times, of effacing Kashmiris from depictions of Kashmir. In Mughal mythic geography, the realm of culture
belonged to the city, while Kashmir could at best hope to graduate,
through their intervention, from a wilderness to the nurtured and controlled garden. Kashmir was 'raw' nature to be 'cooked' suitably for
more discriminating Mughlai palates. Therefore, in Mughal miniatures, Kashmir put in an appearance either in the form of manicured
gardens or of scenery glimpsed incidentally through a window in what
was otherwise predominantly the architecture of the Mughal city.
Kashmiris were barely deemed worth the waste of paint.[5] What is clear
from these portrayals is that it has been easier to depict or speak about
Kashmir than Kashmiris.

[2] Extract from a demi-official letter from Lt. Col. H.M. Lawrence to F. Currie
Esquire, dated 9 November 1846, Foreign Secret/Consultation 26 December
1846/nos. 1240–1 & K.W., NAI.

[3] Ibid.

[4] Hon. Mrs C.G. Bruce, *Peeps at Many Lands: Kashmir* (London: A.&C.
Black, Ltd, 1915), pp. 13, 15–16, 33.

[5] This brief discussion of Mughal miniatures depicting Kashmir has been cul-
led from an examination of paintings printed in the following works: Jeremiah
P. Losty, *The Art of the Book in India* (London: The British Library Reference
Division, 1982); Linda York Leach, *Mughal and Other Indian Paintings*, 2 vols
(London: Scorpion Cavendish, 1995); Norah M. Titley, *Miniatures from Persian
Manuscripts* (London: British Museum Publications, 1977).

The treatment of Kashmir as a landscape without people and the converse move by Kashmiris to reinsert themselves into their 'magnificent frame' lie at the heart of this book. At issue is the legitimacy of a political enterprise, begun by the British in 1846, that placed an 'alien' Dogra Hindu ruling house over Kashmir without consideration for the wishes or interests of the vast majority of its people. Of course, the pre-colonial Mughal, Afghan, and Sikh rulers of Kashmir were no more interested in consulting Kashmiris to determine the latter's acquiescence or otherwise in their own rule. However, the Dogra period ushered in a critical break—in terms of a vital change in the nature of arrangements of power inaugurated at the same time as the state of Jammu and Kashmir was founded by the colonial government of India. This shift endowed the individual ruler with a personalized form of sovereignty, erasing earlier traditions of layered authority shared simultaneously by various levels in Kashmiri society. As a result of changes inaugurated at the moment of transition to 'indirect' colonial influence, Kashmiris, the vast majority of whom happened to be Muslim, found themselves unrepresented in an enterprise of Dogra domination without legitimacy. What is surprising is that the erasure of Kashmiris from the enterprise of governing them survived the establishment of a 'national' government in India after independence in 1947. A popular insurgency erupting into violence in 1989 and continuing into the present has prompted some academic re-examination of the Kashmir dilemma.

As a result, a formidable body of scholarship has emerged, produced predominantly by political scientists and journalists, on the question of Kashmir. Written in crisis mode, the bulk of these works has been concerned with the narrow legalistic question of the validity or otherwise of Kashmir's accession to India in 1947. The preoccupation of this literature has largely been with explaining the three wars fought over Kashmir between India and Pakistan since 1947 and culminating, more recently, in a dramatic game of nuclear brinkmanship by the two nation-states. Reviving a venerable tradition of deliberating about Kashmir with Kashmiris left out of the picture, Alastair Lamb suggested that 'At the very heart of the matter . . . [was] the decision made by the Maharaja of Jammu and Kashmir in October 1947 to accede to India. *From this all else has flowed; and its consequences are with us still.*'[6]

---

[6] Alastair Lamb, *Kashmir: A Disputed Legacy, 1846–1990* (Hertingfordbury: Roxford Books, 1991), p. 2. Emphasis mine.

He also noted that 'until the key issues of 1947 [were] resolved it [was] more than probable that the Kashmir dispute [would] continue to damage seriously the health of the bodies politic of both India and Pakistan.'[7] Pitched at the national levels, Indian and Pakistani, what is patently missing in this study is any consideration of Kashmir and Kashmiris.

Lamb's work is merely one in an entire academic genre that has made only a token gesture at examining the colonial past in Kashmir and, consequently, has ended up demarcating 1947 as an obvious point of departure. Comprehending the 'Kashmir problem' in this approach, albeit with significant internal variations, is reduced to isolating structural factors, all external to Kashmir, that have impeded the state's full integration with India.[8] Explanations are sought, on the one hand, in the post-1947 foreign policies of the Indian and Pakistani states. On the other hand, scholars examining the domestic policies of the Indian state see the Kashmir dilemma as merely the result of unsuccessful or unwise deal-making with pro-accession political parties and personnel in the valley since 1947, regardless of their (un-)representative character. The reluctance to draw links with prior history, beyond a perfunctory recounting of events in the two decades immediately preceding partition/independence in 1947, leads even such erudite authors to overdramatize late-twentieth-century developments in Kashmir.

A recent work by Sumit Ganguly is concerned, in more qualified and historicized ways, with explaining the emergence of the present-day popular insurgency in the valley since 1989. It suggests that this was the result of a profoundly paradoxical exercise engaged in by the Indian state since 1947. The effort was, on the one hand, to entice the Muslims of Kashmir into fuller integration into the (Hindu majority-dominated) Indian nation-state by providing them with every opportunity for full political education and mobilization, while, on the other—because of the threat of potentially separatist inclinations

---

[7] Ibid.

[8] See M.J. Akbar, *Beyond the Vale* (New Delhi: Viking, 1991); Ajit Bhattacharjea, *Kashmir: The Wounded Valley* (New Delhi: UBSPD, 1994); Tavleen Singh, *Kashmir: A Tragedy of Errors* (New Delhi: Viking, 1995); *Perspectives on Kashmir: The Roots of Conflict in South Asia*, ed. Raju Thomas (Boulder: Westview, 1992); Prem Shankar Jha, *Kashmir, 1947* (Bombay: Oxford University Press, 1996).

emerging from such training and the resultant political participation in Kashmir—to stem such trends by muffling the institutions that engendered popular political functioning. The result of these contradictory agendas of the Indian centre was an almost purposeful 'institutional decay' in Kashmir that left no path, other than violence, through which a 'sophisticated' and essentially democratically-educated new generation could either fulfil their aspirations or even express their discontent.[9] While there is little to disagree with in this analysis of the situation prevailing post-1947, still, one cannot but marvel at Kashmiri endurance of such prolonged deprivation. There is nothing new in the thwarting of Kashmiri political mobilization and hopes by an unresponsive government, whether Dogra or Indian: this has characterized the history of the valley for the better part of a century now.

Ganguly's study also raises the important issue of why Kashmiri 'mobilization [took] place along ethnoreligious lines'. He answers his question along four lines, all of which, even if each is qualified in its own way, suggests that 'ethnoreligious' mobilization in Kashmir was the result of a failure of secular politics.[10] Not only does this view take for granted the secular–religious dichotomy—the latter half of the hyphenated dilemma filling the space vacated by the former—it also assumes perhaps unconsciously that 'secularism', as defined by the strand of Congress-dominated nationalism that came to power in Delhi in 1947, had a predestined normative trajectory in Kashmir. That it went off track is read unquestioningly, even if not by Ganguly specifically, as an aberration of the region's history. Once again, this is a view that can be sustained only by an analysis that ignores the pre-1947 past of political mobilization in Kashmir. In as early as the 1930s, overt Kashmiri Muslim resistance was levelled against a Dogra state that had publicly declared and made manifest its Hindu-ness at the same time as it identified its subjects by their religious affiliations. Given the nature of this state, a religious sensibility informing political mobilization by its subjects should not be surprising. However, in fairness to Ganguly, this aspect of Kashmiri mobilization is not a central part of his analysis.

[9] Sumit Ganguly, *The Crisis in Kashmir: Portents of War, Hopes of Peace* (Washington, DC: Cambridge University Press and the Woodrow Wilson Center Press, 1998).
[10] Ibid., pp. 39–42.

Of the corpus of works on Kashmir produced by political scientists, Sumantra Bose's is explicitly concerned with and sensitive to the religious dimension in the recent movement for independence in the valley.[11] He draws our attention to the fact that 'Islamic consciousness' had '*always* been a prominent and integral component, along with other political ideals and forms of identity, of Kashmiri nationalism and its democratic struggles.'[12] However, aside from the fact that the use of the terms 'democratic' and 'nationalism' is ahistorical in any context other than the more recent present, his analysis needs nuancing on two counts.

First, Bose suggests that the 'upsurge of 1931' was to a significant degree 'the revolt of the politicised elements of a subjugated *Muslim* population against a Hindu autocrat, bureaucracy and military.'[13] A mere statement of the difference in the religious affiliations of a ruling hierarchy from those of a subjugated population barely skims the surface of the problem. After all, the Indian subcontinent witnessed nearly seven hundred years of rule by TurkicIslamic groups based in Delhi, similarly separated by their faith from a preponderant non-Muslim subject population. Yet, 'Muslim' rule in India was characterized as much by processes of religious accommodation as by tendencies of religiously informed strife. In the resistance against Hindu rulers by Muslim subjects in Kashmir, what was new was not the discovery of religious identities but the transformation, in the period of colonialism, of the political space in which these affinities came to be articulated. In relation to the Dogra state, specifically, a fundamental distinction to bear in mind is not simply that it entailed rule by Hindus but that it had become a Hindu state.

Second, Bose contends that in the present context mosques have emerged as 'focal point[s] of popular mobilisation' because of the 'total absence of any alternative channels of collective action and protest.'[14] The causality suggested by him is open to question. If, as he argued earlier, an Islamic sensibility was always part of Kashmiri Muslim 'democratic' struggles, then the use of the mosque or Sufi shrine would similarly have always been integral to political mobilization,

[11] Sumantra Bose, *The Challenge in Kashmir: Self-Determination and a Just Peace* (New Delhi and London: Sage and Thousand Oaks, 1997).
[12] Ibid., p. 86. Emphasis in the original.
[13] Ibid. Emphasis in the original.
[14] Ibid., p. 88.

regardless of the availability or otherwise of 'democratic' channels of protest. Inserting history into Bose's otherwise astute analysis reveals that the first half of the twentieth century in Kashmir was marked by acrimonious battles fought between rival groups of Muslims to ride a new political wave through the control of various mosques and shrines.

Probing the role of religion in mobilization for material interests in Kashmir requires, at the same time, the clear demarcation of the nature of the religious references made by Kashmiri Muslims. Were these indeed, as Bose's study also asks, the acts of Muslim zealots sabotaging Indian secularism,[15] or rather the language employed by a vast majority of Muslim subjects waging a struggle against a denial of their basic rights by a 'Hindu sovereignty'? As C.A. Bayly has argued more recently in the context of pre-colonial India, while 'religious community might have salience, even the potential to create division', there were also 'other identities and ideologies which have been in contention with it'. As he puts it further, 'it was the binding force of unevenly developing and differently expressed regional patriotisms and the political discourse of good government . . . that provided the main resistance to those forces in pre-colonial India which stressed the exclusive bonds of the religious community.'[16] If so, we are left with the question of why the protest of a regional people in Kashmir adopted a religious idiom. This book argues that what was patently different in the princely state of Jammu and Kashmir was not only the very recent formation of the state in which a regional patriotism binding its subjects had little salience, but also that the 'discourse of good government' involved only a select group of its subjects.

---

[15] The sociologist T.N. Madan proposes that although the 'militant secessionism of Kashmiri Muslims is more inspired by religious and ethnic (Muslim-Kashmiri) considerations than by pure Islamic fundamentalism, the influence of the latter . . . is not absent.' He suggests further that 'whatever is judged to be the character of Kashmiri separatism, it is perfectly clear that it is against pan-Indian secular nationalism.' He concludes, therefore, that 'it is not going to be easy . . . to accommodate Kashmiri nationalism within the Indian state without imposing a very severe strain upon Indian secularism.' T.N. Madan, *Modern Myths, Locked Minds* (Delhi: Oxford University Press, 1997), pp. 258–9.

[16] C.A. Bayly, *Origins of Nationality in South Asia* (Delhi: Oxford University Press, 1998), pp. 44–5.

Hindu traditions of kingship portrayed a world without a king as a realm of chaos, a time when the weak were left at the mercy of the tyrannically strong. Islamic doctrine and political philosophy, on the other hand, acknowledged the coexistence of three levels of sovereignty: the divine, the spiritual and the temporal. However, this philosophy had also pronounced that, in the interests of proper temporal governance, even a despotic ruler was preferable to a world without a ruler.[17] It must, therefore, be a measure of the lack of recourse available to Kashmiri Muslims from a Hindu king that at the moment of their most dire need they turned to the divine or spiritual realms rather than to the state. Thus, during floods that ravaged the valley in 1893, although 'men were dancing and weeping in their ruined fields and in all directions there was wailing and despair', yet Kashmiris told 'marvellous' tales of the 'efficiency of the flags of saints which had been . . . taken from the shrines *as a last resort*.[18] The invocation of religion by Kashmiri Muslims in the period between 1846 and 1947 suggests a positive cultural and religious affiliation, quite as much as attempts flowing from material concerns to rectify a sense of religiously based discrimination perpetrated by a Hindu state.

A question that needs addressing, then, is how the Dogras were able to maintain dominance over a majority of their subjects in conditions that seemed, otherwise, to spell political suicide. How, in other words, was a project of power without legitimacy sustained relatively undisturbed for the better part of a century? No homogenization of the Kashmiri Muslim community and its experience is implied here. There was indeed a minority of the valley's Muslim élite that was cultivated by even a Dogra-Hindu state otherwise oblivious to culling legitimacy from the Kashmiri society over which it ruled. Another group, even more critically sought after by the Dogras, consisted of the Hindu minority of the valley known as the Kashmiri Pandits. Forming at best a mere 5 per cent of the population of Kashmir, this community exerted influence out of all proportion to its numbers. However, the availability of collaborators only partially answers the question of how

[17] Ayesha Jalal, *Self and Sovereignty: Individual and Community in South Asian Islam since 1850* (Delhi: Oxford University Press, 2001).

[18] Report from Mr W.R. Lawrence on the recent flood in Kashmir, Foreign Department (External A), January 1894, Proceedings nos. 360–2, NAI. Emphasis mine.

Dogra rule was supported, especially since these groups stood significantly discredited in the anti-Dogra movement that erupted in Kashmir in the 1930s.

Understanding the staying power of such a state, as also the predicament of Kashmiris, requires an analysis of the Dogra state as a princely state in the context of colonial India. Princely India was formed out of a series of treaties signed—some voluntarily and some coerced—with Indian rulers. Some of these princes were of antique lineage and some created as the East India Company marched gradually but inexorably into Indian territory between the late eighteenth and the early nineteenth centuries. By the 1850s, a Company strapped for cash had taken to annexing many of these states. In 1858, the aftermath of a mutiny/rebellion that nearly succeeded in overthrowing a hundred years of colonial rule in India called for some pause and reflection on colonial policy towards the princes. Policies of outright annexation were abandoned as the crown took over from the Company, and princes were incorporated into the imperial framework as collaborators and junior partners. This was a political milieu, moreover, in which princely states enjoyed the protection of a paramount colonial power and a queen who had, most articulately in 1858, pledged to 'respect the rights, dignity and honour of the native princes as [her] own.'

India's princes, governing until 1947 some 600 or so states of varying sizes, have been made familiar through a series of mostly non-historical works detailing their amorous peccadilloes, peculiar sexual preferences, sadistic tendencies, profligacy, financial extravagance, and general irresponsibility.[19] These depictions have created the impression of a collection of largely (some literally large) irrelevant, if colourful, political figures whiling away their time in irrelevant pursuits. An examination of the state of Jammu and Kashmir, incorporating a territory larger than France, reveals that the princes of India were far from immaterial to the politics of colonial India.

In 1876 the Dogra ruler Ranbir Singh (*r.*1856–85) is reported to have asked William Digby, a severe critic of British imperial policies,[20]

[19] See, for instance, Khalid Latif Gauba, *His Highness: Or the Pathology of Princes*, revised 10th edition (Ludhiana: Kalyani Publishers, 1971); Diwan Jarmani Dass, *Maharaja: Lives and Loves and Intrigues of Indian Princes* (Delhi: Hind Pocket Book, 1970); John Lord, *The Maharajas* (London: Hutchinson, 1972).

[20] In the 1870s, William Digby had served as the secretary of the Madras Famine Relief Committee and, in that capacity, become known as a critic of the

the following peculiarly phrased question: 'Sahib, what do you call that little thing between the railway carriages? It is like a button stuck on a sort of gigantic needle . . . and when the carriages are pushed at one end or the other . . . bang they go against the poor little button. I felt sorry for this poor little button, but it is doubtless useful in its own way.' Upon being informed that the button was called a buffer, Ranbir Singh exclaimed that that described him precisely and turning to his prime minister, Diwan Kirpa Ram, he insisted that it be recorded as 'one of [his] titles'.[21] Not all of India's princes, and least of all the Dogras, were impervious to the changing politics of the world surrounding them. Fully aware of their critical location between 'the big train of the British possessions', the 'shaky concern of Afghanistan' and the 'ponderous train and engine called Roos [Russia]',[22] the Dogras knew that even a 'button' could derive substantial political advantages from the paramount British power.

Given this context, the argument for a hollowing of the crowns of all Indian rulers under colonial rule requires a re-examination.[23] It is true that the removal of the right to wage war, an essential prerogative of Indian sovereignty appropriated in perpetuity by the colonial state, ensured that the 'circle of kings' would remain forever static. Sovereignty in pre-colonial India had been conceptualized in the form of an unending series of overlapping polities in which the primary political exercise was one of winning over people rather than territory.[24] Wars,

---

Madras government for its passivity in the famine of the 1870s. In 1899, his services as a publicist were engaged by certain pro-Dogra elements in the Jammu and Kashmir state in order to lobby British parliament against the colonial government's decision to deprive Maharaja Pratap Singh of his right to govern.

[21] William Digby, *Condemned Unheard: The Government of India and H.H. the Maharaja of Kashmir* (New Delhi: Asian Educational Services, first pub. London, 1890, repr. 1994), p. 8.

[22] Ibid.

[23] This is an argument made most forcefully by Nicholas B. Dirks who, examining the 'little kingdom' of Pudukkottai in southern India, suggests that colonial rule had reduced Hindu kingship to empty and ineffectual pageantry and kingly polity to a 'theatre state'. Nicholas B. Dirks, *The Hollow Crown: Ethnohistory of an Indian Kingdom* (Ann Arbor: University of Michigan Press, 1996).

[24] Andre Wink, *Land and Sovereignty in India: Agrarian Society and Politics under the Eighteenth Century Maratha Swarajya* (Cambridge: Cambridge University Press, 1986).

'invasions' and 'conquests' had been used as a last resort, when allegiances could not be won otherwise. But what this arrangement ensured was that both the content and the boundaries of sovereignties were kept nebulous and in constant flux. However, the territorial delimitation of sovereignty by the British marked a radical change in the political terrain of India. Insofar as the maharajas' relations with the paramount power and *vis à vis* each other were concerned, they were indeed reduced to 'parodic theatres'[25] of extravagant pageantry and a meaningless competition for ranks and titles devised by and handed down by the colonial government. Yet relations between the rulers and ruled were transformed at the same time and decidedly weighted in favour of the former to a degree unique in Indian history.

The testimony of Kashmir, from the middle of the nineteenth century, contradicts the evidence provided by Dirks for Pudukkottai. While these divergences may simply reflect differences in the historical experience of individual princely states, what they certainly make clear is that the Pudukkottai perspective cannot provide a generalizable model with which to understand the impact of colonialism in princely India.[26] Dirks' study while admirably overturning older conceptions of pre-colonial Hindu states subsumed by religion, overstates the case in contending that it was colonial India which prompted the hollowing of the crown by enabling the dominance of Brahman over king. Dirks builds his argument on the evidence of an increasing bureaucratization of the realm of worship under colonial inducement in Pudukkottai. 'Codified terms of service' regulating the distribution of honours at temples and presided over by Brahman bureaucrats 'displace[d] the older politics', so that the 'Raja no longer arbitrated disputes, and was no longer at the center of political relationships that had once determined hierarchies of status and authority.'[27]

---

[25] Dirks, p. xxv.

[26] This is a claim that Dirks seems to be making. Thus, he writes that his 'book is about the relationship between the Indian state and Indian society in the old regime, and the transformation of this relationship under British colonialism, when the crown finally did become hollow.' Further, he argues that while his study will have to be 'qualified by the fact that [he is] not looking at large transregional states, [yet his] perspective is one that will reveal the complex and integral interrelations of political processes which ultimately culminated in larger kingdoms . . .' Ibid., p. 5.

[27] Ibid., p. 383.

The state of Jammu and Kashmir also witnessed a bureaucratization of the Hindu religious domain. Unlike Pudukkottai, the process here was initiated by and controlled by the maharaja. It was precisely under the aegis of colonial rule that the Dogras established an almost perfect fit between the sway of Hindu religious practice—over which they presided as the chief patrons—and the borders of the political dominion they commanded as maharajas. There was no hollowing of the crown here. In fact, such incontestable control over the Hindu religious domain allowed the Dogras to ride roughshod over the interests and rights of the vast majority of their Kashmiri Muslim subjects.

This calls into question a historiography which suggests an unboundedly interventionist colonial state. This book asserts in contrast that the colonial enterprise recognized layers of Indian society that it could not penetrate, even if it could influence these from the outside. This external position did not make the colonial state's influence any less burdensome, but in such instances colonialism relied very much on the acquiescence of indigenous groups when asserting its position as sovereign. In this particular instance, among the partners—even if unequal ones—of colonialism were the Dogra rulers.

Brought to the fore, once again, is the question of the legitimacy of a state in which a Hindu ruler who was explicitly rather than incidentally Hindu governed a numerically preponderant subject population which was explicitly and not incidentally Muslim. The colonial state was sensitive to the fact that the installation of the Dogras as the new rulers in Kashmir in 1846 would have to be accompanied by some legitimizing device if it was not to appear as an act of brute force. The question of locating these sources of legitimacy is then a critical one and is addressed by this book.

Works such as those by Dirks have sought to make light of the notion of 'indirect rule' in princely India calling it a 'farce' which disguised the grave reality that the 'tentacles of [British rule] were powerful and far-reaching'.[28] Michael Fisher's book on the same subject makes clear that this *modus* of colonial rule was not without its fairly direct means of interference within Indian states through the system of Residents who were perceived as the governor-general's 'personal representative[s] to an Indian ruler'.[29] Yet, as Fisher suggests,

[28] Ibid., pp. xxv, 359.

[29] Michael H. Fisher, *Indirect Rule in India: Residents and the Residency System, 1764–1858* (Delhi: Oxford University Press, 1998), p. 433.

moments of crisis, such as the rise of nationalism in British India in the late nineteenth century, quite as often led to a revision of imperial policies towards princely India. At these times the colonial state acknowledged its need for the princes as important partners in the imperial enterprise and so reverted to permitting them a great deal of internal autonomy.[30] It is significant that the state of Jammu and Kashmir, formed in 1846, did not have a Resident imposed on it until as late as 1885. And even then, although the Resident did indeed become an instrument of colonial interference within the state, there was always a significant lag between the colonial state's 'orders' and their interpretation by the Dogra rulers. Indirect rule, in other words, still provided princely states with substantial leeway to determine their relations with their subjects.

However, this book does not posit a framework suggesting an overbearing exercise of power that left Kashmiri Muslim subjects with no room for manoeuvre. The late nineteenth century saw an insertion into the political vocabulary of Kashmir, spurred in no small measure by the colonial government, of the notion of the obligations of rulers and, conversely, the rights of subjects. In the 1930s a potent movement of political mobilization, led most prominently by the All Jammu and Kashmir Muslim (later National) Conference, took full advantage of the narrow space for 'public' discourse created by the Dogra state under such colonial prompting. This movement consistently displayed an acute religious sensibility, even as it alluded to a wider regional identity bridging the communitarian divide. While it is true that Kashmiri Pandits and Muslims shared many links of common cultural practice and overlapping religious beliefs, this did not prevent them from seeing their political interests as widely divergent. This was largely the result of Dogra patterns of legitimation, which allowed the Hindus of Kashmir to exclude Muslims in the contest for the symbolic, political and economic resources of the state. Therefore, by placing Kashmir within the framework of competing and shifting claims based on location in the regional social structure, the present book seeks to avoid the all-too-common error of reifying religion. Religion cannot be studied in isolation if we are to make any worthwhile sense of the twentieth-century history of Kashmiri Muslim mobilization.

[30] Ibid., pp. 441–54.

Given these theoretical interests, my time-frame extends from 1846, when Dogra rule over Kashmir was first established, to 1947 when the princely state of Jammu and Kashmir was finally dismantled in the process of decolonization in the Indian subcontinent. While the broad structure adopted is chronological, a thematic framework intrudes when relevant. Conceptually, three levels of relationship will be explored: between the Dogra rulers and the colonial state; between the rulers and the ruled within Kashmir; and interactions between different segments of the subject population in Kashmir.

The first chapter probes the transformations in pre-colonial sovereignty accompanying the formation of the princely state of Jammu and Kashmir in 1846. The implications of British attempts to territorialize sovereignty for the relations between the new rulers and their Kashmiri subjects are analysed in the period roughly coterminous with the reign of the first Dogra maharaja, Gulab Singh (1846–56). The result, leaving Kashmiri Muslims unprotected in a state in the making of which they had no say, is also addressed. The concluding section of this chapter traces the combined efforts of the English East India Company and the Dogras to seek a measure of legitimacy to rule for the latter by associating them with the Rajputs of India.

The second chapter develops further the theme of the Dogra search for legitimacy. It investigates how this process was consolidated during the reign of Maharaja Ranbir Singh (1856–85), when the concept of 'Dogras as Rajputs' was broadened to define them also as Hindu rulers. This analysis is set within the context of the relations between princely India and the British crown, which took over from the East India Company in the aftermath of the mutiny/rebellion of 1857. It illustrates how the paramount British power, seeking fresh grounds to buttress the legitimacy of a new phase of colonial rule in India, did so partially in the name of preserving traditional Indian rule represented by India's princes and by investing the latter with religious identities. The crux of the chapter is to highlight how, taking full advantage of this, Maharaja Ranbir Singh presided over the evolution of a novel political form in India—namely a Hindu sovereignty marked by an unprecedented degree of control by the ruler over a territorialized domain of religion and religious patronage.

The period covered by the third chapter corresponds broadly with the reign of Maharaja Pratap Singh (1885–1925). It begins by taking into account a fundamental transformation, beginning in the closing decades of the nineteenth century, in the expectations of the colonial state from its princely allies more generally, and the Dogra rulers more specifically. By insisting that princes acknowledge their obligations to their subjects, regardless of their religious affiliations, subjects were simultaneously endowed with rights and entitled to expect the fulfilment of these. This chapter examines the result of these conceptual innovations, specially since they went against the grain of the earlier framework of legitimation installed by the Dogras and the British.

The objective of the fourth chapter is to present a case study, so to speak, of the functioning of a 'public' department in the state of Jammu and Kashmir. It does so with a view to understanding how, despite the insertion of the new language of the obligations of rulers and the rights of subjects, its vocabulary was unable to override the religious identification of either. By focusing on the archaeological enterprise of preserving historical monuments imposed by the colonial state on the Dogra rulers, it demonstrates the capacity of India's princes to recast aspects of the colonial project to serve their own purpose. At the same time, the chapter explores the ways in which a seemingly innocuous undertaking—such as the archaeological venture—was appropriated by Kashmiri Muslims to wage a struggle against the Dogra state in the name of a denial of rights, and by deploying a resoundingly religious rhetoric.

The fifth and last chapter straddles, as does the previous one, the reigns of Pratap Singh as well as of the last Dogra ruler of Kashmir, Maharaja Hari Singh (1925–47). The principal theme which it delves into is the nature of political mobilization in the valley of Kashmir, beginning in the late nineteenth century and leading up to the moment of the dissolution of Dogra sovereignty in 1947. Through a contextualized account, it scrutinizes the political and cultural deployment of a Kashmiri regional identity, encapsulated in the term 'Kashmiriyat', purportedly overriding religious divisions. It attempts to demonstrate that far from effacing religious differences, Kashmiriyat worked successfully only when such distinctions were acknowledged and such recognition became the basis of accommodation.

To sum up, by focusing on the themes of sovereignty, legitimacy and rights, this book aims at understanding how and why religion and politics became inextricably intertwined in defining and expressing the protest of Kashmiri Muslims against their rulers, whether Dogra or, after 1947, Indian.

CHAPTER 1

Territorializing Sovereignty
The Dilemmas of Control
and Collaboration

Their fields, their crops, their streams
Even the peasants in the vale
They sold, they sold all, alas!
How cheap was the sale.

—Muhammad Iqbal[1]

. . . in no portion of the treaty made with Gulab Singh was the
slightest provision made for the just or humane government of
the people of Cashmere and others upon whom we forced a
government which they detested.

—Robert Thorp[2]

O n 16 March 1846, a treaty conjured into existence the princely state of Jammu and Kashmir in the northern reaches of
the Indian subcontinent. The only fully consenting parties in
this act of creation were the English East India Company and Gulab
Singh, raja of Jammu. Disparate territories stripped by the Company
from the Sikh kingdom of Punjab were cobbled together to bring into
being this state.[3] While the realignment of territorial frontiers to create new dominions was far from unfamiliar in India, the consequences
of this particular act in Kashmir were to resonate for a long time after.

[1] Muhammad Iqbal, cited in Bawa Satinder Singh, *The Jammu Fox* (New
Delhi: Heritage Publishers, 1988), p. 221, fn 115.
[2] Robert Thorp, *Cashmere Misgovernment* (Calcutta: Wyman Bros., 1868),
p. 54.
[3] Including Jammu, Kashmir, Ladakh, Hunza, Nagar and Gilgit.

2: Maharaja Gulab Singh. Add.Or.707.
By permission of the British Library.

Over the following century, this treaty would be frequently revisited and condemnation of it heard from different quarters of Kashmiri society. Indeed the above lines by Muhammad Iqbal, among the most famous expatriate sons of Kashmir, might well have inspired the denunciation of the treaty as a 'sale deed', rallying Kashmiris in 1946 into a final round of uncompromising opposition to their princely rulers. Given this less than propitious history, it is remarkable that such a dominion was established at all, let alone that it lasted for as long as a century and a year. How then did the state of Jammu and Kashmir, so awkwardly constructed and so little accepted, come about?

Gulab Singh: From Raja to Maharaja

Events in the Punjab and the role played by Gulab Singh in their context are critical to explaining the founding of the state of Jammu and Kashmir. After the death in 1839 of Maharaja Ranjit Singh (*r.*1790–1839), the builder of the powerful Sikh kingdom, the court in Lahore spiralled into a period of factional infighting.[4] These circumstances not only provided Gulab Singh with his opportunity for intervention, but also drew the attention of the East India Company, whose territorial control in India had been expanding steadily since the middle of the eighteenth century. During his lifetime, Ranjit Singh and the Company had both found it mutually convenient to rein in their expansionism. Through a treaty of 'perpetual friendship' signed on 25 April 1809, they settled upon the river Sutlej as the frontier separating Lahore's influence from the Company's dominions.[5] This status quo

[4] A detailed history of the Sikh kingdom and the precise circumstances of both its rise to prominence and its decline has been covered in detail by a number of monographs. See, among others, Andrew J. Major, *Return to Empire: Punjab under the Sikhs and British in the mid-nineteenth century* (New Delhi: Sterling Publishers, 1996); Khushwant Singh, *A History of the Sikhs*, 2 vols (Princeton: Princeton University Press, 1963–6); J.S. Grewal, *The Sikhs of the Punjab* (Cambridge: Cambridge University Press, 1990).

[5] In as early as 1803, Ranjit Singh had proposed an arrangement to the East India Company, whereby territories south of the river Sutlej would pass to the Company in return for a 'mutual defence' pact against their 'respective enemies'. For Ranjit Singh the 'enemies' included the Holkars of the Maratha confederacy and various Sikh chiefs in the cis-Sutlej area. While this offer was rejected then, by 1808 there was a convergence of interests between the Sikhs of the cis-Sutlej, increasingly under threat from Ranjit Singh, and the Company 'fear[ing] . . . a

was jeopardized after 1839, when the Company viewed with concern the growing political confusion at the Sikh court. Not only could such instability endanger the delicate frontier between India and Afghanistan, but the Company felt the threat particularly keenly in the context of its balance-of-power strategies that saw a stable frontier in north-western India as the only guarantee against the ever-looming threat of Russian advance.[6] This was a signal for the British to intervene in Punjab and led, in 1845, to the first Anglo-Sikh war. In these hostilities the British alliance with Gulab Singh, an ambitious Dogra[7] chieftain at the court of Ranjit Singh, was of capital importance in turning the tide against the Sikhs. In pinning its strategies on Gulab Singh, the East India Company had not randomly chosen the first aspirant to power at Lahore to come its way. Who, then, was this chief who would be king?

While his chroniclers, as is their wont, inflated the nobility and antiquity of Gulab Singh's pedigree once he had been made Maharaja of Jammu and Kashmir,[8] they failed in the process to do full justice to the individual ingenuity, determination and enterprise that enabled his rise to prominence.[9] Although certainly not of the hoi polloi, Gulab Singh descended only collaterally from the more prominent

---

French invasion of India'. The result was the Treaty of Lahore of 25 April 1809. C.U. Aitchison, *A Collection of Treaties, Engagements and Sunnuds* (Calcutta: Foreign Office Press, 1876), vol. VI, pp. 14-16, 22; J. D. Cunningham, *A History of the Sikhs* (Calcutta: Bangabasi Press, 1904), pp. 202–3.

[6] C.A. Bayly, *Indian Society and the Making of the British Empire* (Cambridge: Cambridge University Press, 1993), pp. 126–8.

[7] The Dogras, broadly stated, are a linguistic group found primarily in the Jammu region. Their language, Dogri, shares many similarities with Punjabi. Although the Dogras also counted Muslims among their members, a later section in this chapter elaborates on the increasing association made between the Dogras and the Rajputs from the early nineteenth century onwards. Chapter Two elaborates on the further process of conceptually equating the categories Dogra Rajput and Hindu.

[8] See particularly, Ganeshdas Badehra, *Rajdarshini*, tr. Sukhdev Singh Charak (Jammu: Jay Kay Book House, 1991), and Diwan Kirpa Ram, *Gulabnama*, tr. Sukhdev Singh Charak (New Delhi: Light and Life, 1977).

[9] For a classic modern biography of Gulab Singh, see K.M. Panikkar, *The Founding of the Kashmir State: A Biography of Maharajah Gulab Singh* (London: George Allen and Unwin, 1930, repr. 1953). For a more comprehensive work on the subject, see Bawa Satinder Singh, *The Jammu Fox*.

Dogra chieftains who had consolidated their hold in the Jammu region in the eighteenth century. The most outstanding of these, Ranjit Dev, who ruled Jammu as its raja from 1750 to 1781, was the brother of Gulab's great-grandfather Surat Singh. Ranjit Dev emerged in the wake of the decentralizing Mughal empire to extend his control in the territories surrounding Jammu. He also allied himself shrewdly with the ascending power of the Afghans under Ahmed Shah Abdali to have his sovereignty confirmed in the area. But the line descended from Surat Singh did not share in these glories and the two branches of the family followed different and sometimes conflicting political trajectories. After the death of Abdali, in 1773, and the loosening of the Afghan hold over Punjab, a number of rival Sikh military confederacies[10] came to dominate the region. Ranjit Dev had to contend with attacks from the confederacies[11] but it was under his son, Brij Raj Dev (*r.*1782–7), that Jammu felt the full brunt of the expanding power of the Sikhs and was forced into a tributary relationship. The Dogra kingdom consolidated by Ranjit Dev had been fragmented once again.[12] Although unfortunate for Ranjit Dev's descendants, these same circumstances provided Gulab Singh's grandfather and father with the opportunity to improve their standing by estabilishing their hold over a few petty estates in the region.[13] While this territorial legacy was modest, Gulab Singh also inherited from his forbears aspirations of raising the prestige of his family by rebuilding a kingdom, centred in Jammu, that would command the hill region.[14]

However, at the time of Gulab Singh's birth (1792), the political landscape of the Punjab had changed once more. By 1790 there was a maharaja in Lahore. Ranjit Singh of the Sukerchakia confederacy had emerged as the most powerful figure of the region by undercutting the other confederacies and balancing the authority of Sikh religious

[10] The word used by the Sikhs is *misl,* which translates roughly as confederacy or brotherhood.

[11] In fact, in 1770, in the wake of an attack by one of the most powerful of the confederacies, the Bhangis, Ranjit Dev had to pay a tribute of Rs 30,000 to parry future threats. Sukhdev Singh Charak, *A Short History of Jammu Raj* (Pathankot and Jammu: Ajaya Prakashan, 1985), pp. 118–19.

[12] Sukhdev Singh Charak, *A Short History of Jammu Raj,* pp.132–8; and Shahamat Ali, *The Sikhs and Afghans* (London: John Murray, 1847), pp. 82–7.

[13] States such as Dyman and Andarwah.

[14] Bawa Satinder Singh, p. 4.

figures and magnates through the recruitment of new men of talent. Having strengthened and modernized his army, he sought to enlarge the resource base of his government through further territorial expansion. Since moving south of the Sutlej would bring him into direct conflict with the British, he turned his attention to the hills and, by 1808, had invaded and incorporated Jammu into the Sikh kingdom. While this foiled Gulab Singh's ambitions in his home province, he benefited from the eighteenth-century ethos that enabled militarily resourceful and intrepid individuals to find gainful employment within what were still loosely bounded state systems. By 1809 the seventeen-year-old Gulab Singh decided, therefore, that his best chances lay with the Sikhs. Within a few years of his recruitment into the Sikh army, he caught the attention of the Sikh maharaja himself. Thus began a partnership that brought extensive benefits both to Gulab Singh and his overlord.

It was mainly through his prowess on the battlefield that Gulab Singh rose in the ranks of the Sikh hierarchy. His ascent was so phenomenal that, by 1831, this sometime non-entity came to be described by Victor Jacquemont, the French naturalist and traveller, as 'the greatest lord in the Punjab', second only to the Sikh maharaja. Jacquemont even suggested that the Dogra chief was 'better obeyed at a distance than Runjeet Singh'.[15] Gulab Singh made his mark through his valiant contributions to a first, but ineffectual, expedition to Afghan-controlled Kashmir in 1813 and the invasion of Multan in 1818. In 1819 he put down, on behalf of the Lahore Maharaja, a revolt in the Jammu hills led by the 'robber' Mian Dido and distinguished himself in the second—and this time successful—Sikh expedition to Kashmir. In the 1820s he was dispatched to the Jammu hills where he engineered the dismantling of the petty chieftaincies of Rajauri, Bhimber, Basohli and Kishtwar. His various successes earned him promotion from soldier to jagirdar[16] with lands assigned to him both

[15] Victor Jacquemont, *Letters From India*, 2 vols (London: Edward Churton, 1834), vol. 2, pp. 1, 166.

[16] A jagirdar was the holder of a non-alienable land revenue assignment. His responsibilities included the preservation of law and order in the territory assigned to him as jagir; collection of revenue on behalf of his overlord from that particular territory, keeping a cut of it as remuneration for his services and the maintenance of himself and his troops; and also the provision of loyalty, more broadly, and armed cavalrymen for the overlord's military campaigns, more specifically.

in the vicinity of Jammu and in the Punjab. Finally, in 1822 he was made raja of Jammu with the signal honour of having his Sikh over-lord travel personally to Akhnur (Jammu province) to preside over the coronation.[17] His brothers Dhian Singh and Suchet Singh and his nephew Hira Singh advanced simultaneously, receiving prestigious appointments at court and numerous jagirs.[18] In 1828 Dhian Singh was, in fact, made prime minister and conferred the title of *Raja-e-Rajgan* (the Raja of Rajas) by Ranjit Singh.[19] His son Hira Singh, lauded frequently for his beauty and described as the 'handsomest man in the East',[20] was a particular favourite of the Lahore maharaja. Ranjit Singh, it is reported, could not bear to be parted from him for long and Hira Singh alone was allowed to sit before him on a chair while other courtiers either stood or took less exalted places on the floor.[21] By all accounts, Surat Singh's descendants, the Jammu or Dogra rajas as they came to be known, had arrived and together become a remarkably pro-minent force at the Lahore court.

But then Maharaja Ranjit Singh died in June 1839. The various so-cial cleavages in the Sikh kingdom caused by his policies of inducting new recruits into the army and the ranks of the nobility now came out in the open.[22] The inauguration of Punjab's new maharaja, Kharak Singh, did not lead immediately to the dispossession of the Dogra rajas. Dhian Singh continued as wazir for a few years but court intri-gues finally caught up with him in 1843, when he was assassinated at the hands of the Sandhawalia faction at the Lahore durbar. Thereafter, the dissolution of the power of the Jammu rajas at Lahore was as rapid as their rise had been spectacular. In March 1844 Suchet Singh died in a military engagement with his nephew, Hira Singh, who had be-come the new wazir at Lahore. They had had a falling out on the ques-tion of who should rightly have succeeded Dhian Singh as minister.

---

[17] Diwan Kirpa Ram, *Gulabnama*, pp. 67–8, 75–6, 83–5, 90–1, 95–7, 104–10, 115.

[18] Lepel H. Griffin, *Punjab Chiefs* (Lahore: C.F. Massey, 1890), p. 323.

[19] Syad Muhammad Latif, *History of the Punjab From the Remotest Antiquity to the Present Time* (Lahore: Progressive Books, 1891, repr. 1984), p. 440.

[20] C. Hardinge, *Viscount Hardinge* (Oxford: Oxford University Press, 1891), p. 71.

[21] Latif, *History of the Punjab*, p. 440.

[22] Bayly, *Indian Society and the Making of the British Empire*, p. 127.

After Suchet's death, there was a parting of ways also between Gulab Singh and Hira Singh. The two had been increasingly locked in a contest for power and control at Lahore and Hira Singh, in collusion with various groups at Lahore, had gone so far as to threaten an invasion of Jammu. Following the death of Ranjit Singh, then, Gulab Singh could no longer rely on the external source of the Sikhs as a *point d'appui*. It was at this time that Gulab Singh, increasingly marginalized at Lahore, made his first, but at the time fruitless, offer of an alliance against the Sikhs to the East India Company. Clearly, he had begun to prepare himself to play a quite different role in the unfolding history of the Punjab and Kashmir. Finally, the split between the Sikh army and Hira Singh led to the latter's elimination in December 1844, leaving Gulab Singh as the only surviving member of the Dogra foursome that had wielded such influence at Lahore.[23]

In the mean time, the Company continued to note with growing anxiety the activities of various rival factions and the plunge of the Lahore court into 'intrigue, debauchery, and riot'.[24] In neighbouring Afghanistan Dost Mohammad, who had engaged in efforts at centralization and military strengthening in the manner of Ranjit Singh, was emir. Never entirely well disposed towards the British, he had even sought alliances with Persia and Russia in the past. Therefore, it was scarcely surprising that instability at Lahore should have triggered British Russophobia and that the need to arrest a Sikh slide into 'anarchy' should have become imperative. It was in these circumstances that the governor-general, Henry Hardinge, gave the go-ahead for the first Anglo-Sikh war in 1845.

While the Sikhs were finally defeated at the battle of Sobraon on 10 February 1846, the British victory proved pyrrhic. The Company realized quickly that a complete subsumption of the Sikh kingdom required greater military thrust and more abundant financial resources than it could then muster.[25] At the time, not only would acquiring the volatile frontier with the Afghans have proven the proverbial albatross, but so too would have the inheritance of other parts of the expansive kingdom that Ranjit Singh had consolidated. For, the legacy of

[23] Bawa Satinder Singh, pp. 54–5, 60, 64–72.

[24] Hardinge, *Viscount Hardinge*, p. 70.

[25] Ibid., pp. 132–3. The power of Lahore was finally dismantled only in 1849 when the former Sikh kingdom passed into British Indian territory.

Punjab included direct control over mountainous territories like Kashmir, difficult to defend and precariously close to the Russian empire. These various considerations led the British, in 1846, to pursue the more limited aim of maintaining the Sikh kingdom but under their firm supervision and in considerably diminished form. The most expedient way of achieving the latter goal was by breaking up the territorial integrity of Ranjit Singh's domains.[26] This would also allow the defence of more onerous areas to be passed on to reliable allies willing to undertake the task. Among these Gulab Singh stood out particularly prominently; he had rendered invaluable service to the Company by remaining neutral during the Anglo-Sikh hostilities.

The diverse but related objectives of the East India Company were achieved through two interlinked treaties signed in 1846. The first was the Treaty of Lahore of 9 March 1846 between the British and the Sikhs. It continued Dalip Singh, a son of the late Ranjit Singh, as maharaja on the Lahore throne under British protection.[27] Earlier, in February, the Sikhs had also been asked to pay one and a half crore rupees to the Company as indemnity for the costs of a war they were held entirely responsible for having provoked by breaching the treaty of friendship the British had signed with Ranjit Singh in 1809. Dalip Singh's inability to pay this compensation was to be made good by his ceding 'in perpetual sovereignty . . . all his forts, territories, rights and interests, in the hill countries . . . between the rivers Beas and Indus, including the provinces of Cashmere and Hazarah' to the British government.[28] Included as Article IV of the Lahore treaty, this demand also provided, quite literally, the opening for the second treaty, the Treaty of Amritsar signed on 16 March 1846 with Gulab Singh. Article I of the latter transferred 'forever in independent possession to [him] and the heirs male of his body, all the hilly or mountainous country . . . eastward of the River Indus and westward of the River Ravee . . . being part of the territories ceded to the British Government by the Lahore state, according to the provisions of Article IV of the Treaty of Lahore.'[29] In return for this bountiful yield of territory, including Kashmir, which he now controlled as maharaja, Gulab

[26] Hardinge, pp. 123–4, 133.
[27] Aitchison, pp. 38–9.
[28] Ibid.
[29] Ibid., pp. 165–6.

Singh agreed to pay the British government the sum of Rs 75 lakhs (half the compensation demanded earlier from the Sikhs). By even the most conservative estimate, Gulab Singh had been munificently rewarded for his co-operation with the East India Company. Indeed, there is a curious element of deliberateness in the way in which these two separate articles were connected, suggesting that the British had already decided, well before negotiating either treaty, to transfer Kashmir and other hill regions to Gulab Singh.[30]

The East India Company chose to view the exercises of 1846 clinically: a simple excision of territories and the most efficient way of managing new circumstances that had arisen in north-western India. And, in many ways, business appeared to be as usual. The Company's expansion in the preceding decades had proceeded through the signing of treaties similar to those of Lahore and Amritsar with a variety of Indian rulers (and often equally coaxed out of them). Also, this was evidently not the first time the valley of Kashmir had been held by 'outsiders', having passed from Mughal (1586), to Afghan (1751) and finally into Sikh (1819) hands. However, what did change critically at the same time as Kashmir was handed over to the Dogras was the nature of the political world of pre-colonial India more generally, and Kashmir more specifically. From an earlier seamless terrain of overlapping and layered sovereignties, the British now claimed a monolithic and territorially bounded sovereignty, a lesser version of which they vested in Gulab Singh. Additionally, in light of its concerns for stability on its north-western frontier, the Company also wished to strengthen the hands of its new ally. Towards this end, the British sought to vacate power held in pockets in Kashmir and transfer it to the new maharaja, in whom alone a personalized sovereignty was now to vest. This underwriting of Dogra rule by the British began a process that enabled the overlooking, if not the outright exclusion, of the elementary rights of the people of Kashmir. The question then is: how was the Dogra state able to ignore the interests of large sections of its Kashmiri population and yet maintain the right, at least in some eyes, to rule over them?

[30] The governor-general, Hardinge, was clearly aware in as early as February 1846 that the Sikhs would be unable to pay the amount of the indemnity, which would then provide the Company with the pretext to compel Lahore to surrender the above territories. Hardinge, p. 123.

A Tale of Two Treaties: Separating Jammu and Kashmir from Lahore

As the Company was soon to discover, carving out territorially distinct political entities from regions that had formerly been integrated, albeit loosely, within one symbolic system of layered and hierarchical sovereignty, required rather more skill with the knife than it possessed. The exercise entailed more than a redrawing of maps and necessitated, in fact, the unravelling of an intricate pattern of intermeshing authority and loyalties extending across porous political boundaries. Reflecting these complexities, the implementation of the two treaties often ended in unintended political retreats which emphasized the inseparability of the two regions and ensured the persistence of Lahore as a significant extra-territorial arena from which the Dogras would continue to derive their legitimacy to rule over Jammu and Kashmir. At the same time, this peculiar arrangement allowed large segments of Kashmiri society to slip quietly out of the minds of their new rulers.

The political imbrication of Lahore and Jammu was apparent in the intertwined nature of the very treaties that were meant to sever the two territories. At the most obvious level, as suggested earlier, this coupling reflected the British strategy of downsizing the Sikh state by assigning tracts from it to a trusty ally. But at another level this arrangement of the treaties of Lahore and Amritsar was also informed by the broader concerns of the Company to legitimate its actions in the Punjab. Hardinge's policy in the north-west, particularly the decision to make Gulab Singh the instrument of Lahore's diminishment, had come under attack from various eminent quarters of British opinion. For instance, Lord Ellenborough, governor-general of India from 1842 to 1844, had forcefully repudiated the policy of 'rewarding . . . Ghulab Singh's treachery to the Lahore State'.[31] Hardinge's riposte insisted that Gulab Singh 'had no cause of gratitude or attachment to the Lahore Darbar, by whose orders and intrigues his own family had been nearly exterminated, his possessions taken, and his own son slain'.[32] However, as his need to exonerate his government's policy along these lines indicates, he may have been protesting too much. The older ties of collaboration and loyalty owed by the Jammu raja to Lahore seemed evidently to weigh on his mind. Viewed from this

[31] Ibid., p. 134.
[32] Ibid., pp. 134–5.

perspective, the treaties of Lahore and Amritsar offer a richer field of interpretation than a purely juridical reading of them might yield.

Article XII of the Treaty of Lahore stated plainly that, far from viewing Gulab Singh as a renegade, the Sikhs, more properly, owed him a debt of gratitude. For it was in '*consideration of the services rendered by Rajah Golab Singh . . . to the Lahore State,* towards procuring the restoration of the relations of amity between the Lahore and British Governments' that Dalip Singh was to recognize the 'Independent Sovereignty' of the Dogra ruler.[33] In other words, the weakened Sikh state was to acknowledge that without Gulab Singh's political nursing and mediation, the East India Company would have taken over Punjab fully in 1846. This was, arguably, not far from the truth. It is reasonable to speculate that had the Company not found in Gulab Singh the sufficiently powerful ally it needed to act as a buffer, it would have been compelled to undertake the defense of the crucial northwestern frontier on its own, no matter how strained its resources.[34] On another but related point, the very order in which the clauses of Article XII were arranged was significant. It ensured that Gulab Singh's sovereignty was, literally, first upheld by Lahore before the British 'admit[ted] him to the privileges of a separate Treaty' with themselves. Since the Sikhs did not realistically have the option of refusing their endorsement, such punctiliousness of form reveals the Company's concern for, and recognition of, the symbolic derivation of Gulab Singh's legitimate sovereignty from Lahore.

The continuing salience of Lahore as a reference point for Gulab Singh was reiterated also by the Treaty of Amritsar. Article VIII of the Amritsar engagement made Gulab Singh's accession to sovereignty conditional upon his respecting various 'Articles of Agreement'

[33] Aitchison, p. 40. Emphasis mine.

[34] It scarcely needs stating that Gulab Singh's decision to intervene in the first Anglo-Sikh war was motivated less by his altruistic concern for the fate of Lahore than by various self-interested calculations about the best means to preserve, if not expand, his power. As he saw it, while overt support of the Lahore durbar against the more powerful British would be injudicious, political seclusion in Jammu was not an option either. This would expose him either to the danger of having 'His territories . . . negotiated away' in the event of an amicable Anglo-Sikh settlement, or to the equal risk of losing them as an act of 'retribution' should the Sikhs win decisively. Bawa Satinder Singh, p. 121. The East India Company did eventually annex Lahore in 1849, but by then Gulab Singh was safely ensconced as Maharaja of Jammu and Kashmir and a valued ally of the British.

concluded between the Company and Lahore on 11 March 1846. Through these articles, the British had undertaken to 'respect the *bona fide* rights' of those jagirdars appointed by the Sikhs in territories now ceded to the Company and 'to maintain' them in 'their possessions during their lives'.[35] Since most of the territories in question, such as Kashmir, were then transferred to Gulab Singh, the Company's obligations towards Sikh-appointed jagirdars within them also devolved upon him. The result, wittingly or otherwise, of this provision of the Treaty of Amritsar was to situate the first Dogra ruler as a 'successor' to the Sikhs in Kashmir rather than as an originally independent sovereign. It did so most obviously by placing Gulab Singh at the pinnacle of a hierarchy of land rights that had been granted by the Lahore durbar. From the new ruler's perspective, this was far from an unqualified boon. The deleterious political effect of such a measure emerged from the fact that jagir grants carried with them duties of service and loyalty owed to the grantor. But, the treaties established a skewed association between the new maharaja and Sikh-appointed jagirdars. While Gulab Singh's responsibility towards them was clear, namely to maintain them during their lives, the relationship was not entirely a reciprocal one since the treaties froze these grants as Sikh gifts, and so also the direction in which concomitant allegiances were to flow. Even if the provisions of Article VIII were to apply technically only for the lifetime of the original jagirdars, it made the very founding of the state that much more perplexing for its new maharaja. It also represented a departure from the primary aim of the treaties of Lahore and Amritsar of severing Jammu and Kashmir from Punjab.

By the same token, even after the formation of the state of Jammu and Kashmir, Gulab Singh continued to claim bases of authority in Punjab through his jagirs and his religious endowments there.[36] In addition to the *Rajgi* (rulership) of Jammu, Gulab Singh had received from Maharaja Ranjit Singh several areas in the Punjab to be held as farms, as also various jagirs in the Jammu hills.[37] This was very much

[35] Aitchison, pp. 42–3.

[36] *Political Diaries of the Agent to the Governor-General, North West Frontier and Resident at Lahore*, 1 January 1847 to 4 March 1848 (Allahabad: Pioneer Press, 1909), p. 66.

[37] The areas to be held in farm were Chukh Huzara, Pukhlee Dhumtour, Djumee, Kuttas and Chakkowall, Sialkot and the salt mines of Pind Dadan

in line with the power-sharing arrangements prevalent in the Greater
Punjab region, and typical also more broadly of pre-colonial India,
by which the spread of sovereignty and the networks of patronage
embodied by it often extended the influence of various layers of
power-holders into each other's territories. As Maharaja Ranjit Singh
explained in 1838 to Frederick Mackeson, the political agent at
Lahore, 'Lahore was the superficial abode of [Gulab Singh] whereas
[Jammu] . . . was the real one.'[38] If this statement was meant to fix
a distinct political hierarchy it also clearly accepted that both Lahore
and Jammu were Gulab Singh's abodes.

Looking for neat equations between sovereignty and territory, the
British were not entirely comfortable with such political thinking,
believing it an 'anomaly [that] the officials or in fact the Ministers
of one State . . . [should hold] independent estates in the lands of a
neighbouring power.'[39] Thus, in 1858, the British went so far as to
purchase a jagir held by Maharaja Gulab Singh and unidentified 'others' in the Hoshiarpur district of the Punjab.[40] British objections in
principle notwithstanding, Dogra rulers continued to hold sovereignty over and extract revenue from areas in the Punjab well into the
second half of the nineteenth century, when their sovereign rights in
these lands were finally surrendered. Yet, even while Dogra sovereignty over territories in Punjab was extinguished at this time in the
narrower political sense understood by the British, the authority derived from religious patronage continued to blur the lines between
Jammu and Punjab. Not only did the Dogra maharajas continue to
use revenues drawn from Punjab holdings to provide for temples
in Jammu,[41] but, in other instances, they also alienated the rent of

---

Khan. The jagirs granted were part of Bhadarwah, Padar, Chenai, Reasi,
Kishtwar, Akh-noor and Rajouri. Panikkar, *The Founding of the Kashmir State*,
pp. 39–40.

[38] Diwan Kirpa Ram, p. 167.

[39] Foreign (Secret), 30 October 1847, Consultations nos. 116–17, NAI.

[40] P/202/47, India Proceedings, Political Consultations, Foreign, 19 February
1858, no. 3, IOL.

[41] Foreign (Revenue B), August 1874, Proceedings nos. 36–7, NAI. The village of Chak Bharat, well within the British side of the boundary line, had been
in the possession of the Maharaja of Kashmir and its revenues had been used to
support the Raghunathji temple in Jammu. Punjab Foreign Proceedings, Pros.
no. 3, August 1874, Part A, IOL.

Punjab villages for the maintenance of temples located within Punjab territory.[42]

Well before the late nineteenth century, the confusion attending the actual implementation of the treaties had already brought home vividly to the British the difficulty of forming geographically delimited dominions. For the Company, having made up its mind to form two new states, the chief concern was to partition territory fairly and following a spatial logic that viewed sovereignty as territorially circumscribable. Thus, Captain J. Abbott, appointed settlement commissioner in 1846, spent considerable energy 'diligently . . . setting up boundary pillars; making new surveys for straightening the boundary line . . . cutting off corners', to ensure the just distribution of areas, bearing in mind their revenue-yielding capacities, on the border between the two domains.[43] The Dogra and Sikh rulers joined the British with gusto in exercises of dividing tracts, haggling vigorously over those considered economically and strategically vital.[44] However, for them, this was more than a competitive struggle for land and revenues. What was at issue was sovereignty itself, understood less as control over territory *per se* and more as the successful management of political loyalties drawn and retained through land-revenue assignments.

The reports of Captain Arthur Broome, deputed to oversee the transfer of power to Gulab Singh, bear witness to the pandemonium accompanying British attempts at territorially demarcating sovereignty. To cite but one example, a principal grievance of Gulab Singh was that 'all those about . . . [him] or in his service' who possessed jagirs now located in the Punjab had been threatened by the Lahore

---

[42] The rent of the village of Golabgarh, for instance, went towards the maintenance of the temple of Raghunathji established by Gulab Singh in Pind Dadan Khan, both places being in Punjab. This continued at least as late as 1891. Punjab Government/Department of Revenue and Agriculture/Pros. no. 10, February 1891/Part B, IOL.

[43] Journal of Captain J. Abbott, Commissioner for the Settlement of the Punjab Boundaries, from the 5th to the 19th April 1846, in *Journals and Diaries of the Assistants to the Agent to the Governor General, North-West Frontier and Resident at Lahore, 1846–49* (Allahabad: Pioneer Press, 1911), pp. 36–7.

[44] Gulab Singh was particularly concerned to acquire territory in the 'plains', more conducive both to the flow of trade and the movement of guns and troops, than in the 'hills' which he seemed to have drawn as his lot. Ibid.

durbar with the confiscation of these 'if they d[id] not quit the Maharajah's service and country.'[45] Such accusations flew in both directions. Thus, in August 1847, a rani at the Sikh court complained that Gulab Singh had confiscated one of her jagirs in Jammu.[46] This was not an isolated incident since Gulab Singh had to be reminded officially that 'all jageers and dhurmurths . . . situated within the territory of [the] Maharaja . . . should remain in the possession of the present holders and that they should not be in any way interfered with.'[47] These various disputes were now to be resolved not by negotiation between the Sikhs and the Dogras but through the mediation of the British, involving the latter endlessly in what they saw as 'the unpleasant feelings roused by the non-reciprocation of favours between the Lahore and Cashmere Governments in releasing each other's jageers.'[48]

Despite evidence calling into question the efficacy of such a policy, the East India Company persisted with its implementation of the new ethos of territory defining the limits of sovereignty. This might have enjoyed greater success if, and assuming this were possible, the Company had exerted itself towards, first, dismantling the entire structure of power and loyalties centred on Lahore and then starting afresh. Instead, in giving Gulab Singh independent sovereignty through a sleight of hand, the British had simply taken a piece out of an infinitely complicated political structure and sought to pass it off as a separate and whole entity. Because they were working on a contingency basis,

---

[45] Letter from Arthur Broome, Artillery on Special Duty, to Henry Lawrence, Governor-General's Agent, North Western Frontier, dated Jummoo, 23 July 1846, Mss. Eur.F. 85, Henry Lawrence Collection, Arthur Broome's Letters to and from Sir Henry Lawrence, dated 1846, IOL.

[46] *Political Diaries of the Agent to the Governor-General, North-West Frontier, and Resident at Lahore*, p. 267.

[47] Ibid., 'Dhurmurths' or 'dharmarths' were grants for religious purposes.

[48] Ibid., p. 331. Also note that Article XIII of the Treaty of Lahore stated: 'In the event of any dispute . . . arising between the Lahore State and Rajah Golab Sing, the same shall be referred to the arbitration of the British Government, and by its decision the Maharajah engages to abide.' And Article V of the Treaty of Amritsar similarly asserted: 'Maharajah Golab Sing will refer to the arbitration of the British Government any disputes . . . that may arise between himself and the Government of Lahore.' Aitchison, pp. 40, 165.

crucial ties between the part and the whole were left intact by the treaties of Lahore and Amritsar.

Gulab Singh continued to count among his personnel men who were employed by him, and so owed him primary political loyalty, but whose sources of income were not only physically located in Punjab territory but were also obtained from the former sovereign in Lahore. Conversely, Gulab Singh, continuing his 'former connection . . . with Lahore' retained 'numerous partisans in that city' and so was in a position to exert considerable pressure there.[49] Besides this, significant holders of land grants in Kashmir who owed their loyalty to Lahore depended, for the preservation of their jagirs, on the new Dogra maharaja. As it turned out, Lahore was liquidated as an 'independent' political centre not long after, in 1849, when the East India Company finally took over the direct administration of the Punjab. Yet the arrangement put in place by the Treaty of Amritsar, which required the preservation of these territorially intermeshed land rights ensured that Punjab, even if no longer merely Lahore, remained an abiding symbolic arena from which the Dogra rulers continued to bolster their legitimacy to rule in Jammu and Kashmir.

As late as 1856, a year before his death, Gulab Singh was reported to be spending hours in public durbar talking chiefly of 'Ranjeet's times and doings'.[50] Even if this is dismissed as the nostalgic reminiscing of an ageing sovereign, it is significant that Gulab Singh's successors were engaged in numerous well-advertised acts of public spending in the Punjab. Thus, in 1873, Maharaja Ranbir Singh (*r.*1856–85), the son and successor of Gulab, had entered into negotiations with the British government to obtain the mortgage of the jagir revenue of Guru Jowahir Singh of Kartarpur (Punjab). The latter was an indebted jagirdar but no ordinary one, being a lineal descendant of the sixth Sikh guru and the head of the 'Sodhi family to which all the Gurus after the third [had] belonged'. And 'as the custodian of what [was] regarded as the original copy of the granth [the Sikh sacred text], the Guru [was] greatly respected by the whole of the Sikhs.'[51] It was

[49] Foreign (Secret), Despatch from the Court of Directors, 19 October 1846, no. 1225, NAI.

[50] MSS Eur.D.974, Hugh Rees James Papers, IOL, p. 58.

[51] Letter from D.G. Barkley, Deputy Commissioner, Jullundur, to the Commissioner and Superintendent, Jullunder Division, dated 29 June 1874, Punjab

undoubtedly with a view to acquiring a 'reputation for liberality with the Sikh Rajahs' that Ranbir Singh had proposed purchasing the mortgage.[52] This gesture stands out particularly conspicuously when considering that the guru had already applied unsuccessfully to the Sikh ruler of Faridkot.[53] The instinct of the Dogra maharajas was not just to spend in the Punjab but to outspend other Punjab princes. Similarly, in 1868, the Dogra ruler made a generous endowment of Rs 6230 towards the establishment of a university for the propagation of literature and science in Lahore.[54] But the competitive impulse was most in evidence in the case of the Lahore University College, established in 1866. The Maharaja of Kashmir's donations were far in excess of those of the 'Maharajas, Chiefs and people of the Punjab' who had subscribed for its foundation. By 1869, the Dogra ruler had spent Rs 62,500 while the Raja of Kapurthala, the only other Punjab ruler to have actually paid up his promised donation, came in a distant second with Rs 10,000.[55] The irony is compounded by the fact that it was not until the early twentieth century that the Dogra maharajas would fund the establishment of institutions of higher education in their own state of Jammu and Kashmir. Therefore, in important ways, the endurance of Lahore and Punjab as a significant site from which to acquire their legitimacy kept the attention of the Dogras concentrated on this extra-territorial arena at the expense of Kashmir and Kashmiris.

Government/Revenue, Agriculture and Commerce Department/Pros. no. 4, March 1876/Part A, IOL.

[52] Marginal note by D.G. Barkley in a letter from D.G. Barkley, Deputy Commissioner, Jalandhar, to the Commissioner and Superintendent, Jalandhar, dated 4 September 1873, Punjab Government/Agriculture, Revenue and Commerce Department/Pros. no. 9, December 1873/Part A, IOL.

[53] Letter from D.G. Barkley, Deputy Commissioner, Jalandhar, to the Commissioner and Superintendent, Jalandhar, dated 23 October 1873, Punjab Government/Agriculture, Revenue and Commerce Department/Pros. no. 9, December 1873/Part A, IOL.

[54] Letter from the Secretary of State for India to the Government of India, dated 1 March 1868, Foreign Department (General A)/ Pros. no. 26/May 1868, NAI.

[55] Statement of donations and subscriptions paid up and still due to the Lahore University College from the commencement of the University up to 31 December 1869, Home Department (Education)/April 1873/Pros. nos. 7–8/Part A, NAI.

The Social Structure of Kashmir

In social terms, as with its territorial composition, the identities of the subjects of the new state were characterized by a patchwork quality. Here, as in other parts of the European empires of the nineteenth and twentieth centuries, redrawn boundaries mapped the history of colonial geo-political and administrative convenience rather more than a commonality of experience shared by the people encompassed within them. As Richard Temple, a Resident in Hyderabad and former governor of Bombay, noted, the 'double title' of the Maharaja of Jammu and Kashmir was 'characteristic of his country . . . a political agglomeration of mountain tracts that have little connection otherwise with each other.'[56]

Of course, during a century of Dogra control, certain segments of Jammu and Kashmiri society had been drawing closer together. As will be discussed, the Dogras, needing at least some dependable allies, sought to co-opt élite sections of Kashmiri society who now competed for the same government and administrative appointments, as well as the same symbolic resources of the state, as their counterparts in Jammu. Moreover, while the rulers were from Jammu, the state itself drew its primary identity from control over Kashmir, most clearly illustrated by the fact that the shorthand resorted to in referring to the state was always Kashmir and never Jammu.[57] However, these instances of integration were limited to the political arena and involved,

[56] Richard C. Temple, *Journals Kept in Hyderabad, Kashmir, Sikkim and Nepal,* 2 vols (London: W.H. Allen & Co., 1887), vol. 1, p. 267.

[57] In her dissertation Chitralekha Zutshi provides fascinating evidence of the importance of Kashmir for the Dogras in a shawl presented by the second maharaja, Ranbir Singh, to the Prince of Wales in 1876. The urban landscape of Srinagar was finely embroidered onto this 'masterpiece of shawl manufacture' and the act of gifting it was meant not only to symbolize the acceptance of British suzerainty but also to make manifest Dogra control over 'the much-coveted valley' as the 'center of [their] kingdom'. Chitralekha Zutshi, 'Community, State, and the Nation: Regional Patriotism and Religious Identities in the Kashmir Valley, *c.* 1880–1953' (Ph.D. dissertation, Tufts University, 2000), p. 63; reprinted with substantial revision as *Languages of Belonging: Islam, Regional Identity, and the Making of Kashmir.* Additionally, as Richard Temple put it, while in the Punjab the maharaja may have been known as the Maharaja of Jammu, 'to the English [he w]as the Maharaja of Kashmir'. Richard C. Temple, vol. 1, p. 267.

at best, only a small minority of the population of Kashmir. Beyond this, Jammu and Kashmir continued to retain their distinctive linguistic traditions, social structures, and patterns of religious interaction. Turning our attention to Kashmir, its social structure had features found nowhere else in the Indian subcontinent.[58] But what is made of this singularity is a different matter. In twentieth-century nationalist or such-prone analyses, what is emphasized is an unparalleled degree of Hindu–Muslim amity, considered by many to be the basis for a unique tradition of regional solidarity, sought to be captured by the designation or feeling of Kashmiriyat. Needless to say, if true, this portrayal makes it difficult to account for the many instances of strained relations between Hindus and Muslims, finally taking a violent form in 1931. However, given the prevalence of this perspective of communal concord and the political uses to which it was put—a theme later sections in this book will expand on—the social structure of Kashmir merits closer analysis, even if only by sketching it in broad strokes.

Most accounts assert that the Hindus of Kashmir were represented by the single caste of the Kashmiri Pandits (Brahmans), a result of the gradual conversion to Islam, beginning in the fourteenth century, of the other castes. Yet even this group was subdivided into at least two endogamous subcastes; the Gors and the Karkuns. The relationship between them was hierarchical in nature, with Karkuns functioning as patrons of the other.[59] A third but much smaller category of Kashmiri Brahmans, present only in the towns of the valley, was called the

[58] According to Walter Lawrence, the British settlement commissioner deputed to Kashmir in 1889, the Hindus comprised about 5 to 6 per cent of the population of the valley, the Sikhs about 0.5 per cent and the Muslims (including the Shias) about 93 per cent. The total population, according to him, amounted to 814,214. Walter Lawrence, *The Valley of Kashmir* (Srinagar: Chinar Publishing House, repr. 1992), p. 284. These numbers remained relatively steady as the 1941 census of India indicated that the Muslims comprised 93.6 per cent and the Hindus about 4 per cent of the total population of the valley. *Census of India*, Jammu and Kashmir, 1941.

[59] P.N.K. Bamzai, *Culture and Political History of Kashmir*, 3 vols (New Delhi: M.D. Publications, 1994), vol. 2, p. 479; T.N. Madan, 'Religious Ideology and Social Structure: The Hindus and Muslims of Kashmir', in Imtiaz Ahmad (ed.), *Ritual and Religion Among Muslims in India* (New Delhi: Manohar, 1984), pp. 23, 41. The word Gor is derived from the Sanskrit Guru and Karkun is the Persian word for civil servants, revenue collectors, etc.

Buher. They formed an endogamous set of their own and were employed mostly as grocers and confectioners. The Pandits neither inter-
married nor interdined with the Buher, often also denying them access
to their temples. However, within these limits, there were still significant ties between these groups of Brahmans. The Gors, for instance,
provided priestly services to the Buher while the latter sought upward
social mobility by emulating Pandit lifestyles and religious practices.[60]

The Muslims of Kashmir, forming about 95 per cent of the population, were also a less-than-cohesive category. The Sunni Muslims
were divided into Shaikhs, Saiyids, Mughals, Pathans, Gujars, and
Bakarwals, and the lowest stratum, comprised of the Doms and the
Watals—regarded as 'untouchables' both by Hindus and Muslims.[61]
The Saiyids, Mughals and Pathans were immigrants and were looked
up to because, even if this was only faintly remembered, they had once
been 'rulers' in the valley, or at least its ruling groups had been drawn
from their ranks. The respect accorded them was also partially in acknowledgement of their having been 'Muslims longer' than the more
recently converted 'native' Kashmiris.[62] In the case of the Saiyids,
specifically, their claim to being descendants of Prophet Muhammad
by itself drew deference.[63] Speaking a different dialect, the Gujars and
Bakarwals, cowherds and goatherds respectively, though important to
the life of any Kashmiri village, were kept on the periphery of the
Kashmiri social structure because their semi-nomadic lifestyle made it
difficult to incorporate them in any but the most transient manner.[64]
The 'natives' of Kashmir, the Shaikhs, were also internally differentiat-
ed along lines determined predominantly by their occupation. These
Shaikhs included, for instance, the zamindars (agriculturists) on the
one hand, and the nangars (the non-agriculturists or artisans) on the
other.[65]

[60] Madan, 'Religious Ideology', p. 40.

[61] Walter Lawrence, *The Provincial Gazetteers of Jammu and Kashmir* (New
Delhi: Rima Publishing House, 1985), pp. 36–9; Madan, 'Religious Ideology',
pp. 53, 57.

[62] Madan, 'Religious Ideology', p. 55. See also Lawrence, *The Valley of
Kashmir*, pp. 308–9.

[63] Madan, 'Religious Ideology', p. 54.

[64] Madan, 'Religious Ideology', pp. 30, 55; Lawrence, *The Valley of Kashmir*,
pp. 316–17.

[65] Madan, 'Religious Ideology', p. 26; Lawrence, *The Valley of Kashmir*,

The Shias formed another subdivision among the Muslims. Introduced into the valley by Shams-ud-din Iraqi as early as in 1450, Shi'ism, however, never gained much ground and its followers formed at best about 5 per cent of the Muslim population in the late nineteenth century. They were concentrated most heavily in the Zadibal quarter of Srinagar and were primarily engaged in the shawl-weaving and papier mâché industries. However, even in their small numbers, they found themselves in conflict with Sunnis quite frequently. A particularly bitter outbreak of violence, often mentioned but rarely elaborated upon by historians of Kashmir, occurred in 1872 in Srinagar. It was ostensibly caused by a dispute over a shrine but was probably also set off by economic discontent in the context of a declining shawl industry pitting mostly Sunni weavers against Shia manufactory owners and traders.[66]

Quite evidently, then, neither the Hindus nor the Muslims of Kashmir formed homogeneous social entities. For both groups the notion of *zat* or *kram*, evoking the concept of birth into a common clan group, was a decisive factor in specifying and living out their identities. As suggested earlier, not only were the Buher separated from the Kashmiri Pandits both socially and religiously, but the two groups among the Kashmiri Pandits, the Gors and Karkuns, also functioned as quite distinct endogamous units. Similarly, the Muslims of Kashmir placed informal restrictions, not sanctioned by their faith but prevalent in custom, on intermarriage between zats or krams. Thus, Muslim marriage practices effectively kept the two occupational categories among the Shaikhs, the zamindars and nangars, separated as endogamous entities. And for the Shaikhs collectively, 'the line drawn' was that they 'must not marry into Saiyad families' accompanied by the dire warning that 'such presumption would bring bad luck'.[67]

Thus regarded, there seems little to distinguish Kashmir from other regions of the subcontinent. However, what made the Kashmiri social structure so singular was the pattern of interaction between the

---

pp. 315–16. Lawrence describes the Nangars as village 'menials' employed in a variety of occupations as carpenters, blacksmiths, potters, weavers, washermen, barbers and others encountered in most other Indian villages.

[66] Lawrence, *The Valley of Kashmir*, pp. 284–5; Bamzai, *Culture and Political History of Kashmir*, vol. 3, p. 691.

[67] Ibid., pp. 306, 308.

Hindus and Muslims deriving from the valley's Hindus consisting solely of the Brahman caste. This forced a relationship of ritual and economic interdependence between Kashmiri Pandits and Muslims. In the absence of the full panoply of jatis that characterized Hindu society elsewhere, the Pandits, whose caste status excluded them from either manual labour or work deemed polluting, relied heavily on Muslim specialist groups for the provision of essential services and liturgical goods.[68] In this sense, as T.N. Madan points out in his seminal essay, from the perspective of the Pandits these Muslim groups functioned as 'caste analogues' and were indispensable for the maintenance of their ritual purity as Brahmans.[69] Kashmiri Muslims, for their part, viewed Pandits as valuable patrons and the relationship as a 'traditional economic transaction'. Thus, while religious differences were fully acknowledged, there were also vital ties that bound these groups in the region. However, Madan may have overemphasized the degree of Muslim acquiescence in this unequal relationship. He goes so far as to suggest that the interaction between the two communities was marked by an asymmetrical pattern of dependence in which the Muslims had the freer hand as they could refuse their services to the Pandits and provide them, instead, solely to their own co-religionists.[70] While this sounds plausible in theory, it looks suspiciously like an attempt at presenting an idealized model of a society extricated from its quotidian functioning and emptied of history.

Although certainly reliant in critical ways on Muslim service groups, what cannot be ignored is the capacity of the Kashmiri Pandits to extract such services. As I suggest later, the Dogra rulers, looking for allies within Kashmiri society, drew primarily on the Pandits. This enhanced the power of the latter, dominant in the administrative structure of the state and especially its revenue department, to bear

[68] Thus the Pandits were dependent on the services of Muslim cultivators, artisans, barbers, washermen and other village specialists. They were dependent on Muslim occupational groups also for the performance of essential religious rites, such as the preparation of terracotta pots for marriage ceremonies (services that would elsewhere have been the task of lower Hindu castes).

[69] Madan, 'Religious Ideology', pp. 35, 42–7.

[70] Madan, 'Religious Ideology', pp. 55–6. Even Madan's suggestion that this Muslim 'sense of security has been considerably heightened since 1947' is open to debate.

down on the rural population, the vast majority of whom happened to be Muslim. An awareness of the privileged position of the Kashmiri Pandits in the Dogra state, and the exploitation this enabled, was never far from the minds of Kashmiri Muslim villagers. Interesting evidence is provided in plays produced by wandering minstrels, known as the Bhaggats or Bands—familiar figures in Kashmiri villages. Bhaggat troupes were almost all Muslim, with the exception of a single company of Pandit performers. Their plays, enacted to the accompaniment of music and songs in Kashmiri, were discerning portrayals of rural society; indeed, Gulab Singh is said to have taken them seriously enough to cull valuable information on village life from them.[71] They reflected the worldview of cultivators, for whose entertainment they were performed at marriage feasts and harvest festivals. The plots were generic and typically began with a raja, 'burning to redress injustice', riding through a village accompanied by his *wazir* (minister), usually identified as a Kashmiri Pandit. On a complaint made by a villager, the wazir would call for the *patwari* (the village accountant), also commonly a Pandit. Eventually, defeated by the combine of the 'wazir and patwari laying their heads together', not only would the laments of the villager grow fainter but the patwari was routinely found innocent and the villager administered a sound lashing. This gloomy depiction of the state of Kashmir's cultivators travelled beyond the valley as the Bhaggats carried their tales even to the Punjab, where their repertoire was presented before émigré Kashmiri audiences.[72]

Colonial observers such as Walter Lawrence, the civil servant deputed to Kashmir as settlement commissioner in 1889, while providing the above evidence about Kashmiri village life, also popularized the image of a harmonious Kashmiri society in which religious differences erased themselves in a blissful world of shared rituals and religious beliefs. Thus, Lawrence wrote of less-than-perfect Muslims who, despite five hundred years of conversion, were still 'Hindus at heart' and so presumably less prone to the supposed fanaticism of their Islamic brethren elsewhere.[73] The Pandits for their part, though Brahmans, were depicted as less scrupulous in the maintenance of their rituals of

---

[71] Walter Lawrence admits that he himself had also 'picked up some hints from them as to the methods of the patwari.' Lawrence, *The Valley of Kashmir*, p. 256.

[72] Ibid., pp. 256, 312–13.

[73] Ibid., pp. 285–6; Lawrence, *Provincial Gazetteers*, p. 35.

purity and pollution than their more 'rigid' counterparts in Hindustan and so more willing to interact with Muslims in a series of common rites and cultural practices. Some of the 'heresies' of the Kashmiri Pandits that would purportedly have horrified orthodox Hindus elsewhere included their willingness to accept water and food from a Muslim and their propensity to eat meat.[74] As evidence of the religious accord Lawrence found characteristic of the Kashmiri religious landscape, he pointed to the many sacred sites at which Muslims and Pandits worshipped together, even if in their own idiom. One such was the imprint of a foot at Fatehpura that Muslims revered as the Holy Prophet's footprint and the Hindus as the mark of Vishnu.[75] While there is probably nothing factually incorrect about any of Lawrence's observations, a historically contextualized examination of Kashmiri society demonstrates that what was at one moment shared had within it the potential for fracture at another. Take for instance the practice common to both Hindus and Muslims, which Lawrence and others delighted in describing, of worshipping nagas (serpent deities) at the many springs of Kashmir.[76] This tradition of collective worship broke down rather dramatically in 1931, in the aftermath of riots in which Kashmiri Pandits and Muslims confronted each other in a competition for the political and economic resources of the Dogra state.[77] A memorial of grievances presented by the Kashmiri Pandits after the riots claimed that since the Muslims had converted out of their original religion, the various springs now belonged exclusively to the Hindus. Muslim devotees were consequently described as encroachers and were sought to be debarred from these sites.[78]

While Hindu–Muslim discord was by no means the inevitable destiny of Kashmiris, neither was a regional identity before which religious differences bowed shamefacedly away. It is true that, for the

[74] Lawrence, *The Valley of Kashmir*, p. 300.

[75] Ibid., p. 386.

[76] Ibid.; R.C. Kak, *Memoirs of the Archaeological Survey of Kashmir, no. 1, Antiquities of Marev-Wadwan* (Archaeological Survey of Kashmir, 1924), pp. 9–11.

[77] The events of 1931 are discussed in greater detail in Chapter Five of this book.

[78] *Memorandum of the Kashmiri Pandits on the Terms of Reference of the Grievances Enquiry Commission* (Srinagar: Sanatan Dharma Youngmen's Association, 1931), p. 5.

most part of Kashmir's modern history, Hindu–Muslim strife tended to express itself less frequently in the form of 'riots', especially when compared with the differently fraught history of both communities in British India.[79] That is probably why Kashmir exercised such a powerful appeal for both the Gandhian and Nehruvian side of the Indian nationalist imagination in the twentieth century.[80] Indeed, as many modern ideologues of Kashmiriyat also remind us, when north India was rocked by religious violence surrounding the trauma of partition, Gandhi looked northwards to Kashmir as a 'ray of hope' and a source of inspiration.[81] As such, this vision of a timeless Kashmir of communal euphony represented, at least to mainstream Indian nationalism, a better past and the prospect that this cherished society had a future in the subcontinent. But this is to make Kashmiris and their history hostages to an Indian nationalism that was working out its own paradoxes from having grown increasingly exclusionary in practice, not least by espousing a unitary national identity intolerant of assertions of religious or cultural difference while holding to its original language of inclusion. As Ayesha Jalal's recent work has suggested, religion has to be prised from the narrow binary, of a monolithic nationalism and

[79] Even on the issue of naming an instance of strife a 'riot', see the illuminating discussion of this question in Gyanendra Pandey, *The Construction of Communalism in Colonial North India* (Delhi: Oxford University Press, 1992). Pandey argues that the history of communalism was itself constructed by a colonial historiography that purposefully read religious motives, at the expense of other more material causes, into a variety of 'disturbances' that erupted in colonial north India from the early nineteenth century on.

[80] With important distinctions, both M.K. Gandhi and Jawaharlal Nehru shared a common vision of the 'secular' basis of the Indian nation. For Nehru, religious affiliation was a pre-modern position that would eventually diminish in importance as Indians were gradually educated into more 'progressive' attitudes. For Gandhi, on the other hand, while religion was important, a vital distinction could be made between its essential and non-essential aspects, the line being drawn between the public and private personae of citizens.

[81] Importantly what was being reified in this compliment to Kashmir was the fact that, despite its Muslim-majority population, the state had rejected the Muslim League's version of statehood based on Islamic commonality. In the process what was already erased, and continues to be effaced today, was that while Kashmir's majority had rejected the idea of Pakistan as insufficiently cognizant of its regional specificity, it had not endorsed the mainstream Indian National Congress's ideal of nationhood either.

a pejorative communalism, within which it has been trapped both in political procedure and academic explication.[82]

If anything, the history of Kashmir challenges such dichotomies. Both religion and region were important ingredients of a Kashmiri sense of self. However, to understand the balance between these elements, shifting at particular historical moments, what seems necessary is an escape from Kashmiriyat defined as it is today. This suggests also an analysis that does not make Kashmir captive to narratives that originated elsewhere and with agendas that were extra-Kashmiri. In other words, what is required is an examination of Kashmiri history on its own terms, delineating those historical contexts in which the pendulum swung from moments in which a regional sense of belonging still encompassed a definite sense of religious difference to those others when religious affiliation fractured regional identity. It is this history of Kashmir that this book aims to let a little light on.

The Treaty of Amritsar and Vacating Power in Kashmir

To return to our narrative: the Treaty of Amritsar provided a disjuncture in several senses in the political functioning of the pre-colonial state system centred on Lahore. The British understood the treaty to transfer the rights, titles and interests possessed by the Sikh government in the territories concerned into their own hands. These were then handed over, along with territory, 'completely and absolutely' to the maharaja, Gulab Singh.[83] Before this novel intervention in the arrangement and distribution of power among various political levels, rights and interests had neither been possessed absolutely and exclusively nor considered transferable in the manner understood by the British. Instead, they had been arranged along a hierarchy that recognized superior and inferior rights, established and maintained as relational entities through accommodative and negotiated processes.

[82] See Ayesha Jalal, 'Exploding Communalism: The Politics of Muslim Identity in South Asia', in Sugata Bose and Ayesha Jalal (eds), *Nationalism, Democracy, and Development: State and Politics in India* (Delhi: Oxford University Press, 1997), pp. 70–103. And, more recently, Jalal, *Self and Sovereignty*..

[83] Frederick Currie's judgement, dated 12 May 1848, cited in K.M. Panikkar, pp. 121–3.

Power at all levels was held by mutual recognition and this pattern of mutuality protected against the complete subsumption of the rights of subordinate levels. As wielders of localized power viewed it, the superior authority of the Maharaja of Lahore was not only compatible with their own authority but necessary to establishing their influence and prestige.

An important dimension in giving symbolic content to this relationship in pre-colonial India was the symbiotic act of gifting a *khillat* (literally a robe) by the suzerain and receiving *nazar* (gold coins) or *peshkash* (valuables, such as horses) from a subordinate. According to Bernard Cohn, these acts of presentation, especially the gifting of a khillat, were key components of political relations founded on the idea that the king stood for a 'system of rule of which he is the incarnation . . . incorporating into his body . . . the persons of those who share his rule.' The implementation of incorporation through the giving of khillats and the receiving of nazars and peshkash made the holders of subordinate honour not just 'servants of the king, but part of him'.[84] The giving of these honours in person carried special significance because the 'hand of the giver left its "essence" on the robe' and as such 'investiture . . . [also] signalled suitability for courtly presence and the solidarity of élite culture.'[85] The reciprocal measure of offering nazar, an acknowledgement of the ruler as the 'source of wealth and well-being', was a reiteration of political allegiance and subordination that carefully graded the rank and status of the presenter.[86] The stakes involved in this relationship between levels of power were those of authority, dignity and symbols of lordship. And this in a political world that relied on personalized relations not inscribed, as would become the norm under the English East India Company, in formally written treaties. The robing ceremony was an enactment of political relations that drew the 'periphery' into the wider world of the 'metropolis' on the basis of the perceived advantages to be drawn by each party from such an association. Moreover, nazar and khillat

[84] Bernard S. Cohn, 'Representing Authority in Victorian India', in Eric Hobsbawm and Terence Ranger (eds), *The Invention of Tradition* (Cambridge: Cambridge University Press, 1989), pp. 168–70.

[85] Stewart Gordon, 'A World of Investiture', in Stewart Gordon (ed.), *Robes and Honor: The Medieval World of Investiture* (New York: Palgrave, 2001), p. 15.

[86] Cohn, 'Representing Authority', pp. 168–70.

'bridged ethnic and familial divisions' as they linked individual 'representatives' of a variety of networks of social belonging to a particular patron.[87] However, investiture ceremonies were also replete with 'semiotic ambiguity' that permitted the giver and recipient to imbue entirely different meanings into the ritual, infusing the 'interchange . . . with the fluid politics of the moment'. Indeed, 'each side could come away satisfied with only a minimal acceptance of what the other side meant.'[88]

An illustration of this system of political functioning at work in the Greater Punjab region was provided by Maharaja Ranjit Singh's visit to Jammu in 1838.[89] It was the occasion for reiterating ceremonially the hierarchy of power in the system which integrated Jammu into the durbar at Lahore. Gulab Singh, we are told, presented a peshkash of 'an elephant with a *haudah* of gold and fleet-footed horses' to Ranjit Singh which the 'world-conquering Majesty accepted . . . with a liberal heart'. So far the incorporation of Gulab Singh into the 'body' of the Maharaja of Lahore had been enacted and noted in Jammu, the Rajgi of the former. Interestingly, the same event became the occasion for Gulab Singh to demonstrate his own power over, and acceptance of it by, a hierarchy of subordinates from Jammu and Punjab. Thus, the *Gulabnama* recounts the granting by Gulab Singh of khillats, according to rank, to 'every one of the chiefs and all the servants, who had become prosperous through [his] respectable favours'. Significantly, the latter act of gifting by Gulab Singh was performed in the presence of Ranjit Singh. Even more significantly, the only instance in which Ranjit Singh made any intervention superseding Gulab Singh was to increase the khillat given to Frederick Mackeson, the political agent at Lahore. He was, as it were, asserting that insofar as the British government was concerned, if there was any symbolic incorporation to be carried out it would be into the 'body' of the Maharaja of Lahore, not that of the Raja of Jammu.[90] At any rate, what this

---

[87] Gordon, 'A World of Investiture', pp. 14, 15.

[88] Stewart Gordon, 'Robes, Kings, and Semiotic Ambiguity', in *Robes and Honor*, p. 380.

[89] Diwan Kirpa Ram, *Gulabnama*, p. 167.

[90] It must be noted that Mackeson's acceptance of the khillat, understood clearly as participation in the ceremonial assigning of hierarchy, was in marked contrast with the very different attitude adopted by the British later. As the

ceremony makes clear is that, at this time, numerous levels of power could coexist without reducing the statures of either the overlord or his subordinates.

The degree of authority and right of independent action allowed to subordinate levels of power was considerable prior to the Treaty of Amritsar. Thus, jagirdars were allowed their own rights of alienation from a jagir's income, placing them at the centre of a network of authority and patronage echoing the position of the maharaja himself.[91] The forging of alliances, an essential component of political functioning, and of the process of establishing and extending authority, could also be carried out autonomously. Although respecting the acknowledged suzerainty of the Lahore durbar, allegiances could even be formed along lines contrary to the suzerain's established policy. For instance, as Henry Lawrence, the agent to the governor-general, North West Provinces, noted, Gulab Singh and his brothers, while affirming the overlordship of the Lahore durbar, also pandered to the 'Mahomedan interest as a check upon the Sikhs', and that too 'in a country, and at a Durbar, where the commonest rites and ceremonies of Mahomedanism were forbidden and outraged'. As a result, 'at Jummoo alone was the call to prayer allowed, though prohibited even at Peshawur and in Huzara'.[92]

The Treaty of Amritsar drew the curtains in the new state on a system in which different groups had held varying degrees of 'nested authority'. After 1846, the structure of relations between superior and subordinate levels of the polity within Kashmir was sought to be

---

nineteenth century wore on, the British were no longer willing to accept khillats and nazars, defining them as bribes and tributes and, as such, markers of illegitimate political functioning.

[91] Thus, we have ample evidence from the Sikh kingdom of dharmarth grants (for the maintenance of religious institutions) made by jagirdars, enabling them to tap into the important symbolic resources of religious shrines. Foreign, 15 October 1852, Consultation no. 116, NAI and Foreign, 14 January 1853, Consultation nos. 212–23, NAI. In addition, land grant records indicate that persons serving the Lahore durbar were granted revenue-free lands by 'other vassal chiefs'. See, for instance, Sohan Lal Suri, *Umdat-ul-Tawarikh*, Daftar III, tr. Vidya Sagar Suri (Delhi: S. Chand & Co., 1961), p. 446.

[92] Minute by H.M. Lawrence, dated 3 August 1850, Foreign (Secret), Consultation no. 116, 27 December 1850, NAI.

taken apart and power held locally to be yielded up to the Dogra maharaja. It was in such a climate, in 1848, that Raja Jawahir Singh, the son of Raja Dhian Singh and nephew of Gulab, put forward a claim to Poonch, Jasrota, a part of the income of Kashmir, and a share in Gulab Singh's private property.[93] His demand, made on the grounds that they were the joint family estate of all the Dogra brothers, was dismissed as preposterous by British arbitrators. So was Jawahir Singh's insistence that he be included by name in the Treaty of Amritsar. An 'agreement' was effected by which Jawahir Singh was given a jagir and the title of 'Raja'. In return, he was to present Gulab Singh with one horse decked in gold trappings every year and also declare himself bound to consult him in 'all matters of importance'. The following extract from Sir Frederick Currie's judgement, dated 12th May 1848, demonstrates the thoroughness with which power was aimed to be swept up and gathered at the apex in the state. Thus Currie wrote that

> . . . whereas it is incumbent to maintain the old and established rights of all rightful persons it is directed that the Mian Sahibs will have no power or authority to dispose of in their own holding any important matter without personal consultation with and advice of the Maharajah Sahib Bahadur. And the Maharajah Sahib Bahadur is assured that the entire administration of the whole country *whether in the possession of the Maharajah Sahib Bahadur or his officers shall remain the Maharajah's sole concern.*[94]

The maharaja himself had declared his willingness to forget the past, and to receive and treat Raja Jawahir Singh with honour and consideration 'provided the latter render[ed] to him the obedience and duty of a subject'.[95]

---

[93] Poonch had originally been given to Raja Dhian Singh, Gulab Singh's elder brother, by Maharaja Ranjit Singh. On the death of Raja Dhian Singh and his eldest son, Raja Hira Singh, the jagir was confiscated by the Lahore durbar on the grounds that the holders had died in rebellion against the Sikh state. In the transfer of territories entailed by the Treaty of Amritsar, Poonch also passed to Gulab Singh.

[94] Panikkar, *The Founding of the Kashmir State*, pp. 121–3. Emphasis mine. Mian was an honorific reserved for those of the Dogras related to the ruling family.

[95] MSS Eur F.231/26, Lyveden Collection, Letter from the President in Council, 17 May 1855, no. 29, IOL.

If the maharaja's own family, who were also his closest allies, were so dealt with, then only the most unrelenting optimist in Kashmir could hope to fare any better. The fate of Sut Ram Razdan, 'a religious character' and one 'always much favoured by all parties',[96] exemplifies Gulab Singh's desire to uproot the authority of significant power-holders in the valley. Razdan, a Kashmiri Pandit, had been venerated by 'all the Hindus of the Valley' and had, in fact, also been patronized by Gulab Singh and his brother Suchet Singh when they had been mere 'vassals', even if powerful ones, at the Lahore court. By 1847, Sut Ram Razdan had no less than 'sixty five villages and portions of villages' which were 'dispersed through fifteen *parganas* in the Valley'. These were held either directly by him or in his name by dependants and friends who had acquired their lands mostly 'without official sanction'. In addition, he also had Rs 4500 worth of dharmarth (revenue-free religious endowment). A certain amount as *zer-i-niaz* or *hanudi* (both being categories of revenue assessment) had been paid to the state through Razdan, who collected it from those under him while the 'latter lived in security under the protection of his name'.[97]

Whereas in the wider political arena of the Sikh kingdom the Dogra brothers had cultivated individuals such as Sut Ram Razdan for the localized sources of authority they provided, with the assumption of direct control over Kashmir such groups now represented a potential threat that had to be kept in careful check. Razdan, being no ingénu himself, fully understood the new game afoot. Therefore, when called upon, along with others, to give an account of his grants, he categorically declined. A valuation was then made of his lands and Razdan was asked to mark off the villages retained by his dependants from those he held directly. This, too, he refused to do, declaring that 'if all was freely given he [would be] willing to take it' and that rather than condescend to explanation, 'if the Maharajah wished he might resume the whole'.[98] Razdan refused to produce, in support of his claims, documents of grants in his possession that might enable the state to legitimately separate villages held by his dependants from his own. What

[96] Political Diaries of Lieutenant R.G. Taylor, Assistant to the Resident at Lahore, on Deputation to Cashmere, May to October 1847, *Lahore Political Diaries*, vol. 6 (Allahabad: Pioneer Press, 1915), pp. 87–90.

[97] Ibid.

[98] Ibid.

was under challenge was his unofficial prerogative of independent alienation of the land rights granted to him. Gulab Singh, striking at a power-holder in Kashmir, was mostly minded to liquidate a network of allegiances that drew in a wider community than the single land-holder targeted in this case. As it turned out, Sut Ram Razdan was able to escape without serious loss, having to suffer only a minor cut in his revenue earnings while managing to retain possession of his sixty-five villages and tracts of land with all the advantages and immunities in areas which he 'had held for many years, and where he was known and he knew the people himself'. It is clear that he managed this because the maharaja, 'a man of his own religion', did not wish to treat him badly.[99]

This is in keeping with what appears to have become a concerted policy of co-opting the Hindu élite of Kashmir, the Kashmir Pandits. If the Pandits were a minority in the valley, their small number was trumped by their influence. This was due to their long tradition of literacy and so their indispensability to the administration of any regime in power in Kashmir. Recognizing this, Gulab Singh conti-nued the Pandits in their dominance of the administrative machinery of the state, most particularly in the revenue department, where an intimate knowledge of tax-gathering procedures was critical. Pandits, such as Sut Ram Razdan, had converted these privileges into the ac-quisition of substantial landed wealth. L.B. Bowring, a British civil servant on vacation in Kashmir, confirmed that Gulab Singh's 'prac-tice . . . [was] to appoint a Dogra Rajpoot of his own clan to exercise authority in his name, while this official was checked in all his acting by a Cashmeri Pandit. The former was the most trustworthy, but was as a rule uneducated, and could not do his work without the aid of the shrewd Brahman of the country.'[100]

On the other hand, Gulab Singh was unwilling to associate Kash-miri Muslims with the upper echelons of his administration and went so far as to let go of Muslim officials in the revenue department.[101] Even in his policy of vacating power in Kashmir, Gulab Singh appears to have targeted Muslim power-holders, such as the Khakka and Bamba rajas from the region of Muzzaffarabad, with particular deter-mination. Of course, it is also true that the Khakka and Bamba rajas

[99] Ibid.
[100] MSS Eur.G.91, L.B. Bowring's Memoir, p. 43, IOL.
[101] Bawa Satinder Singh, p. 171.

had been among the most refractory groups in Kashmir, unyielding before Gulab Singh and supporting the revolt of Sheikh Imam-ud-din, the last Sikh-appointed governor in Kashmir, who had refused to relinquish power in the immediate aftermath of the Treaty of Amritsar.

Henry Lawrence, agent to the governor-general stationed in Punjab, reported on 15 November 1846 that all the Khakka and Bamba rajas had submitted before Gulab Singh. There was nothing unusual in the submission asked of them, which had always been the first step towards 'incorporation'. What was novel was the degree of subservience expected now. The rajas were told by Lawrence that 'that this was their opportunity to *escape from the Maharaja's thraldom*, and that they must now, *once for all*, make up their minds to *submit*, or to *emigrate*'.[102] Further, they were reminded in 'distinct terms' that the 'Maharajah was now master of their fortunes, and that all would henceforward depend on their own good faith and submission'.[103] Those rajas or jagirdars who would not submit absolutely and permanently would be dealt with through the simple and expeditious measure of having them excised from the state altogether. They could either stay and abdicate all real power or opt to reside in British territory, receiving pensions from the British (to be drawn from land assignments made by Gulab Singh for the purpose in areas bordering British territory).[104] By 1856, a year before Gulab Singh's death, those of the Khakka and Bamba chiefs who had opted to remain in Kashmir had reportedly been 'reduced . . . to an abject state of submission'. The taxation on their now unprotected followers was so heavy that it was said, no doubt with some exaggeration, 'they had to sell their wives' and were constantly impressed as coolies to keep them down and incapable of further armed resistance.[105]

Aside from the Khakka–Bamba rajas, there were other Muslim jagirdars, dharmarth holders and *kardars* (revenue collectors) in Kashmir who were also shaken in their hold on power and landholdings

---

[102] Letter from the Agent to Governor-General to F. Currie, dated 15 November 1846, Foreign (Secret), Consultation no. 1248, 26 December 1846, NAI. Emphasis mine.

[103] Ibid.

[104] Letter from H.M. Lawrence to F. Currie, dated 15 October 1846, Foreign (Secret), Consultation nos. 1137–9, 26 December 1846, NAI; Governor-General's Despatch to Secret Committee, Foreign (Secret), no. 4 of 1846, 4 December, NAI; Foreign (Secret), Consultation nos. 1243–7, 26 December 1846, NAI.

[105] MSS Eur.D.974, Hugh Rees James Papers, IOL, p. 92.

upon the inauguration of Dogra rule.[106] George Clerk, the agent to the governor-general, North West Frontier, had reported in 1840 that the Naqshbandis of Kashmir were a reputable family who had been 'held in great esteem far beyond the limits of the country'.[107] This confirmed the account of his contemporary F. Mackeson, the political agent at Lahore, who had earlier assessed that the Naqshbandis were 'the first for respectability in Cashmere'.[108] Yet in 1847, Lieutenant R.G. Taylor, sent by the British to oversee the transfer of Kashmir to Gulab Singh, reported that Shah Ahmed Naqshbandi, one of the scions of the family, complained of 'the extent of injustice caused by . . . the Maharajah's acts'.[109] Similarly Pundit Kunhya Lal, sent on deputation to Kashmir by the British in 1847, reported on many instances of the resumption or the reduction of Muslim dharmarth holdings. At a *khanqah* (Sufi hospice) at Pulhalun, for example, despite proof offered by its votaries of long-standing revenue-free grants made by Maharaja Sher Singh (a son of Ranjit Singh) and others, 'their dhurmurth . . . had been discontinued by the Maharajah [Gulab Singh]'.[110] The shrine of Pulhalun, although an important one in Kashmir, was still not one of the most eminent. Yet even these latter did not escape Gulab Singh's attention. We have further evidence from Kunhya Lal that the officiants of the shrine of the revered Sufi ascetic Baba Payam-ud-din Rishi had 'a *lungur* or public charity room, for which formerly they used to get more, but [that] now the Maharajah ha[d] decreased [the grant]'.[111] P. Sandys Melvill, another British officer dispatched to Kashmir in this period, had described this same shrine at Baba Marishi as an object of devotion for a large number of people and John Ince, a near-contemporary observer, had ranked its sacredness third only after the *ziarats* (shrines) at Charar-e-

---

[106] MSS.Eur.B.369, vol. 5, Journals of T. Machell, Travels in Hindoostan, The Punjab, Scinde and Kashmir, 1855–56, pp. 199–200, IOL.

[107] Letter from George Clerk to Henry Torrens, dated 25 August 1840, Foreign (Secret), Consultations nos. 126–7, 1 March 1841, NAI.

[108] Letter from F. Mackeson, dated 18 July 1840, Foreign (Secret), Consultation nos. 126–7, S.C., 1 March 1841, NAI.

[109] Political Diaries of Lieutenant R.G. Taylor, p. 40.

[110] Diaries of Pundit Kunhya Lal, on deputation to Cashmere, 1847, *Lahore Political Diaries*, 1847–9 (Allahabad: Pioneer Press, 1915), p. 268.

[111] Ibid., pp. 268–9.

Sharif and Hazrat Bal.[112] The maharaja was exercising his newly-acquired power to resume or not to resume not simply over less conspicuous centres of power but also where it would be most visible and have the greatest impact. He was sending the clearest possible messages to power-holders in the valley of Kashmir.

There are strong indications, therefore, that Gulab Singh, on assuming power, threatened to, and in some instances actually did, resume jagirs in Kashmir granted by all previous regimes, apparently flouting the securities provided jointly by the treaties of Amritsar and Lahore. Henry Lawrence wrote in November 1846, in a state of outrage mixed with discomfort, that a jagirdar had come to him in Islamabad (Kashmir) 'to beg his intercession, saying he had heard that it was the intention [of Gulab Singh] to confiscate all jagheers'.[113] However, under pressure from the British, Gulab Singh was persuaded to 'leave all who had grants of land of old standing in possession'.[114] The purpose of such threats on the part of the maharaja seems not to have been to actually resume any jagirs, which the British were clearly going to prevent him from doing. As Dirks has suggested, in pre-colonial India 'giving land away was not really giving it away as much as it was incorporating new people into the moral-political economy in which the king was at the center.'[115] From this perspective, Gulab Singh wished to flex some muscle and assert the primacy of the new maharaja

---

[112] Diaries of Mr P. Sandys Melvill, Extra Assistant to the Resident at Lahore, on Deputation to Cashmere, 1847, *Lahore Political Diaries*, 1847–9, vol. 6 (Allahabad: The Pioneer Press, 1915), p. 205; John Ince, *The Kashmir Handbook* (Calcutta: Wyman Bros., 1867), p. 19.

[113] Letter from H.M. Lawrence to Frederick Currie, dated Cashmere, 12 November 1846, Foreign (Secret), Consultation no. 1241, 26 December 1846, NAI.

[114] Letter from Agent to Governor-General, North West Province, to Maharajah Golab Singh, Foreign (Secret), Consultation no. 1242, 26 December 1846, NAI. Additionally, Gulab Singh agreed to continue to the hill chiefs all jagirs granted to them one year before the death of Sheikh Ghulam Mohiuddeen (the last but one Sikh appointed governor of Kashmir) and further to remit one fifth of the tribute formerly paid by all to the successive Sikh governors. Governor-general's Despatch to Secret Committee, Foreign (Secret), 4 December, no. 4 of 1846, NAI. Also Mirza Saifuddin, *Khulastah-al-Tawarikh*, Urdu translation by Mirza Kamal-ud-din Shaida (Srinagar; Gulshan Publishers, 1984), p. 156.

[115] Dirks, *The Hollow Crown*, p. 137.

as the sole source of such grants. Previous arrangements of power were, figuratively speaking, lapsed and what was sought to be asserted was that their continuation was only at the pleasure of Gulab Singh. All attending loyalty and gratitude were now owed him: for any new sovereign, an important point to make clear.

The British pressure on Gulab Singh to avoid alienating all jagirdars in Kashmir was informed by their concerns for maintaining stability in this newly integrated territory which shared such sensitive 'international' frontiers. The difficulties caused by the 'revolt' of Sheikh Imam-ud-din, who had refused to surrender charge of Kashmir, had brought home the tenuousness of Gulab Singh's position in the valley. The new state had been threatened with ignominious failure at its very inception. The sheikh's rebellion had been a very potent menace as 'the whole resources of the country [had been] at his command, and all the Western Rajahs, Huzaras and Gukkars, [had been] only waiting the raising of his standard to join him.'[116] Indeed, the sheikh was reported to have had an impressively wide base of support in Kashmir. This was confirmed by Arthur Broome's suggestion that he had 'the chief power in the country and [Broome suspected] the popular feeling . . . [was] with him'.[117] Given these circumstances, the British opted for arrangements to bring over the sheikh's more powerful allies, since 'it appeared that if the Hill chiefs were to receive a guarantee from the British Government that they should be continued on the same footing as when under the Lahore Durbar, they would submit at once . . .'[118] Therefore the resolution of this first crisis caused by Imam-ud-din's revolt was limited to arrangements made solely with the more powerful landed interests of Kashmir and through assurances that they would continue to enjoy their former privileges. A select group of people, such as the recalcitrant hill rajas, the Naqshbandi family, or indeed individuals such as Sut Ram Razdan, continued to retain substantial landholdings in the valley of Kashmir.[119]

[116] Foreign (Secret), Consultation nos. 1089–94, 26 December 1846, NAI.

[117] Demi-official letter from Captain Broome in Kashmir, dated 13 August 1846, Foreign (Secret), consultation nos. 1085–8, 26 December 1846, NAI.

[118] Letter from H.M. Lawrence, Agent Governor-General, North West Frontier, to F.M. Currie, Foreign (Secret), Consultation nos. 1089–94, 26 December 1846, NAI.

[119] Hugh Rees James Papers, p. 58.

Clearly then, Gulab Singh did not destroy the entire structure of privileges in Kashmir, but sought systematically to divest localized niches of power of their former effective authority. This attempt at subduing the population of Kashmir may explain why even a tradition of mimic warfare in Srinagar was put an end to by Gulab Singh. An old proverb in Kashmiri designating the people of Ahalamar (a quarter in the city of Srinagar) as being singularly 'quarrelsome' also evokes a pseudo-martial social event, which was an important element in negotiating urban life in Srinagar. We are told that every Friday, the young men of one quarter of Srinagar would challenge those of another to a fight. A rendezvous would be agreed upon and 'youths armed with sticks and slings would assemble' and 'at a signal from their leaders . . . would join combat'. The outcome would range from 'broken limbs' to occasional deaths. And in this war play young men of the quarter of Ahalamar were particularly belligerent, encouraging the formulation of the said proverb immortalizing their pugnacity.[120] However, by the time of the new Dogra ruler, 'life [became] terribly earnest . . . [and] Gulab Singh did not approve of this fighting spirit'; leading him to put a stop to the tradition.[121] Any display of bellicosity even if only for entertainment was to be put down in Kashmir. One suspects that it was in the same spirit that Gulab Singh also launched a vigorous assault on 'dacoits' in the valley—the *galwans*—who were captured, put through summary trials, publicly hanged, and their bodies 'kept suspended for months together on gibbets'.[122] The faintest semblance of militancy in the valley was quashed with determination by Gulab Singh at the same time as the jungle of power holders was being cleared.

To reiterate all power located previously in subordinate levels was given up to the maharaja. This was done through the active intervention of the British, who assessed the proper seat of sovereignty to be located exclusively at the pinnacle of the new state, which was the person of the Dogra ruler. That the British became guarantors of this process is evident from statements by Henry Lawrence. For instance, he writes that 'They [the Rajas of Kashmir] all promised fidelity, first

---

[120] Rev. J. Hinton Knowles, *A Dictionary of Kashmiri Proverbs and Sayings* (New Delhi: Asian Educational Services, repr. 1985, first published 1885), pp. 3–4.

[121] Lawrence, *The Valley of Kashmir*, p. 255; and Knowles, pp. 3–4.

[122] Bamzai, *History of Kashmir*, p. 657.

to me individually and again before the Maharajah, who took their hands, and told them that if they offended he would refer to me, and deal with them as I might advise.'[123] This raises the important question of where the British were placed in relation to the new power structure in Kashmir, a point which caused much confusion in the minds of Kashmiris seeking redress of their grievances in the early decades of the state's existence. Not knowing whom to turn to, Kashmiris at this point in time more often than not fell through the cracks of an ambiguously defined location of power lying somewhere between the Dogra ruler and the overarching authority of the British. Colonial political theory after the takeover of India by the Crown from the East India Company in 1858 had only just begun to explicate the relations between the subjects of princely India and themselves. Even if this anticipates later developments, it still merits discussion here as it throws important light on the dilemmas plaguing Kashmiris at the very foundation of the state of Jammu and Kashmir.

The British, after 1858, held that the subjects of princely states owed a double allegiance to their own rulers and to the British crown.[124] Of course, juridical theories are never quite as simple or straightforward. Acknowledging the nuances of the principle of double allegiance, the British stated that since the position of a princely ruler pre-dated the treaties which then linked his state to the British crown, the prince's authority did not derive from the latter (despite the fact that the ruler held his position at the pleasure of the British

---

[123] Letter from H.M. Lawrence, Agent Governor General, to F. Currie, dated 15 November 1846, Foreign (Secret), Consultation no. 1248, 26 December 1846, NAI.

[124] This position was very clearly enunciated in 1891, for instance, in a telegram dated 28 May from the viceroy to the secretary of state regarding the murder of British officers by subjects of the north-eastern Indian state of Manipur. This missive stated that 'it is essential to our [the British] position in India that the subjects of Native States should understand that the murder of British officers renders the murderers and their abettors liable to punishment of death, whatever orders they may have received from the authorities of the state concerned . . .' By denying the validity of the defense put forward that State subjects in this case were obeying the orders of state officials, the British were articulating a principle of double allegiances by State subjects owed to their ruler and to the British crown. *Documents and Speeches of the Indian Princely States*, ed. Adrian Sever, 2 vols (Delhi: B.R. Publishing Corporation, 1985), vol. 1, p. 324.

monarch). Hence the loyalty of subjects of princely states was owed to their ruler since this allegiance antedated the treaties and was in fact 'an element in the composition of one of the parties entering into the treaty relationship'.[125] However applicable this reading may have been to other princely states in India, the position of Kashmiris *vis-à-vis* the Dogra state was quite different. There was no prior political relationship between the Kashmiris and the Dogras—that being first established through the treaty between Gulab Singh and the East India Company. To whom, then, was the primary allegiance of Kashmiris owed?

The predicament of the Naqshbandi family of Kashmir, referred to earlier, provides one example of the repercussions of such a confused allocation of effective power between the Dogras and the British. In a sense, the Naqshbandis posed a particularly potent threat to Gulab Singh because their authority in Kashmir was derived from sources unbounded by territory. Aside from their local significance in Srinagar as a prominent Sufi family, they owed their notability and influence to their links with powers outside the valley. They had enjoyed the patronage of Ranjit Singh and had been viewed by the British as friends who were of 'real service to European travellers' in Kashmir.[126] Gulab Singh's efforts to strike at their power after the Treaty of Amritsar were thwarted by the British, who persuaded him to continue their jagir grants to the Naqshbandis. Ever since this intervention, the Naqshbandis considered themselves dependent on the favour of the British government and continued to appeal to them directly well into the late nineteenth century.[127]

But they were a prominent family in Kashmir. What of others? When Lieutenant R.G. Taylor, assistant to the Resident in Lahore, arrived in Kashmir in 1847, he was asked four questions by the inhabitants: first, 'whether the British were the heirs to Kashmir'; second, 'whether he [Taylor] . . . had full powers to do what [he] liked'; third, whether in the case of complaint he would 'interfere

[125] Ibid., p. 29.

[126] Letter from George Clerk to Henry Torrens, dated 25 August 1840, Foreign (Secret), Consultation nos. 126–7, S.C., 1 March 1841, NAI and Hugh Rees James Papers, p. 58.

[127] Letter from F. Henvey, Officer on Special Duty, to C. Grant, dated Gulmarg, 3 August 1882, Foreign (A-Political E), nos. 28–31, October 1882, NAI.

authoritatively to procure redress or only intercede'; fourth, whether he would 'save any one who had complained from subsequent ill-treatment' by the maharaja or his officials. A very clear set of questions ostensibly deserving equally clear answers, but in fact obtaining mere equivocation. Taylor's only response was that 'the Maharajah was King of the country and likely to remain so; that [the British] could do nothing but recommend and intercede . . . but that [he] believed that [their] advice would meet with attention'.[128]

The Treaty of Amritsar in fact stood on a different footing from those signed with other Indian states in that no Resident was appointed, giving full internal autonomy to Gulab Singh. While private communications with the maharaja included many British injunctions impressing the importance of the equitable government of his subjects, their implementation was still left to his discretion. Thus the governor-general's instructions to the agent, North Western Frontier, were to insist to 'His Highness that it [wa]s by a just and liberal consideration for the interests of his people that he must hope to maintain his independence.'[129] Such highminded statements aside, the most corrosive aspect of British paramountcy over the state of Jammu and Kashmir was that while inefficient administration would draw the threat of interference from the colonial government, the causes of maladministration would not be relieved since British influence was to remain indirect. In 1847, Reynell G. Taylor, stated candidly that he saw his brief as 'open[ing] the door of complaint . . . [but keeping] the thermometer of hope of redress as low as possible and always represent[ing] [his] powers as extending to advice and intercession and no further.'[130] And in this policy the British sought theoretically to maintain an even-handed treatment towards all in the state. 'As to authoritative interference', stated the Secret Committee, 'the Government of India has no right to interfere . . . [and there could be] no distinction between the case of Jowahir Singh [Gulab Singh's nephew] and the case of any unfortunate weaver in Cashmere who may complain of Golab Sing's oppression.'[131]

Actually, as noted earlier, the British Government of India did use

[128] Political Diaries of Lieutenant R.G. Taylor, p. 42.

[129] Foreign (Secret), 26 December 1846, Consultation no. 1228, NAI

[130] Political Diaries of Lieutenant R.G. Taylor, p. 36.

[131] MSS Eur F.231/25, Lyveden Collection, Secret Letters received 20 March 1855, IOL.

'its good offices' to 'exhort [Gulab Singh] to act towards his nephew justly'.[132] The Kashmiri weaver, on the other hand, would not be a similar beneficiary of the British government's advocacy, although he continued to be enticed by the open door of complaint. The account of a traveller in Kashmir in the closing years of Gulab Singh's reign records the grinding oppressions of that ruler and the poverty of the 'labouring people of Kashmir' who still harboured the hope that the British would take over and bring them relief. He wrote of how 'some men weeding in a field looked up as he passed and called out: "Oh! Sahib! when is the Company's reign to commence? When are we to eat a little of this we labour for?" '[133] Another traveller's account from 1856 noted that many Kashmiris spoke of Gulab Singh as a kind of provincial governor of the British acting frequently on 'Lawrence Sahib's order'.[134] Gulab Singh's public behaviour in fact seems to have encouraged such an impression. Hugh Rees James, visiting the valley in 1856, noted that the letters J.H.S. had been struck on the new coins put in circulation in Kashmir. On inquiring, he was told that these letters were intended for 'Our Saviour's appellation and were placed on the coin by the Maharaja to retain the British alliance more firmly'.[135] Indeed, Gulab Singh seems to have been very conscious of the powers of intercession which the British had, no matter whether present in the valley in an official capacity or simply vacationing. He objected to the presence of Europeans in Kashmir particularly in the winter as that was when he collected his revenues and when complaints by the Kashmiris seemed to multiply.[136] British observers concurred that Gulab Singh was execrated throughout Kashmir, but declared in one voice that they could do nothing about it. With every 'interview' they conducted with the 'ground down oppressed labouring people of Kashmir', they confirmed not only the Kashmiris' consciousness of tyranny but also their realization of having no real recourse. That the Kashmiris had been overlooked in the power-sharing arrangement between the British and Gulab Singh after 1846 was painfully obvious. When

[132] Ibid.

[133] Journals of T. Machell, Travels in Hindoostan, The Punjab, Scinde and Kashmir, 1855–56, p. 198.

[134] Hugh Rees James Papers, p. 38.

[135] Ibid., p. 57. James does not clarify what J.H.S. actually stood for. However, one might reasonably speculate that the letters expand into Jesus Holy Saviour.

[136] Ibid., pp. 43–4.

asked why they did not complain to Henry Lawrence, groups of peasants asserted that 'they were prevented by the myrmidons of the
Maharaja'. Besides, they added that it seemed a futile exercise as 'the
Maharaja [was] so overpoweringly civil . . . to Lawrence Sahib' that it
was not likely he would listen to any complaints from '*us-log, Kunghal*'
(we, indigents). Shrewdly the Kashmiris pointed out that while the
maharaja declared to the 'Burra Sahib "*Sub Moolk ap ka, sub dowlut
ap ka*" [the whole country is yours, all its wealth is yours] . . . he
extort[ed] the last farthing from his peasants and [was] making Kashmir a desert.'[137] Through the Treaty of Amritsar, sovereignty over
Kashmir was negotiated with the person of the ruler and not with the
people of Kashmir.

Although the domination of Kashmir by the Sikh state based in
Lahore had lasted only for about a quarter of a century, it became an
important gauge against which both the British and Gulab Singh were
to measure their own performances as they fashioned the new state.
Henry Lawrence enjoined Gulab Singh in 1846 to 'make liberal arrangements with the Rajahs, chiefs and subjects [of Kashmir], . . .
leaving *no man worse off than he was under the Sikhs.*' As he urged
further, 'If you do so, your rule will be hailed with joy and your name
go down to posterity with blessings . . .'[138] The British were not overly
taxing their new ally, by and large extending the status quo with a
minimum requirement that Gulab Singh ensure his rule simply be 'no
worse' than that of the Sikhs.[139] There is a marked degree of disingenuousness in these professions of concern on behalf of the population of Kashmir, since Sikh rule over Kashmir had already been
denounced in the strongest of terms by the British.[140] It is interesting

---

[137] Mrs Hervey, *The Adventures of a Lady in Tartary, Tibet, China, and Kashmir*, 3 vols (London: Hope & Co., 1853), vol. 2, pp. 229–31.

[138] Letter from H.M. Lawrence, Agent to Governor-General, N.W. Frontier,
to Maharajah Golab Sing, Foreign (Secret), 26 December 1846, Consultation
nos. 1089–94, NAI. Emphasis mine.

[139] Thus we also have John Lawrence, in 1848, echoing H.M. Lawrence when
he wrote that 'the real point is whether his [Gulab Singh's] exactions and interference are greater or less than formerly.' Letter from John Lawrence (Officiating Resident) to H.M. Elliot, Foreign (Secret), 31 March 1848, Consultation
nos. 66–70, NAI.

[140] Note by Major Leech, Foreign (Secret), 18 November 1843, Consultation
nos. 16–19, NAI and Governor-General's Despatch to Secret Committee, Foreign (Secret), 4 December/no. 4 of 1846, NAI.

that, at this time, the comparison made so often from the late nineteenth century onwards between the poor state of affairs in princely India and the benefits available to subjects in British Indian territory, is rarely, if at all, heard. Therefore, in 1846, the British were not demanding the very highest of standards of governance from Gulab Singh. Further aggravating the situation for Kashmiris was the absence of representatives who might have spoken on their behalf. Much of the élite that had any power had either been divested of it, been forced to emigrate, or been co-opted as junior partners of the British or the Dogras. With 'representative' power vacated from the valley, all that remained were lambs meekly awaiting their shearing.

Kashmir as Treasury, Kashmir as Workshop

Had Gulab Singh indeed resumed all jagirs in Kashmir, who could have blamed him? On assuming power, the flustered maharaja 'gazing at the valley from a hill' was said to have noted 'that one part was mountain, one part under water, while the remaining third was in the hands of Jagirdars'.[141] Kashmir had long been envisioned as the endowment from which sinecures were awarded to all loyal servants of either Kabul, under Afghan rule, or Lahore, under Sikh rule. The image of Kashmir as treasury is brought alive by accounts of how all business would seemingly come to a halt at the court in Lahore when the tribute from that land of plenty reached there and provided its annual spectacle. In the words of W.G. Osborne: 'The yearly tribute from Cachemire had arrived, and was, as usual opened and spread upon the floor in the Durbar for inspection of the Maharajah. It consisted of shawls, arms, jewels, &c., to the amount of upwards of thirty thousand pounds.'[142] The opulent resources of Kashmir were valued gifts exchanged between rulers and subordinates in the act of incorporation. Maharaja Ranjit Singh was known to have gifted pashmina worth Rs 30,000 to single individuals.[143] These goods from Kashmir were not merely utilitarian necessities but luxuries that enhanced the stature both of rulers who gave them away and those who received

[141] Lawrence, *The Valley of Kashmir*, p. 201.

[142] W.G. Osborne, *The Court and Camp of Runjeet Singh* (Karachi: Oxford University Press, repr. 1973, first published 1840), p. 77.

[143] Sohan Lal Suri, *Umdat-ul-Tawarikh*, Daftar III, p. 161.

them.[144] The Kashmiris, therefore, must double, toil and trouble to produce the fabled riches of their land.

The issue of the famed Kashmiri shawl had assumed importance in the decades preceding the foundation of the new state. The empress Josephine of France had made it the last word in chic and thereby opened what seemed to be an insatiable market in Europe. Since 1815, the East India Company had been trying to divert to its holdings the Tibetan wool trade, which carried the much sought after *pashm* and *tush* to be woven into carpets and shawls.[145] In this connection, one of the earliest promises made by Gulab Singh to the British was to construct a new road from Kashmir and Jammu to Nurpur (Punjab) with a view to turning the trade of Kashmir, Bultistan, Gilgit, Ladakh and Yarkand through the Jalandhar Doab. He calculated that this would add largely to his own revenue and throw extensive and profitable trade directly into British territories.[146] The reform of the shawl-weaving industry also assumed a high priority with the British government when it sent Lieutenant Reynell G. Taylor on deputation to Kashmir in 1847. More so, because the weavers had struck work in protest against the high taxes levied upon them and about 4,000 of them had fled the valley.[147] The shawl industry was conducted through the *shagird* or weaver bound in conditions of 'near-serfdom' to his *karkhanadar* or 'master of manufactory'. Among other demands the Shagirds had appealed to the new government to fix their wages by law.[148] In the end, in a confirmation of the powerlessness of these Kashmiri artisans and as a testimony to the superior sway of the priorities of the British and Dogra shawl trade, the solution arrived at was in favour of the karkhanadars and at the cost of shagirds. Only those few shagirds who had their own capital resources could hope to break their ties to the karkhanadar; for the others, they had to agree to bind themselves for at least one year. Even this new concession

[144] W.G. Osborne, p. 77.

[145] Robert A. Huttenback, 'Gulab Singh and the Creation of the Dogra State of Jammu, Kashmir and Ladakh', *The Journal of Asian Studies*, 20, no. 4, August 1961, pp. 477–88.

[146] MSS. Eur. F. 85, Henry Lawrence Collection, Arthur Broome's letters to and from Sir Henry Lawrence, 3 April 1846, IOL.

[147] Pannikar, p. 139.

[148] Ibid.

remained a promise on paper, whereas the shawl-weavers were shackled to the same master for their lifetime.[149] Also, the market price of the shawl would now regulate the tax on it. All of these measures were enacted to ensure 'the protection of the karkhanadar' on whom the British and the Dogra maharaja relied for the supply of shawls.[150]

Gulab Singh was minded to reap commercial benefits from his 'purchase' of Kashmir. He enlarged an already burdensome taxation system from the pre-Dogra period to such an extent that his rapacity and avarice assumed legendary proportions. It was said of Gulab Singh in 1850 that, incapable of looking 'beyond his money-bags', he imposed a 'capitation tax on every individual practising any labour, trade, profession or employment, collected *daily*'.[151] Producers of *shali* (unwinnowed rice), the staple crop of Kashmir, were coerced into yielding at least 50 per cent of their harvest,[152] and the maharaja monopolized all trade in the valley, 'from firewood to taking two-thirds of the singhara (water chestnut) which formed the chief portion of food for many Kashmiris'.[153] Gulab Singh used his monopoly over the sale of shali to double its price, thereby leading also to pervasive hoarding and black-marketing among those minded to wring rich profits.[154] The custom of levying fees on marriages was prevalent, and a source of considerable income to the state. The Pandits, however, were exempt from the impost.[155] Such a harsh regime of taxation, not unexpectedly, produced widespread resentment, particularly among the peasantry. However, to dissuade them from quitting their fields—an act of resistance customarily resorted to by peasants as a last and desperate measure throughout India—the government raised the fee 'on the transfer of land' so that it was equal 'to the amount for which it was sold'.[156]

[149] Mohammad Ishaq Khan, *History of Srinagar, 1846–1947* (Srinagar: Aamir Publications, 1978), p. 59, fn 122.

[150] Political Diaries of Lieutenant R.G. Taylor, p. 56.

[151] George H. Hodson as cited in Bawa Satinder Singh, p. 169. Emphasis in the original.

[152] Ibid.

[153] Hugh Rees James Papers, pp. 48, 51.

[154] The price was hiked from one to two rupees per khirwar (a donkey's load). Bawa Satinder Singh, p. 169.

[155] MSS Eur.G.91, L.B. Bowring's Memoir, IOL, pp. 43–4.

[156] Bawa Satinder Singh, p. 169.

In 1856, Saif-ud-din, a news-reporter employed by the East India Company in Kashmir, informed Hugh Rees James that 'the only people who g[ot] a ready hearing from the Maharaja [we]re the "Khair Khwahs" or informers who led to the disgrace of and often supplant[ed] existing authorities by bringing to light their savings or profits: in fact, more attention [wa]s paid to the "farohee" or miscellaneous fees, confiscations etc. than to the legitimate sources of revenue'.[157] The maharaja's fiscal measures had aggravated the Kashmiri peasant's condition to an almost unbearable degree. No wonder, then, that Gulab Singh allowed no one out of his country without a pass or else, as one observer put it, 'his soldiers and zamindars would all bolt'.[158] Another asserted that if each point of exit from Kashmir were not as vigilantly guarded as it was, 'the number of emigrants would be so overpowering; that the province would be entirely depopulated in the course of a year or two.'[159]

Even if some of these statements stray into hyperbole, the predatory nature of Gulab Singh's taxation policies did draw protests and strikes from the Kashmiris. The autumn of 1848 saw Srinagar's shopkeepers temporarily closing down business and demanding reduced prices on goods sold to them by the government. This shut-down by shopkeepers was joined in by some 'industrial workers' as well.[160] And in January 1850 riots erupted in the valley. These isolated instances of protest were effectively put down by the state, on occasion with particular ruthlessness. A story that circulated widely and earned particular infamy for Gulab Singh was of the drowning of an agitator when he was forced to walk across a thinly iced Wular Lake.[161]

It seems quite extraordinary that so many of the British travellers in Kashmir during this period, so sensitive to the condition of the poor, degraded Kashmiri, should have done so little about it beyond criticizing the maharaja's thralldom verbally. In fact, the British cannot be exempted from some measure of responsibility for the plight of the Kashmiris. When Henry Lawrence urged Gulab Singh, in 1846, to behave more like a sovereign and less like a trader,[162] he was acting

---

[157] Hugh Rees James Papers, pp. 72–5.

[158] Ibid., p. 75.

[159] Mrs Hervey, vol. 1, pp. 250–1.

[160] Mirza Saif-ud-din, as cited in Bawa Satinder Singh, p. 170.

[161] Ibid.

[162] Foreign (Secret), Consultation 26 December 1846, nos. 1243–7, NAI.

not solely out of altruism for Kashmiris but also out of the desire to break the maharaja's monopoly over trade, which was impeding the free flow of goods into British Indian territory. British criticisms of the tyrannies of Gulab Singh coincided remarkably with the latter's obstruction of their attempts to break into the pashmina trade.[163] British officials were particularly intent on dismantling Gulab Singh's hold on the 'China trade' conducted from Leh (Ladakh) and including precious commodities from Tibet and Sinkiang.[164]

What became even more odious, and excited the particular ire of the maharaja, was the high-handed attitude adopted by growing numbers of 'junior' employees of the East India Company who began to look to Kashmir as their private holiday resort. Many of them made themselves more than comfortable in the maharaja's territories, particularly in the valley, 'acting as if Gulab Singh was personally indebted to each one of them for the grant of Kashmir'. Their egregious behaviour extended to making off with goods without payment or, in an extreme case, collecting money from Kashmiris 'under false pretenses'. While such outright breaches of propriety finally drew sanction from Henry Lawrence, and the British government sought to put an end to such practices in 1848 by insisting on its officials applying for permission to enter Kashmir, the problem of authorized tourists carrying on in similar vein was more difficult to control.[165] In 1852 and 1856, by arrangement with the maharaja, measures were enacted to ensure that a Company official would be stationed in the valley during the visiting season to 'regulate the conduct of European visitors'.[166]

There were other ways in which the British, travelling in the valley as tourists or junior officials on vacation, perpetuated the oppression attributed to Gulab Singh by actually using to their benefit some of its consequences. For instance, many of them condemned the practice of *begar* (forcible impressment of labour) and, yet, by their own admission, took full advantage of it. Mrs Hervey on a trip to Kashmir in 1853, admitted unabashedly to using the begar system to obtain coolies.[167] Of course, a justification had to be offered for collaborating

[163] H.B. Edwardes and H. Merivale, *Life of Sir Henry Lawrence* (London: Smith, Elder, and Co., 1873), p. 388*n*.

[164] Bawa Satinder Singh, p. 175.

[165] Ibid., pp. 174–5.

[166] Ibid., p. 175.

[167] Mrs Hervey, vol. 1, p.229.

in a practice so close to slavery. So, while many British accounts would, in one breath, condemn the custom they would, in the next, justify it as being the only way to get 'lazy Orientals' to do any work.[168] One way to continue to enjoy Kashmir and still minimize any guilt arising from the visible poverty was by, in some sense, dehumanizing the people of the valley. Witness an example of such a perspective carried to excess: 'There is no great beauty in form or feature, such as the Kashmirians have so long been undeservedly famous for. [But] the little girls are generally pretty . . . I offered to buy a little girl, who was sporting on the banks of the river; but no bribe was sufficient to tempt the mother.'[169]

More often, the Kashmiris were themselves blamed for their plight. Mrs Hervey, who thought pretty little Kashmiri girls were freely available on the market, believed also that the Kashmiri 'race, taken as a whole, are unattractive and contemptible in every way'.[170] But even more sympathetic observers, such as the civil servant L.B. Bowring, remarked that 'a braver race than the Cashmeris would have taken more resolute steps to better their condition'.[171] What makes all this that much more dismal is that the British were, in fact, among the few who articulated any concern for the Kashmiris at the time.

The Search for Legitimacy: Gulab Singh as Rajput Ruler

The relative ease with which large numbers of Kashmiris disappeared from the power arrangements established in the valley after the Treaty of Amritsar is, at the very least, surprising. British strategies that followed the installation of Gulab Singh as maharaja over them were evidently as sensitive to this quandary. Therefore, under British prompting, Dogra-sponsored histories made gestures towards some measure of a historically-based claim to Kashmir. Ganeshdas Badehra, the author of the *Rajdarshini*, a history of the Jammu rulers compiled in 1847, rooted Jammu's claim to Kashmir in 'ancient history'. He asserted that 'the *Vilayat* of Kashmir had long before the era of Kaljug

[168] Ibid., and MSS Eur.D.974, Hugh Rees James Papers, IOL, pp. 41–2.

[169] Mrs Hervey, vol. 2, pp. 113–14.

[170] Ibid., pp. 118–19.

[171] MSS Eur.G.91, L.B. Bowring's Memoir, p. 46.

[dark ages], been favoured by the Rajas of Jammu . . . [where their] rule [had lasted] for . . . fifty-five generations'.[172] With the Treaty of Amritsar, 'after the passage of a period of four thousand nine hundred and forty-seven years, the entitlement [to Kashmir had finally] reverted to . . . [Maharaja Gulab Singh]' thanks to the British.[173] But, except for those easily beguiled by the most blatant inventions of tradition, this was a tenuous and rather unconvincing assertion. It was now time for a shopping spree; the maharaja needed clothes to cover the bareness of his legitimacy to rule.

Writing in 1844, Frederick Currie, Secretary to the Government of India, had suggested that—

> The Government knows generally that the extensive territory now under the Government of Raja Gholab Singh has in very recent times been conquered by him and his late brother Dhyan Singh and the Sikhs, and that the former chiefs of the country have been deprived of their rights of sovereignty and prosperity with every circumstance of treachery and cruelty. Attached as the inhabitants of the hills are, to their ancient rajas it is impossible not to conclude that these acts of injustice and atrocity have left upon the minds of the people feelings of deep rooted animosity against the chiefs of Jummoo . . . It cannot but be supposed that the rule of Gholab Singh is submitted to only from fear, and that he can really command the willing obedience only of the man he pays.[174]

If this had been the thinking of a senior British official in 1844, it is especially significant that only two years later the governor-general, in a stunning volte-face, recognized the 'depredator' Gulab Singh as the representative of a pre-eminent Rajput ruling house. On 3 February 1846 he suggested that 'it may be politic and *proper* . . . to weaken the territorial power of the Government of Lahore, *rendering the Rajputs of the Hills independent of the Sikhs*'.[175]

Having chosen Gulab Singh as the sympathetic force on which to pin their strategies for countering the Sikhs on the one hand, and the

---

[172] Badehra, *Rajdarshini*, p. 228.

[173] Ibid., pp. 229–30.

[174] Broadfoot Papers, vol. III, B.L. MS 40, 129, Letter from Secretary to Government of India to Lt. Col. A.T. Richmond, Agent to Governor-General, North West Frontier, dated 31 January 1844, B.L.

[175] *Calcutta Review*, vol. VI, 1846, pp. 297–301, reproduced as Appendix G in Ganeshdas Badehra, *Rajdarshini*. Emphasis mine.

Afghans on the other, the British now had to give the Dogra raja a veneer of lawfulness. The evidence presented previously of Gulab Singh's spoliations in the hill territories of these 'ancient rajas' had to be swept quickly under some carpet. And the most readily available cover was provided by the newly remembered fact of his 'Rajputness'. James Tod's *Annals and Antiquities of Rajasthan,* published in 1829 and 1832, had made available ample evidence for the natural proclivity among these rulers for internal bickering while at the same time painting the Rajputs as natural aristocrats with a traditional mandate to rule.

Simultaneously, with the waging of war against Lahore and the breaking up of the Sikh dominion in 1846, documentation came to be produced which recounted the histories of ancient Rajput ruling houses in the region termed the 'Punjab Hills'. Until the early nineteenth century, this area comprised thirty-five states. In the seventeenth and eighteenth centuries, a first area was broadly called 'Jammu', including sixteen states and stretching in the north-west end of the hills.[176] A second and central area, lying south-east of the first, was dominated by Chamba and its neighbour, Kangra, and included ten states.[177] The third and last portion, further to the south-east, comprised nine states.[178] Beyond lay the ranges of the Himalayas. British characterizations from the mid nineteenth century sorted this hodge-podge of states under the neat rubric of 'Rajput'. This classification was intended quite as much as a positive identification as for demarcating these regions from the territory of the Sikhs.

It is notable, if not entirely surprising, that the term 'Rajput' was seldom used self-referentially either in the *Rajadarshini* or in the *Gulabnama,* both of which were written at the behest of and using materials in the possession of rulers of the hill states. Even when used,

---

[176] The states in the 'Jammu' group were Jammu itself, Lakhanpur, Jasrota, Samba, Tirikot, Dalatpur, Basohli, Bhadu, Mankot, Bandralta (Ramnagar), Bhoti, Bhau, Chanehni (also called Chaneni in a larger number of the texts examined by me), Bhadarwah, Kishtwar, Poonch.

[177] The eight states included, aside from Chamba and Kangra, were Nurpur, Guler, Kotla, Siba, Datarpur, Kutlehr, Jaswan and Bangahal.

[178] These excluded the Simla hills but included Kulu, Mandi, Suket, Kahlur (Bilaspur), Baghal, Hindur, Sirmur, Bashahr and Garhwal. Of these Kulu and Bashahr lay furthest from the plains, their huge hills making a formidable frontier.

the term was not the most important marker of either identity or prestige for the Dogras or other ruling groups of the Punjab hills. Indeed political, military and even cultural rivalry had characterized the relations between these states quite as much as any unity implied by such a label. It would appear that it is the British who first insistently deployed the category of Rajput to the political communities they meant to separate from the Sikh-dominated realm of the Punjab plains. Even more significant is that this taxonomy gained currency after the break-up of the Sikh kingdom began not only to appear imminent but also to appeal to the British as a desirable course of action. Writing in 1842, G.T. Vigne had derived the etymology of the word 'Dogra' from 'Do Rug' translated literally as 'two veins' and therefore connoting an individual 'of mixed blood and low caste'.[179] The validity of this theory aside, it shows that British and other European observers had not yet endorsed a glorified equation of the Dogras, or other ruling 'clans' of the Punjab hill states, with natural aristocrats just because they were Rajputs. In fact, it is remarkable how often Europeans were unable even to distinguish Dogra from Sikh, asserting frequently and with great authority that 'Golab Singh and his people [were] all Sikhs'[180] or averring that Gulab Singh was an 'oppressive Sikh ruler'.[181] Commentators such as Baron Hugel simply referred to Gulab Singh, his brothers and nephew at the court of Ranjit Singh as the rajas or 'lords' of Jammu.[182] Furthermore, the 'thirty-two petty sovereigns of the Himalayas' were just 'Hindu Rajas', 'imbeciles' all, who had established sovereignties through a 'predatory course' of action.[183]

By 1844 the death of Ranjit Singh's son, Sher Singh, and the 'virtual transfer of all power to the disorganized army' caused the governor-general to feel that the disintegration of the Sikh state was at hand. The East India Company drew out for Queen Victoria a scenario for the separation in Punjab between the government of the plains and

[179] Godfrey Thomas Vigne, *A Personal Narrative of a Visit to Ghuzni, Kabul. and Afghanistan*, 2nd ed. (London: George, Routledge, and Co., 1843), p. 254.

[180] Journals of T. Machell, Travels in Hindoostan, The Punjab, Scinde and Kashmir, 1855–56, p. 189.

[181] Hugh Rees James Papers, pp. 18–19.

[182] Baron Charles Hugel, *Travels in Kashmir and the Punjab* (London: John Petheram, 1845), p. 384.

[183] Ibid., pp. 21–5.

that of the hills, the two regions now being allocated to the Sikhs and the 'Rajputs' under Gulab Singh respectively.[184] Implicit in this view was that the Sikh kingdom artificially extended by a strong ruler such as Ranjit Singh was now bulging out of its seams and could not achieve a comfortable fit until it was pared down into its natural components. The Sikhs themselves had, until recently, held an honourable place in British minds. The latter saw them as having curbed the evils of 'Oriental Despotism' through the 'dispersed sovereignty' of the states they had established in the eighteenth century, before they went 'forth to conquer'.[185] Their fall from grace coincided rather too fortuitously with the British 'reconciling' themselves to weakening and ultimately eradicating Lahore's power as an independent state. Invoking the language of broken promises and dishonourable conduct on the part of the Sikhs, the governor-general issued a proclamation in 1849 announcing that the kingdom of the Punjab was at an end. It declared that

> For many years during the time of Maharaja Ranjit Singh peace and friendship prevailed between the British nation and the Sikhs. When Ranjit Singh was dead and his wisdom no longer guided the Councils of State, the sardars and the Khalsa army, without provocation and without cause, suddenly invaded the British territories . . . the Government has no desire for conquest now, but it is bound in its duty to provide fully for its own security and to guard the interests of those committed to its charge.[186]

But Ranjit Singh too had engaged in expansionist activities. Unlike then, however, the time was now ripe for the British to curb the power of the Sikhs. The containment of the latter would require the return of their 'due space' to the 'Rajputs' who were now seen to have been treacherously deprived of their possessions. The designation of Rajput as applied to the 'hill states' was offered at this point as a counter to that of Sikh. Almost simultaneously, we witness the dissemination of the lore of the ancient claims of the Rajputs to their lands. Thus, in 1846, Charles and Arthur Hardinge, on a visit to the new state of Jammu and Kashmir, described the Dogras as 'the Rughoolbunsee

[184] Bawa Satinder Singh, pp. 59–60.

[185] Thomas R. Metcalf, *Ideologies of the Raj* (Cambridge: Cambridge University Press, 1997), pp. 73–4.

[186] Latif, *History of the Panjab*, pp. 572–3.

Rajpoots descending from the old solar race, and have been in possession of this country [Jammu] since immemorial times'.[187] In 1847, Major G. Carmichael Smyth, a combatant in the first Anglo-Sikh war, included an important last section in his book called *A History of the Reigning Family of Lahore*.[188] This section was titled 'The Lord of the Hills;—A Genealogical History of the Jummoo Family' and opened with words now becoming increasingly familiar in references to the Dogras or indeed to any of the other ruling families of the hills. Explaining the origins of the Dogras, he wrote:

> According to various old Sanscrit manuscripts, corroborated by numerous incidents and historical facts in the traditional legends of the family, about 471 years before the time of the great Vikramadita, about the time of Kyroo (Cyrus) and his vast and great conquests, at which period a great commotion and stir seems to have been excited throughout all Ind . . . at about this period two Rajpoot brothers . . . emigrated with their families and followers . . . from a small village . . . [near] Oude . . . [the younger brother] settled in present Punjaub . . . [the elder] was the . . . supposed head and founder of the Joudpore and Jeypore families.[189]

Of course, tracing the roots of Hill dynasties in antiquity was evolving into a customary theme in British writing on the Dogras. What is surprising is the unusual reliance on sources that were otherwise scarcely considered historical by the British. Presumably, the ends justified the means in this case. Especially interesting in Major Smyth's account was the 'discovery' of a common root for the Dogras with the great families of Tod's Rajputana, Jodhpur and Jaipur. Indeed, when the British wished to persuade Gulab Singh to take steps to put down sati, they did so not only by suggesting that the practice was 'contrary to the Shasters' but also by pointing out that it 'had already been publicly forbidden by the Jeypoor Durbar'.[190] That Gulab Singh would willingly emulate the practice of another great and ancient Rajput ruling

---

[187] V.S. Suri, ed., *Siyahat-e-Kashmir* (Simla: 1955), p. 196.

[188] Major G. Carmichael Smyth, *A History of the Reigning Family of Lahore, with Some Account of the Jummoo Rajahs, the Seik Soldiers and their Sirdars* (Lahore: Government of West Pakistan, repr. 1961)

[189] Major G. Carmichael Smyth, pp. 233–4.

[190] Letter from H.M. Lawrence, Agent Governor General, to F. Currie, dated 15 November 1846, Foreign Dept. (Secret), Consultation 26 December 1846, no. 1248, NAI.

house was taken for granted. The rest of the Major's narrative is even more fascinating. In discussing the representatives of the Dogra house who were his contemporaries, he outlines a tale of a temporary lapse in an otherwise long story of peaceful and independent rule. Smyth's Dogras had 'preserved the independence of the[ir] hill state' by 'stout opposition' throughout a fair part of their history. But the ambitions of Gulab Singh and his brothers had precipitated the loss of liberty for Jammu and other ancient principalities, when they joined the service of Ranjit Singh and conquered in his name. In the mean time, 'the people of the country . . . [had remained] well disposed towards any one who had the will and power to harass and annoy the Seik [Sikh] intruders'.[191]

The claim made by Major Smyth was that, with the Anglo-Sikh wars, the British were restoring their old freedom to Rajputs chafing under the dominance of Lahore. The myth of the 'freeing' of the Rajput hill states from the Sikhs gained such currency from the mid-nineteenth century on that it became a widely accepted orthodoxy and hackneyed reference even for commentators on the artistic traditions of the region. In 1931 J.C. French, a civil servant in India who had conducted extensive research on the paintings of the Himalayan principalities in the best traditions of the enlightened amateur, wrote how he could not

> . . . recall the Sikh conquest of the Kangra Valley without regret. Immemorial tradition and culture were suddenly and violently broken. What makes it all the more pathetic is that immediately afterwards came the first British-Sikh war, which freed the surviving Rajput states from the Sikhs. If only Kangra could have survived till then, we should have a living picture of India a thousand years ago, the India unshattered by Mahomedan invasions, a land of beauty like China and Japan.[192]

Therefore, the other enduring image created in the mid-nineteenth century was of a pristine Hindu India that had survived only in the Punjab hills but that had subsequently been interfered with both by the Muslims and the Sikhs. Indeed, French opened his book by noting how 'when the Mahomedans invaded India, Hindu culture, guarded

[191] Major G. Carmichael Smyth, p. 268.

[192] J.C. French, *Himalayan Art* (Delhi: Neeraj Publishing House, first published 1931, repr. 1983), p. 93.

by Rajput swords, retreated to the hills'.[193] This association of Rajput with Hindu was not new and had begun to circulate among colonial scholars ever since the publication of Tod's *Annals*. For the Punjab hill principalities, elaborate studies had emphasized the Hindu religious basis of the authority of the raja who was 'the head of the State Religion, venerated as divine, either in his own right or as vice-regent of the national god'.[194] And it was this divinity of the raja which ensured that his subjects rendered him 'a ready and willing obedience', making for the 'tranquillity' of these principalities in contrast to the chaos of 'contemporaneous Muhammadan and Sikh rule'.[195] The Punjab hill states were also viewed as having proven better guardians of the Hindu faith than the ruling houses of Rajputana. The latter had adulterated their ancient purity by long and repeated contact with 'Muslim invaders', participating in the power of the Delhi rulers and imbibing freely of their alien culture. The hill states, on the other hand, had remained isolated from trends diluting their ancient faiths and cultures. Pristine Hinduism, which had survived unchanged and protected ever since its retreat to the hills, and which was in turn supported by its Rajput rulers, laid the foundation for 'legitimate' and 'natural' rulerships. 'It was not material force' we are told 'that has given them a perennial stream of vitality. They [had] struck their roots deep as trees grow in the rain and the soft air; they have, as it were, become one with nature, a part of the divine and established order of things, and the simple Rajput peasant no more questions their right to rule than he rebels against the sunshine which ripens his harvest.'[196] For those who held such opinions, Ranjit Singh, being neither Rajput nor Hindu, could not but have represented illegitimate, alien rule over the 'simple Rajput peasant'. The low standing of a Muslim ruler in such visions of legitimate power in the hills needs no further elaboration.

Even the sketchiest study of the history of the Punjab hill states makes it difficult to sustain the idea of this hermetically sealed and virginal domain of a Hindu–Rajput culture and polity. Indeed the evidence from the realm of art points, on the contrary, not only to

[193] Ibid., pp. 1–2.

[194] J. Hutchison and J. Ph. Vogel, *History of the Punjab Hill States*, 2 vols (Simla: Dept. of Languages and Culture, repr. 1982), vol. 1, pp. 65–6.

[195] Ibid., p.96.

[196] Griffin, *Rulers of India: Ranjit Singh*, p. 13.

creative exchanges with the 'Muslims' and 'Sikhs', but also to the existence of a cultural continuum which integrated the hill principalities with the Punjab. Much as the British sought to advance the category of Hindu–Rajput against that of Sikh on the basis of which to divide the Punjab, the paintings of the hills and Lahore foil this enterprise. B.N. Goswamy, one of the most perceptive observers of the 'Pahari' (mountain/hill) style of paintings, powerfully counters attempts to categorize schools of painting on the basis of 'political barriers'.[197] He suggests that these fail to acknowledge the very porous frontiers between states that were constantly breached by migrating families of artists who could serve numerous political masters at the same time. He provides weighty evidence of the connection of the most influential family of artists in the Pahari style, namely that of Pandit Seu, with at least sixteen different political masters, over several generations from the mid-eighteenth to the mid-nineteenth centuries. The most compelling material produced by Goswamy is a 'magic diagram' of a semi-nude female figure with fifteen outstretched arms pointing to the names of sixteen sets of patrons.[198] The diagram, preserved by surviving descendants of the Seu family, is interpreted by Goswamy to be a picture of the *siddhi* or family deity. The arms are 'disproportionately long and skinny' and produce the effect of 'a spider's web'. It is significant that among the patrons recorded to have been served by the family are also three Sikh chiefs. In effect, the web of the siddhi's arms mapped, through a potent religious image, the spread of a style of painting that associated without difficulty the Punjab with the hill states. Had the artists needed to follow up their migrations with radical changes in style, it would be difficult to argue for an artistic continuity between these two regions. But Goswamy demonstrates that the mid-nineteenth century descendants of Pandit Seu continued to work in their 'own family style regardless of the region where . . . [they] were

[197] B.N. Goswamy, 'Pahari Painting: The Family as the Basis of Style', *Marg* (1968), XXI, no. 4, 17–62.

[198] Ibid. The names of the states and patrons whom Pandit Seu's family served are inscribed in the magic diagram. They include Shri Guler (inscribed right above the head of the deity), Chamba, Qila Kangra, Mandi, Suket, Kahlur, Kangra Nadaun, Jaswan, Siba, Datarpur, Shri Gurbaksh Singh, Ramgarhia Jassa Singh, Sujanpur, Mankot, Jammu, Shahpur, Shri Jai Singh, Nurpur and Basohli. These names are the names of thirteen Pahari states and of three Sikh chiefs.

operating'.[199] Moving to Lahore or Patiala did not represent the sort of break that it would in the late nineteenth century. Then, Pahari artists were forced to accommodate themselves to entirely new trends and aesthetic traditions, finding it 'necessary to paint their patrons in Victorian costumes and add to their collection of sketches, photographs of Parisienne models cut out of European magazines'.[200]

Artistic material also counters the perspective of a Hindu bastion in the hills holding out eternally against 'Muslim' swords. B.N. Goswamy uncovers the influences of the Mughal style of painting on the Pahari in the early decades of the eighteenth century. His evidence indicates that while this influence did not manifest itself in any sudden conversion, it was not resisted dramatically either, as might be expected by adherents of the school that held the Pahari states to be resolute defenders of Hindu–Rajput identity from Muslim defilement. Instead, what is presented to us is a process of interchange that modified profoundly the style of Pandit Seu's family, those eminent painters from the hills, but 'only gradually and after a great deal of experimentation and adjustment'.[201] Pahari paintings often linked locales and historic events that have no apparent connection with the subject of a picture. For instance, a picture of 'Raja Balwant Singh (of Jammu) with a party of musicians' bore an inscription that declared it had been painted in 1748 'when Mir Mannu, the Mughal Viceroy, came to Lahore, after having won his victory over the Pathans'.[202] Nainsukh, the son of Pandit Seu, had commemorated a raja in Jammu celebrating with the Mughals in Lahore.[203] And, more notably, the painting had connected temporally two geographic and political spaces. There is no corroborating solace to be found here for those who would wish to draw images of the isolation of 'Rajputs and Hindus' from 'time immemorial' in their mountain fastness. On the contrary, the testimony of Pahari paintings and painters melds plain and hill, Punjab and the Himalayan foothills, 'Muslim', 'Hindu' and 'Sikh',

[199] Ibid., p. 57.

[200] Ibid.

[201] Ibid., pp. 33–4.

[202] Mulk Raj Anand, 'The Pictorial Situation in Pahari Painting', *Marg* (1968), XXI, no. 4, pp. 12–13.

[203] W.G. Archer, *Indian Paintings from the Punjab Hills*, 2 vols (Delhi: Oxford University Press, 1973), vol. 1, pp. 198–9.

one into the other, their seeping colours erasing stark boundaries through the movement of artists and artistic exchange.

British strategies at the time of signing the treaties of Lahore and Amritsar attempted to push Gulab Singh and the Dogras into the realm of the 'Rajput' hills and away from Punjab. However, the ties between Jammu and Lahore were underlined by linguistic connections, the religious traditions embedded in stories of numerous shrines dotting its hilly landscape, as much as by the painting heritage of Lahore and Jammu. G.A. Grierson's linguistic survey linked the two regions firmly by demonstrating the similarities between Punjabi and Dogri, the language spoken in Jammu. Besides the language itself, he directed attention to an oral tradition of folktales forming the substratum of popular culture in both areas—such as the stories of Sassi Punnu or Sohni Mahiwal.[204] Punjab and Jammu confirmed their affinities also in the festivals that they shared but which were unknown in the rest of the subcontinent, such as Basant and Lori. After the creation of the state of Jammu and Kashmir in 1846, these common occasions for celebration continued and were marked by the Dogras with special durbars.[205] The Dogra court also persisted in the special verve with which Holi had been celebrated at Ranjit Singh's court.[206]

Regions that pray together, stay together. This certainly seems in evidence before 1846 if one looks at religious traditions and the patterns of the patronage of religious shrines that further wove the Punjab and Jammu into a single intricate tapestry. We have already noted the patronage of religious shrines by Gulab Singh either in the Punjab itself or the alienation of the revenues of Punjab villages for the maintenance of shrines in Jammu. Similarly, Ranjit Singh had regularly visited and honoured many of the important shrines of Jammu, such as at Uttarbehni and Purmandal.[207] At the latter, Ranjit Singh had the dome of one of the temples (that of Uma Mahapati) painted gold and also built the Eklingaonkar temple, a Shaivite shrine.[208] During his

[204] G.A. Grierson, *Linguistic Survey of India*, 11 vols (Delhi: Motilal Banarsidass, 1967–68), vol. 9, part 1, pp. 637–9.

[205] Frederic Drew, *The Jummoo and Kashmir Territories* (Delhi: Oriental Publishers, repr. 1971), pp. 68, 72.

[206] Ibid., p. 71.

[207] Diwan Kirpa Ram, pp. 164, 166; Frederic Drew, *The Jummoo and Kashmir Territories*, p. 89.

[208] Mira Seth, *Dogra Wall Paintings in Jammu and Kashmir* (Delhi: Oxford University Press, 1987), p. 16.

visit to Jammu in 1838 he made the significant gesture of 'attain[ing] the darshan of Shri Thakaran' in the palace temples of the Dogra rajas.[209] The important religious function of executing wall paintings in temples in Jammu also reflected the links between this region and the Punjab. Murals depicting characters from the *Ramayana* often showed them wearing Sikh hair styles, beards and costume.[210] There were other ways in which the shrines of Jammu had their authority embedded in the Punjab. Ties with Guru Nanak, the first guru of the Sikhs, run through the hagiographical traditions around numerous Sufi shrines in Jammu. To cite but two examples, the shrines of Budhan Ali Shah and of Pir Lakhidata, both in Jammu, derived their legitimacy not only from the revered mysticism of these individual saints but also from their connections with Guru Nanak. Both saints are said to have met with the Sikh guru and engaged in spiritual disquisitions with him. However, in an unusual departure from the hagiographical norm, which claims spiritual victory for its own religious leaders, these Jammu saints are said to have capitulated before the superior moral power of the guru.[211] Not only had Jammu acknowledged its ties to Lahore but it had also successfully evolved a *modus vivendi* that accepted the authority of the Punjab.

This is not to overstate the subordination of Jammu, since Sikh paintings returned the compliment by assigning to Gulab Singh and his brothers a stellar place in their own depictions of the power and splendour of the Sikh kingdom. Indeed, the Dogra brothers at Lahore and especially Gulab Singh, became the centre of what was clearly a 'popular cult'.[212] Gulab Singh was painted repeatedly, in his bath before prayers, in portraits, and more significantly, as an indispensable figure in durbar scenes. The most vigorous phase of the celebration of Gulab Singh lasted until 1846, when he had won extensive territories for his master and when his 'reputation had come to rival even that of Ranjit Singh'.[213] What is most surprising is that this adulation continued, not only after Gulab Singh had been made the independent

---

[209] Diwan Kirpa Ram, p. 166.

[210] Seth, pp. 37–8.

[211] Zohra Khatoon, 'Shrines of the Pirs at Jammu', M.Phil. dissertation, University of Jammu, 1981, pp. 12–16, 36–9.

[212] W.G. Archer, *Paintings of the Sikhs* (London: H.M.'s Stationery Office, 1966), pp. 53–6.

[213] Ibid., p. 55.

sovereign of Jammu and Kashmir, but also into the last quarter of the nineteenth century. While some at the Lahore court would have considered him a traitor, paintings continued to reproduce him as a pivotal figure in nostalgic visual renderings of the lost power of the Sikhs.

Given the intimate association between Jammu and Punjab, the separation brought about by the Treaty of Amritsar seems not to have registered much at first. The *Rajdarshini*, written in 1847 as a Tawarikh-i-Jammu (history of Jammu), deals with the Treaty of Amritsar with surprising brevity. The changes involved are summed up with stunning banality as 'his [Gulab Singh's] boundaries were separated from the kingdom of Punjab, Finish'.[214] As though all that had occurred was simply another one of those tiresome but common family feuds that so often rent joint households, separating property but without ever entirely breaking ties. The text, an eulogy to the ruling house of Jammu, even when discussing the dire hostility of Dogra conflict with Lahore after Ranjit Singh's death, continued to pay due deference to the Lion of the Punjab through references to him as 'Sarkar'.

However, the British government in India had resolved to break up the Punjab and wean away its component parts despite the numerous bonds that held them together. In 1846, in justification of the Treaty of Amritsar with Gulab Singh, 'by which a Rajpoot principality of the Hill districts [had] been constructed,' the governor-general of India stated:

> As it was of the utmost importance to weaken the Sikh nation before its Government should be established I considered the appropriation of this part of the ceded territory to be the most expedient measure I could devise for that purpose by which *a Rajpoot Dynasty will act as a counterpoise against the power of a Sikh prince . . . and both will have a common interest in resisting attempts on the part of any Mahomedan power* to establish an independent state on this side of the Indus or even to occupy Peshawar.[215]

The 'Rajputness' of the Dogras was wielded like the tailor's scissors with which to cut down to size the fabric of a 'greater Punjab' and fashion a new set of clothes to cover the nakedness of Dogra legitimacy,

[214] Badehra, *Rajdarshini*, p. 227.

[215] Foreign (Secret), Governor-General's Despatch to Secret Committee, no. 8 of 1846, NAI. Emphasis mine.

at least in Kashmir. And Gulab Singh was invited to don this newly designed 'line'. If this was the costume the British had fitted him for, then Gulab Singh wore it with enthusiasm. In fact the Dogra rulers of Jammu and Kashmir, through the rest of their history, joined eagerly in a mad competition to 'out-Rajput' the other Rajputs of India, as a way of claiming legitimacy to rule. 'Rajputness' had provided them with a mandate in 1846 and there was no reason why it should not continue to be milked thereafter.

CHAPTER 2

The Consolidation of Dogra Legitimacy in Kashmir

Hindu Rulers and a Hindu State

E ighteen fifty-seven marked the end of a period of experimentation and the consolidation of Dogra power in Jammu and
Kashmir. With the death of Gulab Singh in that year and the
accession to the throne of his son Ranbir Singh a year earlier (*r*.1856–
85), the tentative efforts at tracing bases of legitimacy for the Dogras
within and outside the state were now sought to be given definite shape
and substance. This was a many-faceted endeavour, encompassing
Dogra attempts at intervening in the realm of Hindu religion and the
construction of the social and political prestige of the ruling house on
that basis. Yet no matter how widely the net of legitimacy was cast, it
still excluded the majority of the subjects of the valley of Kashmir who
happened to be Muslims. Insofar as the Hindu minority of Kashmir,
the Pandits, was concerned, there was a distinct effort made at working
with them, founded on a broadly defined religious affinity with their
new Dogra masters.

In this period, the representation of the Dogras as Rajputs was assiduously broadened to identify them also as Hindu rulers; this religious
definition, I argue here, is crucial to understanding the marginalization
of Kashmiri Muslims within this state-(still)-in-formation. The newly
and publicly evident Hindu nature of the state not only allowed at least
the Kashmiri Pandits to feel associated with it, but was partly actuated
with this purpose in mind. This is not to put forward a simplistic argument of a 'clash of religions' in the forging of Dogra state ideology. The
'Hindu-ness' of the state became a critical element of its legitimacy,
particularly in the terms for paramount relations and negotiated

3: Maharaja Ranbir Singh. Add.Or. 3003.
By permission of the British Library.

sovereignty set forth by a crown raj recovering from the tremors of the mutiny/rebellion of 1857.

That year forms a historical turning point in more ways than one. It represents not only a moment of dynastic succession in Kashmir but also the yielding of an old order to a new under British rule in India: a new order in which 'religion' acquired its capitalized initial conceptually, and its capital place in carefully devised policies of non-interference and interference in Indian society. We need to pay close attention to the rule of Maharaja Ranbir Singh, doubling up as a period of the endorsement of the 'Hindu-ness' of the Dogras and the consequent muting of the voice of the largest majority of their subjects, the Muslims of Kashmir.

Queen Victoria's Proclamation and Religious Freedom in Jammu and Kashmir

On 1 November 1858 Queen Victoria, in her famous proclamation, handed down to her Indian subjects what seemed to be a veritable charter of religious freedom. This was an attempt to correct the high-handed nabobism adjudged responsible for precipitating the rebellion of the previous year. Now 'All her Indian subjects were to be secure in the practice of their religions' and to enjoy 'the equal and impartial protection of the law'.[1] Yet it would appear that a portion of India would continue to be left out of its sway. For the queen had simultaneously acknowledged the claims of those loyal 'breakwaters in the storm', the princes of India, guaranteeing 'their rights, dignity and honour' as well as protecting their territorial possessions.[2] Therefore, subjects of the state of Jammu and Kashmir, as in other princely states, would stand poised uneasily between British and not-so-British India in matters of religious (non-)interference and freedom. In British India, Victoria's proclamation was implemented through the construction of a colonial state claiming to arch loftily above religion and the Indian spirit of factionalism. In princely India, however, religion was deemed to form the bedrock of political and social functioning.

---

[1] Bernard S. Cohn, 'Representing Authority in Victorian India' in Eric Hobsbawm and Terence Ranger, eds, *The Invention of Tradition* (Cambridge: Cambridge University Press, 1989), p. 165.

[2] Ibid.

In 1846 the argument offered by H.M. Lawrence, against the British taking over Kashmir directly and in favour of handing it over to Gulab Singh, rested on precisely this sort of reasoning. Explaining himself, Lawrence wrote:

> [Kashmir] would be a pleasant land for a man to dwell in, but I am not a whit more satisfied after seeing it that we were wrong in not taking it . . . Just now the people would be glad to have us for masters, but *being all Mussulmans or Brahmins* they *would* soon prove restive. About four fifths are Mahomedans and would *of course* kill cows while the minority *would* be hostile to the measure . . . between Moollas and Pundits our Raj would not long be declared to be Heaven sent.[3]

In territories where the populace was deemed to suffer from innately ingrained religious identities determining their every intent, purpose and deed, governance was best left to one of them. Viewed in this light, even acts of political rebellion were not perceived as such but determined conclusively to have an underlying religious motivation. For instance, the first transfer of territories to Gulab Singh after the Amritsar treaty of March 1846 had included the Hazara country (later reassigned to Punjab). This move was fiercely resisted by its chieftains, uncomfortable with new arrangements of loyalty and submission. But in the East India Company's astute misunderstanding of India, 'the peaceful submission of wild and turbulent mountain tribes, *of a religion different from that of the Rulers assigned to them, was scarcely to be expected*'.[4] All this to argue that if religious-mindedness was an Indian peculiarity, it was best handled by another Indian.

However, if Queen Victoria's proclamation was not to lose all meaning once caught in the quagmire of that 'other' India of her princes, out-and-out prejudice and 'persecution' would have to be reined in by the colonial administration. The penumbra, in matters of religion, of 'traditional' princely India was assuming shape surrounded by the harsh light cast by pontificating 'modernizing' British Indian officials on the royal anachronisms they were now, however, duty-bound to preserve. The darkest shadow fell over the domain to

[3] Foreign Secret/Cons. 26 December 1846/no. 1240–1 + K.W., NAI. Emphasis mine.

[4] Letter from J.W. Hogg and G. Tucker to the Honourable, the President in Council at Calcutta, Foreign (Secret)/Despatch from the Court of Directors/6 March 1847/no. 1258, NAI. Emphasis mine.

which outright religious 'obscurantists' and 'fanatics', both in British and princely India, were shunned.[5] Indian princes did not form an entirely satisfactory body of imperial partners, especially on the question of religion, but they would have to be tolerated for the greater good of ensuring the sway of *Pax Britannica*. In adopting this stance of resigned tolerance, the British seemed to be overlooking, not always consciously but mostly purposefully,[6] the vital changes introduced in the subcontinent's political dynamic since their first territorial acquisitions in the mid-eighteenth century. However, it is undeniable that, given its brief through the proclamation of 1 November 1858, of desisting from overt interference in princely India, colonial officialdom would do its utmost to follow it to the letter.

The proof lay in the imperial government's treatment of the grievances of missionaries seeking to establish a medical mission in Srinagar. The repeated stymieing of their efforts by a suspicious Maharaja Ranbir Singh, who viewed them as insidious ploys to win converts to

[5] The 'Wahabis' and those of the Indian princes who had participated in the rebellion of 1857 were cases in point. It must be noted that the term 'Wahabi' was used loosely by the British to describe diverse groups of Muslims and Islamic reformist movements that were seen to be implacably opposed to British rule. This category was the product of a feverish British imagination, insecure after the rebellion of 1857, that saw the 'spectre' of Muslim 'conspiracies' everywhere and led to a series of Wahabi trials beginning in 1864. In fact, quite unlike the eighteenth century movement of Abdul Wahab in the Arabian peninsula, reformist movements in India were rarely 'frontal assaults on popular region which stressed the importance of saints, vernacular languages and time-honoured rituals.' Sugata Bose and Ayesha Jalal, *Modern South Asia: History, Culture, Political Economy* (Delhi: Oxford University Press and London: Routledge, 1998), p. 85; Peter Hardy, *The Muslims of British India* (Cambridge: Cambridge University Press, 1972), pp. 83–4.

[6] For instance, attempts at acquiring and holding power over tribes in Orissa in the early nineteenth century, applicable to similar enterprises in Rajputana at around the same time, relied on a very acute sense and application of the principle that 'knowledge is power'. The essence of this strategy lay in the understanding by the colonial establishment that 'The man who correctly understands how a particular structure works can prevent it from working or make it work differently with much less effort than a man who does not know these things.' F.G. Bailey, *Strategems and Spoils*, cited in Robert W. Stern, *The Cat and the Lion: Jaipur State in the British Raj* (Leiden: E.J. Brill, 1988), p. 23.

Christianity, led finally to a complaint being filed by no less a personage than His Lordship the Bishop of Calcutta. In 1867, objections were lodged *via* the secretary to the government in Punjab that 'coercive measures ha[d] been and [we]re used to a greater or lesser extent by the maharaja's establishment to prevent patients attending the Mission dispensary' from a fear that the sick might also receive 'religious instruction'.[7] Later in that year, the civil officer on special duty, Major J.E. Cracroft, reiterated British missionary frustration that 'left to themselves, the sick at Srinugger would more freely resort to the dispensary than they d[id]'. He suggested further that 'everyone holding communication with Europeans, and the civil officer in particular, [wa]s more or less watched', preventing people from 'freely express[ing] their opinions'.[8] The Bishop of Calcutta added to these charges the much graver one of the Kashmir durbar's outright persecution of converts to Christianity. Significantly, he bolstered his case for intervention by the Government of India by asserting that the maharaja's acts represented a 'contravention of the proclamation of 1858'.[9]

In his reply to the Lord Bishop, the viceroy, 'while deeply regretting the pressure to which Christian converts [we]re said to be subjected', made it quite clear that he would be 'unable to take any action under the Proclamation . . . because the terms of that document appl[ied] only to territories included within the limits of British India. In the case of a tributary State like Cashmere' all that could be done was to 'discourage persecution by expostulation and indirect influence'.[10] Therefore, while Kashmir fell within the sway of British paramountcy, religious freedom, in the sense of the religiously neutral functioning of government, or at least an indifference to religion, was deemed a plausible goal of 'modernization' only in British India. Princely India was gradually transformed into a stereotyped 'traditional' India. And,

[7] Letter from T.H. Thornton, Esq., Secretary to the Government of India, to the Secretary to the Government, dated 18 June 1867, Foreign Department (Political A), July 1867, nos. 47–8, NAI.

[8] Letter from Major J.E. Cracroft, Civil OSD in Kashmir, to T.H. Thornton, Esq, Secretary to Government, Punjab, dated October 1867, Foreign Department (Political A), November 1867, nos. 93, 94, NAI.

[9] Foreign Department (General B), August 1867, nos. 119–20, NAI.

[10] Letter to the Lord Bishop of Calcutta, dated 26 August 1867, Foreign Department (General B), August 1867, nos. 119–20, NAI.

as the nineteenth century were on, 'traditional' India came also to be perceived as 'religious' India. Here it was thought that religion, as in the past, would 'continue' to play an important role in determining the terms of sovereignty and the definition of the civil. At the same time, the viceroy on behalf of the colonial government, had also conceded that religious 'prejudice' or the unequal treatment of subjects of religious faiths different from those of the ruler was only to be expected. Such subjects were told indirectly that they could hope for no recourse other than occasional finger-wagging at their ruler by the paramount power when matters went beyond bearing; a state of affairs open to entirely subjective definition dictated by political practicalities and priorities.

Attempts to discourage 'persecution' had been made in as early as 1846 when H.M. Lawrence appealed to Gulab Singh to 'make no difference between . . . [his] subjects of different religions and sects but [to] look with equal favour on Hindoos, Sikhs, Sheeahs and Soonees and allow each and all to follow the precepts of their several religions.'[11] Lawrence had acknowledged, in the same dispatch to the Secret Committee of the East India Company, that on the first Friday following the establishment of Gulab's control over Srinagar, proclamations had been read in the two principal mosques of the city allowing the *azan*, a practice prohibited under the Sikhs.[12] Despite this act of magnanimity satisfactory to British consciences, Gulab Singh's official response to Lawrence's entreaty was qualified by important reservations that were apparently also accepted by the colonial government. He declared that he would 'treat all sects alike *but there [were] certain practices among the Mohummedans distasteful to the religious prejudices of the Hindoos which [could] not be permitted.*' In all other cases Hindus and Muslims would be 'equally at liberty to follow the precepts of their own religions agreeably to which also justice w[ould] be dispensed.'[13]

[11] Foreign (Secret)/Consultation nos. 1243–7/26 December 1846, NAI.

[12] The azan is the call to prayer given by a muezzin five times each day from a mosque. It is interesting that the only extant mosque in Srinagar with any significance at this time seems to have been the Jama Masjid and it too, by all accounts, seems to have been in a pitifully decrepit state. It is difficult to determine to which other principal mosque in Srinagar H.M. Lawrence was referring.

[13] Foreign (Secret)/Consultation nos. 1243–7/26 December 1846, NAI. Emphasis mine.

If princely India was the domain of 'religion', then this stance was neither unexpected nor unreasonable. Gulab Singh's declaration could be treated as a statement of the precedence, rather than the exclusiveness, of the religion of a 'native' ruler. This seemed entirely in keeping with the practice of 'traditional' Indian rulers and so had to be deemed permissible, provided they affirmed their commitment to preserving in other respects the rights of the different religious communities in their state. From this recognition there flowed another unstated one: that the subjects of a ruler who were not his co-religionists could not expect truly equal treatment as they might, theoretically, in British India. That this must have niggled the consciences of the post-1858 British colonial establishment is evident by its feeling pressed to declare that it would 'discourage persecution by expostulation and indirect influence'.[14] Nonetheless, caught between the two promises of Queen Victoria's proclamation, of withdrawing from direct interference in princely India and providing religious freedom to British Indian subjects, the colonial government could do no more than 'reprove' in one of the two Indias over which it was sovereign.

The Imperial Assemblage of 1877 and 'Religious' Princes

In 1877, an Imperial Assemblage was held in Delhi to celebrate the assumption of the title 'Empress of India' by Victoria. The event was also designed to provide an occasion for her Indian subjects to renew their vows of loyalty to her. Although separated in time by nineteen years from her proclamation, the assemblage was the culmination of a process, begun much earlier, of evolving a colonial representation of India's princes, as well as the subjects of British India. The reference point was still the rebellion of 1857, now finally to be laid to rest as 'the tale of panic and revolt may be well forgotten in the story of the Imperial Assemblage at Delhi'. The celebration was to be 'a festival of peace', not a 'paean of triumph', following a suitably long period of amnesia after which the princes and the people of India would either have been won over or chastised enough to retain 'no memories of conquest or defeat'.[15] The training of Indians was deemed to be well on track. *Pax*

---

[14] Foreign (Secret)/Consultation nos. 1243–7/26 December 1846, NAI.

[15] James Talboys Wheeler, *The History of the Imperial Assemblage at Delhi* (London: Longmans, Green, Reader & Dyer, 1877), pp. 42–4.

Britannica as well as the premises and promises of Victoria's proclamation of 1858 could be safely re-enacted on a grand stage bringing together the viceroy, the princes of India and British Indian subjects represented by 'native gentlemen' of various kinds. In 1877, James Talboys Wheeler, the official historian commissioned to record the assemblage, not only detailed the actual ceremonial but did so 'by the light of the history of India . . . in the hope that . . . pictures of India past and present [would] . . . bring out the contrast between the state of India under Native Government and its present condition under British rule.'[16] The assemblage was also to 'make manifest and compelling the sociology of India . . . [and] ideas which the British rulers had about the proper social order in India.'[17] The players on this stage were also its spectators and they included not only all of India's subjects,[18] but also its past and its present. Therefore, statements about India's social order and their implications were meant to be consumed by the widest audience possible, socially, regionally and temporally identified.

By 1877 the British ruling group had developed a double vision of India, perceiving her on the one hand as a feudal society headed by a 'natural aristocracy' of princes, and, on the other, as a society of communities defined variously by religion, region, caste or occupation.[19] The Imperial Assemblage brought into a single line of vision these two perceptions that had hitherto been disconnected, by dividing tradition and change into two realms of separate subordinate sovereignties presided over by the colonial state endowed with the unique capacity for a vision in focus. The former was the India of timeless tradition, whose 'aristocracy' based their status on 'descent', and the latter, helped along

[16] Ibid., Preface.

[17] Cohn, p. 189.

[18] Wheeler tells us that 'The object of the Imperial Assemblage was therefore to bind *princes and people together* in a common loyalty to their Sovereign; to bring European and Native rulers and officials into close communication with each other on a great occasion in which *all* could take part'. Wheeler, p. 46. [Emphasis mine]. And again: 'There were strangers from every land; representatives of every race. There were stalwart Afghans with muscular frames and ruddy faces. There were Beluchis . . . Bengallees in shawls and round flat hats; Hindustanis in quilted jackets . . .' Ibid., p. 49.

[19] Cohn, p. 190.

by the British, was the British India of 'change' where 'native' representatives derived their leadership through their 'actions' and 'achieve-
ments'.[20] Whereas British Indian subjects were also considered to be
ordered along religious lines, these were not, as in princely India,
considered fixed and immutable categories and not the only organizing principle of society. More so, since this was the India 'whose inhabitants ha[d] been for ages accustomed to live more or less in a state
of chronic hostility to each other,' but that the British would be 'modi-
fying unavoidably', even if 'gently, and with sympathy'.[21] India's
princes, on the other hand, were present at the imperial assemblage as
'fossilized embodiments of a past which the British conquerors had
created',[22] but a past born out of and rooted in tradition and unable
to rise above unchanging custom.

This was a past, moreover, coloured in distinguishable religious
shades, as is evident in Wheeler's official chronicle. In three chapters,
he sketched a history of India preceding the establishment of British
rule divided into 'ages' associated with the religion of their respective
ruling groups. Thus, a 'Muhammadan India' interrupted an earlier
'Rajput' and a later 'Mahratta'. But this historic India of religiously
identifiable sovereigns, subordinated ceremonially to the British at
the assemblage, was still not allowed to fade away. Indeed, an important purpose of the assemblage was to derive the authority of the
queen-empress and the British from that of India's erstwhile sovereigns. This required the continuing presence of the past. Wheeler
asserted that the assemblage 'was the only thing wanting to establish
the reality of the British empire in the hearts of the people of India as
the representative of the imperial power which traces back its origin to
Indra and the Sun.'[23] To achieve this it was essential to have modern-
day personifications of 'the three successive ages' in attendance at
the ceremonial.[24] Wheeler clarified, lest there be any difficulties in

[20] Ibid., p. 194.

[21] The Viceroy, Lord Lytton, made a speech at the state banquet on the occasion of the imperial assemblage, reproduced in Wheeler, p. 112. See also Ian Copland, *The Princes of India in the Endgame of Empire, 1917–47* (Cambridge: Cambridge University Press, 1997), pp. 21–4.

[22] Cohn, p. 193.

[23] Wheeler, p. 45.

[24] Ibid., p. 60.

identification, that among the 'flower of the Indian aristocracy' to be seen the 'Rajputs and Mahratta princes are Hindus' while 'the Nizam of Hyderabad is a Muhammadan'.[25] The British themselves were above such categorization, or rather transcended them by subsuming within their imperial power sources of legitimacy deriving from both 'Hindu' and 'Muslim' traditions of sovereignty. For this reason, the question of an appropriate translation of the title 'Empress of India' was thought about long and carefully. Upon the suggestion of G.W. Leitner, the prominent linguist and philologist, the rendition agreed to was Kaiser-i-Hind. This was believed to convey the appropriate degree of imperial grandeur, to enjoy historical currency in the Indian vocabulary but, above all, it 'avoid[ed] the overt association of the title with either Hindu or Muslim titles'.[26]

Insofar as the Dogras are concerned, by the time of the 1877 assemblage they had finally 'arrived' and the task of investing them with the legitimacy to rule deriving from Rajput descent was complete.[27] Wheeler wrote of the Maharaja of Jammu and Kashmir, Ranbir Singh:

> Another Chief presented a striking appearance at Delhi. This was the Maharaja of Kashmir, the ruler of the beautiful valley so often described by poets and travelers. He had been established in his present dominions ever since the close of the first Sikh war in 1846. There is an air of romance about the history of his family. He is the lineal representative of the old Rajput kings of Jummu, whose origin was lost in a remote antiquity before Mahmud of Ghazni invaded India. His father was a cadet of the house, but did not dare to ascend the throne until all the elder

[25] Ibid.

[26] Cohn, p. 201.

[27] Of course, it must be emphasized that re-creating traditions and histories was far from unusual in the late nineteenth century. For instance in Marathi-speaking India, reformers, early revivalists and radical critics of caste each laid claim to the seventeenth-century Maratha warrior Shivaji as 'their' king. Rosalind O'Hanlon, 'Maratha History as Polemic: Low Caste Ideology and Political Debate in Late-nineteenth-century Western India', *Modern Asian Studies*, 17, 1(1983), pp. 1–33. In the southern Indian kingdom of Pudukkottai, too, the Tondaimans re-wrote the story of their origins from the edge of the cultivated spaces. See Joanne Punzo Waghorne, *The Raja's Magic Clothes: Re-visioning Kingship and Divinity in England's India* (University Park: The Pennsylvania State University Press, 1994). However, what was unusual in the case of the Dogras was that the British were so closely implicated and involved in the process.

branches had died out. He is recognized by the hill tribes, not as a nominee of the Sikh government, but as a true representative of the ancient Rajput dynasty. He is a good ruler, and has shown on all occasions his loyalty and attachment to the paramount power.[28]

This representation of the Dogra maharajas served several purposes useful both to the British and the rulers of Jammu and Kashmir. For one thing, it papered over several 'flaws' in the history of this ruling house to bring it in line with the British vision of the princes of India as lawful, because traditional, rulers. The most obvious impediment here was the newness of Dogra rule in Kashmir, dating only to 1846, and therefore difficult to reconcile with principles of legitimacy dependent on the antiquity of sovereignty. The recent provenance of his claim to rule lay Maharaja Ranbir Singh open to accusations of being the descendant of, and by association himself, a 'usurper' and a parvenu. This was whitewashed by hinting at the self-restraint exercised by his father, Gulab Singh, who only reluctantly assumed power after the extinction of the 'elder branches' of his family.

Another way in which the dilemma was resolved was by simply stating the fact of Dogra rule over the valley of Kashmir and then diverting attention to other arenas where their legitimacy as a ruling house might more plausibly be argued. The first was that of Jammu and the 'hills' where Ranbir Singh was allowed to trace his origins in a venerable pedigree suitably 'lost in a remote antiquity'. Second, it is significant that the word 'Dogra' is noticeably missing in this account and the maharajas of Jammu and Kashmir are identified only as Rajputs. This is particularly telling because the same blurring is not permitted in all cases. The reader is gently but firmly coaxed towards greater precision when it comes to 'The Maharaja of Mysore [who] is Rajput, or *akin to Rajput*',[29] or 'another prince of Rajputana . . . the Maharaja of Bhurtpur; *by race a Jat*'.[30] The observer of the assemblage and the interpreter of its chronicle is invited to transfer the legitimacy already established for the representatives of the 'Rajput empire' to Ranbir Singh, his ancestors and successors. They are included when remembering 'the history of the Rajputs . . . [as] a string of traditions of love and war; the relics of an age of Hindu chivalry'.[31]

---

[28] Wheeler, p. 68.
[29] Ibid., p. 60. Emphasis mine.
[30] Ibid., p. 64. Emphasis mine.
[31] Ibid., p. 61.

A third and critical arena for culling legitimacy for the rulers of Jammu and Kashmir was in their 'Hindu-ness' which qualified them generically as original or more 'native' rulers, displaced by the 'Muhammadan empire'. The equation between Rajput and Hindu had already been made by Wheeler. Additionally, the reference to Mahmud of Ghazni's invasions of India, although cursory, was well calculated to evoke impressions of interrupted ancient Hindu rule. This was a fate shared with Rajputs elsewhere in India, where 'the old heroes and heroines of Rajput romance were swept away by the Muhammadan invasions' and 'princes and nobles . . . driven out of their ancient thrones in the valleys'.[32] Wheeler drew attention to the fact that the rulers of Jammu and Kashmir were Hindus also by setting off the Dogras from both Muslims and Sikhs 'whose nominee Ranbir Singh was not'. This, then, was the chief achievement of the imperial assemblage for the Dogra rulers of Jammu and Kashmir. As recompense for their 'loyalty and attachment to the paramount power' they were guaranteed their continued rule over their territories but also given a roadmap on how to do so 'legitimately'. And in this, their being Hindus was to play an important role.

A significant feature of the assemblage had been that while Victoria's British Indian subjects were addressed directly and so, figuratively speaking, were present in the audience, the subjects of princely India were nowhere to be seen. The assemblage confirmed the double subjecthood of the latter, to the British crown and to their 'native' rulers. The princes were 'cordially welcomed' by the viceroy at the assemblage, not as representatives of their subjects but because their 'presence, on this great occasion, [was] conspicuous evidence of . . . [their] sentiments of attachment to the Crown of England.' In return, 'Her Majesty regard[ed] Her interests as identified with those of the princes,'[33] clearly leaving out the interests of their subjects. The 'native' subjects of the empress of India were admitted at the assemblage to 'have a recognised claim to share largely with . . . English fellow-subjects . . . in the administration of the country', and this was acknowledged for all subjects, 'whatever [their] race, and whatever [their] creed'.[34] Religion, in the sense of providing a constant and cri-

[32] Ibid., p. 62.
[33] Ibid., pp. 83–4.
[34] Ibid., p. 84.

tical reference point, had not disappeared in the least from the colonial arena. However, in British India religion was, even if only theoretically, relegated to a space subordinate to the 'secular' and the 'public'. In princely India, offering a convenient contrast to the beneficence of British rule, it was seen as continuing to define the various states. The crown had negotiated sovereignty with the individual personages ruling over their states. And a gradually evolving colonial sociology finding expression both in the proclamation of 1858 and the Imperial Assemblage of 1877, had invested in Indian rulers a religious identity, linked crucially to their legitimate rights to govern.

Maharaja Gulab Singh as a 'Hindu' Ruler

So H.M. Lawrence could do little when Gulab Singh declared, in 1846, that while there would be no active interference in the religious beliefs of the Muslims, as a Hindu ruler he would have to give priority to the religion of the Hindus. As mentioned, his statement could be viewed as an affirmation of the precedence of a ruler's religion. This was entirely usual among pre-colonial rulers and formed the substance of sovereignty, intertwining politics and the public patronage of religion.[35] As the previous chapter has also shown, the Sikh maharaja Ranjit Singh had permitted divergent expressions of regional sovereignty and religious affinity among his subordinates and subjects, so long as they were underwritten by the understanding that the overarching sovereignty and religion of the Lahore ruler would have symbolic pre-eminence.[36] Thus, while Ranjit Singh, in consolidating his power, had made the obligatory references to the Sikh Khalsa,[37] the founding guru of the faith (Nanak), and the holy scripture (the *Granth*), he also extended his sovereignty over the Muslims of the Punjab by patronizing, rather than extirpating, their religious leaders and learned men. There seemed to be no difficulty in reconciling two visions of the Sikh kingdom; as the political expression of the sovereignty of the Sikh *panth* as well as Dar-ul-Islam, a land in which Islam

[35] Cf. C.A.Bayly, 'The Pre-history of "Communalism"? Religious Conflict in India, 1700–1860', *Modern Asian Studies*, 19, 2 (1985), pp. 177–203.

[36] Ibid.

[37] The military brotherhood established by the tenth guru, Guru Gobind Singh.

could be publicly practised. Nevertheless, the precedence of the Sikh faith was clearly asserted in that 'Muslim' practices such as cattle slaughter, considered irreconcilable with Sikh worship, were prohibited, as was the calling of the azan from mosques in the Sikh sacred centre of Amritsar.[38] The insistence on the 'primacy' rather than the 'exclusiveness' of a ruler's faith within the Sikh kingdom of Ranjit Singh eased the political assimilation of Gulab Singh as yet another level of politics-through-religious patronage. As long as the 'ceremonial primacy' of Ranjit Singh as 'donor-in-chief' was not challenged by Gulab Singh, the latter was allowed to construct his own, albeit subordinate, sovereignty as a protector of the Hindu faith under the shelter of Sikh authority. Thus, Ranjit Singh would preside over worship and patronage at Purmandal and Uttarbehni, in the Jammu province, and even in the temples in the inner quarters of the Dogra palaces in Jammu city.[39]

In a world of imbricated sovereignties, control by a political overlord was transitory unless it could rely on the allegiance of regional lords and their capacity to make their own local arrangements and compromises to incorporate distant peripheries into the centre. Conversely, a regional raja's success in a locality rested on his ability to reflect the glory of his overlord and this was achieved partly by his replicating his political master's system of incorporation. Therefore, the microcosm of Gulab Singh's subordinate sovereignty duplicated Ranjit Singh's insistence on the 'primacy' of his own faith and its forms of worship, without excluding those of other religious communities. In this, Gulab Singh was following the example not only of Ranjit Singh but also of his own eighteenth-century forbear, the Raja Ranjit Dev, who had been determined to buttress his political power by shoring up the economic prosperity of Jammu. In order to implement this strategy, Ranjit Dev had taken great pains to attract Muslim traders to the city by carefully building up the reputation of Jammu as a centre in which 'religious freedom' could be enjoyed by all on a level unknown in the region.[40] Therefore, like Ranjit

[38] Ibid., pp. 186–7.

[39] Diwan Kirpa Ram, *Gulabnama*, pp. 164, 166; Frederic Drew, *The Jummoo and Kashmir Territories*, p. 89; Mira Seth, *Dogra Wall Paintings in Jammu and Kashmir*, p. 16.

[40] George Forster, *A Journey from Bengal to England*, 2 vols (Patiala: Punjab Languages Department, first published 1808, repr. 1970), vol. 1, pp. 283–5.

Dev, Gulab Singh made his own locally expedient compromises with groups of Muslims and permitted the calling of the azan in Jammu. This decision was no doubt facilitated by the fact that the latter did not hold quite the same significance as Amritsar did as a holy city for the Sikhs.[41] G.T. Vigne, a European traveller to the territories of Gulab Singh during the 1830s, and none too admiring of his host, could not help being impressed by the fact that Jammu was 'the only place in the Panjab where the Mulahs may call the Musulmans to prayers. Runjit

---

Forster who visited Jammu during the reign of Brij Raj Dev, the son of Ranjit Dev, praised the latter's far-sightedness in building up the economic power of Jammu. He suggests that Ranjit Dev, seeking to take advantage especially of the prosperous Kashmir trade passing through Jammu, provided every advantage to merchants, the vast majority of whom happened to be Muslim and Kashmiri. He suggests that Ranjit 'went farther than the [mere] forbearance of injuries' by allot-ting to Muslim merchants a separate quarter of the town called 'Moghulpour' and so 'that no reserve might appear in his treatment of them, a mosque was erected in the new colony'. If riding through the colony during the time of prayer, Ranjit Dev would stop until worship was over. Forster further recounts an occassion when some Hindus of the town had complained that the public wells were being contami-nated by the Muslims dipping their vessels in them. In response, Ranjit replied that 'water was a pure element, designed for the general use of mankind, and could not be polluted by the touch of any class of people'. Hence, Forster admired Ranjit Dev for his 'liberality of disposition the more conspicuous . . . as it is the only instance of the like toleration in this part of India . . .' By contrast, Forster has portrayed the Sikhs as subjecting Muslims to all manner of insults such as the throwing of carcasses of hogs in mosques. He is also among a series of European travellers who have attested to the fact that the Sikhs had forbidden the azan in their territories. Ibid., pp. 338–9. Reinforcing this portrayal of Jammu as a city in which Muslims were treated with consideration, Ganesdas Badehra, the chronicler of Gulab Singh's rise to power, tells us that Ranjit Dev's Jammu had in fact become the home of Malika Zamani, a queen of the Mughal emperor Muhammad Shah, where she built elegant mansions and, in typical Mughal style, laid the foundations of pleasure gardens on the banks of the Tawi river. Ganesdas Badehra, *Rajdarshini*, p. 163. It is important to remember that Ranjit Dev had strengthened his political position, during a period of growing Sikh power, by forming an alliance with Ahmad Shah Abdali who had established Afghan hegemony in north-western India at the time. Shahamat Ali, *The Sikhs and Afghans* (London: John Murray, 1847), p. 79; and Ganesdas Badehra, *Raj-darshini*, p. 173.

[41] This in contrast with the position the city was sought to be given under Ranbir Singh, who wished to build Jammu into a 'second Benares'.

had forbidden them to do so; but Gulab Singh, his powerful vassal, allowed them to ascend the minars of Jamu, in the exercise of their vocation.' So much so that when a 'pious Brahmin, or Sikh . . . complained that the Mulah's cry disturbed his devotions', Gulab Singh replied with his characteristically acerbic wit 'that he would order . . . [the muezzin] to desist, if the applicant would take the trouble to collect the flock for him.'[42]

Granted that the permission for the azan in Jammu was an act of liberality unusual in the wider Sikh territories, Gulab Singh was nevertheless anxious to be seen as a Hindu raja and a protector of the Hindu dharma. Therefore, even when in the service of the Lahore durbar, he had taken pains to mark himself out as a man devoted to religious duties. John Honigberger, a German physician at Ranjit Singh's court, remarked that, unlike his brothers at the court, who would eat with their retinue, 'Gholab Singh, however, d[id] not dine in company but invariably [took] his meals alone . . . having previously passed an hour or two in performing his ablutions and repeating his poojah [prayers].'[43] This fastidiousness represented apparently more than either personal idiosyncrasy or an instance of exceptional piety. It seemed to be part of a widely broadcast image, becoming the subject of at least one painting 'executed for the public at large' by a Pahari artist resident in the Punjab plains. In this depiction Gulab Singh is shown taking his bath before performing his religious rites, with a priest waiting to assist him and various ingredients of worship set out in the courtyard before him.[44] W.G. Archer, in whose volume on *The Paintings of the Sikhs* this image is described, is struck by the uniqueness of this picture in that 'no other Sikh minister was ever portrayed in such informal surroundings' and deduces from this that a 'mysterious aura was attaching to [Gulab Singh's] presence'.[45] It is intriguing that Archer views this painting as an instance of 'informality'. On the contrary, this portrayal serves the important purpose

[42] Godfrey Thomas Vigne, *Travels in Kashmir, Ladak, Iskardo*, 2 vols (New Delhi: Sagar Publications, first published London 1842, 1st Indian reprint, 1981), vol. 1, p. 184.

[43] John Martin Honigberger, *Thirty-Five Years in the East* (London: H. Bailiere, 1852), pp. 163–4.

[44] W.G. Archer, *Paintings of the Sikhs* (London: H.M.S.O., 1966), p. 54.

[45] Ibid.

of marking not only Gulab Singh's claim to sovereignty but also to sovereignty within Hindu traditions of kingship dating back to early medieval India. It also explains why no other 'Sikh minister' would have been depicted in the same manner.

Traditions of Hindu kingship and authority in early medieval India were linked intimately to the royal rituals through which they were enacted and made manifest, such as those surrounding the installation ceremony (*rajyabhisheka*)—according to Ronald Inden, an archetypical ceremony.[46] It was, in fact, 'the most important of royal rituals . . . by which both regional kings and imperial overlords were created' and a man changed into a king.[47] Rituals forming its substance were meant to convey the very significant message of a king's dual role: in his more earth-bound form as a temporal sovereign, but also as a mediator between God and his subjects. The king was conceived as a 'master' over the land, the people and his ministers. As the master, however, he was also deemed to represent his servants before God and this made him the chief worshipper and sacrificer (*yajnaman*) on their behalf. However—and this distinguishes the Hindu tradition of kingship from the other historically prominent form in South Asia, namely the Muslim[48]—a king's effectiveness as a plausible mediator was relied upon only because of his image as a god. A Hindu king was 'commonly perceived as a "partial descent" of the great God Vishnu, the preserver of dharma, the natural and moral order, and himself a form of the Cosmic Overlord.'[49] Muslim sultans and *padshahs* of the subcontinent could, at best, get away with titles such as Zillallah (the Shadow of God on Earth) without incurring the wrath of the religiously orthodox and accusations of having forsaken the faith.[50] The

[46] Literally the 'affusion' (*abhisheka*) into kingship (*rajya*), as Ronald Inden informs us. Ronald Inden, 'Ritual, Authority, and Cyclic Time in Hindu Kingship', J.F. Richards (ed.), *Kingship and Authority in South Asia* (Madison: University of Wisconsin-Madison South Asia Publication Series, no. 3, 1978).

[47] Ibid., pp. 37, 41.

[48] Peter Hardy, 'The Growth of Authority Over a Conquered Political Elite: The Early Delhi Sultanate as a Possible Case Study', in ibid., pp. 192–214.

[49] *Kingship and Authority in South Asia*, p. 31.

[50] One of the Delhi Sultans, Balban (1265–84) had added the title of Zillallah to his other exalted ones, in a concerted effort to build up the prestige of the monarchy. By the time of the Mughal emperor Akbar (r.1556–1605), as described by his famous historian and publicist Abul Fazl, royalty was seen as 'a light

performance of royal rituals on the part of a Hindu ruler, equally significantly, had to be mediated 'through the agency of his *purohita* or
priest', thereby marking an important dimension of power-sharing
between the ruler and the Brahmanic religious hierarchy.[51]

The bath was a vital component of the *abhisheka* and the protocol
for this ritual, accompanying almost every significant political event
involving the Hindu king,[52] was laid out in the *Vishnudharmottara-
purana*, a text compiled around the eighth and ninth centuries. Inden
suggests these rules were probably followed by most imperial Hindu
rulers in the early medieval period, including the Karkota dynasty of
Kashmir (625–1003), and seem to have survived for centuries, observed even by the Maratha warrior Shivaji during his coronation in
1674, and by the Hindu king of Nepal, Birendra, as late as 1975.[53] The
royal priest or purohita began the first half of the rajyabhisheka ceremony with 'a series of baths' in the most private quarters of a ruler's
palace by making offerings of a number of ingredients that were stock
components of any religious ceremony, especially those derived from
Vedic sacrificial worship. Without delving in further detail into the
intricacies of this ceremony, it seems quite clear that the painting referred to by Archer is far from displaying informality. It seems intended
as a statement of sovereignty, with a very respectable pedigree in
Hindu traditions, to which Gulab Singh was laying claim. All of the
important props of the (rajya)abhisheka are in evidence: the bathing
pavilion and the bath, the ingredients of worship and the priest. This
image, therefore, by evoking the ceremony in the minds of people who
were still familiar with its idiom was also an important assertion of the
political power of this ambitious Hindu raja at the Lahore court.

By 1846, Gulab Singh was formally established in independent

---

emanating from God, and a ray from the sun, the illuminator of the universe'.
This light was also called '*farr-i-izidi* (the divine light) . . . communicated by
God to kings without the intermediate assistance of any one.' Abul Fazal Allami,
The Ain-i-Akbari, H. Blochmann (Calcutta: The Asiatic Society of Bengal,
1927), vol. 1, p. 3. However, neither Balban nor Akbar could claim to be God
or even an incar-nation, nor could they be mediators between God and the ruled.

[51] *Kingship and Authority in South Asia*, p. 31.

[52] Inden suggests that the abhisheka, as a ceremony establishing the universal
sovereignty of a king, would be performed before a wide range of political activities such as holding court or waging battle. Inden, p. 38.

[53] Ibid., p. 39.

sovereignty over the territories of Jammu and Kashmir. However, as noted in the last chapter, the substantiation of this independent sovereignty proceeded at snail's pace, with only a gradual extrication of Jammu and Kashmir from the sway of Lahore. In fits and starts, and 'against his will', Gulab Singh would occasionally 'release [some] . . . rent-free holdings in Cashmere' or 'resign all claim to the religious endowments' granted by the Lahore durbar's governors in his territories.[54] Unravelling the networks of religious patronage that wove Jammu, Kashmir and Punjab together was a gradual process ensuring that Gulab Singh's actions as maharaja differed little from his actions as raja and that he proceeded with caution.

Ruling over a state with predominantly Muslim subjects, especially in Kashmir, the external boundaries of which were still in flux, Gulab Singh was hesitant to antagonize too far. This concern was more pronounced in the context of the links between powerful sections of Muslims in Kashmir and Lahore established by the last two Muslim governors, Ghulam Mohi-ud-din and Imam-ud-din, astutely stationed in Srinagar by the Sikhs in the years immediately preceding Gulab Singh's accession. Both Ghulam Mohi-ud-din and his son Imam-ud-din had used their prerogatives as governors to win over substantial sections of the Kashmiri Muslim élite by making a large number of revenue-free grants to them. Imam-ud-din had done so even more liberally in order to sustain support for his 'revolt' against the British decision to hand over Kashmir to Gulab Singh in 1846.[55] Gulab Singh's attempts to resume these grants had met with spirited resistance and although he succeeded in large measure in revoking the more 'indiscriminate' ones made by Imam-ud-din, he was alert to the need of not alienating entirely the Kashmiri Muslims, particularly the more prominent among them. Gulab Singh, through the brief ten years of his reign as Maharaja of Kashmir, would tread a fine line between angering powerful sections of Muslims in Kashmir with plausible recourse either to Lahore or Calcutta, and the pressing imperative of still basing his sovereignty on his claim to rule as a protector of the Hindu dharma.

While the question of the azan did not exercise him as much as it

[54] *Political Diaries of the Agent to the Governor-General, North West Frontier and Resident at Lahore*, pp. 31, 66.

[55] Mirza Saif-ud-din, *Khulastah-al-Tawarikh*, tr. from Persian into Urdu by Mirza Kamal-ud-din Shaida (Srinagar: Gulshan Publishers, 1984).

did the Sikh rulers, the litmus test for the sovereignty of non-Muslim rulers in pre-colonial India was the issue of the 'sacred' cow and its slaughter. To allow it was considered an abdication of sovereignty since it was viewed, almost uniformly, as a clear contravention of Hindu or Sikh religious beliefs.[56] The azan was tied in intimately to the practice of their faith by Muslims, since denying it was also to hamper the performance of the *namaz* (prayer), one of their five principal religious duties. Ringing out five times a day, the azan represented a much more public act than the consumption of beef.[57] To permit it could be sufficient in itself to convince those content with even cosmetic assurances, such as H.M. Lawrence on behalf of the British,[58] of the religious 'liberality' of any particular government. And, conversely, prohibiting it would constitute a much more visible denial of 'religious freedom' to Muslims. There was an element, involved in these decisions, of weighing the relative significance of various practices to the different religions of the subcontinent. So while the azan was acknowledged to be crucial to Muslims, the banning of cow-slaughter was deemed by non-Muslim rulers as critical to their own dharma and so also to their sovereignty relying on its protection.

It is over the latter that lines seem to have been drawn most strictly and often with morbid consequences for violators. Mirza Saif-ud-din, the newswriter employed by the East India Company, noted that dire punishments were meted out to 'cow-killers'. These chastisements ranged in degrees of discomfort, from the cutting off of noses to the chopping off of ears, and from the capital reprisal, so to speak, of burning an offender's hair to the torching of their houses.[59] Sometimes, occasioning a flurry of correspondence at the highest levels of a horrified British establishment, punishments were inflicted with 'gross cruelty'

---

[56] See Bayly, 'The Pre-history of "Communalism"?'

[57] Yet, by the end of the nineteenth century the question of cow-slaughter and the controversy around it became far more 'public'(-ized) as an issue over which riots broke out. Muslims in India, including Kashmir by the early decades of the twentieth century, rallied around their right to slaughter a calf asserting that they were being denied the performance of an important religious duty, namely *qurbani* (sacrifice) during *Eid*.

[58] Foreign (Secret)/Consultation nos. 1243–7/26 December 1846, NAI.

[59] Saif-ud-din Diaries, cited in Bawa Satinder Singh, *The Jammu Fox*, p. 176.

on the mere suspicion of intent to injure a cow.[60] However, even then, it would appear that Ranbir Singh, while still only heir-apparent, was the greater 'fanatic' and an extremely 'cruel fellow'. Thus, it is said that 'he slit a woman's tongue for beating a cow which had torn some clothes she had hung out to dry'.[61] Gulab Singh, for all the inclemency with which he punished open violations of the injunction against cow-slaughter, stopped short of a blanket award of the death sentence, limiting the punishment instead to life imprisonment.[62] Ranbir Singh, unhappy with this 'liberality', took his own measures to ensure that imprisonment would translate, in effect, into the death penalty. For instance, on one occasion, while inspecting a state prison, Ranbir Singh was appalled by the 'goodness of fare' given to a 'stout man' incarcerated for cow-slaughter. He ordered that salt be mixed in his food so that he died of dehydration.[63] In 1853, well before he had been crowned Maharaja, Ranbir Singh also urged Hindus and Sikhs to 'boycott' the shops of Muslim butchers and patronize, instead, the shops of Sikh butchers.[64] His actions can be interpreted as personal religious zeal on the part of an important individual within the state. On the other hand, he may have provided the loophole for his father Gulab Singh, as maharaja, to assert his status as a Hindu ruler in the face of the concessions that he would have been forced to make towards the Muslims of Kashmir.

Whatever the case, Gulab Singh too was undoubtedly careful to emphasize his standing as a Hindu ruler by ordering the closing of butchers' shops on Hindu religious festivals such as Dussehra and Diwali, by celebrating these occasions with great fanfare, and by performing pilgrimages to the sacred sites of Haridwar, Benares and Amarnath.[65] In other equally public gestures, he denounced Hindu–Muslim marriages and conversions from Hinduism to Islam, although

---

[60] Letter from Lord Dalhousie to the Secret Committee, Foreign Department/Despatch to Secret Committee/no. 67 of 4 October 1853, NAI.

[61] Hugh Rees James Papers, pp. 56–7, IOL.

[62] Ibid.

[63] Ibid.

[64] Saif-ud-din Diaries, cited in Bawa Satinder Singh, p. 177.

[65] Saif-ud-din Diaries, cited in Bawa Satinder Singh, p. 176. Also Hugh Rees James Papers, p. 46.

he never banned these practices.[66] Insofar as Muslims in Kashmir were directly concerned, Saif-ud-din records one instance of Gulab Singh permitting the erection of a temple on the site of a mosque. But the newswriter also makes clear the maharaja's explicit disapproval of such practices. Gulab Singh, in fact, actively intervened on another occasion to save a mosque from demolition.[67] However, while he may not have approved of the destruction of Muslim shrines in Kashmir as a general policy, he was evidently reluctant to actively patronize them. Not only was the Jama Masjid at Srinagar in ruins,[68] but we also have the testimony of Muslim maulvis claiming that 'since Golab Singh's accession, they ha[d] been deprived of the water which flowed to the mosque in a small channel from Naoshera on the plea of its being required for the rice cultivation there.' Hugh Rees James, a British visitor to Kashmir in 1856 who evidently got his information from Mirza Saif-ud-din (with whom he was in touch), suggests that this was 'a mere pretext and the act was purely one of annoyance . . . and is severely felt by the Mussalmans.'[69] Similarly, at the shrine of Aish Muqam, James heard the complaint of *Rishis*, one of the most venerated Sufi orders among Kashmiris, against 'Golab's meanness in stopping the allowance formerly made for oil at the shrine, as well as rice for the poor people who visit it. Many of [the Rishis had] in consequence taken to agriculture, and there [were] only fifty who live[d] at the ziarut and upon a religious income'.[70]

---

[66] Saif-ud-din Diaries, cited in Bawa Satinder Singh, p. 177.

[67] Ibid. Unfortunately, Saif-ud-din does not mention which mosque was destroyed for the construction of the temple and so it is impossible to comment fully on the reasons informing Gulab Singh's action. Such acts of the destruction of the religious shrines are quite commonly encountered in the pre-colonial history of India. Many were really attempts by rulers to impose their political sovereignty on the religious spaces of the adherents of faiths other than their own. There were other instances of clearly politically motivated destruction of shrines, such as the Mughal emperor Aurangzeb's attack on the temple of Keshava Rai in Mathura which had allegedly developed into a centre of sedition and rebellion against Delhi. Cf. Richard Eaton, 'Temple Desecration and Indo-Muslim States' in David Gilmartin and Bruce B. Lawrence (eds), *Beyond Turk and Hindu: Rethinking Religious Identities in Islamicate South Asia* (Gainesville: University Press of Florida, 2000), pp. 246–81.

[68] MSS.Eur.A.129, 'Journals of Edward Moffat', 1858–77, p. 134, IOL.

[69] 'Hugh Rees James Papers', pp. 17–19.

[70] Ibid., pp. 55–7.

For the Muslims of Kashmir the contrast was particularly stark in relation to the earlier Sikh-sponsored patronage of Muslim shrines. After the Sikh defeat of the Afghans in 1819, when Kashmir passed into the control of Lahore, Ranjit Singh is reported to have affirmed that the 'Kashmiris are worshippers of the universal Almighty and their prayer shall bring the Maharaja and his kingdom prosperity and felicity'.[71] This spirit, typical of pre-colonial attitudes, animated the decision to spend about two lakhs of rupees annually from the Sikh dharmarth department on shrines, saints, learned men, religious festivals, alms and other such charitable purposes in Kashmir.[72] The beneficiaries were both Hindu and Muslim. Insofar as the Muslims were concerned, some of the important shrines patronized were indeed among the most revered, such as Hazrat Bal and Maqdoom Sahib in Srinagar, and the shrine of Baba Pam Rishi. They profited from generous land grants, and employees at the shrines were paid regularly from the dharmarth fund, which was also used for financing free kitchens.[73] With the installation of the new Dogra rulers this tap suddenly ran dry and with it possibly also the source of comfort arising from the belief that Kashmiris were, with the Dogras, worshippers of a common 'universal Almighty'. Submitting to a different God from their rulers appeared increasingly to spell the temporal eclipse of the faithful of Islam as worthy recipients of patronage, and as consequential participants in the new state. The 'neglect and dilapidation visible in all the Mohammedan buildings', in all fairness not directly attributable to the Dogras since they would simply not have had the time to perpetrate such ruin, would nevertheless have irked all the more as, simultaneously, 'on every side Hindoo temples [were] being erected'.[74] Hugh Rees James points to numerous instances of repairs made at several ruined temples in Kashmir, especially at ancient and important sites such as Mattan, lying on the route to the pilgrimage centre of Amarnath. The slipshod quality of the repairs left much to be desired but bespoke the haste of

---

[71] Sohan Lal Suri, *Umdat-ut-Tawarikh*, cited in D.C Sharma, *Kashmir Under the Sikhs* (Delhi: Seema Publications, 1983), pp. 101–2.

[72] Vigne, *Travels in Kashmir,* vol. 2, p. 120.

[73] *Tarikh-i-Kalan*, cited in Sharma, *Kashmir Under the Sikhs,* pp. 113–14.

[74] Lieut. Col. Henry Torrens, *Travels in Ladak, Tartary and Kashmir* (London: Saunders, Otley & Co., 1862), pp. 305–6. The account of another traveller, T. Machell, is similarly rife with evidence of the decay of mosques in Kashmir. MSS.Eur.B.369, vol. 5, 'Journals of T. Machell', 1855–6, IOL.

Gulab Singh in making his presence felt as the new Hindu ruler at the helm of affairs in the valley.[75] Perceptions of indifference, read as discrimination, towards the Muslims of Kashmir by their new Dogra rulers had become prevalent enough to lead Rees James to prophesy, in 1856: 'The reaction when it does come, and come it must and will, will be powerful: the emancipation of a religion long forcibly kept down is ever attended by such result.'[76]

If the patronage of the Muslim religious domain in Kashmir by Gulab Singh was gradually on the decline, the control of Hindu shrines was a complicated exercise. Most aspirants to political power in pre-colonial India, whether of old standing or on the make, had had to deal with the familiar quandary of building their political power with the widest social reach possible. At the same time, they had to pander to that other dominant 'political' section in society, the religious hierarchy, with limited social following but capable of lending or withdrawing legitimacy from kings. No pre-colonial Indian ruler ever managed to entirely control the domain of religion and worship. Thus, Ganeshdas Badehra, writing in 1847, tells us of the great reverence and even impressive degrees of autonomy enjoyed by Brahmans in Jammu particularly in the reign of Ranjit Dev. For instance, a Brahman or Brahman villages, called *patholi*, could provide asylum to a rebellious or destitute subject; this was a harbour no government would dare breach even if sheltering an individual owing money to the state. Another custom, called *parah*, prevalent among Brahmans ensured their continuing sway in society. It was deployed to great effect against individuals who either failed to show deference 'traditionally' due them or generally refused to grant demands made. Brahmans would retaliate by fasting in front of the offender's house. Should their strike prove unsuccessful, their resistance would take more extreme paths, with Brahmans either immolating themselves or thrusting daggers into their own bellies to extract their intestines and bleed to death! Few would hazard carrying the burden of such gory deaths on their consciences, and not even rajas were immune against this drastic form of blackmail.[77] Mercifully Ranjit Dev's reign, we are told, witnessed no such incidents as he was careful to conciliate Brahmans who 'commanded great respect and

---

[75] 'Hugh Rees James Papers', pp. 42, 47–8, 52–3, 82–4.

[76] Ibid., pp. 18–19.

[77] Badehra, *Rajdarshini*, pp. 166–7.

reverence' under his just disposition. Ganeshdas, commenting on the reign of his patron Gulab Singh, noted (with a remarkable ability for quantifying such assessments) that even though 'only a fraction or one-thousandth of the earlier reverence for the Brahmans is left' yet the institution of the patholis and customs of resistance such as the parah continued in the Jammu area.[78]

The strength of the religious domain, requiring placating, drew from the fact that any temple or religious order in pre-colonial India usually enjoyed the sponsorship of numerous political patrons at one time. The location of a shrine in the territory of a particular ruler did not necessarily ensure primary loyalty from its officiants or worshippers to that ruler. The networks of religious patronage had very little do with territorial frontiers and much to do with the overlapping nature of layered sovereignties characterizing pre-colonial India. Propping each other up, neither Brahmans nor kings were autonomous groups. No ruler could rest comfortably in the knowledge that he had done his bit by his land grant or temple building and rely on this keeping his primacy intact. There were always other political patrons with the capacity to do more, or less, in a political world in which neither polities nor sacred benefits, gained from religious patronage, were bounded by horizontally perceived geographic frontiers.[79] If one were to consider the number of patrons at the holy temple city of Purmandal (Jammu province) alone, the potential for Brahmans to play one benefactor off against the other becomes clear. It is reputed that among the many important worshippers at the Kasi-Visvanath temple in Purmandal was Raja Man Singh of Amber (in Rajputana) who had vowed to build a new temple should the deity grant him victory in Kabul, where he was about to engage in battle on behalf of the Mughals. Since he did win, he repaid the divine favour by constructing and endowing the Uma Mahapati temple dedicated to Shiva.[80] As mentioned earlier, in the nineteenth century Ranjit Singh had been

[78] Ibid.

[79] See Thongchai Winichakul, *Siam Mapped: A History of the Geo-body of a Nation* (Honolulu: University of Hawai Press, 1994). Winichakul provides a fascinating elaboration on the difference between frontiers perceived and conceptualized horizontally and those, characteristic of the non-Western world of pre-colonial polities, viewed and perceived vertically.

[80] Seth, p. 17.

another of the distinguished patrons at Purmandal, where he built the Eklingaonkar temple and donated 1300 *gumaons* of land to Mahanta Motigar Ji, a Shaivite sanyasi, for its maintenance.[81] Spurred on by Ranjit Singh's patronage, many of his courtiers also built their houses there. These houses were inhabited by Brahmans by the time Frederic Drew saw them in around 1874,[82] indicative of the manner in which the Dogra rulers had chosen to re-orient former Sikh patronage at Purmandal after the 'fall of Lahore'.

Following in the footsteps of these esteemed political figures, Gulab Singh, as a raja bidding for sovereignty in Jammu, had made his own contributions to the Purmandal temple complex and to the Brahmans there by donating land for the maintenance of the Kasi-Visvanath temple. Seeking to assert some measure of control over this significant temple, he installed within it images in a Pahari iconographic style peculiar to hill states such as Jammu. Thus, the image of Shiva that Gulab Singh placed within the temple is shown sporting a moustache, a vision rare in the rest of India.[83] Gulab Singh had spared no expense in his construction and endowments of temples, spending for instance close to a lakh of rupees on gilding the dome and cornices of a Shivala[84] and placing in it about 360 *lingas* brought all the way from the Narmada river in Central India.[85] In 1840 Gulab Singh also commissioned the construction of the Shiva-Parvati temple at Purmandal and the wall paintings within it were significant attempts to associate the temple with his own claim to political sovereignty. Although this was a temple dedicated to Shaivite worship, the walls of the *garbha-griha*[86] had two panels depicting the durbar of the Vaishnavite deity Rama,[87] from whom the Dogras claimed descent. Gulab Singh's brother, Suchet Singh, not to be left behind, was also prompted to build a *dharamsala* (a rest house) at Purmandal, while Ranbir Singh erected

[81] Ibid.

[82] Drew, *The Jummoo and Kashmir Territories*, p. 89.

[83] Seth, p. 17.

[84] A high-domed temple, usually associated with the worship of Shiva.

[85] Lala Ganeshi Lal, Tehsildar, *Siyahat-i-Kashmir*, tr. Vidya Sagar Suri (Chandigarh: Punjab Itihas Prakashan, 1976), p. 14.

[86] The inner sanctum in which the images of the chief deities to whom the temple is dedicated are housed.

[87] Seth, p. 18.

many small temples there. Joining in were a number of rich merchants and traders, also seeking merit at Purmandal by constructing shrines such as the Radha Krishna temple in 1897.[88] The effect of these competing sources of endowments was that no sovereign or individual aiming at the assertion of power monopolized either the finances of these temples or their capacity to allot sacred merit.

In a symbiotic relationship, Purmandal was considered particularly holy and so drew widespread patronage and, in turn, the patronage of so many potent political figures there further enhanced its importance as a hallowed centre. Thus, Lala Ganeshi Lal in 1847, while praising the magnificence of Gulab Singh's constructions at Purmandal, added that 'other splendid buildings stand here . . . belonging to the several chiefs of the country and give the place an imposing appearance.' The importance of Purmandal was so great that though the river was dry at most times, except during the rainy season, devotees went to the extent of digging holes in the desiccated bed in order to bathe there.[89] Drew tells us that by the 1870s 'the atoning power of [bathing at Purmandal] . . . is considered in these hills to be second only to that of a visit to Haridwar on the Ganges'.[90] In pre-colonial India centres such as Purmandal, therefore, attracted endowments and patronage from many influential figures and so provided an intersection of several networks of political sovereignties. With so many influential figures vying with each other to sponsor worship and endow temples at Purmandal, the Brahmans associated with the various temples there suffered only from an embarrassment of choice.

Therefore, any raja worth his salt not only made concerted efforts to outdo his rivals in his patronage of priests and ascetics but did so with clear regard to the political boons earned from such sponsorship. The link between the political arena and the temporal power of the religious domain was clearly established at the Rama temple at Tandon Khu in Jammu province. The structure was erected by Raja Dhian Singh, the elder brother of Gulab, in honour of Naraindas, an ascetic belonging to the Ramanandi order. The 'history' recounted by the *mahantas* of the temple about its construction was inaccurate in its details but summed up the capacity of Brahmans and ascetics to

---

[88] Ibid.

[89] Lala Ganeshi Lal, p. 14.

[90] Drew, *The Jummoo and Kashmir Territories*, p. 89.

intervene decisively in political rivalries. According to the legend
Dhian Singh, imprisoned by the Sikhs in Lahore, saw Naraindas one
evening when he was taken for a walk by his guards. When he paid his
respects to the ascetic the Sikh soldiers accompanying him mocked his
act of obeisance to a mere impoverished faqir. As a reward for Dhian
Singh's reverence, the faqir gifted him with an enormous treasure,
hidden under a simple mat, with which the raja bought his release
from the Sikhs. Subsequently, Dhian Singh convinced Naraindas to
move to Jammu, where he built the Tandon Khu temple for him.[91]
This tale bears evidence of not only the religious but also the political
and financial capital controlled by priests and ascetics and their capacity to transfer them from an unsatisfactory patron to a suitably de-
ferential one. The wall paintings inside the temple further reiterated
the message of the veneration in which the Dogras held the Hindu
priesthood. They did this through numerous panels portraying the
respectfully hierarchical relationship between *guru* and *chela* (teacher
and disciple), ranging from depictions of such relations in the *Mahabharata* to images of Guru Nanak and his disciples.[92] Should these
allusions have escaped the more obtuse observer, a panel depicting the
three Dogra brothers, Gulab Singh, Dhian Singh and Suchet Singh,
kneeling reverentially before a sadhu, makes the point abundantly
clear.[93]

The exercise of patronizing religious orders was not a simple one.
Aside from the regionally tangled nature of political pecking-orders in
pre-colonial India, religious orders were themselves tied up in hierarchies defying territorial comprehensibility. The intricate web meshing
the Thakurdwara[94] of Suba Gir at Mirpur in Jammu, within a hierarchical relationship with the alleged 'parent' Thakurdwara Sanglanwala
of Dinga in Punjab, would truss up the courts of Jammu and Kashmir
in legal disputes until almost the middle of the twentieth century. The
Thakurdwara at Mirpur traced its origins in a grant made by Ranjit

[91] Seth, p. 16. Raja Dhian Singh was never imprisoned by the Sikhs.

[92] Ibid. In referring to Guru Nanak within the larger context of the story of the
temple, the suggestion seems to have been that the Dogras were better devotees
than even the Sikhs, the actual adherents of Nanak's faith.

[93] Ibid., Fig. 46.

[94] A temple dedicated to Vaishnavite worship, specifically to the worship of
Rama as an incarnation of Vishnu. The Dogras traced their descent from Rama.

Singh, who set it up as an independent institution. But the appointments of its mahants were, at various times, made in compliance with the wishes of authorities at the Dinga Thakurdwara in Punjab.[95] This geographically imbricated nature of the lineage of religious orders forced political patrons to go beyond the straightforward expedient of outspending their rivals.

Maharaja Ranbir Singh: The Making of a 'Hindu State'

The Dogras were evidently well aware of the significance of temples and Brahmans, both in the political realm as well as in the domain of religion. They were also alert to the complications arising from the territorially perplexing nature of attempts to control this elusive religious domain. This explains the alacrity with which, at a time of political upheaval in 1846–7 when Sikh power was being gradually dismantled, the Dogras of Jammu intervened to cut off Lahore's patronage and worship at Purmandal. On several occasions in 1847, the widow of Ranjit Singh, Rani Jinda Kaur, complained bitterly to the British in Lahore that Brahmans sent by her to Purmandal to pray for the Sikh maharaja's 'health and prosperity' had been turned away by Ranbir Singh. The Dogras had insisted that the Brahmans not return without the permission of Gulab Singh or the British Resident at Lahore. The British viewed with sympathy Ranbir's suspicion 'that the Brahmins had come to pray for the restoration of [the Sikh] Rajah Lall Singh and the downfall of the Jummoo Raj' and agreed with his recommendation that the rani 'send instead to Umritsur or Benares'.[96] Purmandal, as also other important sacred centres located in the Jammu and Kashmir state, was now perceived as 'belonging' to the newly defined Dogra territory and the merit of prayers offered there would have to accrue primarily to its own rulers.

This incident marked a fundamental change in the relations between religion, religious patronage and territory that would find full

[95] *The Jammu and Kashmir Law Reports, Volume 1, Baisakh to Chet, Samvat 1999,* Appellate Civil, Before the Chief Justice, Civil 1st Appeal no. 6 of Samvat 1997, pp. 445–51.

[96] *Political Diaries of the Agent to the Governor-General, North West Frontier and Resident at Lahore,* 1 January 1847 to 4 March 1848, pp. 124, 138–9.

expression in Ranbir Singh's rule and underlie his construction of a Hindu state in Jammu and Kashmir. Ranbir Singh would territorialize the Hindu religious arena in ways in which it had never before been territorially circumscribable, even as late as during the rule of Gulab Singh. He would devise a carefully regulated system of control for every temple located within his state, actualizing a hierarchy linking each temple to the Dogra maharaja himself. Ranbir Singh worked towards establishing a fit between the sway of the Hindu religion over which he would preside as chief patron, and the borders of his political dominion, which he would command as maharaja.

To a significant extent this was both facilitated and necessitated by increasing British efforts at making the frontiers of native states binding. By the time of the Imperial Assemblage of 1877, the right to make war, a substantial factor in keeping the frontiers of sovereignty in pre-colonial India in political flux, had been expunged from the princely domain. Thus, as Wheeler noted, 'such was one result of the Imperial Assemblage. The ruling chiefs and notables at Delhi strove to accommodate themselves to the new era . . . they were lavish in their expressions of good-will towards each other. Hereditary feuds were forgotten; the Imperial Assemblage made them friends.'[97]

The imperial government had also settled, as a necessary concomitant, the question of precedence which ranked the princes of India. Interestingly, however, they had resolved this vexing problem, arising as early as 1869 and defying solution then, by effectively avoiding it. On the occasion of the assemblage, in anticipation of 'discontent and heartburning' arising from potentially bruised princely egos, the British 'avoided the difficulty by grouping the chiefs in *territorial* sections'.[98] Additionally, appellations expressing the 'majesty' of sovereigns were now reserved solely for the British monarch: Indian princes would have to rest content with the humble address of their 'highness' and a hierarchy of other titles designed and handed down to them authoritatively by the British. The critical instruments of negotiated

[97] Wheeler, p. 89.

[98] Memorandum by S.H. Butler, Secretary of State, dated 21 January 1909, R/1/1/370, CRR, Political Department (Foreign Department/Secret I/Pros. April 1909, no. 1) IOL. Emphasis mine. Also, Confidential Memorandum by Viceroy, dated 11 May 1876, MSS.Eur.F.86/166, Temple Collection, Imperial Assemblage Proceedings, IOL.

stature, incorporation and accommodation which had kept the political milieu of pre-colonial India in a fluid state no longer existed. In a world of frozen relations between princes who *would* be 'friends', none could ever again be a 'great king' overlord to 'little' kings; no ruler could ever again build his kingship by claiming prestige as a 'universal monarch'. Their sovereignty circumscribed and relegated to a subordinate level, India's princes were now increasingly wedded to their inviolable territorial frontiers.

Colonial authorities were themselves concerned to tidy up the clutter left behind from pre-colonial India's layered and overlapping sovereignties. Through the second half of the nineteenth century, British officials worked slowly but doggedly towards demarcating the lines separating directly governed areas from those under 'native' rule. Areas lying in British India but providing revenues that sustained the intersecting religious sovereignties of rulers located elsewhere presented one set of bewildering overlays that needed sorting out. An instance of this dilemma was presented by 'the village of Chak Bharat . . . [lying] well within the British side of the boundary line . . . quite separated from all villages belonging to Jammu,' but which had 'remained all along in the possession of the Maharaja of Kashmir' to support the temple of Raghunath in Jammu. By 1874 a solution was arrived at, exemplifying the spirit of the age. Effecting a compromise with the Maharaja of Kashmir, the British Indian government acquired full sovereign rights over the village, and so over its inhabitants, while its revenues alone would continue to accrue to the 'Kashmir government for the support of the temple of Raghunath in Jammu during the maintenance of such institution.'[99] The line dividing the sovereignties of British India and the state of Jammu and Kashmir had been established. The Maharaja of Kashmir retained a purely economic prerogative, but one that reinforced his control over the purse-strings of a temple critical for his status as a patron of the Hindu religion *within* the state of Jammu and Kashmir.

The British Indian government's preoccupation with the clear delineation of boundaries, marking off sovereign spaces, extended be-

---

[99] Letter from C.M. Rivaz, Officiating Secretary to Government, Punjab, to the Secretary to the Government of India, Foreign Department, dated Lahore, 3 August 1874, Punjab Foreign Proceedings/Pros. no. 3, August 1874/Part A, IOL.

yond lines traced in soil to less solid ones cut in rivers. Of course, this concern with riparian frontiers is not unfamiliar to modern-day governments, but it certainly disconcerted 'native' states and their subjects, as well as British Indian subjects, who had only barely begun to understand the vogue of tangible political borders in the first place. Thus, we are told that Captain J. Abbott, the settlement commissioner sent to Jammu and Kashmir in 1846, had 'given almost the whole bed of the Chenab, opposite Upper Bajwat, to Jummoo territory'.[100] The problem exercising British authorities in this particular instance arose because Abbott's line appeared to have dissected rather arbitrarily a village called Kundal on an island lying somewhere in the middle of the river, which in turn appeared determined to confuse issues by changing its course. The result was a cacophony of proprietary claims to lands extending on either side of the Abbott line. Besides the concern for 'the rights of the zamindars of our [British] villages in lands in their possession, or to which they have a title', there was, as might be expected, another underlying economic motive. In this case, it was the loss of 'control of the river islands on which much drift timber is cast, and which is speedily annexed and marked with the sign denoting the Jummoo Maharaja's proprietorship'. The economic imperative added to the urgency of settling what was simultaneously a political problem of clearly defining frontiers. Disputes continued to crop up for sometime afterwards, leading British colonial officials to ask whether they should tell the Kashmir durbar 'anything about *half* the river *bed* being ours and half Kashmir, or shall we only speak of . . . the banks?'[101] Bank or bed, the sanctity of a territorial frontier was conveyed to India's princes in unambiguous terms.

The colonial government's concerns extended also to the territorial differentiation of the subjects of British India from those of native states. Described as 'foreign vagrants', groups of Kashmiri Muslims trading in British India were repeatedly 'returned to their country'.[102] On one occasion a large 'gang' of 111 Kashmiris was accused of causing 'some inconvenience in consequence of disturbances which [had] recently broken out in the adjoining districts' of Sholapur in Bombay

---

[100] Punjab Foreign Proceedings/no.10, April 1881/Part A, IOL. The Chenab shared its banks with British Punjab and sections of the Jammu province.

[101] Home Department (Forests)/March 1883/Pros. nos. 5–23, Part A, NAI.

[102] Home Department (Public)/15 January 1870/Pros. nos. 195–7, Part A, NAI.

Presidency.[103] This irritant led to their being promptly incarcerated until such time as they could be deported. The precise nature of the disturbances was not described in this particular instance, an oversight that is surprising given the usual scrupulous attention to detail in the colonial government's files. All that are available are hints at how 'their presence even in small parties, is a nuisance; in large gangs, they are manageable only when placed under close restraint; and even granting their ostensible trade to be a legitimate one, it supplies no want.'[104] Quite simply then, they ought not to have been there, no matter why they were. However, even more intriguing was the inability of these 'vagrants' when interrogated, to provide 'all detailed information as to the[ir] nationalities', vastly complicating the exercise of 'separating foreign vagrants . . . from those who might be British subjects'.[105] Confusion reigned as the colonial authorities in charge of deporting these 'foreigners' to their 'own country' were confronted with a bevy of options, ranging from Herat to 'a place called Cashmere in Beluchistan' to their 'real habitat' in the Nizam of Hyderabad's territories.[106] There was a clear discrepancy here in the understanding of the term one's 'own country'. In the end, the issue was resolved by simply determining the place of birth in order to then settle on the territorial lines that bound them and to which they were sent under British escort.

Maharaja Ranbir Singh took the message about the confines of geographic boundaries very seriously. As a recognized ruler of his state, he was given a territory whose frontiers could not err into British domains but which was, simultaneously, all 'his', as were the subjects which came with the territory. At the same time, he was both instructed and reassured by his paramount masters that his legitimacy to claim this territory and to govern its populace was founded on his being a

[103] Home Department (Public)/October 1875/Pros. nos. 268–77/Part A, NAI.

[104] Letter from Captain H.W.H. Cox, Superintendent of Police, North Arcot, to the Magistrate of North Arcot, dated 15 February 1875, Home Department (Public)/October 1875/Pros. nos. 268–77/Part A, NAI.

[105] Letter from W. Lee Warner, Acting Under Secretary to the Government of Bombay, to the Resident at Hyderabad, dated 8 June 1875, Home Department (Public)/October 1875/Pros. nos. 268–77/Part A, NAI.

[106] Letter from W.S. White, District Magistrate of North Arcot, to the Acting Chief Secretary to the Government of Madras, dated 17 February 1875, Home Department (Public)/October 1875/Pros. nos. 268–77/Part A, NAI.

'traditional' and 'Hindu' ruler. Most pre-colonial rulers, seeking to establish the widest possible social bases for their power and sovereignty, had defined their stature as religious patrons in the most ambiguously interpretable terms possible without riding too close to the accusation of heresy by the orthodoxy. Similarly, one might have expected Ranbir Singh to have sought the widest religious, and therefore social, insurance possible. However, after Queen Victoria's proclamation there were only three paths for rulers or governments to follow: Hindu, Muslim, or religiously neutral. The politically convenient ambiguity of the category 'neither' with precedence for one or the other was progressively erased. And a 'Muslim' ruler Ranbir Singh neither would nor could be. Insofar as the category of religiously neutral went, had he sought such a qualification, he would not be allowed it. This latter characterization, while put out in the domain of politics in India, was increasingly intended to be an inappropriable concept reserved for the colonial state. With the setting of these important ground rules, Ranbir Singh's efforts were directed wholeheartedly towards matching the political dominion allowed to him and the religious identity demanded of and embraced energetically by him, within territories demarcated for him.

There were two important and exhaustive documents drawn up under orders of Ranbir Singh in the years immediately preceding his death in 1885. The first of these was the *Dastur-ul-Amal*, loosely translated as 'the will of His Highness the Maharaja of Kashmir', and the second was the *Ain-i-Dharmarth* or 'The Regulations for the Dharmarth Trust'. Taken together, they represent a formalization of the various measures Ranbir Singh had undertaken through his reign to ensure the high standing of the Hindu religion in his state and the affirmation of the adherence to that faith by the ruling family as a basis for their sovereignty. Thus, the *Dastur-ul-Amal*, drawn up in 1882 and printed at the Punjab Government Press as a 'confidential document', opens with the following words:

> Whereas this State was acquired by the late Maharaja [Gulab Singh] under the treaty of the 16th March 1846, without the participation of any other person (i.e. in sole sovereignty), and has since, by the grace of the Almighty been in the process of improvement, it is hereby considered expedient that, with a view to avoid misunderstanding and dispute between the descendants, heirs and successors . . . a law and

procedure be laid down in order that they should act up to, and abide by it *for ever*. . .[107]

A primary purpose to be served by this document, therefore, was to assert the independent sovereignty of the descendants of Gulab Singh over the state of Jammu and Kashmir by emphatically sidelining not only the British paramount power but also, and probably more importantly, any claims to sovereignty that may have been made by distant or close relatives of the ruling family. Ranbir Singh was also concerned in his 'will' to impart the prescription that would ensure the continued sovereignty of the descendants of the late Maharaja Gulab Singh. Alongside a series of articles designed to prevent succession disputes and intra-family feuds, was an injunction emphasizing 'Hindu-ness' and 'tradition' as the basis of their rule. Thus, Ranbir Singh made it 'incumbent on all the members of the family that they should not make any departure from the old customs, usages, traditions and religion as they involve *the reputation and honour of the family.*'[108]

Having acclaimed the importance of being Hindu in order to rule in Jammu and Kashmir, Ranbir Singh went on to devise an intricate framework in which a religious centre in Jammu would correspond with a political centre overseen by the Hindu maharaja and extending to the territorial limits of the Jammu and Kashmir provinces. The outline for this project can be culled from the *Ain-i-Dharmarth*, drawn up in 1884.[109] Probably taking as its model Abul Fazl's *Ain-i-Akbari*, the *Ain-i-Dharmarth* addressed, in as minute detail as possible, the regulation of the public performance of religious rites within the Hindu Dogra state of Jammu and Kashmir. The idea of a dharmarth department was not new, taking its cue from the Delhi sultans and the Mughal emperors who had similarly supervised the grant of revenue-free incomes to learned and pious men and appointed officers of religion. As mentioned earlier, the Sikhs had also sponsored an active

[107] The 'Dastur-ul-Amal', the English translation of the will of His Highness Maharaja Ranbir Singh, Maharaja of Jammu and Kashmir, dated 1st Sawan Samvat 1939 [AD 1882] in R/2/1067/88, Crown Representative's Residency Records, Kashmir Residency Office, F. no. 107/1921, IOL. Emphasis mine.

[108] Ibid. Article Twenty Two. Emphasis mine.

[109] *Ain-i-Dharmarth* or Regulation for Dharmarth Trust Fund (Jammu: Ranbir Press, 1884).

dharmarth department that had supported acts of charity, men of learning and piety. Modelling himself on his erstwhile political overlords in Lahore, in 1826 Gulab Singh had also invested funds for the purposes of dharmarth,[110] yet the nature of this enterprise was qualitatively different from that under Ranbir Singh's supervision. Under Gulab Singh it had remained a private concern of the ruler, even though it had been transformed formally into a regular department of the state by 1846 with an initial donation of five lakhs of rupees made by him to the 'Treasury of Shri Raghunathji' for the permanent maintenance of *sadavarts* (public charitable institutions).[111]

It was not until Ranbir Singh's reign, though, that a permanent and systematic arrangement was made for the administration of the dharmarth funds. Announcing new beginnings, and with a singular lack of modesty, Ranbir Singh declared that although he had 'until now executed the said trust in a very satisfactory manner . . . it [wa]s now [his] desire that the sadavarts and their management, should . . . be placed on a permanent footing'.[112] Clearly, there was a transition afoot. The Dharmarth Trust was no longer to remain a private fund bearing testimony to the piety of an individual ruler. Instead, Ranbir Singh enjoined his 'sons, heirs, descendants *and officials and administrators of the State* to lend their help and assistance to the arrangement.'[113] He related the Dharmarth Fund and sadavarts to the goal of providing 'his own spiritual redemption as well as that of his august family'. This would follow from honouring the arrangements of the trust founded with 'a view solely to ensure the advancement of the sacred religion of the Hindus'.[114] Oblivious to any contradiction between the personal spiritual redemption of the ruler and the greater good of the polity, Ranbir Singh had no difficulty in enlisting the assistance of state officials. And though, with the formal appointment of a council, the Dharmarth Trust was sought to be given an independent and self-regulating life of its own, the maharaja still loomed

---

[110] Sukhdev Singh Charak, *Life and Times of Maharaja Ranbir Singh* (Jammu: Jay Kay Book House, 1985), pp. 275–6.

[111] Letter from Raja Amar Singh, Prime Minister, to the Resident, dated 26 December 1890, OER, JKA; General and Political Department, 1890, File no. 18, JKA.

[112] Ain, p. 1.

[113] Ibid.

[114] Ibid., p. 2.

quite clearly as the directing force behind it. Thus, Article Three of the 'Regulations Regarding the Great Council' asked its members to see to it 'that all orders and regulations of His Highness are dully [*sic*] carried out and they should themselves also act upon them.'[115] Dully or with alert readiness, the officials and administrators of the state were conscripted also for the purpose of conducting the business of a 'government department' founded with the single aim of securing the glorification of the Hindu religion in the state. Potential embezzlers of the fund were confronted with Ranbir Singh's doom-filled threat that they would 'incur the sin of having killed one crore of cows' or be considered 'guilty of having committed sins against all *tiraths*'.[116] Further tying the dharmarth to the state, Ranbir Singh ordered the members of the council to 'attend Durbar twice a day: for two and a half hours in the morning and four hours in the afternoon'.[117] The association of the trust, and by extension the officials and administrators of the state, with the Hindu religion was difficult to miss.

Confined within the narrowest religious premise, the implementation of the trust's duties was envisioned in the broadest terms possible. The members of the Dharmarth Trust council were asked to inspect regularly the religious institutions and schools in their charge; supervise the jagirs and land belonging to the trust, as also the income from the trade and business spun off from the capital of the fund; and oversee *paths* (recitation from sacred books) and *prayogs* (meditation and penance performance performed on behalf of others).[118] Aside from these onerous duties, members of the council were also expected to aid the maharaja in maintaining his politically and religiously important role as chief dispenser of charity and gifts. Thus, the council was instructed that 'if any *pandit* or *sadhu* (ascetic) or *mahatma* (saint) arrives [in the state], for the first time, he should be examined first and a report made to His Highness, and then he should be brought to His Highness and hospitably treated. They should be bestowed gifts on departure according to their position.'[119]

The chief concern of Ranbir Singh was to establish control over the domain of Hindu worship and its officiating priests *within* his state.

[115] Ibid., p. 3.
[116] Ibid., p. 2. A *tirath* is a place of pilgrimage.
[117] Ibid., p. 9.
[118] Ibid., p. 4.
[119] Ibid.

At one level, the goal of ensuring 'the advancement of the sacred religion of the Hindus' implied an unending frenzy of building, repairing
and more building. Thus, Article Twenty One of the *Ain* required
that a 'well, a *baoli* [a step well], a tank or a temple should every year
be erected on behalf of the State, but after one work is completed, the
other should be taken in hand.'[120] At another level, the major purpose
of the *Ain* was to structure this complex of Hindu shrines throughout
the state, newly built or of old standing, within one common regulated
framework of worship. Rules for the conduct of worship at almost
every 'state temple' were handed down, in painstaking detail, to the
pujaris (priests) at each one of these shrines. Thus the *Ain* instructed
that 'For every god, a separate *padati* (directions about and functions
to be carried out at *puja* service) should be prepared here [in Jammu]
and sent to every temple concerned. The *puja* (prayers dedicated to a
personalized God) should be correctly performed in accordance
therewith.'[121]

Fanning out from Jammu, the *Ain* included within its fold temples
in Kashmir (both those preceding Dogra rule and new ones built there
since) as well as temples in the remotest mufassils of Jammu province.
Regulations regarding the latter provided for the diffusion of a central
plan guiding not only the design of new temples to be erected there but
also the learning requisite for their priests.[122] Headmen of villages and
villagers themselves, many of whom would have been Muslim, in the
distant outposts of the state were ordered to 'render proper help in the
erection of temple-houses'.[123] Through the ceaseless raising of new
temples in the mufassils, Ranbir Singh's control over the religious domain sought to extend to the farthest reaches of his territory. Interestingly, the duties of priests at the mufassil temples included reporting
'every month to the Dharmarth office at Jammu, through the police,
all occurrences, good or bad in the villages concerned.'[124] In this way,
the Dharmarth Trust made possible Ranbir Singh's goal of a religious
centre in Jammu coinciding with a political centre and expanding to
fill up the territorial outlines of the state.

[120] Ibid., p. 5.
[121] Ibid., p. 14.
[122] Ibid., pp. 115–16.
[123] Ibid., p. 117.
[124] Ibid., p. 116.

Ranbir Singh also attempted to ensure that the Dogra maharajas would have no rivals to their authority in the state. Already rendered subservient by being put on the payroll of the Dharmarth Trust, Brahmans were also warned against resorting to the practice of parah, which had both provided them with and reflected their considerable bargaining power in the past.[125] The custom of patholi was also attempted to be done away with when the *Ain* expressly forbade the harbouring of 'offenders' at any of the temples in the state.[126] Furthermore, potential competitors for the maharaja's status as the chief patron of the Hindu religion in Jammu and Kashmir were sought to be neutralized. Thus, any person who wished to build a temple in the state territories and have it named after him would have to apply for permission from the maharaja.[127] Similarly with prayog, the ritual of meditation and penance performed on behalf of others, the standing order in the *Ain* was that if 'any State servant or a native of the country, or a foreigner or any other . . . wish[ed] to perform prayog or get a prayog performed on his behalf . . . he [would] not be allowed to do so without first reporting to His Highness.'[128] The *Ain* provides a list of temples at which if prayog was performed, a report was to be submitted to His Highness at once. They included a large number of those in Jammu and four of the principle temples in Kashmir.[129] Essentially, then, any religious act involving a dedication within the state would have to be vetted by the maharaja. In this context, a very significant decree in the *Ain* ordained that any 'person who is disloyal to the State, should not be allowed to perform prayog even if he wishes to perform it for his own health'.[130] Tying in Hindu worship to the state of Jammu and Kashmir, making loyalty to the latter a precondition for the former, Ranbir Singh territorialized the Hindu religious universe in an unprecedented manner.

And the centre of this religious universe was the Raghunathji temple built in Jammu. Raghunathji, an epithet for the god Rama, was the tutelary deity of the Dogras who were primarily Vaishnavite. The

[125] Ibid.
[126] Ibid., p. 10.
[127] Ibid., p. 97.
[128] Ibid., p. 44.
[129] Ibid., p. 48.
[130] Ibid., p. 44.

foundation stone for the Raghunathji temple in Jammu was laid by
Gulab Singh in 1852 but it was finally completed and consecrated by
Ranbir Singh in 1857. It was in fact a temple complex, the chief structure in it being dedicated to Rama, and enshrining along with this
deity, his wife and brother, Sita and Lakshman. This main edifice was
surrounded by the temples of the four Vedas and several others dedicated to a wide range of Hindu deities, numbering according to the
Ain an impressive 24 lakhs.[131] Yet the heart of this web was the Raghunathji temple and the routine of worship prescribed at it presents an
interesting exercise in centring the religious universe. The pujaris of
each of the temples dedicated to the 24 lakh deities, though decreed
their own separate rites, were to gather together to perform the *arti* at
the chief temple. There was a strict order of precedence laid out for this,
enjoining upon all the priests to first visit each of the temples of the
Vedas in turn, picking up their respective priests along the way, to
finally congregate for worship at the Raghunathji shrine. Absenteeism
during the time of this particular ceremony was not tolerated and any
of the 'temple people' who absconded were threatened with nothing
short of expulsion.[132] The chief ceremony at this principal temple was
to radiate outwards to unite also the world beyond. According to the
Ain, during the '*arti* big gongs and conch shells should be . . . heard
at a distance of . . . about 2 miles'.[133]

Ranbir Singh made unequivocally manifest his status as the chief
donor and so the chief recipient of sacred allocations from the Raghunathji temple. Thus, he commanded that the 'dishes of offering
(*naived*) for *Thakurji* should be brought to the big temple of Shri
Raghunathji and should first be offered to the *Thakurji* and then eaten
by the *pujaris* [priests offering worship]', but before the priests sat
down to their meal, 'one *thal* (dish) . . . after it has been offered to Shri
Thakurji . . . should be sent to His Highness daily'.[134] Additionally,
wall illustrations on the entrance to the chief temple made barely
disguised associations between Hanuman and Ranbir Singh as the
chief worshippers of Lord Rama, the former being the divine devotee

[131] Ibid., p. 27.
[132] Ibid., p. 27.
[133] Ibid., p. 28.
[134] Ibid., p. 15.

while the latter was his temporal counterpart.[135] While every state temple received detailed instructions as to the proper performance of worship, what texts recitations were to be drawn from, how money should be spent and so on, the most painstaking management was reserved for the Raghunathji temple. It should come as no surprise that the regulations for worship at this temple paralleled closely Ranbir Singh's own daily routine as maharaja and vice versa. This was so from the time of rousing the deity, appropriately referred to as Thakurji, his afternoon rest, his holding of a 'durbar', to the daily processions when the deity's image would be carried on a 'throne'. Raghunathji's durbar included not only the personnel usual in the court of a temporal ruler, with mace-bearers who 'should keep standing, while the officers and clerks should carry on their work', but also included activities such as music, singing and dancing in the evenings.[136] As the location of Raghunathji's and Ranbir Singh's durbars, Jammu was the centre of both the divine Thakur's cosmic realm and the more earthly one's temporal domain.

The political control over the valley of Kashmir by the Hindu maharajas of Jammu was matched by the extension to it of the sway of Raghunathji's temple and forms of worship associated with it. This was effected by bringing together the Vaishnavite ruler's Rama cult with the Tantric Shaivite beliefs and shrines of Kashmiri Pandits. The means employed encompassed both the construction of new temples dedicated to Rama and Hanuman in the territory of the valley as well as appropriating through patronage and regulation the Tantric Shaivite

---

[135] Madhu Bazaz Wangu, 'Hermeneutics of a Kashmiri Mahatmya', in Jeffrey R. Timm (ed.), *Texts in Context* (Albany: State University of New York Press, 1992), p. 153.

[136] *Ain*, pp. 90–2. Arjun Appadurai's illuminating work presents a very similar picture in the context of south Indian temples. Thus he points out that 'South Indian ethnographic evidence . . . suggests that the deity is conceived to be the paradigmatic sovereign. The Tamil word koyil means both temple and royal palace . . . [and the paraphernalia of the] deities . . . is indistinguishable from the paraphernalia of human kings: conches, palanquins, umbrellas, elephants, fly whisks . . . The language of service is the idiom of bonded servitude . . . and the deity is referred to explicitly in terms that indicate universal lordship and sovereignty'. Arjun Appadurai, *Worship and Conflict Under Colonial Rule* (Cambridge: Cambridge University Press, 1981), p. 21.

4: 'Hindu Festival, Cashmere'. P1363.   By permission of the British Library.

5: 'Priest and Worshippers at the Shiva Temple, Srinagar',
Kashmiri Artist, *c.* 1850–60. Add.Or. 1745.

By permission of the British Library.

shrines already in existence in Kashmir. The success in the approximation of these two forms of Hinduism was facilitated by the fact that it served the mutual interests of the parties involved. The Dogra maharajas needed to substantiate their claim to legitimacy in Kashmir as Hindu rulers by associating with them its powerful Hindu minority, while the Kashmiri Pandit community was concerned to hold on to its privileged access to government employment. Charles Girdlestone, who had visited Kashmir in 1871, wrote that 'trading on the Maharaja's veneration of the Hindoo religion the Pundit employee rather affects long prayers and the narrating of stories from their mythology in the hope of worldly advantage.'[137]

Needless to say, it was not always plain sailing between Kashmiri Pandits and Dogra rulers; between Shaivite, Shakta and Vaishnavite practices. George Buhler, the German Indologist visiting the valley around 1877 to collect Sanskrit manuscripts, reported that Ranbir Singh disapproved of aspects of the religious practices of the Kashmiri Pandits. Some segments of the community evidently appeared too lax for Ranbir Singh's taste in following 'the rulers of the Sastras.' So much so that the 'performance of the prayaschittas, or penances for breaches of the commandments of the Smriti, [was] looked after by the Government' and 'the Maharaja himself' intervened to ensure that 'Brahmanical offenders expiate their sins in the manner prescribed by the Sastras'. However, determining the 'exact nature and amount of the penances' was left to 'five Dharamadhikaris, who belong[ed] to the most respected families among the . . . Pandits.'[138] Furthermore, Buhler noted that

> In former times both the Kasmirian Saktas and Saivas were famous for their proficiency in the black art . . . Now it is said that only a few *Abhicharikas* [sorcerers] exist and that these carefully hide their art, as the Maharaja is opposed to them and punishes them . . . It may be that witchcraft is now not much practiced in Kashmir, but the belief in its

[137] Charles Girdlestone, *Memorandum on Cashmere and Some Adjacent Countries* (Calcutta: Foreign Department Press, 1874), pp. 25–6.

[138] George Buhler, 'Detailed Report of a Tour in Search of Sanskrit MSS Made in Kashmir, Rajputana, and Central India', *Journal of the Bombay Branch of the Royal Asiatic Society of Great Britain and Ireland* (Extra Number), vol. XII, no. 34, 1877, pp. 21–2.

efficacy, in *yoginis* who celebrate their foul rites on the desert mountain sides, and in *Bhuts*, is perhaps stronger and more universal in Kasmir than in India proper.[139]

His objections notwithstanding, Ranbir Singh proceeded to patronize the worship of the Kashmiri Hindus, making allowances for some of their specific customs. Both funding from and the regulations of the Dharmarth Trust were applied to the principal Kashmiri Hindu shrines such as Khir Bhawani, Shri Jawalaji and Sharkaji. Taking into account the practices of the Kashmiri Pandits, the *Ain* prescribed the serving of 'zarda and mutton' at the shrine of Sharkaji.[140] This was clearly a local concession since the cooking and serving of meat would have been considered sacrilegious at shrines in Jammu. As Buhler had been told by his Pandit informants, 'the custom of eating meat is based on a *desaguna*' or 'a virtue of the country'.[141] Additionally, in a clear attempt at appropriating the merit, political and religious, of the shrine the Brahmans there were told that they 'should by turn perform *parkarma* (circumambulation) every day on behalf of His Highness.'[142] The domain of painting also witnessed efforts at affiliating Vaishnavite and Tantric Shaivite practices, drawing together Jammu and Kashmir. An illustrated Kashmiri manuscript of a Devi *mahatmya*,[143] probably painted and compiled during Ranbir Singh's reign, demonstrated not only a fusion of styles from the two regions but, given its subject, also the patronage increasingly extended by the Dogra rulers to the Shakta cult of Kashmir.[144] In fact, insofar as the goddess Khir Bhawani is concerned, although she was 'highly cherished by the local Kashmiri Hindu population', it was only under the aegis

---

[139] Ibid., pp. 24–5.

[140] Ain, p. 152.

[141] Buhler, p. 23.

[142] *Ain*, p. 152.

[143] Mahatmyas are Hindu sacred texts that narrate myths and legends of important deities, eulogize the deity's pilgrimage centre and prescribe the rites to be observed by the pilgrims.

[144] Karuna Goswamy, *The Glory of the Great Goddess* (Zurich: 1989). It is also noteworthy that Ranbir Singh had commissioned Pandit Sahebram, a respected Sanskritist of Kashmir, to 'prepare a trustworthy copy' of the great text of the Kashmiri Pandits, the *Nilamatapurana* 'for edition'. Buhler, pp. 32–3.

of the Dogra maharaja that a *mahatmya* was first composed and an island temple built in her honour.[145] Having embraced the patronage of Khir Bhawani, the Dogras would continue to do so with verve into the twentieth century. Protecting the sanctity of her shrine, Maharaja Pratap Singh (*r.*1885–1924) repeatedly issued orders against the desecration perpetrated by Europeans who insisted not only on walking on the island with their shoes on but also on fishing in the waters surrounding it.[146]

In addition to the patronage of Kashmiri shrines and deities, very gradually Ranbir Singh also began to embed aspects of the Rama cult in the valley in order to associate Jammu and Kashmir within a common frame of worship. One way in which the Dogras did this was by erecting temples dedicated to Vaishnavite, especially Rama, worship on Kashmiri soil. Among the prominent ones were the Gadadharji temple dedicated to Hanuman and the Ranbirswamiji temple, both in Srinagar.[147] Along with the temples came the celebration of religious festivals honouring Rama, such as Rama Naumi (Rama's birthday), and Dussehra, celebrating Rama's victory over the demon king Ravana.[148] These festivals had never been celebrated in Kashmir before the Dogras. The composition of the mahatmya for Khir Bhawani provided Ranbir Singh with fresh occasion to superimpose the Rama cult on Kashmiri beliefs and to do so by enlisting the help of Kashmiri Pandits funded by the Dharmarth Trust. Thus, in the mahatmya, which was completed in the reign of Pratap Singh, Khir Bhawani was described as 'the one who grants *Ramarajya . . .* and has made Satidesa her abode'.[149] By the time Pratap Singh ascended the *gaddi* (throne), the religious boundaries of the Hindu faith united the provinces of Jammu and Kashmir in a state that not only had a Hindu ruler but that itself also had a distinctly Hindu identity.

The following chapter examines what it meant for a Kashmiri Muslim to live in such state. A summary assessment suggests that, seen from the perspective of Muslims, 'Kashmir [was] literally overrun by

[145] Wangu, p. 148.

[146] Memorandum for submission to the Maharaja Sahib Bahadur, dated 20 August 1908, OER, Political Department, 1908, File no. 258/V-87, JKA.

[147] *Ain*, pp. 129–34 and pp. 141–9.

[148] Ibid., p. 130. Also Drew, *The Jummoo and Kashmir Territories.*

[149] Wangu, pp. 155–7.

Hindoo faqueers, detested by the people they prey upon, but supported and encouraged by the Government and their numbers . . . rapidly increasing.'[150] What was probably even more galling was that, since part of the dharmarth funds were raised as a portion of the land revenue from 'all the people irrespective of religion',[151] Kashmiri Muslim cultivators had been obliged to contribute to the construction of a Hindu state, seemingly oblivious to them when searching for its legitimacy to rule over them.

[150] Torrens, *Travels in Ladak, Tartary and Kashmir*, pp. 305–6.
[151] Charak, *Life and Times of Maharaja Ranbir Singh*, p. 278.

CHAPTER 3

The Obligations of Rulers and the Rights of Subjects

The ignorant Mohammadan cultivator has not only no one he can call friend, but everyone, whether Hindu or Mohammadan, of any influence is against him, for cheap bread by the sweat of the cultivator's brow is a benefit widely appreciated.

—A. Wingate.[1]

Ranbir Singh sought his legitimacy to rule, and had been encouraged to do so by the paramount British authority, in his Hinduness. This basis for his legitimacy was deemed sufficient at the time. It could be unfurled generously enough to include not only a large section of the population of the Jammu province but also the Pandits in Kashmir. But even as this became a mandate for Dogra power, Ranbir Singh's successor Pratap Singh (r.1885–1925) was instructed that he would have to find yet another framework for establishing his political legitimacy. In the late nineteenth century the British imposed on the Dogra maharaja the new obligation of a demonstrated concern for 'the good of his people', Hindu as well as Muslim. From being a ruling dynasty whose legitimacy had until then relied on its association with one religious community, the Dogras were now required to make themselves more 'representative' of a subject population encompassing different religious affinities. For the Dogras this requisite leap of faith, so to speak, was greater than patterns of legitimation set in place since the founding of their state would permit. The result was a confounding exercise in transposing the notion of rulers with obligations, and subjects with rights, on patterns of governance

[1] R/2/1061/3, Crown Representative's Residency Records, Kashmir Residency Office, File no. 28 of 1888, A. Wingate, 'Preliminary Report of Settlement Operations in Kashmir and Jammu', p. 26, IOL.

that were, at the same time, unable to transcend the narrower religious definitions of either. This was still a Hindu state but one which would perforce have to concern itself with the whole body of its subjects. Conversely, the subjects also continued to be identified by religious affiliations that determined both their experience of and their access to the resources of the Dogra state. This anomalous position created the conditions for the mobilization of Kashmiri Muslims in defence of rights they now understood they possessed. But, more importantly, it inscribed both this mobilization and the understanding of rights firmly within the language of religion.

Maharaja Pratap Singh, 'unfitted in character', small in stature and sickly in health, was apparently not up to the new political gymnastics required of him. In 1885 he was allowed to accede to his father's powers on strictly defined conditions of internal reform; in 1889 he was deprived of the power to govern, though allowed to reign, for not conducting the reforms demanded of him by the colonial government; and then, finally, in 1905 his powers were fully restored to him by the viceroy, Lord Curzon. However, it was no accident that Pratap Singh became the object of colonial contumely. His reign coincided with a period of questioning in the colonial metropolis, in Europe, and in India, of aristocrats and dynastic rulers who failed to 'naturalize' themselves in the face of a growing onslaught from popular nationalist sentiments.

From 'Breakwaters in the Storm' to 'Naturalized' Rulers

In 1895, in preparation for a public durbar organized in honour of the viceroy's visit to Lahore, short summaries were written identifying the various ruling chiefs who were to attend. Similar in form to those written by Talboys Wheeler for the imperial assemblage of 1877, the assessment of the ruling chiefs of Jammu and Kashmir, however, had undergone a sea change. This was indicative of the alteration in the terms for legitimacy expected of princely rulers. The princely state of Jammu and Kashmir was described as

A Native State in political connection with the Government of India . . . The founder of the ruling family was Gulab Singh, a Dogra Rajput, who had begun his life as a horseman under the Maharaja Ranjit Singh . . . he

was confirmed in possession of the State which he had held as feudatory
of the Sikhs . . . [Ranbir Singh] was a munificent patron of education
and literature. He contributed Rs 93,478 to the Punjab University College, and arranged in his own territory for the translation of English
standard works into Sanskrit. The present Chief is His Highness Maharaja Partab . . . The Administration of the State is at present carried on
by a Council . . . guided by the advice of the Resident in all matters of
importance. As to his character and projected alterations in the administration of his State, his attention and that of the Government of India
have recently been directed, nothing need be said here.[2]

This account had collapsed into a single one the two categories of
Indians conceptualized as separate at the imperial assemblage of 1877:
those deemed legitimate 'natural aristocrats' on the basis of 'descent'
and those recognized as representatives on the basis of their 'achieve-
ments'.[3] Ranbir Singh was rewritten in this rendition of the Dogras
and given praise for his accomplishments in the public interest as 'a
patron of education and literature'. Never mind that the translation of
English works into Sanskrit, a language only a few spoke or read at any
point in India's history, could serve no real public good. Similarly,
Gulab Singh's glory no longer derived purely from his being the scion
of an 'ancient Rajput dynasty'. Instead he was remembered as a man
who began his career as a mere 'horseman' in the service of the Sikhs
but who rose through the ranks by dint of effort and attainment. Pratap Singh, however, was castigated for his weaknesses of character and
had yet to prove himself as deserving the honour of governance bestowed upon him by the paramount power. Gone were the days when
he would be entitled to his sovereignty solely by virtue of his descent
from a long lineage 'lost in a remote antiquity'. Where Ranbir Singh
had been allowed to cull his legitimacy from being a devout Hindu,
in Pratap's case adherence to religion earned him the reproof of being
notoriously 'sunk in the most besotted superstition and the lowest
vice'.[4] Being a Hindu would continue to provide him with a mandate
to reign but his ability to rule would depend on the fulfilment of his
obligations as a ruler to his subjects.

[2] Foreign Department (Secret-I)/Pros. May 1895/nos. 65–115, NAI.

[3] Cohn, 'Representing Authority in Victorian India', p. 194.

[4] Note in the Foreign Department, dated 27 March 1888, Foreign Department (Secret E)/Pros. March 1889/nos. 107–200, NAI.

Ian Copland has pointed to demands increasingly made, beginning already in the 1860s, from both a British trading lobby as well as from 'the evangelical fraternity', for a change in the post-rebellion colonial state's decision to preserve India's princes. They were allegedly speaking in the interest of large numbers of Indians left beyond the pale of benign direct British rule. 'Was it right', they asked 'that some of India's people should prosper while others languished in poverty and ignorance and suffered oppression just because they happened to be subjects of a dependent prince?'[5]

These changing perceptions about princely states in general, and about Jammu and Kashmir's rulers in particular, were in line with a wider trend discernible not only in colonial India but also more globally. Benedict Anderson has written about a process of 'naturalization' engaged in by Europe's ruling dynasties in the course of the nineteenth century. A strategy for survival in an age when the 'national idea' and popular nationalist movements were increasingly widespread, dynasts aspired to make themselves more 'representative' of their subjects. In Europe, the 'official nationalism' resulting from this acknowledged that the legitimacies of rulers would require a stronger basis than their 'putative sacrality and sheer antiquity'.[6] In those parts of Asia that had successfully resisted colonialism, such as Thailand, and even more consequentially in Japan, ruling dynasties had also adopted variants of this 'official nationalism' to pre-empt their marginalization in a 'nationally-imagined community'.[7] Obviously, the difference in the case of the princely state of Jammu and Kashmir is that the impulse for the 'naturalization' of its rulers, far from being voluntarily realized and produced, came from the external stimulus of a British paramount power whose hand could always bear down more directly on them. India's princes had long ceased to be in a position to 'determine' state ideology at such exalted levels. However, the rulers of the larger states among them, such as the Dogra maharajas, still enjoyed considerable latitude in making politically pragmatic adjustments of imperial agendas in the domains that were still theirs, even if the terms for

[5] Ian Copland, *The Princes of India in the Endgame of Empire: 1917–1947* (Cambridge: Cambridge University Press, 1997), pp. 17–18.

[6] Benedict Anderson, *Imagined Communities: Reflections on the Origin and Spread of Nationalism* (London: Verso, 1991), pp. 83–6.

[7] Ibid., pp. 95–101.

controlling that domain were changing in ways beyond their independent control.

In the colonial metropolis itself the decade of the 1880s witnessed a period when the privileges of Britain's own aristocrats were under attack. The decline of agrarian incomes that had constituted the territorial base of Britain's patrician classes, and the rise of an urban financial and industrial middle class as well as the emergence of a rural and urban underclass demanding greater political rights combined to assail the power and status of Britain's aristocratic élite. That it still took Britain's aristocracy a hundred years 'a-dying' was a testimony to its willingness, in the following decades, to adapt to these changing circumstances.[8] In the late nineteenth century, then, there was a growing and proliferating sense of discomfort with dynasts and nobility incapable of performing the more modern representative roles required by an age of rising nationalisms. The principle of descent and tradition providing legitimacy would have to be complemented by the ideal of service and accountability to populations deemed to possess political rights.

If these stricter standards were demanded of truly sovereign monarchs and even of the metropolitan aristocracy, then no less could be expected of Indian rulers. More so since the British had taken it upon themselves to guarantee the rule of India's princes in 1858, when they had been perceived as 'breakwaters in the storm' of the Indian rebellion. Therefore it was the British who felt the onus of compelling princely states to adopt more responsible positions towards their subjects, particularly at a time when British India saw the emergence of movements of Indian nationalist assertion. Failing this the colonial paramount power would stand accused of promoting tyrannical native regimes—as they were in any case by Indian nationalists—in India while not permitting the same at home. It is in this context that rulers reluctant or slow to adapt were painted as depraved and irresponsible while those less unwilling were acclaimed as being 'progressive'.[9]

[8] David Cannadine, *The Decline and Fall of the British Aristocracy* (New Haven and London: Yale University Press, 1990), pp. 25–32.

[9] However, even on the British designating some of the princely states 'progressive', see the fascinating work of Manu Bhagavan on the state of Baroda. He shows how the British construction of Baroda and the Gaekwad as models of 'ideal progressive' and 'enlightened' rule was inverted to resist colonialism itself

The Colonial State, the British Resident and the Obligations of the Dogra Rulers

A necessary first step, however, in effecting this colonially sponsored metamorphosis of the Dogras into a semblance of 'naturalized' rulers had to be the appointment of an overseer. In other princely states such a supervisory function was performed by the colonial man on the spot, the Resident. However, as we saw, the Treaty of Amritsar was unique in that, unlike treaties with other princely states, it made no provision for the appointment of a British Resident, leaving the Dogra rulers internal autonomy.[10] This was an act of magnanimity that many in British India wanted withdrawn immediately after Victoria's proclamation. And, as just mentioned, a vocal lobby emerged that went further to urge the annexation of Kashmir in the interests of the benighted Kashmiris.[11] While the colonial government consistently opposed the demand for outright annexation, the need for a Resident in Kashmir became more pressing as the nineteenth century wore on.

No small role was played by the increasing pressure placed by British trading interests on the colonial government to intervene more decisively in Kashmir affairs. Since the formation of the state and its handing over to the Dogras, a growing number of British subjects had been clamouring for the extension of greater facilities to conduct free trade in Kashmir, especially the right to acquire property there. This demand had been resisted by Ranbir Singh but was revived under his successor. In 1886, Pratap Singh had written to the viceroy that the state had already taken all possible steps to promote the free course of trade and provided suitable houses to be had on rent for this purpose. Allowing British traders to acquire and hold land, on the other hand, he argued would 'affect the peaceful administration of the country' by

---

by creating spaces 'in which Western ideas could be reclaimed and (re-)cast as Indian' and in the process 'reconstitut[e] modernity in a way that subtly undermined its use in colonial ideologies'. Manu Bhagavan, 'The Rebel Academy: Modernity and the Movement for a University in Princely Baroda, 1908–49', *The Journal of Asian Studies* 61, no. 3 (August 2002), pp. 922–3.

[10] Aitchison, *A Collection of Treaties,* vol. VI, pp. 165–6.

[11] See Arthur Brinckman, 'The Wrongs of Cashmere' and Robert Thorpe, 'Kashmir Misgovernment' in S.N. Gadru (ed.), *Kashmir Papers* (Srinagar: Free-Thought Literature, 1973).

creating a large colony of resident Europeans immune from the jurisdiction of his courts. This, he suggested, would 'eventually affect the
integrity and undiminished enjoyment of [his] ancestral rights solemnly guaranteed by the British government.'[12] The response of the
viceroy was swift and sharp. He pointed to what he perceived was an
inconsistency in the maharaja's argument, namely that a colony of
resident Europeans in Kashmir 'would be equally free from the jurisdiction of [his] courts, whether they lived in houses supplied by [him]
or in houses belonging to them'. But, most of all, the viceroy insisted
that 'it [wa]s not possible that any Native State in India c[ould] be
allowed to prevent European British subjects from enjoying in any
part of the empire so common and necessary a right.'[13] Nevertheless,
the maharaja had his way in this particular instance and British traders
were informed that while they would be permitted to lease a house or
land, 'they could not acquire immovable property in the State'.[14] In the
process, what was also apparent was that the 'ancestral rights' of native
princes could no longer guarantee them unfettered enjoyment of
sovereignty within their states. Representing appropriately the interests of their people alone would protect the maharajas of Kashmir from
the colonial government taking measures 'extremely unpalatable to
the Darbar'.[15]

A famine that devastated the valley of Kashmir in 1877–9 had already prompted serious reconsideration of the colonial policy of non-
interference in Kashmir. It had made apparent the inefficiency of the
Kashmir administration in a moment of dire crisis. In 1879, the wor-
rying condition of the country had caused certain colonial officials
and the lieutenant-governor in Punjab to contemplate placing British officials in charge of relief operations, though well aware that the

---

[12] Letter from Maharaja Pratap Singh to the Earl of Dufferin, Viceroy, dated
14 January 1886, Foreign Department (Secret E)/Pros. July 1886/nos. 423–8,
NAI.

[13] Letter from the Viceroy to the Maharaja of Kashmir, dated 16 March 1886,
Foreign Department (Secret E)/Pros. July 1886/nos. 423–8, NAI.

[14] Foreign and Political Department (Internal)/Part B (Secret)/Pros. July
1918/no. 289, NAI.

[15] Memorandum of Conservation between the Viceroy and the Maharaja,
dated 15 January 1886, Foreign Department (Secret E)/Pros. July 1886/nos.
423–8, NAI.

maharaja would not willingly consent to such intervention.[16] In the end, this was deemed an unwise step and the project abandoned in favour of assisting the Kashmir state by supplying large quantities of grain from Punjab.

Yet the writing was on the wall, and it was simply a matter of time before the colonial government would demand a firmer foothold within the state through a Resident. The pressure to do so grew stronger after 'the ill-starred Afghan war of 1878' which made control over the north-western boundaries of the empire more urgent than ever.[17] In 1884 the viceroy, Lord Ripon, argued that the appointment of a Resident in Kashmir was 'called for' both 'by the need for assisting and supervising administrative reforms' but also to obviate disturbances on the Afghan frontier.[18] Nevertheless, the British were reluctant to force such an innovation during the lifetime of Ranbir Singh, who had made clear his opposition to such egregious interference.[19] By April 1884 Ranbir's death appeared imminent and the British government believed that the time was ripe for intervention.[20] While waiting for the maharaja to breathe his last, they made their preparations for the succession of Pratap Singh, imposing their terms on the new ruler as a condition for his accession. Exhibiting almost unseemly haste, the

[16] Letter from A.C. Lyall, Secretary to the Government of India, to the Secretary to the Government of Punjab, dated 24 February 1879, Home Department (Public)/February 1879/Pros. no. 211/Part B, NAI.

[17] William Digby, *Condemned Unheard* (New Delhi: Asian Educational Services, first published 1890, repr. 1940), p. 46.

[18] Letter from the Government of India to the Secretary of State for India, dated 7 April 1884, Foreign Department (Secret E)/ Pros. May 1884/nos. 354–7, NAI.

[19] Thus, in August 1884, the Foreign Department of the Government of India instructed the Officer on Special Duty in Kashmir that 'so long as Maharaja Ranbir Singh is alive, the Government of India do not propose to make any change in their existing policy . . . [avoiding] anything which is calculated in the Maharaja's present state of health unnecessarily to disturb his mind'. Letter from the Secretary to the Government of India, Foreign Department, to the Officer on Special Duty in Kashmir, dated 1 August 1884, reproduced in William Digby, p. 130.

[20] Letter from the Government of India to the Secretary of State for India, dated 7 April 1884, Foreign Department (Secret E)/ Pros. May 1884/nos. 354–7, NAI.

British officer on special duty in Kashmir was instructed that 'immediately after the news of Maharaja Ranbir Singh's death reache[d] the Government of India, a letter addressed by . . . the Viceroy to the new chief w[ould] be sent to [him] for delivery.' Upon which no time was to be lost in 'invit[ing] the [new] Maharaja to indicate the reforms which he may consider it necessary or desirable to introduce.'[21] The invitation was of course one which the new maharaja would be given no opportunity to decline and the reforms indicated included the appointment of the officer on special duty as the new Resident in Kashmir. At the same time, the Government of India made it clear that the Resident would have virtual *carte blanche* in Kashmir and impressed on the maharaja 'the necessity for consulting [him] at all times, and following . . . [his] advice'.[22] That the British were successful in forcing these terms on the new ruler was due, in large part, to Ranbir Singh's reluctance to name Pratap Singh, his eldest son, as his successor; he was leaning instead towards the younger raja, Amar Singh. Taking advantage of Pratap's resultant political insecurity, the colonial government imposed its conditions on him in return for upholding the principle of primogeniture in the succession.[23]

The appointment of a Resident in Kashmir was a necessary prelude to the implementation of wide-ranging reforms in the Dogra state. These included the introduction of a lighter assessment of revenue to be collected preferably in cash; the abolition of the system of revenue farming; the cessation of state monopolies; the revision of existing taxes and dues (especially transit and customs dues and taxes on various trades and professions); the introduction of a modern and salaried bureaucracy manned by qualified individuals; a reorganization of the army, which was also to be paid regular salaries; a system of proper financial control; improvements in the judicial administration of the

[21] Letter from the Secretary to the Government of India, Foreign Department, to the Officer on Special Duty in Kashmir, dated 1 August 1884, reproduced in William Digby, p. 131.

[22] Ibid.

[23] Letter from the Government of India to the Secretary of State for India, dated 7 April 1884, Foreign Department (Secret E)/ Pros. May 1884/nos. 354–7, NAI. Incidentally, Raja Amar Singh would never be Maharaja of Jammu and Kashmir but his son, Hari Singh, who was adopted by Pratap Singh, would rule over the state from 1925 to1947.

state; the construction of proper roads; and the removal of all restrictions upon emigration.[24] Giving the maharaja a face-saving device, the British Indian government agreed to leave the initiation of such reforms to him and a liberal time-frame within which to do so.[25]

Reforms were demanded by the colonial government in the name of impressing upon the Kashmir government 'its *obligations* to its *own* subjects',[26] and it was made clear that the maharaja would not be permitted to shirk these. The Resident was to act as a watchdog on behalf not only of the British government but also of the 'people at large' in Kashmir, who were to see in his appointment an 'assurance of substantial reforms to come'.[27] As officially and publicly justified, the installation of the Resident was in order to serve the interests of state subjects deemed to be suffering from a long and now intolerable history of 'misrule'.[28] In this way the appointment and its rationale provided a heightened awareness among Kashmiri Muslims of their disadvantages. Additionally, it made available to Kashmiri Muslims a platform for the expression of their grievances. The number of petitions addressed to the Resident, rather than or in addition to the Kashmir government, proliferated dramatically from the end of the nineteenth century onwards.

Despite the changes inaugurated upon his succession, Pratap Singh was divested by the British government of his powers to govern on 17 April 1889. Relying on the evidence of certain anonymous forged letters received by the Resident, Pratap Singh was accused of conducting treasonable correspondence with Tsarist Russia and of plotting the assassination of the Resident in Kashmir, as also of his own brothers, the rajas Ram Singh and Amar Singh. As a result, the maharaja was

[24] Foreign Department (Secret E)/Pros. October 1886/no. 725, NAI.

[25] Letter from Government of India to Lord Randolph Churchill, Secretary of State for India, dated 19 October 1885, reproduced in William Digby, p. 129.

[26] Letter from the Government of India to the Secretary of State for India, dated 7 April 1884, Foreign Department (Secret E)/ Pros. May 1884/nos. 354–7, NAI. Emphasis mine.

[27] Letter from Resident in Kashmir to the Secretary to the Governmet of India, Foreign Department, dated 6 September 1885, reproduced in William Digby, p. 135.

[28] Letter from Government of India to Lord Randolph Churchill, Secretary of State for India, reproduced in William Digby, p. 129.

presented with an *irshad* (order) which forced him to 'voluntarily' abdicate his powers to govern even while he was allowed to continue as the titular chief of the state.[29] A State Council, whose members were to be appointed by the Government of India, was formed to take over the administration. It consisted of the maharaja's two brothers, Ram Singh and Amar Singh, two of his ministers, Pandit Suraj Koul and Rai Bahadur Bhag Ram, and a British officer nominated by the Government of India. And although the Council was given full powers of administration, it was 'expected to exercise these . . . under the guidance of the Resident . . . [taking] no steps of importance without consulting him, and follow[ing] his advice whenever it may be offered.'[30] Clearly, there was more to this action on the part of the British government than the mere evidence of the letters, the authenticity of which they themselves doubted.

As with the decision to appoint a Resident and the foisting of reforms on the new maharaja, the stripping of Pratap's powers was also justified in terms of protecting the subjects of the Dogra state. As early as in March 1888, the Resident, Mr Plowden, had 'thought that the time had come when, *for the sake of the State*, it was essential to effect some reduction of the Maharaja's authority.'[31] He had written a highly critical assessment of the maharaja, failing to find in him any 'capacity for governing his country, or any genuine desire to ameliorate its condition.' Allegedly incontrovertible proof of this lay in the failure of the maharaja 'to introduce those reforms which he ha[d] acknowledged to be necessary'.[32] The British government appeared to have decided to deprive the maharaja of all effective authority almost a year before the actual 'abdication'. In fact, Colonel R. Parry Nisbet, Plowden's successor, had admitted frankly to his superior in the foreign department that he did not 'attach much importance to the letters but they strengthen[ed] . . . [the British] right to intervene.'[33] Yet, if the

---

[29] Foreign Department (Secret E)/Pros. August 1889/nos. 162–203, NAI.

[30] Ibid.; Foreign Department (Secret E)/Pros. April 1889/nos. 80–98, NAI.

[31] Letter from the Government of India to the Secretary of State, dated 18 August 1888, reproduced in William Digby, pp. 145–6. Emphasis mine.

[32] Report on the Affairs of the State of Jummu and Kashmir by the Resident in Kashmir, dated 5 March 1888, reproduced in William Digby, p. 146.

[33] Letter from Colonel R.P. Nisbet, Resident in Kashmir, to H.M. Durand, Secretary to the Government of India, Foreign Department, dated 16 March 1889, Foreign Department (Secret E)/Pros. April 1889/nos. 80–98, NAI.

intervention itself was not to appear an instance of imperiousness, the British government was keen to reiterate that it was 'the existing misgovernment in Kashmir' that had rendered it inevitable.[34] Critics at home had also to be assuaged and the Government of India persistently avowed that it 'deprecated any interference in the affairs of the State beyond what [was] necessary for the reform of the administration.' It was with regard to '*the interests of the people of Kashmir, and of the ruling family itself*' that the colonial government 'no longer [considered it] right or possible to leave the affairs in the hands of the Maharaja.'[35]

The maharaja spent sixteen years appealing to the British Indian government for the full restoration of his powers. In 1902 the viceroy, Lord Curzon, while not rejecting outright the maharaja's requests, had repeated that full restitution would depend on the maharaja himself.[36] Although Pratap Singh's powers were reinstated in 1905,[37] the precondition of responsible rule placed by Curzon on the maharaja had important consequences for the subjects of the state. Both the acts of depriving and then restoring his powers as well as the justificatory rhetoric set off a competition between the maharaja on the one hand, and the colonial government represented by the Resident on the other, for championing the cause of the subjects of the state. However, the two sides diverged in the classes of subjects whose interests they advocated.

Pratap Singh had declared upon his accession in 1885, and in public durbar, that 'next [only] in importance to [his] obligations to the paramount power . . . [would] be the duty of governing [his] country with justice and moderation.' He had also sworn that in performing this duty he would adopt only such measures as would 'secure to [his] subjects their greatest good and the fullest enjoyment of their rights . . . *without any distinction of race or rank, creed or colour.*'[38] Despite this

[34] Ibid.

[35] Letter from the Government of India to the Secretary of State for India, dated 3 April 1889, reproduced in William Digby, pp. 155–6. Emphasis mine.

[36] Foreign Department (Secret E)/Pros. December 1902/no. 112, NAI.

[37] Foreign Department Notes (Secret I)/Pros. November 1905/nos. 32–40, NAI.

[38] Manifesto of the Maharaja of Jammu and Kashmir, Enclosure B in the letter from the Resident in Kashmir to the Secretary to the Government of India, Foreign Department, dated 27 September 1885, Foreign Department (Secret E)/Pros. December 1885/nos. 192–245, NAI. Emphasis mine.

promise, the constituency he backed was still the narrow one of the Dogra and Kashmiri Hindus.[39] This was in keeping with older patterns of legitimation installed in Jammu and Kashmir since the reign of Gulab Singh and buttressed under Ranbir Singh. Strengthening his links with the most privileged segment among his subjects and promoting their interests was particularly advisable if he was to counter the increased powers of the State Council and the Resident, both backed by the imperial government. Thus, in 1897, he criticized the state council for filling the higher rungs of the state bureaucracy with 'aliens' at the expense of the natives of Kashmir and the Dogras.[40] This had become a common cause for resentment, particularly among the Kashmiri Pandits, who had been losing out increasingly on official appointments to either Indians from the Punjab[41] or Englishmen recommended by the British government.[42] Although Pratap Singh's criticism had been couched in the language, to use C.A. Bayly's term, of 'regional patriotism' and in the name of defending the rights of 'natives' against foreign elements, he was in fact representing the interests of only the small Hindu segment of his Kashmiri subjects. As discussed

[39] In fact, the only social segment in the state which seemed to have demonstrated any sense of outrage when their ruler had been deprived of powers in 1889 had been the Dogras of Jammu. This is proven by the fact that even the Calcutta newspaper *Amrita Bazar Patrika*, which had been conducting a campaign in favour of the restitution of full powers to the maharaja, could find no other group to include in its evidence of popular resentment against the measure. Extract from the *Amrita Bazar Patrika*, Thursday, 30 January 1890, reproduced in Foreign Department (Secret E)/Pros. December 1890/nos. 232–424, NAI.

[40] Letter from McMahon to Talbot, dated 8 July 1897, Foreign Department (Secret E)/Pros. February 1898/nos. 183–286, NAI.

[41] While some Bengalis had been appointed in the administration of the state, by 1886, the British were convinced that they were 'useless and mischievous', contaminated by nationalist sentiments and egging the maharaja on to resisting colonial demands for reform. By the late nineteenth century, the colonial government therefore adopted a clear policy of excluding the Bengali element from the Jammu and Kashmir administration, replacing them instead with Punjabis. Foreign Department (Secret E)/Pros. October 1886/nos. 235–300, NAI.

[42] This new concern for the rights of 'natives' of the state demonstrated by Pratap Singh was not usual. More usually, the employment of foreigners had the advantage of giving the princes 'a certain leverage over them' as well as obviating 'their having to make difficult choices between competing elite communities'. Copland, *The Princes of India*, p. 7.

later, protecting the access of Kashmiris to the highest rungs of the bureaucracy held as yet little interest for the vast majority of the state's subjects who were Muslim and largely uneducated.

There were other measures instituted by the maharaja, and passed by the State Council, that made even more transparent the state's narrowly construed definition of subjects whose interests were to be promoted. In 1894, the maharaja and the council inaugurated the 'Pratap Code', this being 'a regulation to ameliorate the condition of the Dogra Rajputs'. Specifically, the code was intended to provide Dogra Rajputs greater access to land, on revenue-free terms for the first five years and at only half the rate subsequently; access to education; exemption of their villages from begar, and of their cattle from taxation. Such anxiety for their 'circumstances' was reserved for the Dogras as they were the maharaja's 'brethren'.[43] For them belonging to the 'same caste as the ruling family' excepted them not only from capital punishment,[44] but Dogra jagirdars settled in Kashmir were released also from the requirement of obtaining licenses to possess firearms on the grounds that 'they could not be treated like the general public'.[45] This was a significant concession in a state that had, since Gulab Singh's days, worked assiduously towards appropriating a monopoly of coercive powers. Special consideration was extended also to Kashmiri Hindu landed interests so that while Muslim jagirdars were required to pay nazrana on their succession to a jagir, Kashmiri Pandit jagirdars were confirmed, in 1910, in their exemption from similar payments.[46]

On the other hand, the subjects whose interests were most actively supported by the imperial government were the Muslims of the valley of Kashmir. This was prompted in large measure by growing public disapproval of the treatment of Kashmiri Muslims both in Indian and in British circles. The mishandling by the Dogras of the famine of 1877–9 shone the spotlight particularly brightly on the plight of Kashmiri Muslims. Newspapers in the Punjab, particularly those owned by

---

[43] OER, Political Department, General and Political, 1894, File no. 67, JKA.

[44] Extract from the *Civil and Military Gazette* of 19 August 1890, included in Foreign Department (External A)/Pros. October 1890/nos. 176–80, NAI.

[45] Order of His Highness Maharaja Pratap Singh, dated 1906, Political Department, 1936, File no. 209, JKA.

[46] Order of the Maharaja Pratap Singh, dated 20 July 1910, OER, C.S., Political Department, 1910, File no. 59/H-1, JKA.

Muslims, were unrelenting in their criticism of the Dogra state and also of the British for having permitted such gross neglect by a protected prince. Some Muslims in the valley had made their own attempt to voice their discontent with prevailing conditions. In 1877 'some unknown Kashmiris' had submitted a memorandum to the viceroy. It was never published but sections of it had made their way into the accounts of some British writers and into the Indian press. The accusations of maladministration levied in it were of the gravest character. The most serious charge made was that 'in order to save the expense of feeding his people' the maharaja, Ranbir Singh, had preferred to drown boat-loads of Muslims in the Wular Lake. The British government had taken these allegations seriously enough to appoint a commission of enquiry but Kashmiri Muslims had, supposedly, been too frightened to come forward to provide corroboration.[47] Although the maharaja was exonerated, the outrage aroused by this advertisement of the shocking condition of the valley's Muslims called for some measure of intervention by the colonial government. Even more critically, the Kashmir durbar's attitude during the famine had demonstrated its incapacity to rise above the preferential treatment of its already privileged Hindu subjects to the detriment of Muslim cultivators who were the greatest sufferers.

The political volatility presented by a large discontented Muslim population in Kashmir fuelled an abiding anxiety among the British, evident since the very founding of the state. In handing over Kashmir to the Dogras, the governor-general, Lord Hardinge, had wished to build up a Hindu buffer to prevent a uniting of Muslim interests, Kashmiri with Afghan, in the north-western 'entrance into India'.[48] The Afghan debacles of 1878 and the early 1880s had rekindled this apprehension of the British, leading (as mentioned earlier) Lord Ripon to fear that 'any disturbances which continued misgovernment might create in Kashmir would be acutely felt on the frontiers of Afghanistan.'[49] Clearly, the influence of European balance-of-power strategies, focussed on blocking Tsarist Russia, also remained instrumental in driving colonial interference in Kashmir. By 1884, when the

[47] Bazaz, *The History of the Struggle for Freedom in Kashmir*, p. 132.

[48] Bawa Satinder Singh, *The Jammu Fox*, p. 129.

[49] Letter from the Government of India to the Secretary of State for India, dated 7 April 1884, Foreign Department (Secret E)/Pros. May 1884/nos. 354–7, NAI.

appointment of a Resident seemed possible, colonial officials at the highest level were asking 'whether, having regard to the circumstances under which the sovereignty of the country was entrusted to the present *Hindu* ruling family, the intervention of the British Government on behalf of the *Muhammadan* population ha[d] not already been too long delayed.'[50] And in 1895, upon inaugurating the Jammu and Kashmir State Council, the colonial government stressed once more the 'desirability of Muhammadan interests in Kashmir being attended to'.[51]

Kashmiri Muslims also commanded the attention of the colonial state by the sheer virtue of their numbers. It would have been unreasonable for the imperial government to object to the Dogra rulers championing the rights of the Hindus among their subjects in the context of earlier bases of legitimation they had colluded in establishing. Yet, this still presented the problem of the rights of the vast majority of subjects remaining unaddressed. This was untenable in light of the new obligation to play a 'representative' role towards all their subjects being pressed on the Dogra rulers. At the same time, by the closing years of the nineteenth century there was mounting evidence of political mobilization among certain Kashmiri Muslims, not just against the Dogra Hindu government but also the British Indian government. In 1897 a 'mullah' had been expelled from the state for engaging precisely in such activities,[52] and, as the last segment of this chapter elaborates, there were other more widespread instances of resistance. As an immediate palliative, the Government of India exhorted the council to appoint a Muslim among their ranks who could be projected as a defender of specifically 'Muslim' interests.[53] Yet it was clear to the British that the time for tokenism had passed, and farreaching reforms alone might keep Kashmiri Muslims quiescent in imperial and Dogra arrangements of power.

To sum up, the late nineteenth century witnessed the assumption of a new responsibility on the part of both the colonial state and the maharaja for the interests and rights of the subjects of the state of

---

[50] Letter from the Earl of Kimberley, the Secretary of State for India, to the Government of India, dated 23 May 1884, Foreign Department (Secret E)/Pros. December 1885/nos. 192–245, NAI. Emphasis mine.

[51] Foreign Department (Internal A)/Pros. January 1905/nos. 82–94, NAI.

[52] OER, 1897, File no. 39, JKA.

[53] Foreign Department (Secret E)/Pros. February 1898/nos. 183–286, NAI.

Jammu and Kashmir. However, unlike the Dogra rulers, the corpus of subjects about whom the greatest anxiety was demonstrated by the British government and in whose name reforms were demanded in the state's administration was its largest number, the Muslims of Kashmir. The question the colonial government now posed was not whether there should be a Hindu prince in the state of Jammu and Kashmir but on whose behalf he should rule. At the same time, a result of first divesting Pratap Singh of his powers and then restoring them to him was the introduction of a conceptual hiatus between the person of the maharaja and the office. Thus, some in the foreign department of the Government of India had suggested allowing the maharaja to follow his own procedure 'as regards his private and family affairs and . . . his morality . . . so long as these ha[d] no influence in State affairs'.[54] Separating his private from his public persona, as ruler the maharaja would have clearly defined and obligatory duties of ensuring the welfare of his subjects. Ranbir Singh's assertion in his *Dastur-ul-Amal* of 1882 that measures enacted by the rulers be guided primarily, if not solely, by considering their effect on the 'reputation and honour of the [ruling] family' was under some challenge.[55] And although the Dogra ruler would still be permitted to derive legitimacy from his being Hindu, this would have to be accompanied by a demonstrated concern for the rights of all categories of his subjects. Of course, as the following segments will demonstrate, there was still a significant lag between the Dogra maharaja's undertaking to be more 'representative' and the actual dismantling of a state structure in which privileges were organized along religious lines. Nonetheless, a vital shift had been made: a perception had been created among the subjects of the state, particularly the hitherto neglected Kashmiri Muslims, that they were entitled at least in principle to have their rights represented on a level of parity with those of other subjects.

Reforming the State or Protecting Privileges?

The imperative of correcting years of 'misrule' within the state of Jammu and Kashmir led the Government of India to lend the servi-

---

[54] Demi-official letter from H. Henvey to H.M. Durand, dated 5 April 1888, Foreign Department (Secret E)/Pros. March 1889/nos. 107–200, NAI.

[55] See Chapter Two of this book.

ces of a number of its officials to investigate and reform its economic, financial and administrative structures. It is in this context that R. Logan, the accountant-general of the Bombay Presidency, was sent in 1890–2 to inquire into the Kashmir durbar's finances. His inspection put on the agenda the issue not only of how much was spent in the state but also for whose benefit the money flowed. The verdict he returned was that the maharajas of Jammu and Kashmir had egoistically spent on themselves rather than on the state and for the public good of their subjects. A particular focus of Logan's investigations had been the Dharmarth Trust's funds. By the time he completed his examination and made his recommendations, the maharaja's place as chief Hindu worshipper in the state lost some of its gloss, following from a tightening of the pursestrings that had bankrolled it, but still none of its former power to legitimate his rule.

When a Resident was first foisted on Jammu and Kashmir the British government had been fairly ignorant about the dharmarth fund and the purpose it was meant to serve. Writing in 1885, the Resident reported that according to ministers of the state 'the public treasury [of Jammu and Kashmir was] practically empty.' Yet the Resident had also heard that 'the late Maharaja [had] regularly diverted the revenue of certain districts to his private chest', some of which was 'devoted to religious purposes'. Moreover, he had been told that Ranbir Singh had 'solemnly enjoined that this money should never be used to meet the current expenditure of the State.'[56] The notion that public revenues from the state could be funnelled to a ruler's private, secret treasure and be spent on 'no [more] useful object' than religious purposes was appalling enough to the British.[57] But that this should continue at a time when the state's finances had hit rock-bottom appeared so flagrant that it prompted the investigations by R. Logan.

In 1890 the Resident in Kashmir intimated to the State Council that he required a clearer explanation of the precise reasons for the establishment of the Dharmarth Fund.[58] He was particularly

[56] Letter from the Resident in Kashmir to the Secretary to the Government of India, Foreign Department, dated 16 September 1885, reproduced in William Digby, pp. 132–7.

[57] Ibid.

[58] Letter from the Resident to Raja Amar Singh, Prime Minister and President of the State Council, dated 15 December 1890, OER, General and Political Department, 1890, File no. 18, JKA.

concerned to find out whether the fund was reserved purely for 'charitable' purposes or whether it could be put to other public uses. The first response of the council was a deft play on the Resident's words, defining the specific religious purposes of the trust's fund as 'charitable' and therefore sufficiently public.[59] However, there remained the matter of the Dharmarth Trust's capital, amounting to close to twenty lakhs of rupees at the time, but which, according to the *Ain* could not be touched.

Arguing on the grounds of financial soundness and public usefulness, Logan suggested to Raja Amar Singh—the prime minister and brother of Pratap—that the state borrow part of these reserve funds to pay off arrears of salaries owed to officials and soldiers. Amar Singh, while 'not object[ing] to the money being used', viewed the particular uses suggested as 'unremunerative or unproductive' and as such certain to be opposed by 'public opinion'.[60] At loggerheads were two very different ideas of public utility. The Dogra ruling family was still wedded to deriving its legitimacy to rule from their status as chief patrons of the Hindu religion. It was towards fulfilling this role that they felt 'public opinion' would wish to see the dharmarth money 'belong[ing] to the Maharaja and his brothers' being spent. The British government, on the other hand, was concerned with principles of a larger public good and of sound financial management to serve that purpose. Logan considered Amar Singh's response ludicrous since, in his view, neither the settlement of salaries in arrears nor expenditure on 'public works . . . having regard to the *material and political requirements* of the state' could be considered unprofitable.[61] He had also pointed out the incongruity of such large sums of a 'circulating medium' lying unutilized while money was so scarce in the interior of Kashmir that trade had to be conducted mostly by barter.[62]

The irreconcilability of an accountant's utilitarian principles with those of a ruling house relying on its status as religious patrons resulted

[59] Letter from Diwan Janki Pershad, Officer in Charge of Dharmarth, Jammu, to Pandit Suraj Koul, Revenue Member of the State Council, dated 30 December 1890, OER, General and Political Department, 1890, File no. 18, JKA.

[60] Letter from R. Logan to W.J. Cunningham, dated 26 August 1891, Foreign Department (Secret E)/Pros. March 1892/nos. 100–5, NAI.

[61] Ibid. Emphasis mine.

[62] Ibid.

in a compromise which became the hallmark of Pratap Singh's tenure as ruler. But it took some juggling of account heads. The Dharmarth Trust fund was included within the public revenues of the state but placed under the special category of an 'excluded local fund' which could not be appropriated for the general public spending of the state. However, the expenditure of this fund now had a fixed annual ceiling and included the maintenance of the dharmarth establishment (such as salaries of its officials), which Ranbir Singh had previously and cleverly shifted on to the general revenues of the state. Any unspent balance of the fund's revenues was to be 'devoted to Education and Medical heads',[63] columns in an account book carrying no religious distinction.

The position of neither the Dogras nor of the colonial government on notions of the 'public good' and how it was to be brought about was abandoned. Logan was sensitive to 'the Maharaja and his brothers . . . tak[ing] alarm at the idea of the fund being dealt with in . . . a manner . . . reduc[ing] its transactions to ordinary rule [and thereby contravening] . . . its quasi-sacred nature.' Yet his solution enabled a satisfactory arrangement also for the fund being put to a more generally beneficial public use as understood by the colonial government.[64] In return, the Dogras were allowed to retain considerable control over funds acknowledged to be (quasi-)sacred, and devoted to the promotion of the Hindu religion, while being afforded the opportunity, at the same time, of appearing to fulfill more widely defined public needs. The Dogra maharaja would be the chief worshipper in Hindu terms within the state but, when he was sitting on the throne, would also acknowledge responsibility for his subjects as a whole, irrespective of religious affiliation.

Of all the measures of reform proposed by the colonial government in the state of Jammu and Kashmir, none was as thoroughgoing as the land settlement operations instituted between 1889 and 1895 and overseen by the British civil servant Sir Walter Lawrence. The apparent sympathy with which he treated the plight of the cultivating classes of Kashmiri Muslims earned him a degree of respect in evidence

[63] Ibid.

[64] Letter from R. Logan to the Secretary to the Government of India, Foreign Department, dated 25 November 1891, Foreign Department (Secret E)/Pros. June 1892/nos. 133–5, NAI.

to this day in Kashmir. The book he wrote summarizing his land settlement but functioning also as a colonial-style gazetteer, titled *The
Valley of Kashmir*, seems never to have gone out of print in the state.
However, even before Lawrence's appointment, another settlement
officer, A. Wingate, had been sent by the British to Kashmir to conduct a preliminary survey between 1887 and 1888.[65] As a result of the
investigations of both Wingate and Lawrence it was as though a veil
had suddenly been lifted and the life of the Muslims in the valley revealed, in a barrage of detail, as one of unmitigated oppression suffered
through the years.

Walter Lawrence condemned the 'administration of Kashmir [for
being] opposed to the interests of the cultivating classes and to the
development of the country' and asserted 'that the officials systematically endeavoured to make themselves feared by the people'.[66] In similar vein, Wingate had suggested that the Kashmiri cultivator had been
'pressed down to the condition of a coolie cultivating at subsistence
allowance the State property' and that the responsibility for this lay
with the 'influential pandit' servants of the state.[67] Wingate and Lawrence had spent many months in the rural hinterland of Kashmir. They
brought to the fore, in an unprecedented manner, the tensions that
underlay Kashmiri society, pitting the interests of the Hindu Pandit
community against those of the numerically preponderant Kashmiri
Muslim cultivators within the framework of the Dogra state. However, beyond agreeing about the nature and causes of the Kashmiri
Muslims' oppression, the solutions offered by Wingate and Lawrence
were at significant variance. While both acknowledged the responsibility of the Kashmiri Pandit community in exacerbating the situation
of the Muslim cultivating classes, Wingate was far more uncompromising in demanding the elimination of the exemptions and privileges of the former. In contrast, while Lawrence's land settlement also
sought to provide relief to the cultivating classes of Kashmir, it did so

[65] R/2/1061/3, Crown Representative's Residency Records, Kashmir Residency Office, File no. 28 of 1888, A. Wingate, 'Preliminary Report of Settlement
Operations in Kashmir and Jammu', IOL. Henceforth referred to as Wingate.

[66] Note by Walter Lawrence on the 'Position of the Cultivating Classes in
Kashmir', Keep-with no. 3 in Foreign Department (Secret E)/Pros. February
1890/nos. 106–10, NAI.

[67] Wingate, p. 19.

without entirely dismantling the privileges of the Kashmiri Pandit community. As a result, some of his innovations were more so in form than in actually providing a parity of rights to the agrarian classes of the valley. And, probably for this reason, it was Lawrence's blueprint for reform that was accepted over that of Wingate. However, a fuller discussion of the land settlement effected by Lawrence and its consequences requires an examination first of the agrarian structure, land tenure patterns and agrarian relations prevailing in the valley in the period preceding it.

Once again, it was the Kashmir famine of 1877–9 that had provided the impetus for the colonial government's demanding an overhauling of agrarian rights and relations in Kashmir. The death toll from the famine had been overwhelming by any standards. Some authorities had suggested that the population of Srinagar had been reduced by half (from 127,400 to 60,000), while others had estimated a diminution by three-fifths of the population of the entire valley.[68] The famine had brought to light the inadequacy of the protection afforded to Kashmiri cultivators by the agrarian arrangements of the Dogra state. Lawrence had shown that substantial quantities of rice could have been salvaged and the staggering loss of life averted if cultivators had been permitted to cut their crop before the start of the rains that destroyed the autumn harvest of 1877. But the rigid adherence to the old revenue system, in which assessments were made on the standing crop, delayed the reaping operations.[69] To paraphrase an older Irish saying, the famine had shown that while God made the rain it was the Dogras who made the hunger.

A perception given much currency from the late nineteenth century on was that the Dogra maharaja was the owner of all the land in Kashmir. This was a claim asserted by most pre-colonial Indian rulers and had survived in 'native states' under colonial rule.[70] However, this assertion did not amount to a 'modern' Western understanding of full private property rights carrying with it the absolute right of alienation. The statement that all land belonged to the ruler was simply the conceptual foundation of a hierarchy of rights, extending from the ruler

[68] Lawrence, *The Valley of Kashmir*, p. 213.

[69] Ibid., p. 214.

[70] B.H. Baden-Powell, *The Land Systems of British India*, 3 vols (Delhi: Oriental Publishers, repr. 1974), vol. 1, pp. 320–32; vol. 3, p. 122.

to the individual cultivator, over the revenue of the land rather than over land itself. Assertions of 'ownership' never precluded a recognition of the right to occupy and cultivate land enjoyed by primary producers. In Kashmir too a similar understanding informed claims to the land made by various rulers from the Mughal conquerors down to the Dogra rulers.

Rights over land were held, on the one hand, by the ruler and his assignees and, on the other, by zamindars. The term zamindar in Kashmir held a meaning different from other parts of the Indian subcontinent. In the valley the term denoted not an intermediary class of revenue collectors but the cultivators themselves. The Dogra state employed its own tax-gathering agency to collect the revenue directly from the cultivators. This hierarchy began at the village level with the accountant, the *patwari,* whose chief duty was to maintain records of the area of holding and revenue-paying capacity of each villager. Over the patwaris stood a group of Pandits who, in various capacities as revenue officials, dealt with villages as a whole. Over these were the *tehsildar* and one or two *naib-tehsildars* (deputy tehsildars) who controlled the revenue collection from the fifteen *tehsils* (districts or groups of villages) into which the valley had been divided. The tehsils themselves were grouped into three *wazarats* presided over by *wazir wazarats* (ministers). This entire revenue establishment, known as the Daftar-i-Diwani, was composed almost entirely of Kashmiri Pandits and was ultimately subordinate to the Hakim-i-Ala, or Governor, who was also often, if not always, a Kashmiri Pandit.[71] Lawrence provided evidence that while many of the Pandit officials might be 'individually gentle and intelligent, as a body they were cruel and oppressive . . . and their combination [wa]s of so perfect . . . a nature as to make it impossible to break . . . by any half measures.'[72] This *esprit de corps,* as well as their remarkable level of literacy, ensured they had a virtual stranglehold on the revenue administration and members of the department's hierarchy could count on their misdeeds being shielded by other Pandit officials within it.[73]

[71] Lawrence, *The Valley of Kashmir,* pp. 400–1.

[72] Note by Walter Lawrence on the 'Position of the Cultivating Classes in Kashmir', Keep-with no.3 in Foreign Department (Secret E)/Pros. February 1890/nos. 106–10, NAI.

[73] Ibid.

The fatal results for Muslim agriculturists of this capacity for combination among the Hindu Kashmiris was demonstrated most clearly during the famine of 1877–9 when the office of prime minister was also held by a Kashmiri Pandit, Wazir Punnu. According to reports received by Lawrence, not a Pandit died of starvation during these annihilative years for the Muslim cultivators. Undoubtedly reflecting a selective Pandit view of the famine, Wazir Punnu is said to have declared that there 'was no real distress and that he wished that no Mussulman might be left alive from Srinagar to Rambhan [in Jammu].' A remark the callousness of which makes Marie Antoinette's about bread and cake pale in comparison, it also justified incidents of extreme cruelty towards Muslim cultivators, including the humilation of stripping them naked for their failure to pay revenue.[74] Yet even members of the Kashmiri Pandit community who had been 'disgraced during the . . . famine' for embezzlement, continued to hold office owing to the unity among the Pandits dominating the state administration.[75]

The Dogra state under Gulab Singh had taken three-quarters of rice, maize, millets and buckwheat and nine-sixteenths of oil-seeds, pulses and cotton from the zamindars. In 1860, the state reduced its share to a little over a half but the benefits of this reduction were more than countered by the employment of *chakladars* (contractors) speculating in the collection of revenue. These individuals, being outsiders and with no interest vested in the land beyond the annual contract, made large profits from defrauding the cultivators. In 1880, an assessment based on the average production of three years was introduced. It was in theory a cash assessment; however, in practice the Hakim-i-Ala of Kashmir was given full discretion to decide how much of the revenue would be taken in cash and how much of it in kind. No actual survey of the villages of the valley preceded the new assessment. As a result, those villages that had somehow managed to survive the famine paid a heavier price than those others that had broken up and where cultivation had been abandoned. There was much room also for collusion between the Kashmiri Pandit-dominated revenue department

[74] Letter from Walter Lawrence, Settlement Officer, to Colonel R.P. Nisbet, Resident in Kashmir, dated 2nd December 1889, Foreign Department (Secret E)/Pros. February 1891/nos. 295–326, NAI.
[75] Ibid.

and influential headmen for passing the burden of heavier assessments on to poorer and weaker villages. In 1882, a system of *izad-boli* or auctioning villages for the purposes of revenue collection was adopted. Pandits, boatmen and other 'adventurous spirits' from the city, ignorant of the actual revenue-paying capacity of villages and with no interest beyond the particular year's collections, bid at the highest rates. After extracting all they could from the villagers, they absconded without paying the state on the grounds that the year's harvest had been a bad one. The most harmful result of the system of auctions was that the unrealistically high sums offered at them came to be regarded as the actual revenue demand of the village.[76]

Not only was the high revenue demand of the state an odious burden placed on the Kashmiri Muslim cultivator (while Pandits and Pirzadas were assessed at much lighter rates),[77] but it was made heavier by the food control system operating in the valley. The main crop grown in Kashmir was rice. However, no market truly existed for this commodity as its export had been prohibited since the early days of Dogra rule.[78] Even internally the state had established itself as the sole grain dealer and kept the price of shali pegged at an unvarying and artificially low rate. Although there may not have been a direct prohibition against selling shali on his own account, Wingate recorded that the cultivator was distinctly afraid to do so.[79] Rice would be collected in large granaries and rationed to the city population. Instituted in the early years of Dogra rule, the purpose of this system of food control was to make cheap rice available to the residents of Srinagar and in the 1890s these state-controlled rates were at one half of the real market price. More specifically, this system had been intended primarily to maintain the shawl weavers of Srinagar, whose product had brought an annual revenue of between Rs 600,000 and 700,000 to the state. This incentive, as also the exemption from begar granted to them, ensured a steady stream of labourers for the shawl industry coming from the countryside. Although this meant a loss of manpower to the agrarian sector, and while the policy of collecting the greater part of the revenue in kind curtailed cultivation and the development of agricultural

[76] Lawrence, *The Valley of Kashmir,* pp. 402–5.

[77] *Gazetteer of Kashmir and Ladakh* (Delhi: Vivek Publishers, first published 1890, repr. 1974), p. 106. Pirzadas were Muslim religious figures.

[78] Wingate, p. 16.

[79] Ibid., pp. 16–17.

resources, the bountiful profits to the state from the Kashmiri shawl more than justified the sacrifice. With the decline in the demand for Kashmiri shawls after the outbreak of the Franco-Prussian war of 1870, the financial rationale for the system disappeared. It was continued nevertheless at the behest of the large and influential Kashmiri Pandit citizenry of Srinagar grown used to obtaining cheap rice.[80] Even among the urban beneficiaries of this system, the Kashmiri Pandits were among the few who did in fact obtain shali at the state rate, while most of the poorer classes in Srinagar often paid twice as much.[81]

This system of food control ensured that at least part of the revenue would continue to be collected in kind from the zamindars. However, the flexibility that systems of collection in kind might have allowed was lost in Kashmir where the revenue demand of the state was fixed irrespective of variations in actual production from a good to a bad year. Although, after 1880, part of the revenue was theoretically allowed to be collected in cash, it rested entirely with the governor to determine the proportions. In the absence of a market for foodgrains, their prices were also fixed by the state. The compensation paid to the cultivator for shali, for the reasons mentioned above, was kept low with a 'perfect indifference to harvests'. On the other hand, the value of agricultural commodities, such as cotton, pulses and oilseeds, was fixed at higher rates than justified by the demand. Cultivators were concerned above all to induce revenue officials to take as much of the revenue demand in the higher priced goods than in shali, which they needed for their own subsistence. The manipulation of the market by the Dogra state had ensured that cultivators had compulsorily to sell rice below the proper market price and pay higher rates in order to buy it back for their consumption needs. By contrast, they were paid higher rates for cotton and such products than they cost in the market, making it more economical for them to give these up as revenue and buy back the quantities of these goods that they needed from the bazaar.[82] Much depended therefore on the capacity of the cultivators to propitiate the Kashmiri Pandit revenue official with 'loans'. The more 'complaisant' the official the greater the proportion of the revenue taken in cotton and oilseeds rather than in shali and the larger the bribe required.[83]

[80] Ibid.; Lawrence, *The Valley of Kashmir*, pp. 409–10.

[81] Wingate, pp. 17–18.

[82] Ibid., pp. 25–6.

[83] Lawrence, *The Valley of Kashmir*, p. 406.

The dependence of the Kashmiri Muslim cultivator on the Pandit-controlled revenue department was also ensured by the system of begar or the forcible and usually unpaid impressment of labour. In a still vastly underpopulated territory where labour was a scarce and valuable commodity, the Dogras had made an art of obtaining it for free. How to escape begar was a constant preoccupation for the Kashmiri cultivator most especially since it was levied without consideration either for the ability of individual families to spare the labour otherwise required for agricultural purposes or for the particular phase of the agricultural cycle in which it was demanded. Typically, impressment for begar would come in the summer months of June and July, when barley and wheat were cut and threshed. Even more critically for the staple food, this was also the time of the crucial operation of *khushaba* or rice weeding. A particularly labour-intensive manual exercise, it required teams of cultivators to stand in flooded fields 'on all fours . . . scuffling with the mud, and kneading it as the baker does'.[84]

But significant sections of the Kashmiri population also enjoyed exemptions from begar. As mentioned earlier, the urban Muslim artisanal classes such as the shawl weavers of Srinagar fell into this category. This ensured that whereas in other parts of the subcontinent the demand for begar labour might have been met in urban areas, this was not the case in Kashmir. Other groups exempted were the cultivators working on the lands of Kashmiri Pandits, Sikhs, jagirdars and the dharmarth department. Also released were the Muslims working on the lands of Pirzadas or Muslim religious figures. However, exemptions in this particular instance appear to have been won with greater difficulty and the gain was always somewhat tenuous. Thus, a story prevalent in Kashmir when Lawrence conducted his survey recounted that a servant of the powerful Rishi saint Zain-ud-din had been seized by officials for forced labour. In deference to the power of the saint, the servant was released from begar but the followers of the Rishi divine were told to wear a distinctive headdress if they were to ensure against future impressment.[85] No such distinguishing mark was required of the cultivators who laboured on the lands of Pandits or of the dharmarth department. At any rate, the result of these various exemptions was that the burden of begar fell more heavily on a population of

[84] Ibid., p. 327.
[85] Ibid., p. 288.

414,241 out of a total of 814,241 and the vast majority of these constituted the class that could least afford it, namely the cultivators.[86]

The begar system provided great opportunities for graft to Pandit revenue officials through whom demands were channelled. If a requisition for the labour of a number of coolies was made in Srinagar, the tehsildar would double the number asked for and his subordinates quadruple it. This left room for three-fourths of the zamindars in the village to buy off their freedom, paying up to Rs 70 to 90 per head, making a tremendous profit for the hierarchy of Pandits, and still meeting the state's requirements.[87] In other instances, as recorded by Lawrence, cultivators who could not pay for their release would go to horrific lengths to escape their impressment for the tasks of the state. The most notorious of these latter was the transport of the baggage of troops going to and from Kashmir to Gilgit, so much so that the very name of Gilgit struck terror in the hearts of zamindars. When word spread that state agents were on rounds to collect men, 'there was a general stampede among villagers' and 'whole villages would bivouack in the mountains', many dying there of the cold or maimed from frostbite.[88]

The baneful aspects of begar prompted many cultivators to leave *khalsa* (government) lands to work on begar-free lands. And although this meant a loss of revenue to the state, the Dogras were unwilling to take on the powerful entrenched interests of the Pandits and of other Hindu beneficiaries of dharmarth grants.[89] For Muslim cultivators, freedom from begar was obtained at the cost of reinforcing their dependence on Pandit officials. In many instances, the revenue officials used this opportunity to acquire the occupancy rights of the Kashmiri agriculturists. Any sum paid for such 'purchases' to state officials was more than made up by extortion from cultivators.[90] For those Muslim cultivators who worked on dharmarth villages in order to obtain release from begar, there was another kind of price to pay. As Lawrence had suggested, the existence of dharmarth villages constituted a

---

[86] Ibid., p. 412.

[87] Wingate, p. 37, and Lawrence, *The Valley of Kashmir*, p. 412.

[88] Lawrence, *The Valley of Kashmir*, p. 413.

[89] Note by Walter Lawrence on the 'Position of the Cultivating Classes in Kashmir', op. cit.

[90] Ibid.

divided authority in the state, an '*imperium in imperio*'.[91] The *Ain* had placed the dharmarth villages and villagers within a virtually separate judicial hierarchy over which its own officials presided. It suggested that 'in judicial proceedings in which the parties [were] . . . servants of Dharmarth' the powers of the members of the council would be 'equal to those of local courts.'[92] Considering that the vast majority of the servants of the dharmarth were Muslim cultivators, this meant their subjection to the laws of an institution with a very clear Hindu religious identity.

Aside from its labour aspect, begar had another pernicious side to it, namely the requisition of village produce regularly made by revenue officials, from which even Muslims working on begar-free lands were not exempt. These included giving up produce such as wood, milk, and blankets. And whether working on khalsa or begar-exempt lands, the cultivator was obliged to pay not only a heavy burden of official taxes to the state but also a series of unofficial perquisites (*rasum*) to Pandit revenue officials. Lawrence made a rough calculation of approximately Rs 1300 per annum paid by one of the villages to the state, including payment to the Dharmarth Trust fund, and an additional Rs 410 to Pandit officials.[93]

The position of privilege held by Kashmiri Pandits, Lawrence argued, had been enhanced considerably since the time of Ranbir Singh who had given them greater authority and encouraged them to traffic in land. By all accounts, large tracts of land in Kashmir lay uncultivated until the early decades of the twentieth century. In 1862, Ranbir Singh, introduced the system of *zer-i-niaz chaks* (grants on easy terms of assessment) in an effort to extend cultivation to fallow lands in the valley. Beside the obvious merits in agrarian terms, the *chakdari* system was also a device for the Dogras to brace their 'alliance', political and cultural, with the Kashmiri Pandits. The *chaks* (or allotments of waste land) were granted on comfortable terms, for ten years, and carried the proviso that *chakdars* were to employ only such persons as

[91] Memorandum on the Dharmarth Department by Walter Lawrence, dated 23 May 1891, Foreign Department (Secret E)/Pros. March 1892/nos. 106–12, NAI.

[92] *Ain*, pp. 20, 60.

[93] Note by Walter Lawrence on the 'Position of the Cultivating Classes in Kashmir', op. cit.

were not already cultivators or by 'attracting cultivators from the Punjab'. In 1866–7, Ranbir Singh introduced yet another kind of chak in the valley, granted on even more favourable terms and known as the *chak hanudi* or chaks granted to Hindus. Among the conditions to be fulfilled by the beneficiaries of such grants was that they not employ cultivators of khalsa lands; that they extend cultivation only into waste land; that they agree to the terms of assessment (which were very generous and rising only very gradually); and, very importantly for Ranbir Singh, that they 'remain Hindus and accept service nowhere else'.[94] In 1880, the chakdaris were extended further to include a new category of *mukarrari* chaks 'under which a great deal of land [was] held' when Wingate surveyed the valley in 1888. The assessment rates, though slightly higher than on the chaks hanudi, were still very generous. And quite evidently, mukarrari chaks were also intended as grants to Hindus since one of the conditions imposed was that the 'holder [remain] loyal to the state and true to his caste'.[95]

The chakdari system became an important mechanism for the Kashmiri Pandit community to acquire control over extensive tracts of land in the valley. Although chaks were allotted under strict and elaborate conditions, most of these were regularly violated by their Pandit beneficiaries. When lands fell fallow temporarily during the Kashmir famine of 1877–9, Pandits took over substantial tracts of them claiming that they constituted uncultivated waste. Numerous Kashmiri Muslim cultivators who had left the valley for Punjab, to escape the devastation of those years, found upon their return that they had been ousted from lands they had cultivated over generations.[96] Chakdaris, at the inception of the system, were granted through *pattas* (deed of grants/assignments) issued directly by the durbar, as a means of establishing and extending the latter's authority over powerful political allies. However, this formality gradually lapsed and *diwans* (revenue ministers) and wazir wazarats in Kashmir made such grants under their own authority.[97] These officials tended to be Kashmiri Pandits and so schemed with their co-religionists in the consolidation of large landed estates in the valley. The condition about not using extant

[94] Wingate, pp. 27–8.
[95] Ibid.
[96] Ibid., p. 29.
[97] Ibid.

cultivators, instituted to ensure a true increase of cultivation, was also consistently disregarded. Evidence suggests that the rates owed to the state were not paid either, since most Pandits held land in 'excess of what they pa[id] for'. And while some fallow land was indeed brought under cultivation, the Kashmiri Pandits also included substantial portions of already cultivated lands, ousting old cultivators to 'destroy any proof of prior farming.[98]

The Pandits devised numerous ingenious strategies for an almost 'annual' accretion of lands to their chaks. The help of the local tehsildar was frequently summoned by the chakdar for the acquisition of cultivated lands adjoining his assignment. Common machinations included the threat of raising the revenue demand or instigating imaginary boundary disputes to compel cultivators to abandon their lands, which were then 'legitimately' transferred to a chakdari. The moment the durbar announced the desirability of resettling these 'waste or semi-waste villages . . . by leasing them out on easy terms', the Pandit revenue officials 'would have possession of a valuable patronage'. The assessment was low since it was made on the land considered waste, and the 'cultivators . . . waiting in surrounding villages' would be allowed to come back on terms favourable to the chakdar. The Kashmiri Pandit thereby made large profits *vis-à-vis* both the state and the cultivators.[99]

In his preliminary report on settlement operations, Wingate attributed too much naïveté to the Dogra durbar. Undoubtedly the state would not have wished to be defrauded of its revenues. However, it seems highly unlikely that the Kashmir durbar was such a helpless victim of Kashmiri Pandit officialdom.[100] In creating chaks hanudi and mukarraris assigned mostly to Hindus in the valley, the Dogras were quite clearly seeking to provide Kashmiri Pandits with a stake in supporting their rule. They abdicated voluntarily the supervision of the actual working of these grants in favour of the Pandit-dominated revenue department. A rap was administered on knuckles only in instances of the situation spinning out of control, or when the British

[98] Ibid., pp. 29–30.

[99] Ibid., pp.29–32.

[100] Wingate suggested that 'It is to be clearly understood that the interests of the Darbar and the interests of the cultivators are identical . . . The cultivators desire more food and the Darbar, more revenue, and the whole pundit class live by shirting both'. Ibid., pp. 33–4.

raised questions about the 'rights' of cultivators being trampled too palpably (as they did via Wingate and Lawrence).

By Wingate's own admission, at the time of his visit to Kashmir 'a suspicion of the truth' about the misappropriation of cultivated land by chakdars had arisen in the durbar circles as a result of which chaks had become progressively more difficult to obtain. It is remarkable that despite these misgivings that should have made the durbar more vigilant, Pandit officials were still able to transfer lands to themselves with astonishing ease and impunity. Some of the stratagems employed were too artless to constitute acts of concealment but appear instead to be gestures of merely keeping up appearances. In some instances cultivators were coerced into acknowledging the fictitious assertions by Pandits that certain villages had been the ancestral property of the latter. As much as the claims, the deeds recording them were also manufactured and asserted that 'somehow possession was lost, but the villagers unanimously recognise[d] him [the Pandit in question] as proprietor'.[101] Not only were forged deeds not unknown to the Dogra regime, but the rulers were also certainly capable of, and in other contexts had been self-interestedly diligent in,[102] investigating records of land grants. That they did not do so is either explained by their gullibility or by their deliberate decision to turn a blind eye. Wingate's proposal that both applied at the same time is untenable. The Dogra rulers provided too many loopholes for the Kashmiri Pandits to exploit for this not to be part of a conscious policy aimed at winning support for their exercises of legitimation. Recording another 'very simple method' of obtaining control over revenue, Wingate suggested that the Trakiyat or land improvement department was instituted in Kashmir to 'work waste lands that nobody would take up by means of hired labour'. He proposed further that 'it was most useful in conferring the management of small estates upon numerous needy pundits' since 'any bit of land could be transferred to this convenient department and made over to a friend to cultivate'.[103] However, when the Trakiyat had become 'too notorious', Wingate also admitted that it was abolished.

This was not a government run by an oblivious dupe but one which knew when and to whom its sovereign rights of revenue collection

[101] Ibid., pp. 30–1.

[102] As Gulab Singh did in the case of Sut Ram Razdan, also a Kashmiri Pandit and a prominent one at that. See Chapter One.

[103] Wingate, p. 32.

could and should be devolved. The governor of Kashmir at the time of Wingate's survey was fully conscious that cultivators sold and mortgaged their rights fairly regularly. However the position he adopted was that since the 'durbar [wa]s the only owner [of land], it d[id] not matter if people [did] buy and sell their land.'[104] The Kashmiri Pandits, in turn, were well aware of the correct form to be observed. 'However possession [of revenues] was got', Wingate observed, 'great ingenuity and co-operation we[re] displayed [by the Pandits] in building up a title. *To please the durbar and allay any apprehension* every official glibly agree[d] that the land belong[ed] to His Highness.'[105] Though cognizant of Kashmiri Pandits contravening the principle that all land in Kashmir belonged to the ruler, the durbar was equally conscious that any attempt at 'dispossessing' them would result in large expanses of revenue-paying lands falling out of cultivation. Many of the original cultivators had disappeared and others would be too intimidated by the Pandit officials to take them over.[106] In this manner, some of the richest lands of the valley were acquired by the Pandits through sale and mortgage and, undoubtedly, with the conscious acquiescence of the Dogra durbar.

The Dogra state's policy of granting Hindus privileged access to Kashmiri revenues was not confined to the Pandits alone. Beginning in 1877, Ranbir Singh had created service grants in portions of the valley for members of his own caste of the Dogra Mian Rajputs.[107] The objective was to encourage them to settle in Kashmir so that the maharaja would have 'a certain body of his own people ready at hand in the event of any disturbances in the valley.'[108] The particular Dogra Mians selected were required to live in Kashmir along with their *sowars*

---

[104] Ibid., pp. 32–3.

[105] Ibid., p. 32. Emphasis mine.

[106] Ibid., pp. 32–3.

[107] The term 'Mian' was reserved for members of an endogamous sub-group among the Hindu-Dogras. The Dogra rulers had traditionally married into this group but, by the end of the nineteenth century, also had matrimonial alliances outside of it with a variety of other 'Rajputs'. The category of Mian Dogras was, itself, divided and ranked along a loose hierarchy depending on the place of origin. Thus, the Raipuria Mians were regarded as superior to the Mians from Jandral who, in turn, were considered more elevated than the Mians from Jasrota. The Dogra rulers of Jammu and Kashmir were Jamwals (from Jammu).

[108] J.L. Kaye, *Preliminary Report on H.L. Rivett's Assessment Report on the Mian*

(cavalrymen), the families and servants of both. The grantees were given the produce of certain villages in lieu of payment of salaries in cash. They were also given free wood to build houses and granted exemption from taxation on their sheep and ponies, dry trees and brushwood, and rights and privileges in the state forests (as were enjoyed by Kashmiri villagers).[109] These grants carried with them several conditions, most of which were observed more in the breach and for which the durbar rarely punished the Mians. It was for a clear project of colonizing Kashmir that these grants were created by the Dogra maharaja, and so it should not be surprising that the greatest leeway was permitted the grantees.

The requirement of military service had quite evidently lapsed by 1888. When Dogra grantees were summoned in that year, it was discovered that they had no horses fit to do sowars' work.[110] Although failure to render service did sometimes result in the resumption of grants, more often than not they were restored after a few years. In other instances Dogra beneficiaries continued to draw payment even after their grants had been registered as *zabt* (confiscated). Vaguely phrased pattas granted to the Dogra Mians allowed for an undefined number of claimants such as those naming an individual and '*waghaira*' (literally '*et. cetera*'). In some cases deeds entirely omitted to enter the name of a grantee so that they could be claimed by anyone. That such lapses were not accidental is proven by the fact that one such patta was issued by no less a personage than Ranbir Singh's Pandit prime minister, Wazir Punnu. The condition that the Rajputs and their families reside permanently in Kashmir was also seldom respected. Families rarely accompanied the grantees, preferring instead to remain in the more familiar and familial domain of Jammu. The grantees themselves remained absent from the valley, visiting only at harvest time and employing 'false substitute[s] to answer whenever a roll was called'.[111] In 1897, J.L. Kaye, the settlement commissioner in Kashmir, pointed out that it was a misnomer to call the Mians jagirdars when they were in fact merely recipients of salaries paid in kind (instead of

---

Jagir Villages Situated in Kashmir Proper (Lahore: The 'Civil and Military Gazette' Press, 1897), p. 4.

[109] Ibid., p. 5.

[110] Ibid.

[111] Ibid., p. 6.

cash). The claim by the Dogra Mians that their grants constituted jagirs had enabled them to extend their privileges and (mis-)appropriate the right to collect revenues themselves from the villages assigned to them.[112] In fact, all that the grants had entitled them to was to obtain produce in kind to a value equal to their salaries. There is little doubt that the Dogra durbar was aware of these violations by the Mian Rajputs of the terms of their grants. Even if they could claim ignorance in the past, they certainly could not continue to do so after Kaye's report. However, the settlement commissioner's suggestions to the maharaja that the durbar clarify the true nature of the grants as also that it insist on a strict adherence to their conditions fell on deaf ears. The durbar declared that there was 'nothing more to be said' about 'the privileges which His Highness the Maharaja and the Raja Sahibs [his brothers] ha[d] thought fit and expedient to accord the Mians.'[113]

The maharaja and his brothers were not quite as united in the case of zer-i-niaz and jagirdari grants claimed by the Naqshbandi family of Kashmir.[114] When the latter were informed that their zer-i-niaz villages would be assessed at full rates or failing that be resumed, they complained to the Resident that they were entitled to revenue-free possession on the grounds that these villages formed part of their jagirs. Whereas zer-i-niaz chaks (hanudi and mukarrari) had been continued to Hindus on easy terms of assessment despite obvious infringements of the conditions of their grant and the Dogra Mians had been allowed to overstep the definition of their endowments and claim jagirdari rights, the Naqshbandis were not allowed the same indulgences. Their claims were subjected to detailed scrutiny by the State Council in 1898. At issue were four villages granted on zer-i-niaz terms, but 'understood' as jagirs, to the Naqshbandis by Ranjit Singh. The State Council had wished to resume these.

The maharaja, however, chose to differ in this instance from the council with a view to preserving the goodwill of one of the most prominent Muslim religious families of the valley. He chose to read the

[112] Ibid.

[113] Letter from Rai Bahadur Pandit Bhag Ram, Revenue Member of the Jammu and Kashmir State Council, to the Vice President of the Jammu and Kashmir State Council, dated 25 January 1897, OER, C.S., Political and General Department, 1896, File no. 117, JKA.

[114] OER, C.S., Political and General Department, 1896, File no. 117, JKA.

nature of the grant as 'zer-i-niaz villages treated as jagirs by the late ruling chiefs'. In this instance of disagreement between the maharaja and his council, the Resident's opinion was solicited. The latter agreed, having only recently endorsed Lawrence's careful investigation of land rights, that the distinction made by the council was technically correct and that treating them as jagir would mean a loss of Rs 9500 per annum in state revenues. The matter was referred to J.L. Kaye, the settlement commissioner. What is interesting is that in the examination which ensued of older documents of grants to the Naqshbandis, dating from Ranjit Singh's times all the way to the era of Wazir Punnu, it became apparent that they had a clearer title to the jagirdari rights, under condition of payment at zer-i-niaz rates, than any that could be established by the Pandit chakdars or the Mian 'jagirdars' in Kashmir. In the end, the maharaja won out and the state council was dissuaded from resuming the four villages on the condition of the payment of Rs 1000 per annum. This was a significant concession accorded to the Naqshbandis on the basis that their villages formed a 'separate' category of zer-i-niaz villages occupying a position of 'conditional jagir villages'. However, it was founded on the grounds of exceptionalism and had required the intervention of the British Resident's office, which had urged that the matter be investigated carefully by the revenue department before the 'parties [were] actually dispossessed'.[115] It had also taken the Naqshbandis threatening to leave the valley and 'weeping like children' before the council members and, more importantly, declaring that their grants originated in British intervention with Ranjit Singh.[116] Although the Naqshbandis continued as a substantial landed group of Muslims in the valley until 1947 with jagirdari profits of at least Rs 8500 per annum, their status depended on the goodwill of the maharaja and the British Resident.

The same position of dependency applied to other Muslim jagirdars, such as the Bambas, whose assignments had been continued with great

[115] Letter from Captain Stuart Godfrey, Assistant Resident in Kashmir, to Raja Amar Singh, Vice President of the Jammu and Kashmir State Council, dated 4 October 1898, OER,C.S., Political and General Department, 1896, File no. 117, JKA.

[116] Confidential Note by Raja Amar Singh to the Resident in Kashmir, dated 13 September 1898, OER,C.S., Political and General Department, 1896, File no. 117, JKA.

reluctance by Gulab Singh under the terms of the Treaty of Amritsar. Although they held revenue-free grants, principally in the Machipura district of Kashmir, by the time Lawrence encountered them in 1889 the Bambas had 'degenerated into a feeble, ridiculous, and most pitiable condition'. They were impoverished and 'quarrelsome' and almost pathetically, but with very little resonance in reality, held on to the title of 'raja' and the tract in which they lived was still called 'Rajwara (the land of the Rajas)'.[117]

Among the few Muslim figures prominent in the agrarian structure of the Dogra state were the *lambardars*, or village headmen. A hereditary office dating to the Mughal conquest of Kashmir (1586) when it was created by Akbar's revenue minister Todar Mal, the lambardar under the Dogras received a salary of 5 per cent on the revenue, which he was responsible for collecting. However, he was caught between the clichéd rock and a hard place. On the one hand, he was a respected figure, occasionally performing the important religious duties of a preacher in some of the more inaccessible villages that could not afford a resident mullah for their mosques.[118] On the other hand, the role he played in the revenue arrangements of the Dogras made him a much reviled figure among Kashmiri Muslim villagers. In theory, his position was one of great responsibility, but in practice he was made fully subordinate to the Pandit dominated revenue department. He was treated with contempt by revenue officials and regarded as little more than an ordinary cultivator. 'There [was] no honour attaching to the office and [he was] as meanly dressed and as meanly housed as the rest of the village.'[119] To remedy this situation, the more successful lambardars collaborated actively with the revenue machinery of the state and against the cultivators. For instance they would forcibly bring back runaway *assamis* (cultivators) or collude with Pandit tehsildars in manufacturing figures for the arrears of a village and share in the profits.[120] In the end, the lambardar was in 'a false position', having little real authority over the cultivators, while in relation to the revenue

[117] Lawrence, *The Valley of Kashmir*, p. 309.
[118] Walter Lawrence, 'Assessment Report of the Lal Tehsil', p. 35, included in Foreign Department (Secret E)/Pros. February 1891/nos. 295–326, NAI.
[119] Ibid., p. 37.
[120] Ibid.

officials he could either be 'powerless, and insulted' or consent to 'intriguing' with them'.[121] For the cultivator what this meant was that there was no recourse against illegal extortion as long as the formidable revenue department controlled agrarian relations and undermined the stature of the lambardar as the one figure potentially capable of speaking on their behalf.

Paradoxically, with the land settlement carried out by Lawrence the position of privileged holders of land rights, primarily Hindu, became more fully entrenched in the agrarian hierarchy of Kashmir. Zamindars in Kashmir, from the time of the Mughals onwards, had possessed the undisputed right to cultivate and hold land. However, there were two slightly different concepts of this right prevalent in the valley. The first was denoted by the term assami used from the time of the Mughals to describe any person recognized by the state as a lawful occupant of the land. In the perception of the village community, however, an assami was one who also held a *miras* or hereditary right to certain plots of cultivable land and irrigated land within the boundaries of the village. While a succession of rulers from the Mughals to the Dogras gradually etiolated the miras rights, these were 'kept alive by the village'.[122] This discrepancy in the two concepts had enabled the Dogras, through the second half of the nineteenth century, to recognize a variety of people as lawful occupants (assamis) of the land, regardless of the hereditary principle recognized in the village community.

Lawrence's settlement sought to revive the greater legitimacy of miras rights. His efforts were in line with the new direction taken by tenancy legislation in British India from the 1870s onwards that, recognizing the 'historical primacy of the village community', sought to 'stabilise the position of those enjoying immediate and customary possessory dominion'.[123] In his settlement, Lawrence acknowledged the superior rights of *mirasdars* but found that weeding out assamis with miras rights from new occupants of land was fraught with considerable difficulties. This was particularly true after the famine of

---

[121] Ibid.

[122] Lawrence, *The Valley of Kashmir*, p. 428.

[123] Eric Stokes, *The Peasant and the Raj: Studies in Agrarian Society and Peasant Rebellion in Colonial India* (Cambridge: Cambridge University Press, 1980), p. 4.

1877–9 when large numbers of Kashmiri cultivators had emigrated provisionally to the Punjab. In 1880, in the wake of the famine and in an effort to stabilize cultivation in the valley the Dogras, under Ranbir Singh, announced a land settlement through which all cultivators *then* in occupation of land, and willing to pay the new assessment, were recognized as assamis. While many of these were mirasdars who had survived the disaster, some of whom had extended their title over abandoned lands, the newly recognized assamis also included a number of entirely fresh claimants such as the Pandit chakdars discussed above. Lawrence, while wishing to accommodate cultivators who had abandoned their lands temporarily to escape the famine, could not in all fairness 'turn out' those who could prove that they had accepted the assessment of 1880.[124] However, he elaborated only on the cases where mirasdars who had remained in the valley had encroached upon the occupancy rights of those others who had left for the Punjab. These, he suggested, were sorted out relatively smoothly because of the ease with which fugitives with genuine miras claims were recognized by village communities and the willingness of mirasi assamis to voluntarily relinquish fields to them.[125] In the course of his survey each person in undisputed occupancy of cultivated land was registered as an assami. And after Lawrence's settlement, permanent hereditary occupancy rights were given to all persons who agreed to pay the assessment fixed on the fields entered in their name.[126] However, what the settlement also did was to grant the status of assamis and permanent hereditary occupancy rights to privileged holders such as the Kashmiri Pandit chakdars. As Wingate suggested, the prerequisite of 'undisputed occupancy' in order to qualify as assami was easily overcome by chakdars compelling cultivators to testify to that effect. Although Lawrence did not directly address the issue, his dilemma of sorting mirasdar assamis from newly created ones evidently involved recently sprung groups of Hindus asserting non-hereditary claims of occupancy in the land. His statement that 'he ha[d] never found it difficult to ascertain whether a fugitive was a mirasdar or not'[127] implies a number of fraudulent claims being made. Wingate had already suggested that the Kashmiri

[124] Lawrence, *The Valley of Kashmir*, pp. 428–9.
[125] Ibid.
[126] Ibid., pp. 429–30.
[127] Ibid. p. 429.

Pandit chakdars were among the worst offenders in instances of grabbing occupancy rights over lands vacated during the famine. Lawrence himself had acknowledged elsewhere that the 'Pandits ha[d] a great desire to become landholders' and that if the 'Pandit [wa]s an official or the distant relative of an official, the acquisition of land [wa]s relatively simple'. Tehsildars used their official prerogatives to call in the free labour of Muslim cultivators to 'break' new land and installed themselves as the 'owner[s] of a handsome estate'.[128] In one fell swoop, through Lawrence's settlement, the rights of all of these new bidders, whether mirasdars or not, were recognized on par with those of hereditary Kashmiri cultivators without, however, levelling the playing field for the latter.

Ultimately, Lawrence's settlement left privileges in the land more or less undisturbed. To a large extent this was guaranteed by his argument that even a reformed revenue department would have to rely on a Kashmiri Pandit staff since the state was too poor to afford the expense of 'imported' Punjabi officials.[129] He was also wary of the political consequences of turning the powerful 'Pandits adrift'. Of course, he insisted that the Kashmiri Pandits employed in the revenue department would have to be carefully trained, supervised and disciplined.[130] To this end he recommended the appointment of a

[128] Letter from Walter Lawrence, Settlement Officer, to Colonel R.P. Nisbet, Resident in Kashmir, dated 13 November 1889, Foreign Department (Secret E)/Pros. February 1891/nos. 295–326, NAI.

[129] Letter from Walter Lawrence, Settlement Officer, to Colonel R.P. Nisbet, Resident in Kashmir, dated 2 December 1889, Foreign Department (Secret E)/Pros. February 1891/nos. 295–326, NAI. Lawrence had also recorded elsewhere that there was a 'natural apprehension among all Kashmiri officials that a proper revenue administration would mean the dimunition of all Pandits . . . holding office, and that [he was] doing [his] best to reassure the more decent of the Pandits . . . that the administration [would have] on financial reasons alone [to] be carried on through a Kashmiri agency'. Letter from Walter Lawrence to Sir Mortimer Durand, dated 29 June 1889, Foreign Department (Secret E)/Pros. September 1889/nos. 204–8, NAI.

[130] Lawrence did not believe that the Pandits were 'past reclamation, and . . . felt that if they were] properly paid, supervised and encouraged, they would probably be as useful public servants as the ordinary'. Letter from Walter Lawrence to Sir Mortimer Durand, dated 29 June 1889, Foreign Department (Secret E)/Pros. September 1889/nos. 204–8, NAI.

'controlling officer', who would spend most of his time in camp and have full powers to dismiss and fine. The inability to dismantle Pandit dominance over the revenue machinery, then, was sought to be countered by greater reliance on a presumably non-partisan outsider. However, treading on egg-shells *vis-à-vis* the Kashmiri Pandit community and undermining the full effectiveness of a truly supervisory role, Lawrence also suggested that, should it become necessary to dispense with the services of an unqualified revenue official, the latter should be compensated with the grant of waste land. In the end, the cosmetic nature of Lawrence's changes was made most evident by his admission that even among his own staff any relaxation in his watchfulness resulted immediately in graft and fraud.

Privileged rights in land enjoyed by some groups of Kashmiris were not only maintained but means were devised to strengthen them after the settlement. Lawrence himself had kept the chakdars and mukarraridars in place. In theory they were turned into assamis of the villages in which their estates lay. But while admitting that there was 'nothing in the deeds which entitle[d] them to privileged rates [of assessment]', Lawrence applauded the state's decision to continue the concessionary rates for a further ten years.[131] The ten-year limitation was obviously disregarded since the chakdars and mukarraridars continued to enjoy beneficial terms of access to land until as late as 1948 when their grants were finally abolished.[132] Jagir villages were not even included in Lawrence's survey.[133] However, in subsequent years the British Resident encouraged the introduction of the rule of primogeniture in inheritance to protect the integrity of this class. Thus the assistant to the Resident wrote to the chief minister in 1913, approving of 'the policy underlying the state council decisions' that sought to prevent the 'frittering away of a Jagir into small portions' resulting in a 'reduction in the status of Jagirdars to that of the ordinary indigent zamindars'. The desired result of the policy was to be 'the establishment of a class of landed gentry, loyal to His Highness the Maharaja, influential in

---

[131] Lawrence, *The Valley of Kashmir*, p. 426.

[132] Mirza Afzal Beg, *On the Way to Golden Harvests, Agricultural Reforms in Kashmir* (Jammu: Government of Jammu and Kashmir, 1950), pp. 7–9 and Government of Jammu and Kashmir, Ministry of Revenue, *Jagirs, Muafis and Mukarraris* (Srinagar, February 1956).

[133] Lawrence, *The Valley of Kashmir*, p. 239.

their local districts, and capable of exercising a wholesome effect on the surrounding peasantry.'[134] The new rights granted to cultivators by Lawrence's settlement were balanced by bolstering a set of more conservative, compliant and favoured groups within the Kashmiri agrarian structure.

Agricultural indebtedness had been marginal in the period before Lawrence's settlement. Indeed both Wingate and Lawrence had commented on the uniqueness of Kashmir in that 'the Banya [Hindu moneylender] of India [was] practically unknown in Kashmir.'[135] This did not, however, mean that there was no credit mechanism in operation. Most of the larger villages had their *wani* or *bakal*, who was usually a Muslim peddler running a modest retail business in salt, oil, spices, snuff, sugar, tea and occasionally cotton piece-goods. The wani also doubled as a small-scale moneylender under the system known as *wad*. Being a Muslim, theoretically he was not permitted to take interest on loans. Through the wad system, therefore, the borrower repaid his loan in kind through goods such as blankets, fruit and grain. These would be evaluated by the wani at a lower rate than that at which he sold them on the market.[136] In some other larger villages in the valley, there were also Hindus who carried on the business of petty shopkeepers and, like the Muslim wanis, obtained their supplies from the city. They also made advances to cultivators on the security of their crops.[137] Nevertheless, it is clear that this system of credit did not lead the cultivator to becoming hopelessly indebted since, as Lawrence recorded, wanis were 'unanimous in saying that they never ma[de] a bad debt and that they were never obliged to sue a debtor.'[138]

Conditions changed in the post-settlement period, with a marked increase in indebtedness. This was a direct result of Lawrence converting the payment of at least part of the revenue owed to the state from kind into cash. Precise figures about agrarian indebtedness are hard to come by, but that it had grown into a significant problem is attested to by Maharaja Hari Singh (successor to Pratap Singh) when he

[134] Letter from the Assistant to the Resident, to the Chief Minister, dated 14 November 1913, OER,1913, File no. 162/H-13, JKA.

[135] Lawrence, *The Valley of Kashmir*, p. 387; Wingate, pp. 16–17.

[136] Lawrence, *The Valley of Kashmir*, p. 5.

[137] Walter Lawrence, 'Assessment Report of the Lal Tehsil', p. 33.

[138] Lawrence, *The Valley of Kashmir*, p. 5.

promulgated the Agriculturists' Relief Act in 1926/7 with a view to 'freeing agriculturists from the clutches of moneylenders and protecting them from usurious rates of interests'.[139] By this time indebtedness affected more than 70 per cent of the rural population of Kashmir.[140] The provisions of the act were to ensure that the interest charged was paid in instalments related to the capacity of debtors after they had met the needs of cultivation and subsistence and that the total amount of the interest was in no case to exceed 50 per cent of the capital.[141] In 1932, the wanis had claimed exemption from this Act on the grounds that they were 'in no sense moneylenders' but simply made a 'living by supplying agriculturists with ordinary every day commodities'. Even the British official to whom this appeal was made acknowledged that only the strictest application of the law would include them in this category and admitted of a distinction in actual practice between 'trade of this nature' and the 'business of moneylending'.[142]

It is clear that other groups, predominantly Hindu, had joined the wanis and bakals as the bigger players in the profitable venture of moneylending.[143] The strongest protest made against the Agriculturists Relief Act had come from a Hindu-dominated 'Protest Committee of Jammu and Kashmir' and from the Hindu Yuvak Sabha, a predominantly Kashmiri Pandit body. They claimed that the Act 'affect[ed] the interests of the Hindu community and [was] against the principles of Justice and equity as they benefit[ted] one community at the expense of another.' This objection was dismissed by the state on the grounds that the enactment was made in the interests of the agriculturists and so disqualified protest from the Hindu Yuvak Sabha, 'no

[139] B.J. Glancy etc., *Report of the Commission Appointed Under the Orders of His Highness the Maharaja Bahadur Dated 12th November 1931 to Enquire into Grievances and Complaints* (Jammu: Ranbir Government Press, 1932), pp. 35, 36. See also Gwash Lal Kaul, *Kashmir Then and Now* (Srinagar: Chronicle, 1967), p. 101.

[140] P.N. Bazaz, *Inside Kashmir* (Srinagar: The Kashmir Publishing Company, 1941), pp. 253–4.

[141] Government of Jammu and Kashmir Law Department, 'The Agriculturists' Relief Regulation', p. 7, in General Department, 1929, File no. 1248/AG-5, JKA.

[142] Glancy etc., *op. cit.*, p. 36.

[143] Bazaz, *The History of the Struggle for Freedom in Kashmir*, p. 562.

member of which . . . [was] an agriculturist or [had] . . . anything to do with land.'[144] Quite obviously, contrary to the state's ruling, this had everything to do with the Hindu groups who had been lending money to cultivators. The memorialists' complaint was that agriculturists were shielding themselves behind this latest enactment to 'take forcible possession of lands which they had mortgaged', thereby leading 'to strained relations between [the two] classes'.[145] Nevertheless, that agrarian indebtedness in Kashmir in no way disappeared in the wake of the Act of 1926/7 is shown by the fact that debts in Kashmir amounted to Rs 310 lakhs in 1949.[146] Moneylenders compensated themselves for the restrictions on the rates of interest by making an agriculturist sign for sums that were sometimes double the amount of the actual loan.[147] As late as 1946 a British writer had observed that, in a typical Kashmiri village, 'every household was in debt, and the usual rate of interest was 48 per cent' and that the tiller was indebted to the moneylender who might also be the landowner.[148] The scaling down of the cultivators' debts became a central part of the radical reforms instituted by the popularly backed National Conference-led government that took power in Jammu and Kashmir after 1947 (more fully discussed later).

Related to the escalation in indebtedness of Kashmiri cultivators was the increasing pressure placed on the land in the early decades of the twentieth century. In the period before and during Lawrence's settlement, a good deal of land had been available in Kashmir so that greater premium had been placed on labour and it was possible to force zamindars to till the land.[149] Otherwise, the system of *rahdari* (passports), in operation since the time of Gulab Singh, preventing cultivators from leaving Kashmir without the permission of the ruler and binding them to the land, would have made little sense. Although it

[144] Letter from the Chief Justice to the Prime Minister, dated 26 November 1932, General Department, 1929, File no. 1248/AG-5, JKA.

[145] Memorial Presented by the Protest Committee of Jammu and Kashmir to the Maharaja, General Department, 1929, File no. 1248/AG-5, JKA.

[146] *Administrative Report of the Jammu and Kashmir State* (1949), p. 37.

[147] Glancy etc., p. 36.

[148] H.M. Brailsford, cited in Jammu and Kashmir Ministry of Information and Broadcasting, *Five Years* (New Delhi: Caxton Press, 1953), p. 10.

[149] Lawrence, *The Valley of Kashmir*, pp. 411, 426.

was abolished after the famine of 1877–9,[150] the services of the lambardars and tehsildars had often been enlisted to bring fugitive zamindars back to cultivate the land.[151] This situation changed quickly due in large part to population growth[152] that led to 'agriculture outgrowing its resources' and the decreasing availability of new cultivable areas in the valley.[153] The pressure on land was aggravated by a steady decline in handicraft production in the towns and rural areas. Artisans were affected detrimentally by competition from machine-made goods increasingly available in the valley after the construction of the Jhelum Valley road (connecting Kashmir with Punjab) in 1890 and the Banihal Cart Road (connecting Srinagar with Jammu more directly) in 1922. Agriculture began to provide the only escape to the artisanal classes.[154] As a result, in the early decades of the twentieth century the value of land increased as much as the demand on land from among non-agriculturists, particularly Kashmiri Pandits resident in Srinagar.[155]

Walter Lawrence, anticipating this, had sought to counter the ill effects of this increase in the worth of land combined with the growing indebtedness of the Muslim cultivator by making the permanent and hereditary occupancy right in land strictly inalienable. He had hoped that even if the state found itself forced in the future to 'give the fatal gift of alienation to the Muslims', that it would ensure that at least some portion of the holdings would continue to remain inalienable.[156] However, the conferral of a permanent hereditary occupancy right by Lawrence's settlement had within it a loophole. It was subject to the caveat that the occupant paid in full the revenue fixed at the time of assessment on his land.[157] Before the settlement, the accumulation of a revenue deficit against villages, known as *bakaya*, had been permitted

---

[150] Wingate, p. 16.

[151] Lawrence, 'Assessment Report of the Lal Tehsil', p. 37.

[152] The population of Kashmir, which was estimated at 814,241 in 1891, had increased to 1,190,977 by 1921. *Census of India*, 1921 (Kashmir), pt 1, p. 25.

[153] Ibid., p. 63; *Census of India*, 1931 (Jammu and Kashmir), pt 1, pp. 16, 62.

[154] *Census of India*, 1931 (Jammu and Kashmir), pt 1, p. 222.

[155] Petitions by Pandit Sri Kanth Khazanchi, dated 13 September 1911, 4 August 1912, 16 October 1912, 12 August 1913, OER, 1911, File no. 14/B-168, JKA.

[156] Lawrence, *Valley of Kashmir*, p. 6.

[157] Ibid., pp. 429–30.

without entailing that such arrears would necessarily result in the eviction of cultivators from the land.[158] After the settlement, and in conditions of growing pressure on the land, the non-payment of revenue (collected increasingly in cash), led to a proliferation of what was known euphemistically as the *dustbardari* (voluntary relinquishment) of occupancy rights.[159] While the land so 'relinquished' was not put on the market, since technically there was no right of alienation until 1932, the effect was only mildly different. The state reassigned them to any person who would agree to pay the arrears. This process resulted in the continued consolidation of large estates by the privileged landed classes and the creation at the same time of a class of landless labourers well in evidence by 1931.[160]

The British themselves were alert to the gradual course these reforms would have to take. For instance, in 1892, the Secretary to the Government of India in the foreign department wrote about the inability of the colonial government, despite its disapproval of the practice, to do away with the system of begar. He suggested that the 'small alteration' in the system that he had made was limited to the aim of 'correct[ing] abuses, but not the abolition of begar altogether'. The latter, he suggested, would be 'impossible for many a long day'. Regardless of the public demand for the 'abolition of begar [to enable] the immediate transition of the Kashmiri villager from a condition of "status" to a condition of free contract', this official believed that it was 'an impossible thing to achieve, and . . . disastrous to try'.[161]

That there had been no substantive change in the position of the Kashmiri cultivator or of the privileged classes was made evident most poignantly in 1929 by Sir Albion Bannerji, a Bengali Christian civil servant who had been employed in the state as its Foreign and Political minister. Disgusted by the conditions prevailing in the valley and the inability of even conscientious members of the administration to effect

---

[158] Ibid., pp. 407–8, 448–50.

[159] U.K. Zutshi, *Emergence of Political Awakening in Kashmir* (Delhi: Manohar, 1986), p. 141. The euphemism was important since the settlement had granted cultivators permanent hereditary occupancy rights of which they could not be deprived theoretically.

[160] Ibid.

[161] Note by the Secretary to the Government of India, Foreign Department, dated 15 March 1892, Foreign Department (Secret E)/Pros. June 1892/ nos. 133–5, NAI.

a change, he resigned the post he had held for two years. So much for Lawrence's sop of appointing a 'controlling officer' who would correct, through vigilant supervision, the ills of an agrarian administration and a hierarchy of privileges otherwise left largely untouched. Bannerji followed up his resignation with a much-publicized statement to the representative of the Associated Press in Lahore that ignited protests not only in Kashmir but also in the Punjab newspapers. He bore witness to the fact that the

> Jammu and Kashmir State [wa]s labouring under many disadvantages, with a large Mohammedan population absolutely illiterate, labouring under poverty and very low economic conditions of living in the villages and practically governed like dumb driven cattle. There [wa]s no touch between the Government and the people, no suitable opportunity for representing grievances and the administrative machinery itself require[d] overhauling from top to bottom . . . It ha[d] . . . no sympathy with the people's wants and grievances.[162]

Lawrence's settlement had only theoretically provided a parity of rights in land for Kashmiris. In practice, and typical of Pratap Singh's reign and the British-inspired reforms at the time, privileges in the state that followed the broad lines of religious divisions among the subject population were not only continued but reinforced by having gone through the supposed trial by fire of reform. However, an important principle that had been put into place by the British was that, at least notionally, 'Kashmir [would] no longer be governed solely to benefit the ruling family and the rapacious horde of Hindu officials and Pandits, but also for its people, the long suffering indigenous Muhammadans.'[163]

The Subjects of the State: Separate and Unequal

Accompanying the new emphasis on the Dogra rulers making themselves more representative of their people, Pratap Singh's reign also saw the attempt to popularize a 'national anthem'. Composed in 1911 by a certain C.J. Burnow, it was played as a substitute for the 'general

---

[162] Bazaz, *The History of the Struggle for Freedom in Kashmir*, pp. 140–1.

[163] Letter from Colonel R. Parry Nisbet, Resident in Kashmir, to the Secretary to the Government of India, Foreign Department, dated 29 January 1890, Foreign Department (Secret E)/Pros. February 1891/nos. 295–326, NAI.

salute' to receive the maharaja on public occasions. Embarrassingly, a full two years later, in 1913, the officials of the state were still struggling to make it recognizable to the state's subjects.[164] In addition to these efforts, a new coat of arms was devised for the state, modified considerably from the one designed for it by the British for the purposes of the Imperial Assemblage of 1877. In response to a query by the Resident in 1911, the chief minister of the state explained the various components of the coat of arms thus:

> The sun at the top of the hills designates the solar descent of the Ruling family of the Jammu and Kashmir state. The three peaks of mountains represent the three peaks of the hills in Jammu Province below one of which is the sacred place of Trikuta Bhagwati, the family Goddess of the Jammu Ruling family. Next, below the mountains, there was a representation of a saffron flower designating Kashmir. Below the flower is the State shield showing four rivers that flow in this State . . . On both sides of the shield stand the figures of Dogra soldiers representing the Kashmir Army. The soldiers are connected by two bows one mentioning the name of the present Ruler . . . Pratap Singh and the other the Motto of the family . . . which means that heroism on the battle-field is commendable.[165]

It is quite remarkable how the association of the state with the religion of the ruler was still quite evident in this emblematic representation of it. In fact, although Pratap Singh had declared in 1885 that he would treat all his subjects 'without any distinction of race or rank, creed or colour', this was by no means to suggest that either the ruler or the ruled would lose their religious affiliations.

The emergence of a collective body of subjects but with clearly demarcated religious identities was reiterated in the increasingly public celebration of festivals patronized by the Hindu ruling house. As rulers more representative of their subjects, the Dogras provided occasions for the participation of all Kashmiris in their public rituals, such as the celebration of Ankut, the harvest festival. Although this was an agricultural festivity without any specific religious association, in point of fact it was inaugurated with the carrying in procession of the idol of Shri Gadadharji from his temple to a marble terrace, where a military

---

[164] OER, Political Department, 1911, File no. 58/E-19, JKA.
[165] OER, Political Department, 1911, File no. 133/R-7, JKA.

guard of honour waited. Here religious ceremonies were performed in the presence of all the civil and military officers of the state. The chanting of Vedic hymns coupled with the 'touching notes of the national anthem . . . duly impressed upon the people the gorgeousness and dignity of this auspicious occasion and the hearts of all joined in one fervent prayer for the welfare, health and longevity of [His] Highness and the Royal family and the prosperity of the state and its subjects.'[166] The ceremony was followed by a public feast but one in which separate arrangements were made for the different 'classes of people'. Thus, state officials, Kashmiri Pandits, Sunnis, Shias, Punjabi Hindus and European 'ladies and gentlemen' would eat in tents kept distinctly apart from each other. The public creation of a body of subjects, therefore, involved a melding of religious particularism with 'national' commonality, a superimposition on a Hindu ruler of a more 'representative' maharaja for whose health and 'longevity' all the subjects would pray with one collective heart.

The juridical definition of subjects in Kashmir also sought to emphasize and maintain their separate religious identities. In parts of British India through the nineteenth century, customs and various legislative enactments by the colonial state[167] had begun in practice to supersede the personal law of both Hindus and Muslims in important civil matters. Thus, between 1827 and 1876, the legislature had provided that 'subject to certain conditions, customs prevailing among any body or class of persons [would] form the rule of decision by the court.'[168] In Kashmir, on the other hand, the historical trend flowed in the opposite direction. Before the enactment of the Laws Consolidation Regulation of 1872, the general rule governing succession to landed property and other family matters was custom and not the personal law of either the Hindus or Muslims. In 1872 a first conscious attempt was made to apply Hindu and Muslim personal law to the respective religious communities. This regulation was later enacted as

---

[166] State telegram from the Governor of Kashmir to the Maharaja, dated 13 November 1901, OER, Political Department, 1901, File no. 43/85, JKA.

[167] Such as the Caste Disabilities Removal Act of 1850 which abolished the civil disabilities suffered by members of one religious community upon conversion to another religion.

[168] Hakim Imtiyaz Hussain, *Muslim Laws and Customs* (Srinagar: Srinagar Law Journal Publication, 1989), p. 72.

the Sri Pratap Jammu and Kashmir Laws (Consolidation) Act of Samvat 1977 (AD 1920).[169] Henceforth the law courts of the state were assiduous in insisting that the personal law of the various subjects of the state would govern all decisions, unless one or the other party to a suit proved successfully that 'personal law [was] abrogated by such customs as [were] found to be prevailing'.[170]

The burden of proof lay on parties claiming the operation of custom and it was a heavy burden. The state's determination to dissuade its subjects from resorting to custom was made evident by its placing conditions that were almost impossible to meet in their entirety. It was stated, therefore, that a custom to be treated as valid could not simply be argued to have existed since time immemorial,[171] a principle which in English law formed the very definition of custom. Nor could isolated instances prove the existence of an established custom,[172] but had to be corroborated by the independent and reliable evidence of a member of the 'community' to which the litigant belonged.[173] This member of the community, assumed evidently to be literate and therefore among its upper classes, who would argue against the application of personal law, was becoming rarer at a time when religious identifications were becoming increasingly rigid.

Yet, as late as the mid-twentieth century, the state's courts were repeatedly confronted with litigants who failed to see any contradiction in their being governed both by custom and personal law. In the past, the operation of customary law had resulted in the sharing of certain inheritance laws between the Kashmiri Muslims and Pandits. Yet, this ambiguity in the juridical personalities of the state's subjects was increasingly discouraged. Kashmiri Muslims were told that these shared laws dated to the period preceding their conversion from the Hindu

---

[169] *Laws of Jammu and Kashmir: Being a Collection of all the Enactments . . . in force in Jammu and Kashmir State*, 2 vols (Jammu: Ranbir Government Press, 1941), vol. 1.

[170] Civil suit brought before the Appellate Civil Court, dated Samvat 2001, *The Jammu and Kashmir Law Reports*, vol. IV, pp. 264–7.

[171] Mst. Subhani v. Nawab, *All India Reporter*, 1941, Jammu and Kashmir, P.C. 21.

[172] Laju *v.* Sansaro, 1939, *Punjab Law Reporter*, Jammu and Kashmir, 10.

[173] Mst. Bhagan *v.* Haveli Singh, 1940, *Punjab Law Reporter*, Jammu and Kashmir, 14.

religion in 'medieval' times and so were no longer truly applicable to them as Muslims. Furthermore, what was emphasized was that since the Pandits had themselves abandoned many of these customs, the Muslims had even less of a right to claim their enforcement.[174] In effect, the decisions of the courts consistently informed litigants that, insofar as the state was concerned, they were either Hindu or Muslim and as such governed by their respective religious traditions. That they could be both or neither was no longer a valid position.

The reign of Pratap Singh, therefore, witnessed a combination of the diligent maintenance of separate religiously-informed identities among the state's subjects with the assertion that the representation of the interests of subjects, so defined, was a duty of the ruler. One important result was an increasing spirit of assertiveness among Kashmiri Muslims with regard to the rites and rights of their faith. If the state was now defined as 'their state', then the Muslims were demanding that their religion be given equal treatment within it. This was a vital change from the time of Ranbir Singh, who had died as he had lived: the Hindu ruler of a Hindu state. The incidents surrounding the observation of his death ceremonies, in many ways, summed up the position occupied by the Kashmiri Muslim throughout his reign. It was reported that out of deference for the performance of the maharaja's last rites, all business in the state was brought to a halt for the period of thirty days required by Hindu tradition. Not only were all shops closed but no slaughter of any sort of animal was permitted. Unfortunately, this period coincided also with the Bakr-Eid in that year, when Muslims are called upon to sacrifice a young ram or goat. The state felt no hesitation in interfering with the celebration of this important festival by Muslims, emphasizing once more the privileging of Hindu ceremonies over those of Muslims.[175] Such an unabashedly partisan stance would no longer be possible without severe qualifications in the time of Pratap Singh's rule.

In fact, the last decade of the nineteenth century and the first two of the twentieth saw a proliferation of instances of cow-killing and a revival of the issue of the azan. While the Dogra rulers from Maharaja Gulab Singh onwards had officially permitted the calling of the azan

---

[174] *All India Reporter*, 1972, Jammu and Kashmir, p. 105.

[175] Report by the Special Correspondent in *The Statesman* (Calcutta), dated Tuesday, 29 September 1885, cited in D.C. Sharma, *Documentation on Kashmir* (Jammu: Jay Kay Book House, 1985), pp. 25–6.

in the state, unofficially and in more remote villages, this entitlement seems to have been quietly sidelined. But there was a new mood of militancy that would not permit Muslims to remain silent. In 1897, the Hindus in a village called Arnia in Ranbirsinghpura tehsil, had prevented Muslims from making their call to prayers on the grounds 'that it was not borne out by previous usage'. What is both surprising and telling is that even at this late date, the government of Jammu and Kashmir had to ask itself '*whether* the Mohammadans of Arnia should make the Azan' and 'if so *whether* the Hindus should be prohibited from making any interference with the performance of that rite'.[176] The Muslims confronted this denial of their religious 'rights' with violence and rioting in the village and, upon pressure from the Resident's office, the state authorities reinstated the right of Muslims to call the azan.[177]

In 1913, the maharaja had written to his chief minister, Diwan Amar Nath, that 'cow-killing cases ha[d] become more frequent and [that] it [wa]s absolutely necessary to bring to book the offenders and to take . . . steps . . . [to] stop . . . offenders committing this *heinous* crime.' What worried him above all was that 'a reference to the number of such cases w[ould] show that their number [wa]s daily increasing.'[178] Upon inquiry by the governor of Kashmir, it was found that it was not so much actual instances of cow-killing as rumours about such incidents that were on the rise. But these rumours, spreading rapidly and through the valley 'by some sort of wireless telegraphy', were fuelled by 'religious sentiment'[179] and clearly reflected a growing desire among Muslims to 'remove or to minimize the significance of the legal prohibition against cow-killing in the State'.[180]

---

[176] State Council Resolution no. 33 dated 17 April 1897, OER, Political and General Department, 1897, File no. 68, JKA. Emphasis mine.

[177] Letter from the Judicial Member and Secretary to the State Council, to the Vice-President of the Jammu and Kashmir State Council, dated 30 July 1897, OER, Political and General Department, 1897, File no. 68, JKA.

[178] Letter from the Maharaja of Jammu and Kashmir to the Chief Minister, Rai Sahib Diwan Amarnath, dated 9 July 1913, OER, Political Department, 1913, File no. 91/P-56, JKA.

[179] Note on Cow-killing by Khushi Mohamed, Governor of Kashmir, OER, Political Department, 1913, File no. 91/P-56, JKA.

[180] Letter from Pandit Narendranath Koul, Governor of Jammu Province, to the Revenue Minister, Jammu and Kashmir State, dated 13 September 1913, OER, Political Department, 1913, File no. 91/P-56, JKA.

A note prepared by the home minister on the subject reiterated the point. His assessment, based on investigations in Srinagar and in Sopore, was that cows were not slaughtered for 'food purposes' since those accused 'of this offence [we]re in easy circumstances' and could afford more expensive meats. His conclusion was unequivocally that the

> incentive for cow slaughter [was] therefore generally purely religious . . . [and] for sacrificial purposes, on certain religious festivals, chiefly the Id-i-Qurban. The relatives and friends and the *Village Baradari* join[ed] in performing the rite and the beef slaughtered in this manner . . . supposed to be conducive to spiritual good [wa]s also sent to relatives and connections at a distance . . . As such, cow-killing [wa]s a communal *crime* in which the whole village community [took] part probably with the connivance and knowledge of the Lambardar and Chowkidar . . . It is . . . feared that the recent agitation, the increasing tendency towards crime as well as *the endeavours of some irresponsible persons to lessen the gravity of the offence in the sight of the people* may tend to increase this offence.[181]

There was, then, a perceptible change in the stance of Muslims in the valley of Kashmir. In evidence was the burgeoning of a new attitude towards the treatment of their religion and their religiously-defined community within this Hindu state. While cow-slaughter was obviously not essential to the performance of their religious duties, it was not prohibited by their faith either. The circumscription of any aspect of their right to freely practise their faith was coming to be viewed as a constraint on their faith as a whole. They were going further and asserting that a particular 'spiritual good' attached to beef slaughtered by a community of Muslim villagers or, by extension, of the faithful on an especially holy occasion.

The spark fuelling this 'riot' of investigation and writing in the Dogra state was the rumour not only that Muslims in the Baramulla district of Kashmir had slaughtered cows but that the meat was being sold in Srinagar butchers' shops and consumed by an unwitting Kashmiri Hindu clientele. The Muslims interrogated by the state authorities seemed as willing as the Kashmiri Pandits to admit that Hindus

---

[181] 'Note on Suppression of Cow-killing in the Jammu and Kashmir State', by A. Mitra, Home Minister, OER, Political Department, 1913, File no. 91/P-56, JKA. Emphasis mine.

should not be forced through ignorance to eat the beef. The adherence of Hindus to their religion prohibited them from consuming beef, but that this should then become the premise for prohibiting, by force of law, the slaughter of cows by members of another religious community was being called into question by the Kashmiri Muslims.

That at issue were the legal disabilities suffered by Kashmiri Muslims *vis-à-vis* the full freedom to practice their faith is borne out by an earlier incident involving cow-slaughter. In 1897, about three hundred Muslims in Mirpur had joined together to assert their religious right to sacrifice a cow. Although this eventuality was forestalled by the state, what seemed to exercise the authorities even more was that the incident was followed by large groups of Muslims gathering in a khanqah (Sufi hospice) to raise subscriptions to fight cow-killing cases in the state's courts. Additionally, enquiries by the superintendent of police revealed, possibly some of it fed by paranoia, that the Muslims in Mirpur seemed not so much to have slaughtered a cow but wished instead to 'make away with Hindus who prosecute them for cow-killing'.[182]

In response to this increasing outspokenness on the issue of cow-slaughter, the state came down harder on Kashmir's Muslims. One of the measures suggested by the home minister for suppressing cow-killing was to issue a police notification 'prohibiting all such utterances in public meetings, societies and Anjumans and contributions and articles by inhabitants of the State to papers outside the State as advocate cow-killing on any grounds within the State or may criticise the law which makes it a heinous offence.'[183] In addition, the 'crime', which had been made bailable in 1896, was now declared non-bailable and imprisonment, which had tended to average no more than two to three years, was sought to be extended to the full term of ten years (and a heavy fine) permissible by the state's law. A relaxation in the application of the law in 1896, under pressure from the Resident, was deemed responsible for the increased tension caused by cow-killing, whether real cases or rumours, and so justified the tightening up.

The Shias of Kashmir too had joined in moves to assert their right

---

[182] OER, Political and General Department, 1897, File no. 20/L-59, JKA. Also, copy of a telegram from Raja Ram Singh to the Resident in Kashmir, dated 4 July 1897, OER, Political and General Department, File no. 70, JKA.

[183] 'Note on Suppression of Cow-killing', op. cit.

to the free practice of their faith on par with the Hindus. Thus, by 1922, cases were reported of Shias in Srinagar contravening past practice and publicly taking out processions in broad daylight during Muharram. The numbers participating in the processions were also unusually large, involving close to five thousand people. They went further and demanded that, since Muharram was a period of mourning, the state shut down cinema theatres for the duration out of respect for the religious feelings of this group of the Maharaja's subjects.[184] The reaction of the state authorities advertized the inequities suffered by Muslim communities in the state. The response of the maharaja was that 'as regards stopping the cinema, the whole community [could not] be asked to observe mourning for the sake of the Shias.'[185] The disparity implied in the expectation that Bakr-Eid take a back seat to maharaja Ranbir Singh's funerary rites in a state in which the 'whole community' was overwhelmingly Muslim seemed not to matter in the least. The stand taken by the Dogra ruler both on the issue of cow-slaughter and *vis-à-vis* the Shias of Srinagar clearly belied his declaration made before a gathering of Muslims in Srinagar that 'it had always been one of the first principles of [his] rule that the fullest liberty should be enjoyed by [his] subjects in religious matters'.[186]

The actions of Muslims were, at this stage, still countered effectively by more stringent legislation by the Dogra state. However, the issue was to become one of unrelenting opposition on the part of the Muslims of the valley. The situation grew more explosive over the next few decades, when the sense of the unequal treatment of their religion in the state combined with the growing consciousness among Kashmiri Muslims, fed by socio-religious reform groups and new political parties, of the economic and political disabilities suffered by them despite being supposedly equal subjects of the state of Jammu and Kashmir.

[184] Telegram from the Arwat Shiahi to the maharaja, dated 29 August 1922, General Department, 1922, File no. 719/P-5, JKA.

[185] Order of the Maharaja of Jammu and Kashmir, General Department, 1922, File no. 719/P-5, JKA.

[186] His Highness the Maharaja's speech before a gathering of Muslims of all shades of opinion in the Durbar Hall, Srinagar, OER, Political Department, 1910, File no. 144/P-91, JKA.

CHAPTER 4

Contested Sites

Religious Shrines and the
Archaeological Mapping of Kashmiri
Muslim Protest

I n the early decades of the twentieth century, pitched battles were
   fought in the princely state of Jammu and Kashmir over historical
   monuments, particularly religious shrines. These contests invoked
the language of archaeology and history in their defense. Yet, as late as
the end of the nineteenth century, the attitude prevailing at all levels
of Kashmiri society towards historical antiquities had been one of indifference. In 1889 Walter Lawrence had reported on the multitude
of ancient relics to be found in every village. Much as in the rest of
India, no villager, when asked by him, was remotely informed about
the 'history' of these remains 'save the vague guess that they were the
works of the Buddhists or of the Pandus [sic]'.[1] What accounts for this
striking transformation in outlook?

This chapter examines the functioning of a specific 'public' project
of the state, namely the archaeological enterprise that it was encouraged to adopt as a duty by the colonial government in 1904. The impact of this purportedly religiously neutral venture was paradoxically
to amplify religiously defined identities within Kashmir. The extension of the archaeological project of the British Indian government to
Kashmir also galvanized, unwittingly, a movement of rising Muslim
self-assertion against their princely rulers. The colonial state's archaeological enterprise was refashioned and appropriated both by the
Dogra-Hindu princely state to legitimate its own authority as also by

---

[1] Lawrence, *The Valley of Kashmir*, p. 161. The Pandavas were the heroes of the
Mahabharata, an epic that describes events that probably occurred between 1000–
700 BC. However, the versions that survive today were compiled much later, in the
first half of the first millennium AD.

a nascent Kashmiri Muslim political leadership to reclaim sites of Kashmiri religious and cultural affinity. The latter's reclamation of physical sites and political space was used to formulate a sense of community-in-neglect.

The Colonial Politics of Archaeology and Conservation in British India

The colonial government established the Archaeological Department of India as an important handmaid of the state. Opening in 1862 under the direction of General Alexander Cunningham, it was fraught with organizational and financial tribulations in its first forty years or so, until it was thoroughly revamped under Curzon's tenure as viceroy (1899–1905). The latter believed that the conservation of India's historical monuments was 'one of the primary obligations of government' and deplored the fact that this 'imperial responsibility' had been allowed to fall by the wayside through the inertia and lack of interest of his colonial predecessors.[2] By carrying out the preservationist mission with 'biblical fervour' and meticulous personal attention,[3] Curzon, gave a new importance to the department and a prestige for its work derived directly from the viceroy himself.

The archaeological undertaking of the Government of India was shaped by several interlinked impulses. At one level, it was influenced by the passion felt by individuals such as Curzon for the preservation of historic monuments, whether in India or indeed in Britain. Curzon's sensitivity to the aesthetic combined with his 'powerful historical imagination' had led him to buy a number of dilapidated patrician houses and castles in Britain, and to study and restore them at great personal expense.[4] His preservationist instinct found more than ample room for play in India when he served as viceroy.

More importantly, the archaeological project in India was informed by intellectual developments in nineteenth-century Europe. The

[2] Speech delivered by H.E. the Viceroy and Governor-General of India (Lord Curzon) at a meeting of the Bengal Asiatic Society at Calcutta, on Tuesday, the 6 February 1900. Reproduced as Appendix II in Dilip K. Chakrabarti, *A History of Indian Archaeology* (New Delhi: Munshiram Manoharlal, 1988), pp. 227–36.

[3] David Gilmour, *Curzon* (London: John Murray, 1994), pp. 179–80.

[4] David Cannadine, *Aspects of Aristocracy: Grandeur and Decline in Modern Britain* (New Haven and London: Yale University Press, 1994), p. 80.

evolution of a new 'scientific history,' relying especially on the 'science' of archaeology, revealed the exciting potential for uncovering every minutia of life in antiquity. Armed with this new branch of knowledge, men such as William Jones, James Prinsep, James Fergusson, Alexander Cunningham and others went about reconstructing ancient Indian alphabets, deciphering inscriptions and translating manuscripts to make the silences of Indian history speak. The spirit animating them was a zeal for adding to the wealth of a common body of human knowledge.

Finally, the archaeological enterprise also served a political purpose, making it a vital instrument for the establishment of the colonial state in India. While this aspect may have existed only unconsciously in the minds of many of the officials who went about uncovering and preserving India's monumental legacy, political utility was a significant element in the functioning of the department. In contrast with Europe, where private wealth often funded the conservation of ancient monuments and archaeological research, in India archaeology began as and remained a responsibility of government.[5] As a result, it was woven into the legitimizing mechanisms of the colonial state and statements on archaeology were also political assessments of enlightened government.

The colonial government, linked directly to the crown and parliament in the metropolis after 1857, actively distanced itself from the now reviled days of the East India Company's trading Raj.[6] The new regime displayed its archaeological sensitivities to accentuate the contrast with its predecessor, in whose official mind 'the barbarian still dominated the aesthetic', concerned as it was 'with laying the foundations and extending the borders of a new Empire, [thinking] little of the relics of old ones.'[7] In the heyday of company rule, trader-officials

[5] Speech delivered by H.E. the Viceroy and Governor-General of India (Lord Curzon) at a meeting of the Bengal Asiatic Society, op. cit. Also, Letter from J. Fergusson to the Under-Secretary of State for India in Council, dated 10 June 1868, Home Dept. (Public), 22 August 1868, Pros. 90–1, Part A, NAI.

[6] As discussed in previous chapters, in 1858, in the aftermath of rebellion, the East India Company was abolished and control of India transferred to the British crown and parliament.

[7] Speech delivered by H.E. the Viceroy and Governor-General of India (Lord Curzon) at a meeting of the Bengal Asiatic Society at Calcutta, op. cit., p. 232.

had been concerned primarily with physically transferring to Britain the historical and cultural wealth of India, especially that obtained through warfare and standing as trophies marking its conquests.[8] Increasingly after 1857, the 'civilizing mission' of the colonial state focused on constructing its legitimacy on the ground and in full view of Indians who were to be its beneficiaries.

In India, through the task of archaeological conservation, the colonial government placed itself in a dual pattern of historical succession to previous indigenous rulers. At one level, it asserted continuity with Indian precursors and thereby tapped into their legitimacy. At another, it maintained its qualitative separateness from them and simultaneously also from the subjects whose governance it had inherited. Curzon's enlightening speech to the Bengal Asiatic Society in February 1900 represented the culmination of a process under way since 1858. He gave voice to a linear vision of history in which one ruler followed another with equal right to rule, pinning the legitimacy to govern not only on the inheritance but also the safekeeping of a historical legacy shared in common with Indians. Thus, with regard to the conservation of ancient monuments, as Curzon put it:

> We have a duty to *our* forerunners, as well as to *our* contemporaries and to *our* descendants . . . since we are the custodians for own age of that which has been bequeathed to us by an earlier . . . Moreover, how can we expect at the hands of futurity any consideration for the productions of our own time . . . unless we have ourselves shown a like respect to the handiwork of *our* predecessors.[9]

The archaeological remains of India also had their uses for the colonial government in demonstrating that the age of what they considered a genuinely Indian rulership had long passed. Thus Curzon suggested that a 'remarkable feature of the majority of Indian antiquities—of those at any rate that belong[ed] to the Muhammadan epoch' was that they did not 'represent an indigenous genius or an Indian style.'[10] Archaeology, therefore, provided plentiful evidence

---

[8] Bernard S. Cohn, *Colonialism and Its Forms of Knowledge* (Princeton: Princeton University Press, 1996), pp. 76–105.

[9] Speech delivered by H.E. the Viceroy and Governor-General of India (Lord Curzon) at a meeting of the Bengal Asiatic Society at Calcutta, op. cit., p. 227. Emphasis mine.

[10] Ibid., p. 229.

that India's historical legacy was a mosaic patterned by rulers 'foreign' like themselves and thus made for an easier succession to the governance of India by the British.

Yet, while part of its efforts were directed towards asserting historical continuity, the British Indian state engaged at the same time in the contradictory exercise of affirming its separateness from India. The capstone of the colonial state's legitimacy-building exercise, manifested in the high noon of empire under Curzon, was the claim to inheriting the entire sweep of India's past, Hindu and Muslim. This was justified by the contention that the British were endowed with a unique vision of India's history. Thus, Curzon suggested that a foreign 'race' such as the British were 'better fitted to guard, with a dispassionate and impartial zeal, the relics of different ages, and of sometimes antagonistic beliefs' than Indians—seen to be locked eternally in religious rivalry. Only the British could see that the relics of India represented the 'glories or the faith of a branch of the human family'.[11] The British were not just foreign but more foreign than any of their predecessors, being the representatives of a peerless and modern Western tradition towering loftily above the spirit of fractiousness deemed typical of Indians. They were successors to India within the framework of a Universal History but one of which they alone had an understanding and into which they alone were qualified to incorporate India. Of course, this made the burden of the colonial government only heavier. Any lapse in its task of archaeological conservation would lay it open to the accusation of 'merely . . . forging a fresh link in an unbroken historic chain' of Indian rulers prompted by 'religious fanaticism, or restless vanity, or of dynastic and personal pride'.[12]

Archaeology in India, then, was to a significant degree a political undertaking that, like the colonial state initiating it, sought to function within Indian society by keeping itself above it. Here the archaeological enterprise dovetailed neatly with a sociology of India invented by the colonial state also for the purposes of self-legitimation. The image of Indians trapped in a timeless cycle of religious strife had become conventional wisdom and served to put into greater relief the Solomon-like justice ushered in by *Pax Britannica*. The excessive attachment to religion by Indians was extended also to their buildings. In the

[11] Ibid., pp. 229–30.
[12] Ibid., pp. 230–1.

colonial vision, historical monuments, whether secular or religious, were divided into the 'communal' categories of Hindu (including Buddhist and Jain) and Muslim. Classificatory complications arising from the contradictory evidence of an admixture of 'Hindu' and 'Mohammedan' architectural styles were artfully dodged by reference instead to the faith of their patrons.[13] Against this backdrop, it was felt that if Indian society were allowed to take over, Hindu–Muslim antagonism would inevitably intervene to destroy each other's memorials.[14] This allowed the Archaeological Department to arrogate to itself the duty of laying down the principles of conservation and to continue to exercise the strictest management.

By Curzon's time, the department's task came to be defined in very clear religiously neutral terms as the preservation of historical and aesthetically worthy monuments, without reference to the faith of the communities that had built them. Reflecting this spirit of impartiality, Curzon told the Asiatic Society of Bengal:

> If there be any one who says that there is no duty devolving upon a Christian Government to preserve the monuments of a pagan art, or the sanctuaries of an alien faith, I cannot pause to argue with such a man. Art and beauty, and the reverence that is owing to all that has evoked human genius or has inspired human faith, are independent of creeds, and, in so far as they touch the sphere of religion, are embraced by the common religion of all mankind. [15]

Curzon's suggestion, further, was that the concern of archaeology should be purely with 'tear[ing] the mask off the face of the past' rather than with 'the dogmas of a combative theology'.[16] Buildings chosen for repair were described as 'national' monuments and the criteria for selection were solely their 'architectural merit or historic associations'.[17] In the same manner, the inscriptional records of the religions

[13] Thomas R. Metcalf, *Ideologies of the Raj*, (Cambridge: Cambridge University Press, 1995), pp. 151–3.

[14] Foreign Department (Internal B), October 1908, nos. 108–15, NAI.

[15] Cited in Gilmour, *Curzon*, pp. 178–9.

[16] Ibid.

[17] Note on Archaeology by Sir John Marshall, p. 4, OER, 1915, F.no. 45/E-73, JKA; Note in the Foreign Department, dated 8 August 1908, Foreign Department (Internal B), October 1908, Pros. nos. 108–15, NAI.

of the subcontinent had their experts represented equally in the department by two government epigraphists, one who dealt with Persian and Arabic, the other with Sanskrit and linguistically cognate materials. A similar scrupulously even-handed treatment was meted out by the two official journals of epigraphy printed by the department: the *Epigraphia Indica* and *Epigraphia Indo-Moslemia*.[18] Therefore, at least theoretically, the colonial state attempted to divest the objects of its attention of all religious association. However, this was a profoundly contradictory exercise. The colonial state's credentials as a non-partisan adjudicator were founded on first clothing monuments in religion to then denude them of it. The link between religion and history, and indeed the colonial state, was far from broken.

This paradox was rooted in the very principles of conservation and the purpose for which the Archaeological Department had been created. Its founding rationale had been the deployment of a new science to unlock the secrets of India's remotest past. However, a colonial historiography of India itself depicted the ancient period as the Hindu/Indian epoch preceding Muslim conquests. In 1870, Lieutenant H.H. Cole, superintendent of the Archaeological Survey of India, in justifying his task suggested that 'as bearing on our knowledge of India the study is important to those who wish to know who the people of this great country are and what state they existed in before the Mahomedan invasion'.[19] By 1906, the Director-General of Archaeology clearly enunciated the principle of 'preserving every class of monuments in the country whether they belong to the Christian, Muhammadan, Hindu or Buddhist creeds.'[20] However, in privileging antiquity, the department's focus on the oldest remains available also preserved the theme of correcting the depredations visited by 'fanatical' Muslim sovereigns, later arrivals, on Hindu temples. In 1901, Lord George Hamilton, the Secretary of State for India, accepting Curzon's argument that the conservation of Indian monuments was an 'imperial responsibility', had stipulated against spending money on buildings in an advanced state of ruin or on those that had

[18] Note on Archaeology by Sir John Marshall, p. 2

[19] Lieutenant Cole's Report on the Archaeological Survey of India for the year 1869–70, Home (Public), 4 June 1870, Pros. nos. 72–3, Part A, NAI.

[20] Note in the Foreign Department, dated 8 August 1908, Foreign Dept. (Internal B), Pros. nos. 108–15, October 1908, NAI.

been desecrated by 'natives' generations earlier.[21] Although prompted
by considerations of economy, the last injunction also made eminent
political sense. But little heed was paid to these restrictions. In 1915
the Director-General, Sir John Marshall, wrote of the urgency of
protecting those 'sacred edifices that [had] escaped destruction at the
hands of the Moslem invaders' and to preserve them as 'national heir-
loom[s] for posterity'.[22] Therefore it is open to speculation how truly
religiously neutral the archaeological department came to be viewed in
its actual operation despite its stated commitment to being so. A result
of its devotions was not only to preserve historical remains but also to
bring to public attention 'relics' that had faded from the 'national'
memory, as also stories of conflict embedded in them and now read as
purely religiously motivated. Yet the colonial state was undoubtedly
committed to the *principle* of the separation between religion and
archaeology, reiterating the historical importance of edifices and vacating them of people and their faiths.

Yet, since for the enterprise to be effective it could not function in
a vacuum, it became necessary for the Archaeological Department to
strike some roots within Indian society. The superior right of the British to rule could not merely be asserted but had to be recognized by
the subject peoples. However, Indian attitudes towards their monuments provided poor raw material for British conservationists to work
with. Curzon was appalled by 'a local and ignorant population, who
s[aw] only in an ancient building the means of inexpensively raising
a modern one for their own convenience.'[23] Thus, the sixteenth-
century fort in Delhi built by Sher Shah had been 'encumbered' with
'squalid' villages until the intervention by the Archaeological Department.[24] For Indians the weight of history sat lightly on their ancient

[21] Gilmour, *Curzon*, p. 179.

[22] Note on Archaeology by Sir John Marshall, pp. 6–7.

[23] Ibid., p. 228. It must be noted here that Curzon directed a great deal of his
vitriol not only at Indians but quite as much, if not more, at British officials and
soldiers who had occupied many monuments and so caused their deterioration.

[24] Note on Archaeology by Sir John Marshall, p. 4. Similarly, the department
cleared villages that had sprung up around other buildings in Delhi such as the
Khirki masjid (mosque) and the Moth ki Masjid, 'a singularly fine example of the
late Pathan work'. In 1847, Alexander Cunningham witnessed in Srinagar the
removal of materials from the ruins of the Mughal empress Nur Jehan's palace for

edifices. When structures could be recycled they were either put to new uses or were indeed 'vandalized' without qualms, and when they could not, they were allowed to fade away along with their builders. It became imperative, therefore, for the archaeological department to impart a new consciousness in the minds of Indians of the value of their monuments. In 1903, attempts were made to involve Indians themselves in the enterprise by encouraging the study of archaeology through the offer of state scholarships. By 1915, this programme registered a modest degree of success, as there were eight Indian scholars in archaeological posts, five in British India and three in the 'native' states of Hyderabad, Gwalior and Kashmir.[25] The hope was that through these measures and in collaboration with new museums, universities, colleges and schools, 'a much wider public interest . . . [would] be awakened, and [the] veneration for the remains of antiquity, . . . [would] become as marked a trait of the [Indian] cultured classes as it [was] in western countries.'[26]

Despite the need to involve Indians, however, the archaeological enterprise had to remain ultimately Western and inappropriable by Indians. This alone can explain the searing attack by James Fergusson, the British art historian, against Rajendralal Mitra, the most prominent Indian antiquarian of the nineteenth century. In his work, *The Antiquities of Orissa* (1875), Mitra demonstrated that he had evidently learnt his archaeological lessons too well. He marshalled his British training to refute, in an expression of nationalist pride, the view held by Fergusson and others that Indian stone architecture owed its origins to the Greeks. Fergusson's reaction was venomously racist. In the prefatory remarks to his book, *Archaeology in India With Especial Reference to the Work of Babu Rajendralal Mitra,* Fergusson asserted that 'the real interest of . . . [his] volume' was not 'in the analysis of the archaeological works of . . . Mitra'. Instead, he argued that at a time of 'the discussion on Ilbert Bills . . . the question as to whether the Natives of India [were] to be treated as equal to Europeans in all

---

the construction of annexes to the new Dogra ruler's palace at Shergarhi. Alexander Cunningham, *Description of the Temples of Kashmir*, pp. 5–6 and OER, F.No. 182/K-13, 1908, JKA.

[25] Note on Archaeology by Sir John Marshall, p. 3.

[26] Ibid.

respects' was of greater significance.[27] Indians were qualified neither to judge Europeans nor to presume to be their scholarly peers. Here was an exposition of what Partha Chatterjee has called the 'rule of colonial difference', according to which the colonial state was 'a modern regime of power destined never to fulfill its normalizing mission because the premise of its power was the preservation of the alienness of the ruling group'.[28] The process of evolving what had of necessity to remain an alien consciousness of the 'historical' value of their antiquities among Indians justified the imperial government's keeping close control over the nature of the 'veneration' to be inculcated.

Archaeology in the Service of the Dogra-Hindu State

Therefore, the British viewed the supervision of the archaeology of India as too important a task to be left entirely to Indians and insisted that it had to emanate from the colonial state and ultimately the viceroy himself.[29] There was a difficulty, though, in that many of these edifices lay within the territorial jurisdiction of native states. Victoria's proclamation of 1858 ending the East India Company's rule had also confirmed the remaining Indian princes in their sovereignty, albeit subordinated to British paramountcy, and the territorial integrity of their states. Therefore, in 1901, the Government of India could only 'invite' the co-operation of the native states in its archaeological enterprise and offer them advice or financial assistance.[30] But an invitation issued by the colonial state and the viceroy was no mean tool of persuasion, and in May 1904 the Jammu and Kashmir state resolved to

---

[27] James Fergusson, *Archaeology in India With Especial Reference to the Work of Babu Rajendralal Mitra* (New Delhi: K.B. Publications, first published 1884, reprinted 1974), pp. vi–vii. The Ilbert Bill, mooted in 1883, had attempted to make Europeans in India subject in criminal matters to the jurisdiction of Indian judges. It had to be revised substantially in the face of widespread and virulent protests by Europeans resident in India.

[28] Partha Chatterjee, *The Nation and Its Fragments* (Princeton: Princeton University Press, 1993), p. 18.

[29] Note by Lord Minto, dated 27 July 1907, Foreign Dept (Internal B), Pros. nos. 108–15, October 1908, NAI.

[30] Note on Archaeology by Sir John Marshall, p. 3.

create its own Archaeological and Research Department for the care of ancient monuments in its territory.[31]

However, it soon became clear that the native states would not be allowed immoderate degrees of independent action and that the Government of India would continue to arrogate to itself the final supervisory authority. The location of historical edifices in princely territory notwithstanding, they were deemed 'national' monuments and a 'definite duty' was placed on India's princes, regardless of their own views, to preserve them.[32] The Government of India laid down the principles of preservation and prepared lists of monuments of historical interest not only in British India but also in the princely states.[33] And by 1908, the Director-General of the Archaeological Department of India warned that the inability or reluctance of the Kashmir durbar to conserve its monuments would compel the colonial state 'to interfere and assert its own responsibility in maintaining them'.[34]

A tide of British criticisms about its inefficiency and the general apathy of the durbar towards its monuments soon followed the establishment by the Jammu and Kashmir state of its own archaeological and research department.[35] The Director-General of Indian Archaeology complained that the neglect of monuments in Kashmir was unrivalled in any other native state[36] and the viceroy himself noted with despair the durbar's reluctance to preserve its monuments.[37] However, colonial accusations of incompetence reflected a more fundamental disagreement with the durbar over three important areas of what was

[31] Note on Archaeological Work in Kashmir, OER, F.No. 293/E-8, 1909, JKA.

[32] Note by the Director-General of Archaeology, dated 6 August 1908, Foreign Dept (Internal B), Pros. nos. 108–15, October 1908, NAI.

[33] Note in the Foreign Department, dated 8 August 1908, Foreign Dept. (Internal B), Pros. nos. 108–15, October 1908, NAI.

[34] Foreign Dept (Internal B), Pros. nos. 108–15, October 1908, NAI.

[35] Note in the Home Department, Archaeology and Epigraphy Branch, dated 22 September 1909, Foreign Department (Internal B), October 1909, Pros. nos. 180–2, NAI.

[36] Note by the Director-General of Archaeology, dated 6 August 1908, Foreign Dept (Internal B), October 1908, Pros. nos. 108–15, NAI.

[37] Note by Minto, dated 1 October 1909, Foreign Department (Internal B), October 1909, Pros. nos. 180–2, NAI

at heart a political enterprise. First, the archaeological undertaking became enmeshed in a battle over sovereignty and control. Second, the Kashmir durbar objected particularly to British intervention in the realm of research and exploration and, finally, even when the durbar was willing to assume the task of archaeological conservation, it resisted having to conduct it within the idiom of a religiously neutral enterprise as defined by the British.

The Dogra state had grasped quickly that it would have no choice but to support in some form the colonial government's archaeological mission, now significantly also enshrined as a 'duty' of the state. However, having accepted its responsibility for monuments in its 'charge', the durbar was concerned precisely to retain charge. That its anxiety was not entirely misplaced was evident from the periodic threats of intervention that the colonial state issued. In its role as the ultimate guardian of India's historical memorials, the colonial state seemed in effect to reserve the right to breach the *de jure* political separation between British India and the princely states that it had recognized in 1858. In his report for 1908–9, the archaeological surveyor for the Frontier Circle, Dr Spooner, condemned in blunt language the inactivity of the Kashmir durbar in preserving its monuments. Significantly, his account also suggested that the only time Kashmiri officials 'display[ed] any energy at all' was when the British Indian department was 'trying to help' and then it was 'directed to putting difficulties and obstacles' in its way.[38] Spooner had travelled to the state to 'superintend personally' work being done on a ruined temple near the town of Rampur (Jammu). While the durbar had no objection to Spooner's offering recommendations or touring in the state, it felt that all 'active field work, whether conservation or excavation' must be reserved for its own officers.[39]

Similarly, 'obstructionist' proclivities resurfaced over the ownership of the finds of archaeological exploration. A dispute had erupted in 1910 when the colonial state sponsored an expedition to survey the archaeological remains of Ladakh. While the durbar had permitted

[38] Note in the Home Department, Archaeology and Epigraphy Branch, dated 22 September 1909, Foreign Department (Internal B), October 1909, Pros. nos. 180–2, NAI.

[39] *Annual Report of the Archaeological Survey of India, Frontier Circle, for 1908–9*, Foreign Department (Internal B), October 1909, Pros. nos. 180–2, NAI.

the survey, it insisted that the British would not be allowed to remove any antiquities from the state. Taken aback by this unusual
'solicitude of their antiquities', the British Director-General of Archaeology went so far as to question the right of the durbar to them. The
claim of the durbar was contested by arguments that it had not
financed the expedition and that in the past tourists had carried off
antiquities without interference. Moreover, the colonial government
demonstrated that the state had no proper provisions for the secure
housing of ancient artefacts. The durbar's cause was scarcely strengthened by the curatorial arrangements at its museum in Srinagar that
classified sculptures under the heading of Geology, 'presumably on
account of their being carved in stone'.[40] In the end the British Indian
government had to acknowledge that, although princely states had
not in the past contested its acquiring archaeological artefacts found
in native states, the pugnacity of the Kashmir government had been
provoked partly by the Director-General's attitude. Making a virtue
of necessity, the colonial state acknowledged the Kashmir durbar's
claim to 'objects found within [its] territories' but got in the last word
by 'express[ing] the wish that the durbar will take measures to ensure
the safe custody of the objects found'.[41] Within a decade the newfound
concern of the Kashmir government was enshrined in a notification
that upheld unequivocally the primary title of the state to objects of
archaeological, historical or literary interest in its territories.[42] At stake
was more than the supervision of archaeology itself but in fact the control of a political enterprise in which both the colonial and the princely
state of Jammu and Kashmir were involved.

The colonial government had noted regretfully also the durbar's indifferent disposition towards research.[43] However, it would appear
that the Government of India had not fully understood the Dogra
state's attitude. The Kashmir durbar's efforts, far from uninterested

[40] Note by Dr Vogel, Officiating Director-General of Archaeology, dated
1 June 10, Foreign Department (Internal B), June 1910, Pros. nos. 162–5, NAI.

[41] Note by L.W. Reynolds in the Foreign Department, Foreign Department
(Internal B), June 1910, Pros. nos. 162–5, NAI.

[42] As noticed by the judge of the High Court, Jammu and Kashmir State, this
notification even encroached upon the right of private owners of antiquities to sell
them. Note by Judge, High Court, Jammu and Kashmir State, dated 4 July 1919,
OER, F.No. 206/IV-3, 1919, JKA.

[43] Foreign Department (Internal B), June 1910, Pros. nos. 162–5, NAI.

in research, were directed to cordoning off this domain from British intervention. In 1910, Pratap Singh reorganized the state's archaeological department to separate the tasks of archaeology and research.[44] Justified in the interests of efficiency, the division had another fortuitous result. While conservation in the state continued to be supervised by an official trained by the Archaeological Department of India, the research branch was placed under a separate hierarchy headed by a linguist trained in Sanskrit, and manned overwhelmingly by Kashmiri Pandits.[45] In this way, the durbar attempted to guard the task of research, and the 'knowledge' produced by it, from colonial intrusion. Such a usable knowledge was to serve the Dogra rulers, rather than the colonial state, to bolster their legitimacy as patrons of Hindu learning and worship.

The research department of the Kashmir durbar promptly invented a genealogy for itself that reiterated its separateness from the colonial archaeological enterprise. It traced its origins to 1857, in the second year of Ranbir Singh's reign, a period pre-dating direct British involvement.[46] It was Ranbir Singh's accomplishments in 'foster[ing] Hindu learning' through his establishment of a Sanskrit library in the Raghunath temple in Jammu[47] that allegedly served as the model for the research department. And it drew its inspiration from his 'pious regard for the inherited religious traditions and enlightened interest in Indian learning,'[48] rather than from a colonially inspired interest in history

---

[44] Foreign Department (Internal B), September 1910, Pros. nos. 11–12, NAI and OER, F.No. 293/E-8, 1909, JKA.

[45] Letter from Dr. Vogel, Officiating Directory General of Archaeology in India, to The Secretary to Government of India, Home Department, dated 27 July 1910, Foreign Department (Internal B), September 1910, Pros. nos. 11–12, NAI. Also, Memorandum by the Committee appointed by His Highness the Maharaja Sahib Bahadur to Report on the Archaeological and Research Department, dated 2 August 1911, OER, F.No. 293/E-8, 1909, JKA.

[46] J.C. Chatterji, *A Report of the Archaeological and Research Department, Jammu and Kashmir, for the Sambat year 1960–62* (Jammu, Ranbir Prakash Press, 1909).

[47] Letter from G. Buhler, Educational Inspector, Northern Division, to the Director of Public Instruction, Bombay, dated 19 April 1875, Home Department (Public), May 1875, Pros. nos. 203–5, Part A, NAI.

[48] Cited in J.C. Chatterji, *A Report of the Archaeological and Research Department*, p. 1.

uninformed by religion. Thus, by 1910, Pratap Singh too had declared the objective of the research department to be the establishment 'once more [of] the reputation Kashmir enjoyed in Sanskrit learning as in the days of old'.[49] As a list of the tasks undertaken by the department demonstrates, it continued to focus on works associated with 'Hindu learning'.[50] An indication of the different path research might have taken under firmer British direction can be gleaned from Sir John Marshall's reproach that 'nothing had been done during this period towards elucidating the political history of the State' as understood by the British.[51] Although subsequent history proved them wrong, at this stage the durbar probably also hoped that the zeal with which work was carried out in the realm of research would disguise a marked imbalance in the area of archaeology. Whatever the calculation, while considerable work was done in collecting, translating and publishing Sanskrit texts, very little energy was expended on the conservation of monuments.[52]

The third and perhaps most significant point of contention by the Dogra state was over adopting the religiously neutral idiom that the British privileged. In fairness, to demand this would have been to ask the Dogras to reverse canons of governance based on 'tradition' the paramount power had itself aided in installing after the rebellion of 1857. As elaborated earlier, there was a vital difference in the relations between rulers and ruled in the British and Dogra states that underlay the work of archaeology. The colonial state claimed indifference to religion by placing itself above Indian society, whereas the Dogra state could neither be indifferent to religion nor above society. As 'native' rulers the Dogras were expected to derive their legitimacy to govern from 'traditional' relationships within society. However, as they were also constructed as traditional 'Hindu' rulers, they sought their legitimacy more narrowly from the Hindu segment of their subjects. While

[49] Memorandum by the Committee appointed by His Highness the Maharaja Sahib Bahadur to Report on the Archaeological and Research Department, dated 2 August 1911, OER, F.No. 293/E-8, 1909, JKA.

[50] J.C. Chatterji (ed.), *The Kashmir Series of Texts and Studies; Being a Prospectus of the Publications of the Archaeological and Research Department of the Jammu and Kashmir State*, Srinagar, 1911.

[51] Note on Archaeological Work in Kashmir, OER, F.No. 293/E-8, 1909, JKA.

[52] Ibid.

adherence to the precept of religious neutrality, or at least its myth, was essential for the functioning of any colonial institution, it went against the grain of Dogra arrangements of power and legitimacy.

While bending before the necessity for archaeological conservation, the Dogra state, however, resisted the application of a principle that would include Muslim monuments within its liability. In this context, the 'List of Ancient Monuments in Kashmir' drawn up in 1886 by the Archaeological Survey of India embodied a critical predicament. All eleven monuments enumerated were religious shrines, some in current use, and of these, two were Muslim shrines.[53] Reconciling their status as 'Hindu' rulers with the new demand that they undertake the maintenance of what were and had been Muslim tombs and places of worship was an enterprise replete with contradictions. This is neither to suggest that the Dogras were singularly bigoted rulers nor indeed that bigotry had anything to do with it. In 1901, the Begum of Bhopal had similarly declared her inability to preserve the Buddhist stupa at Sanchi on the grounds that by doing so 'she would be encouraging idol worship', a position irreconcilable with her status as a Muslim ruler.[54] While the colonial state had handed down the preservation of archaeological legacies as an obligation, princely rulers were left to devise their own framework within which to fit the project without undermining the ideological underpinnings of their claims to legitimacy. The archaeological scheme of the colonial state chose to view religious shrines as purely historical monuments, vacant of people and stripped of religious associations. For the Dogra rulers, on the other hand, that these historical monuments happened to be religious shrines was of inescapable significance.

Before the intervention of the colonial archaeological enterprise, custom in Kashmir had placed the burden on the various communities

[53] List of Ancient Monuments in Kashmir, Foreign Department (Internal B), May 1886, Pros. nos. 335–7, NAI.

[54] Note in the Foreign Department, Foreign Department (Internal B), October 1908, Pros. nos. 108–15, NAI. It is important to note that while the much-publicized policy of the Taliban government of Afghanistan in 2001 towards the Buddha statues in Bamiyan seems to echo this claim there is a vital difference between the two positions. The Begum of Bhopal, while disputing the state's duty in maintaining the Sanchi stupa, neither prevented other groups from undertaking this task nor advocated the destruction of the shrine.

themselves for the upkeep of their places of worship. Sunni and Shia shrines were looked after by *mutwallis* (managers) accountable to their respective local communities and notables. In the case of Hindu shrines, the maintenance of private temples was the responsibility of the individuals or families who had founded them. The care of 'state temples', on the other hand, was committed to the Dharmarth Trust.[55] Even though it had been transformed by the late nineteenth century into a department of the Kashmir government, at no stage was the upkeep of Muslim shrines considered the duty of the Trust or, by extension, the Dogra rulers. The regulations of the Dharmarth had merely stipulated that '*tiraths* (places of pilgrimage) . . . attached to the mosques and shrines of the Mohammadans, should not be disturbed',[56] with no further responsibility accruing to it. The dharmarth department, unlike the archaeological, was not founded on notions of religiously neutral functioning and so had no difficulty in excluding the shrines of other religious communities from the purview of its 'proto-conservationist' activities.

By the early twentieth century, Dogra proclamations increasingly asserted that the condition of all temples was of broader relevance in reflecting on the standing of the Hindu faith in the state to which was also attached the prestige of the ruling family. Therefore, even the theoretical separation between the state and private temples was increasingly obscured as the Dogra state, using the good offices of the dharmarth, took over the latter when they fell into disrepair. For instance, in 1908, a question had arisen about the maintenance of two temples in the sacred town of Purmandal built by Hakim Ganga Ram, who had died heirless and without making adequate provisions for their upkeep. Pratap Singh insisted on the state bearing the necessary expenses for maintaining these private temples on the grounds that 'it was not considered desirable to leave them in a neglected condition, a thing hardly permissible from a religious point of view.'[57] Not only

---

[55] Sant Ram Dogra, *Code of Tribal Custom* (1917), reproduced in Syed Tassadque Hussain, *Customary Law and Indian Constitution* (New Delhi, 1987), pp. 245–9.

[56] Ibid., p. 6. Interestingly, the word 'tirath' was part of Hindu religious terminology rather than Islamic.

[57] OER, F.No.117/G-34, 1908, JKA. In 1906, Pratap Singh had also stated: 'The maintenance of the temples where no aid in the form of *Mokarrari* is given

were a slew of similar acts of taking over the care of private temples justified for reasons of state, but they were also seen as consistent with the custom of religious communities caring for their own shrines. What was increasingly clear was that the Hindu community and the state were becoming coextensive. The Dogra ruler saw his role not only as a head of state but, *via* the dharmarth department, also as the leader and chief patron of the Hindu community.

The maintenance of Muslim shrines, then, remained the responsibility of the Muslims themselves, whether from the state or from British India. In 1886, the Nawab of Dacca provided funds for repairs to the Hazrat Bal mosque and Khwaja Naqshbandi's tomb, two revered Muslim shrines in Srinagar. The Kashmir State Council acknowledged that these works had been long desired by Kashmiri Muslims but that they had been unable to undertake them from a lack of finances.[58] Prior to the interjection of the archaeological mission in Kashmir, there seems to have been no expectation within the Muslim community either that the maintenance of their shrines was the responsibility of any but their own community and its leaders. Even Muslim-owned newspapers published in the Punjab but widely read in the valley, and which later levied the most vituperative criticism of the Hindu rajas of Kashmir, endorsed this point of view. For example, the *Koh-i-Nur* suggested that it was the obligation of Muslim *anjumans* (societies), whether in Punjab or in Kashmir, to repair Kashmiri mosques and raise funds for the purpose.[59] In 1881, the *Punjabi Akhbar,* another

---

from the state, should be provided from the Dharmarth Funds. If not, then for what purpose does the Dharmarth Funds exist?' [*sic*]. OER, F.No. 82-B-38, 1901, JKA.

[58] OER, F.No.1, 1886, JKA.

[59] *Koh-i-Nur,* Lahore, 13 November 1900, *Selections From the Vernacular Newspapers Published in the Punjab,* p. 640.

[60] *Punjabi Akhbar,* Lahore, 18 March 1881, *Selections from the Vernacular Newspapers Published in the Panjab, N.W. Provinces, Oudh, Central Provinces & Berar,* p. 157. This is not to suggest that the Punjabi Muslim press of the nineteenth century was entirely free of criticism of the Dogra state's withholding patronage from Muslim mosques. Indeed, in 1880 the *Rahbar-i-Hind* complained that despite the fact that the Muslims contributed most of the revenues of Kashmir, the state spent no money on mosques compared to the fortunes which were expended on temples and even on the Cathedral Church at Lahore. *Rahbar-i-Hind,* 4 May 1880, *Selections from the Vernacular Newspapers Published in the*

Muslim-owned paper, exhorted Kashmiri Muslims to be grateful to Ranbir Singh for his contribution of Rs 3000 towards repairs at the Jama-i-Masjid in Srinagar (a gesture of dubious effectiveness since this mosque was still in a dilapidated state at the turn of the century).[60] This was not, yet, an act of generosity expected by Kashmiri Muslims of their sovereign. This makes the contrast with what followed even sharper.

By the end of the first decade of the twentieth century, however, Kashmiri Muslims and the same section of the Punjab press fired repeated volleys of censure at the Kashmir durbar for neglecting mosques within its territory. They spoke and wrote in defence of edifices identified not only as religious shrines but also as historical monuments and emphasizing their antiquity.[61] They deployed a vocabulary given currency by the colonial state's archaeological enterprise to demand that the Dogra maharaja perform his duty and 'pay due heed to . . . *ancient* buildings and monuments.'[62] This was an indication of the remarkable rethinking about religion, legitimacy, the duty of the state and the rights of subjects that followed in the wake of the introduction of the archaeological enterprise in Kashmir.

The archaeological undertaking had undergone vital changes by the time it opened shop in Kashmir. Instituted to conserve historical monuments, the first deviation from its founding principles had

---

Panjab, N.W. Provinces, Oudh, Central Provinces & Berar, pp. 324–5. However, at this point, these were not only relatively isolated censures, but also qualitatively different from the more widespread complaints from the first decade of the twentieth century onwards. At this later point, not only was the demand made for more even-handed treatment of Muslim religious shrines but this was demanded as a right within the framework of a complex of conceptual tools provided by the Archaeological Department of India.

[61] *Paisa Akhbar*, Lahore, 27 April 1910, *Selections from the Native Newspapers Published in the Punjab*, p. 382. For instance, the *Paisa Akhbar*'s lament that 'a part of the magnificent Idgah at Srinagar, *which has been in existence for about the last 800 years*, is being built on by the State.' Emphasis mine.

[62] *Kashmiri Magazine*, Lahore, 14 August 1917, *Selections from the Indian Newspapers Published in the Punjab*, p. 690. The *Kashmiri Magazine* bemoaned the poor condition of mosques of specifically antiquarian interest such as Dara Shikoh's mosque, Sultan Fateh Shah's tomb, and particularly asked that the archaeological department of Kashmir look after them and improve their condition.

become apparent when colonial archaeology itself had categorized monuments as Hindu and Muslim. As suggested earlier, this was linked to the British Indian government's project of founding its superior right to rule on the carcass of a society discredited for its inherent religious divisiveness. To demonstrate its own lack of prejudice, colonial archaeology had to first identify the antagonists and then highlight its own equal treatment of them. The terms of reference were religious even in the case of structures that were clearly secular. Since the selection of important monuments for conservation was made by the colonial department, this classificatory scheme was extended also to Kashmiri monuments even in princely states, accounting for the inclusion of Mughal gardens in lists of 'Muhammadan' monuments.[63] However, while colonial archaeology demonstrated its impartiality by first investing monuments with religion to then strip them of it, Kashmiri edifices lay outside its territorial jurisdiction. Therefore, once they were given religious identities by the British-drawn lists, Kashmiri monuments continued to retain them as they were incorporated in the Dogra rulers' search for legitimacy as patrons specifically of Hindu worship.

The next shift in the working of the archaeological enterprise followed easily from this first. Objects selected for archaeological attention in Kashmir were not just buildings with religious associations but were, in fact, primarily religious shrines. This resulted partly from a scarcity of secular monuments of 'historical importance' that survived in Kashmir, aside from a handful of forts and Mughal gardens. However, the archaeological department of Kashmir carried its focus on the religious significance of ruins much further to preserve even sites that were barely visible. A telling instance was the energy devoted to protecting a stone plinth of twenty feet identified as the ancient site of the worship of Hatkeshwara, a Hindu deity.[64] This begs the question of how the archaeological department of Jammu and Kashmir defined its task. The significance of what was, from a strictly conservationist point of view, little more than a pile of stones stemmed only from the

<hr />

[63] Note in the Home Dept. by H.A. Stuart & H.A. Adamson dated 12 August 1908, Foreign Dept (Internal B), Pros. nos. 108–15, October 1908, NAI.

[64] Note on the Hatkeshwar Temple by the Superintendent, Archaeology, Research & Museum, dated 19 January 1940, Political Department, F.No. 146/G1-41, 1939, JKA.

Hatkeshwar shrine's having drawn, 'from hoary times', the veneration of Kashmiri Pandits.[65] It appears that the Kashmiri archaeological department had come to see its duty as that of protecting places of worship, particularly of the Hindu community.

Significantly, Hatkeshwar Bhairo had been the centre of a dispute between the Hindus and Muslims of the valley. In 1912, when some Muslims had removed stones from the Hatkeshwar shrine, believing it to be part of an adjacent mosque, the Hara Masjid, the dharmarth department had brought criminal proceedings against them. It had built its case by consulting 'authentic historical records' to determine that the site in question belonged to the Hatkeshwar shrine. When the dispute was revived in 1916, the maharaja asked the dharmarth department to erect a fence around the Hindu shrine. He added the admonition that 'Mohammedans have no right to interfere with Hindu shrines' and suggested that a temple be constructed at the site at once to prevent a 'breach of peace between the two communities'.[66] The attempt by a Pandit to implement this decision in 1923 drew Kashmiri Muslim protest. In that year Muslims from the Mallah Khan quarter of Srinagar petitioned the governor of Kashmir to stop the work of temple construction claiming that it was destroying the foundation of the mosque and disturbing the graves of religious leaders surrounding it.[67] Finally, the Kashmir state resolved the crisis by recommending that 'no sect be allowed to interfere with the site in any way' and placing the responsibility for its preservation on the archaeological department.[68]

Several motifs emerge strikingly in the narrative of this dispute indicating the extent to which the archaeological enterprise had become variously appropriable and available for deployment by all parties to

[65] Ibid.

[66] Letter from the Governor of Kashmir Province dated 1 May 1923 to the Senior and Foreign Member, Jammu and Kashmir State Council, General Department, F.No. 697/Ar-7/A, 1923, JKA.

[67] Vernacular Application dated 10 Baisakh 1980 (AD 1923) submitted by Mohammedans of Mohalla Mallah Khan etc., through Rajab Kak Lambardar to the General Assistant to the Governor of Kashmir, General Department, F.No. 697/Ar-7/A, 1923, JKA.

[68] Note by the Foreign Member of Council, dated 21 November 1923, General Department, F.No. 697/Ar-7/A, 1923, JKA and General Department, F.No. 33/C-38, 1923, JKA.

a dispute over religious shrines. Interestingly, the arguments employed by the Muslims in this echoed closely British archaeological ideas. In keeping with the Archaeological Department of India's principles of conservation, the Muslim petitioners pointed to the fact that, though in ruins, the foundations of the Hara Masjid were still extant in contrast with the meagre remains of the Hatkeshwar shrine.[69] Unlike the mosque and tombs, in compliance with colonial archaeological principles, the Hatkeshwar platform should have been viewed by Kashmiri archaeologists as 'already too decayed to be preserved'.[70] Instead, the Dogra state fulfilled its obligation to protect a Hindu place of worship by decreeing that the archaeological department take it under its wing.

Indeed throughout this dispute the archaeological department appeared to be synonymous with, or an extension of, the dharmarth department. The arrangements for the preservation of the site made by the archaeological department after 1923 merely replicated the previous actions of the dharmarth department in fencing off the stone plinth to prevent encroachment. That this was a measure directed against Muslims is clear from the archaeological department's awareness that, as late as 1940, Kashmiri Pandits continued visiting the Hatkeshwar Bhairo shrine.[71] It is also clear that, whatever the facts may have been regarding the temple of Hatkeshwar in the past, sites of Muslim veneration had sprung up around it in the centuries since. However, the state upheld the right of the Hindus over that of the Muslims and did this by privileging the antiquity of sites and adopting colonial principles of conservation useful for its own legitimizing structures. In some ways, Curzon himself had sanctioned the primacy of antiquity when he suggested that the 'work of the archaeologist in India' would lie in 'the exploration of purely Indian remains [presumably as opposed to the more recent and foreign Muslim ones], in the

[69] Vernacular Application dated 10 Baisakh 1980 Submitted by Mohammedans of Mohalla Mallah Khan, etc., op. cit.

[70] Dilip K. Chakrabarti, *A History of Indian Archaeology* (New Delhi: Munshiram Manoharlal, 1988), p. 105.

[71] In 1940, the Superintendent, Archaeology, had remarked that 'Pilgrims to the Sarika Parvata on their return homewards even now go round the place to offer their respects to Hatakeshwara'. Note on the Hatkeshwar Temple by the Superintendent, Archaeology, Research & Museum, dated 19 January 1940, Political Department, F.No. 146/G1-41, 1939, JKA.

probing of archaic mounds, in the excavation of old Indian cities, and in the copying and reading of ancient inscriptions.[72] This, coupled with Sir John Marshall's emphasis on preserving those structures that had survived destruction by Muslim invaders, could conceivably justify the durbar's action in connection with the Hatkeshwar Bhairo shrine as being legitimately within the parameters of the function of archaeology.[73] The services of the research department were availed of to confirm the authenticity and antiquity of the temple through references to the twelfth-century chronicle, *Rajatarangini*, and learned disquisitions on the etymological derivation of the word 'Hara' (as in the mosque) from the word 'Hataka' (as in Hatakeshwar).[74]

In fact, the research branch of the Kashmiri archaeological department played a critical role in strengthening the hands of the Dogra state in its selective protection of Hindu shrines. It did so by providing plentiful documentary evidence of the destruction by past Muslim rulers of Hindu temples in Kashmir. In 1905, the List of Ancient Monuments drawn up by the archaeological and research department of Kashmir, before its separation into different branches, meticulously listed those temples of the valley that had been converted into mosques and ziarats.[75] Ram Chandra Kak, a former director of the department, took up the theme of the destruction of temples by Muslim rulers so bluntly in his book, *Ancient Monuments of Kashmir*, that he was forced to expunge certain passages before it could be published by the India Society in London. These sections, it was suggested, were bound to offend Muslims, 'while they [were] irrelevant to the study of Kashmir archaeology'.[76] Here too, the research department could claim to be

[72] Speech delivered by H.E. the Viceroy and Governor-General of India (Lord Curzon) at a meeting of the Bengal Asiatic Society at Calcutta, on Tuesday, the 6 February 1900, op. cit.

[73] Note on Archaeology by Sir John Marshall, OER, F.No.45/E-73, 1915, JKA.

[74] General Department, F.No. 697/Ar-7/A, 1923, JKA; General Department, F.No.33/C-38, 1923, JKA, Political Department, F.No. 146/G1-41, 1939, JKA.

[75] A List of Ancient Monuments in Kashmir, Appendix A of J.C. Chatterji, *A Report of the Archaeological and Research Department*, op. cit. Ziarats are shrines built at the grave sites of prominent Sufis.

[76] General Department, F.No. 117/R.S.-3, 1928, JKA. One of the deleted excerpts compared Sultan Sikander of Kashmir to Charles IX of France responsible

taking its lead from the British. In 1848, Alexander Cunningham had written the earliest learned thesis on the temples of Kashmir, in which he had dedicated several pages to theorizing on the destruction by gunpowder of ancient Hindu shrines at the hands of Muslim rulers. His work, and that of many others, was part of a purportedly dispassionate historical exercise of providing the genealogies of Kashmiri Muslim shrines but which also traced their origins in the destruction of temples.[77] The literary productions of a research department manned almost entirely by Kashmiri Pandits, carrying with them the supposed sanctity of textual and archaeological evidence endorsed by the British, were important tools in decreeing Hindu precedence over shrines disputed between the Kashmiri Pandits and Muslims.[78]

If this were not enough to taint the archaeological department of Kashmir as a body working in the interests of the Hindu community, the outright refusal of the durbar to spend money on Muslim mosques and tombs would leave only the most naive in doubt. In July 1908, the British Resident reported that the Kashmir state could not 'find funds for their restoration' and that it did not 'care to throw away money on

---

for the massacre of St Bartholomew. Kak drew a grim picture of a blood-thirsty Muslim ruler whose 'perpetual cry' was to 'slay, burn, destroy' Hindus, Hindu images and shrines.

[77] Alexander Cunningham, *Description of the Temples of Kashmir* (1848, no other bibliographic information available), pp. 3–6; H.H. Cole, *Illustrations of Ancient Buildings in Kashmir* (London: W.H. Allen & Co., 1869).

[78] There were myriad such shrines the possession of which were disputed between the Hindu and Muslim communities of Kashmir. The Khanqah-i-Mualla (Shah-i-Hamadan mosque) and the adjacent Maha Kali shrine in Srinagar involved the two communities in repeated altercations. Whereas in the past the Pandits had been content to continue to worship at the site of the shrine over which the Khanqah-i-Mualla mosque had been established in the reign of Sultan Qutb-ud-din (1373–94), by 1924 they were demanding the right to erect a covering over the shrine. Political Department, F.No. 35/R-59, 1924, JKA. Pandit Anand Koul, *Archaeological Remains of Kashmir* (Srinagar: The Kashmir Bookshop, 1935?), pp. 22–4. Sanatan Dharm Youngmen's Association, Kashmir, *Memorandum of the Kashmiri Pandits on the Terms of Reference of the Grievances Enquiry Commission* (Srinagar: 1st December 1931), pp. 4–5; Political Department, F.No. 195/P.S.-323, 1932, JKA. The Kashmiri Pandits also laid claim to the whole of the Shankaracharya (Takht-i-Sulaiman) and Hari Parbat hills. *Report of the Commission Appointed Under the Orders of His Highness the Maharaja*

Muhammadans'.[79] That the durbar's tightfistedness was reserved specifically for Muslim religious shrines is evident from the large sums of money it spent at the same time on the maintenance of Hindu places of worship. For instance, only four years later, in 1913, the durbar provided an outlay of Rs 20,000 for repairs to the Shakta shrine of Khir Bhawani, justifying it in terms of its 'historical and religious importance'.[80] The colonial state could not tolerate such a blatant display of religious partisanship, especially when associated with a project it had originated and lent its name to. Embarrassed by growing public condemnation about the neglect of Kashmiri Muslim monuments, it was time for the British to pull up the Dogras. The durbar's shortage of finances was dismissed as a poor pretext since, as the colonial state pointed out, measures for the preservation of Muslim monuments suggested in 1906 by W.H. Nicholls, the archaeological surveyor for the Northern Circle, could not cost much. 'The durbar', the British warned, 'ought not to be permitted to neglect . . . remains merely because they [were] Muhammadan'.[81]

The result of the colonial government's intervention was the reiteration of the 'definite duty' of the Dogra state towards all ancient edifices within its charge. However, in the context of Kashmir where monuments were equated with religious shrines, the colonial state's contention implied that the Kashmir durbar also had a duty towards the mosques and shrines of Muslims and therefore towards its Muslim subjects. And where duty is assigned, certain rights are assumed.

Archaeology, Kashmiri Muslim Protest and the Reclaiming of Religious Sites

The Government of India had, albeit unwittingly, suggested to Kashmiri Muslims that if the durbar had a duty to preserve their religious

Bahadur, dated the 12th November 1931 to Enquire into Grievances and Complaints (Jammu: Ranbir Government Press, 1932), p.4.

[79] Letter from Sir Francis Younghusband, Resident in Kashmir, to the Secretary to the Government of India in the Foreign Department, dated 15 July 1908, Foreign Department (Internal B), October 1908, Pros. nos. 108–15, NAI.

[80] Chief Minister's Memorandum dated 11 July 1913, OER, F.No. 31/M-275, 1913, JKA.

[81] Foreign Department (Internal B), October 1908, Pros. nos. 108-15, NAI.

monuments, they in turn had the right to expect such protection. However, all evidence pointed to the archaeological department of Kashmir functioning as an instrument of Dogra sovereignty, asserted through the exclusive preservation of Hindu shrines. Therefore, since the Kashmir state had been negligent of its duty to conserve the ancient shrines of Muslims, the latter insisted that those of their monuments under the control of the state be returned to the community so that they could be cared for appropriately. The hiatus between colonial archaeological principles and their application in Kashmir provided a space and a vocabulary that Kashmiri Muslims manoeuvred to excise their shrines and, by extension, their community from the authority of the Dogra state. The tying in of archaeology and religious shrines made disregarded ancient mosques and Sufi shrines admirable battle-grounds for an emerging Kashmiri Muslim political leadership challenging the legitimacy of the Dogra state to rule over them.

Appropriating the archaeological project in order to control shrines also enabled a younger generation of Muslim politicians searching for new social bases of mobilization to challenge an older, more socially exclusive and élite leadership centred on the *mirwaiz* (chief preacher) of the Jama Masjid in Srinagar. As will be discussed more fully in the next chapter, from the late nineteenth century onwards, Sunni Muslims in Kashmir were increasingly divided along the lines of which of the two mirwaizes in Srinagar they supported. Besides the Jama Masjid mirwaiz, the other figure drawing the allegiance of Kashmiri Muslims was the mirwaiz of Khanqah-i-Mualla (or the Shah-i-Hamadan shrine).[82] This was an indication of a cleavage growing among Kashmiri Muslims between those relying on a tradition of Sufism and 'saint worship' and those turning increasingly towards more orthodox 'Wahabi' doctrines represented by the 'Jama Masjid faction.'[83] Even though Sufi Islam was more widespread in the valley than the Wahabi 'wave', the Kashmir Durbar nevertheless chose to co-opt the latter faction. Yet, while in the state's perception the Jama Masjid mirwaiz commanded a substantial following among Srinagar's Muslims, the religious affinity of a majority of Kashmiri Muslims was still oriented

[82] The Khanqah-i-Mualla was the shrine of Mir Saiyid Ali Hamadani of the Kubrawiya silsilah of Sufis, also known as Amir-i-Kabir, who is credited with having first brought Islam to Kashmir in the fourteenth century. The shrine and the mosque attached to it were held in great reverence among Kashmiri Muslims.

[83] Lawrence, *Valley of Kashmir*, p. 286.

towards Sufi shrines such as Hazrat Bal, Chrar-e-Sharif, Dastgir Sahib
and Maqdoom Sahib.[84] This rivalry intensified once the popular acti-
vist Sheikh Abdullah chose to support the Hamadani mirwaiz as the
leader of a more broad-based religious constituency. In the dual struggle for the leadership of Kashmir's Muslims and for autonomy from
the state, shrines were to play a vital role.

However, not all Muslim places of worship were equally available
for the mobilization of public opinion against the Dogra-Hindu state.
The Jama Masjid, for instance, remained the preserve of its mirwaiz
and his supporters locked in a comfortable relationship of mutual dependence with the durbar. In 1906, the British archaeological surveyor had tagged this mosque for conservation and leading sections of
the Muslim community of Srinagar had come forward to raise subscriptions for the purpose.[85] Although the maharaja also contributed
Rs 40,000 towards the repairs, most of the expenditure was raised from
the Sunni peasantry of the valley. The subscription was levied as a tax
on each of them and realized along with the land revenue.[86]

Though the durbar's contribution was undeniably generous, this
was the only Muslim monument of any significance to the preservation of which it made any benefaction, and that too bowing to pressure from the Government of India. Even then it is of significance that
the work was not carried out under the aegis of the archaeological department of the state.[87] The latter's role in this case was limited to
ensuring that no part of any Hindu temple was demolished for the
repair of the mosque.[88] And, since the maharaja's grant was conditional upon 'his Sunni subjects' bearing the brunt of the financial
and organizational responsibility for the repairs,[89] to all intents and

[84] Walter Lawrence, as we saw, mentioned the special reverence in which these
shrines were held in Kashmir. Lawrence, *The Valley of Kashmir*, p. 292.

[85] Report by W.H. Nicholls, Archaeological Surveyor, Northern Circle, dated
September 1906, and Note in the Foreign Department, dated 8 September 1908,
Foreign Department (Internal B), October 1908, Pros. nos. 108–15, NAI.

[86] Khan Bahadur Sheikh Muhammad Maqbool Hussain, *Halat-e-Masjid-e-
Jama* (Urdu) (Srinagar: Kashmir Pratab Steam Press, 1916).

[87] Diwan Bahadur Diwan Amar Nath, *Administration Report of the Jammu and
Kashmir State, 1912–13*, p. 98.

[88] Letter from the Superintendent of Archaeology, Jammu and Kashmir State,
to the Home Minister, dated 7 July 1913, OER, F.No. 234/FC, 1913, JKA.

[89] Memorandum by the Home Minister on the Measures for Repairing the
Jama Masjid (Srinagar), OER, F.No. 104/B-125, 1911, JKA.

purposes the onus still lay with the Muslim community for the maintenance of its religious structures. The framework within which the repairs to the Jama Masjid were conducted was amenable, therefore, to the Dogra state's pattern of funding religious shrines. This particular royal donation was merely an occasional and unexpected gesture of magnanimity towards Kashmir's Muslims.

A committee to supervise the work was set up that consisted of the Muslim social and economic élite of Srinagar and headed by such luminaries as the mirwaiz and the renowned merchant Khwaja Saad-ud-din Shawl. Well-publicized work on the mosque was, of course, an opportunity for these members of the élite to advertise their leadership position in the valley. When the committee volunteered their subscriptions for the repairs, it claimed the authority to speak on behalf of all Sunni Kashmiris who were never, in fact, consulted in the matter. The committee declared without hesitation that no Muslim would object as 'the work [was] entirely in their interest and in accordance with their wish.'[90] At the same time, never failing to articulate appropriate expressions of gratitude to the maharaja, this committee behaved rather more like petitioners than as subjects demanding a right they were entitled to. Which is probably why the durbar, once forced into it, had no further objection to funding the repair of the mosque. The conservation of the Jama Masjid and the committee supervising it had allowed itself to be co-opted within a pattern of patronage acceptable to the maharaja.

It is clear that the position of the Jama Masjid *vis-à-vis* the Dogra state was at least unusual, if not unique, for sites of Islamic worship in the valley. Most other Muslim shrines were kept outside the compass of state patronage and were overlooked by the Kashmiri archaeological department. Among them was the Patthar Masjid (stone mosque) located in Srinagar. This edifice is especially interesting, for it was transformed from a mosque in which worship had been abandoned centuries earlier to a symbol and rallying call for the Muslims of Kashmir struggling for the protection of rights defined in broader terms than the purely religious. From all accounts it would appear that the Patthar Masjid had occupied no place of particular significance in the

[90] Ibid., and Khan Bahadur Sheikh Muhammad Maqbool Hussain, *Halat-e-Masjid-e-Jama.*

religious practices of the Kashmiri Muslims for several centuries before the first decade of the twentieth. This mosque, built by the Mughal empress Nur Jehan, had been declared desecrated and unfit for worship soon after its construction. One of the many apocryphal explanations offered for this is that when asked how much it had cost to build it, she had pointed to her shoe intending to indicate that the expense was equal to the value of the pearl embroidered on it. Some later historians have suggested that worship at the mosque was discontinued because it had been erected under the patronage of a woman. Whatever the reason, it is clear that at the time of the transfer of the valley to the Dogras in 1846 it had long ceased to be used for prayer and had done duty as military stables and afterwards as a state granary.[91] The historical record is remarkably lacking in any evidence of protest from the Muslim community over the secular uses to which the mosque had been put. That is until the colonial archaeological department turned its attention to the edifice in 1906, declaring it to be a 'Mosque, in pure Moghal style . . . very precious in Srinagar, where so few stone buildings exist' and called for its preservation.[92]

In 1910, under pressure from the colonial department, the director of the Kashmir archaeological department asked the state to transfer the mosque to its care arguing that it was 'a Mohammadan Monument of considerable importance.'[93] Nevertheless, after calling for a report on the 'history and archaeological interest' of the mosque and despite it, the maharaja ordered that it house an orphanage dedicated

[91] Letter from Lt. Col. J. Manners-Smith, Resident in Kashmir, to Mr J.B. Wood, Political Secretary to the Government of India in the Foreign and Political Department, dated 28 August 1916, Foreign and Political Department (Internal B), September 1916, Pros. nos. 192–6, NAI. Also, Note by the Chief Minister, Jammu and Kashmir State, dated 13 January 1911, OER, F.No. 55/E-3, 1911, JKA. As late as 1903, there is evidence that the State rented out the Patthar Masjid to individuals for the storage of grain. Letter from C.M. Hadow, Esq., to the Revenue Member of Council, dated 22 October 1903, OER, F.No. 154, 1903, JKA.

[92] Report by W.H. Nicholls, Archaeological Surveyor, Northern Circle, dated September 1906, Foreign Department (Internal B), October 1908, Pros. nos. 108–15, NAI.

[93] Letter from the Director of the Archaeological and Research Department, Jammu and Kashmir State, to the Public Works Minister, Jammu and Kashmir State, dated 23 December 1910, OER, F.No. 55/E-3, 1911, JKA.

to the Hindu deity Sri Gadadharji (Hanuman).[94] Now Kashmiri Muslim protests over the 'sacrilege' committed at this shrine erupted out of all proportion to the preceding silence. In February 1912, the Muslim revenue minister of the state had suggested to the Dogra maharaja that judging from his 'own feelings as a Mohammedan, [he could] have no doubt that the use of the Pather Masjid as a habitation will hurt the susceptibilities of His Highness' Mohammedan subjects. The mosque [had] already been misused in the past, but it was so far used only as a store for grain. Its use now as a dwelling house will . . . be generally regarded as a desecration'. He advocated the state's placing the mosque under the charge of the archaeological department. A year earlier in 1911, the same minister had been approached with a request from Kashmiri Muslims to have 'the mosque restored to its *legitimate* purpose'.[95] This signals a discrepancy between the archaeological mission and the aims of the Muslim community. The archaeological department sought to reclaim the mosque from the maharaja for its preservation as an ancient monument, whereas the Muslims of Kashmir were demanding that it resume its function as a mosque.[96] For instance, a petition submitted by A.S. Rafiqi, a Srinagar merchant, suggested that, as he had heard the maharaja intended to clear the mosque of grain and transfer it to the archaeological department, he might consider allowing the Muslims to read their prayers there 'without hitch or hindrance'. He added that he was prepared to bear all the expenses for lighting the structure and for the maintenance of an imam and a muezzin.[97] Of course, the Kashmiri Muslim petitioners conveniently chose to forget that their own forefathers had discarded this religious structure centuries earlier.

In 1912, in utter disregard of the wishes expressed in these petitions, the maharaja upheld his decision to locate the Sri Gadadharji

---

[94] Orders of the Maharaja dated 30 August 1911 and 13 February 1912, OER, F.No. 55/E-3, 1911, JKA.

[95] Letter from the Revenue Minister, Jammu and Kashmir State, to the Chief Minister, Jammu and Kashmir State, dated 13 February 1912, OER, F.No. 55/E-3, 1911, JKA. Emphasis mine.

[96] Ibid.

[97] Application submitted by A.S. Rafiqi, Srinagar, to the Revenue Minister, Jammu and Kashmir State, dated 28 September 1911, OER, F.No. 55/E-3, 1911, JKA.

Orphanage within the mosque. This sparked off searing attacks on the Dogra rulers, and since no newspapers were allowed publication in the state until 1932, Muslim-owned newspapers from the Punjab became the forums for the campaign against the Kashmir durbar. The reaction focused not only on the religious offense, but the treatment of the Patthar Masjid was seen as symptomatic of a variety of non-religious disabilities suffered by the poorest classes among Kashmiri Muslims. The horror of a Hindu idol being 'worshipped in the mosque' was linked more broadly to the powerlessness of the vast majority of the Dogra-Hindu state's Muslim subjects. As the press incanted, not only were they deprived of proprietary rights in land, but subjected to arbitrary acts of eviction, oppression by the 'pettiest officials' and the compulsory and unpaid requisition of their labour, from all of which disabilities Hindus were exempt.[98] These critics also bemoaned the state's failure to provide for the education of its Muslim subjects, thereby disqualifying them from lucrative jobs in administration, monopolized by Hindus, and keeping them in the most abject condition of poverty. A significant part of the reaction also took the form of severe castigation of the inadequate leadership provided by the Kashmiri Muslim élite. The *Zamindar* of Lahore suggested not only that 'their spiritual leaders and well-to-do co-religionists stand in the way of the [Kashmiri] Muslim community receiving education [but that] . . . the Maulvies also prevent grievances . . . being laid before the state authorities.'[99] This potent critique seemed especially apropos when considering that this is the time when sections of the Kashmiri Muslim élite, claiming to speak on behalf of all the Sunni Muslims of the valley, had been subscribing to repair the Jama Masjid.

By 1913, the maharaja dropped the idea of the orphanage and officially declared his intention to transfer the Patthar Masjid to the state's archaeological department.[100] However, not only was this measure not put into effect but it sparked off a fresh round of agitation in which the demands of Kashmiri Muslims shifted subtly but crucially. Petitions

[98] *Paisa Akhbar*, Lahore, 11 September 1912, *Selections from the Native Newspapers Published in the Punjab*, p. 764.

[99] *Zamindar*, Lahore, 8 October 1912, *Selections from the Native Newspapers Published in the Punjab*, pp. 850–1.

[100] Order passed by the Maharaja on 25 June 1913, Political Department, F.No. 55/E-3, 1911, JKA.

from this period showed a remarkable replication of the colonial state's language in advertising the historical worth of the shrine. In the words of one supplicant, writing to the viceroy, the destruction of 'an ancient mosque called Pathar Masjid in Srinagar . . . a very good specimen of . . . architecture of the time of the late Jahangir, Emperor of India' would mean that 'a valuable old architectural monument [would] disappear.' This would also 'hurt the feelings of thirteen lakhs of Muhammadan subjects of Kashmir'.[101] Another petition from the same period expressed surprise that the durbar could consider converting the mosque to any other use when its priority should clearly be to 'maintain the ancient buildings'. To prevent such an action, 'injurious to the Muslims', the petitioners appealed to the British Resident not only to order that the building continue as a mosque but that the Muslim community be allowed to undertake its repair.[102] Not only did these petitions condemn the Dogra state for its failure to perform its duty in preserving the mosque but the request was that Muslims be given the opportunity to rectify this 'disgrace for Islam [*sic*]'.[103] Given that the state had only recently contributed funds for repairs to the Jama Masjid, it is significant that a similar demand was not made for the Patthar Masjid. Growing numbers of Muslims now demanded autonomy from the state for newly rediscovered sites of their historical and religious affinity. Mobilization around the Patthar Masjid, which had been accompanied by the assembling of parties of Muslims to offer prayers within its premises,[104] insisted not that it be maintained as a historical monument alone, but that it be returned to the Muslim community as a mosque under its own control.

Echoes of this demand were also heard in the Punjab press, with newspapers such as the *Vakil* of Amritsar mobilizing behind the resumption of the Patthar Masjid's function as a mosque. This newspaper raised it as 'a question of principle which the state should duly consider'. It suggested that the maharaja 'issue a general proclamation

[101] Abstract translation of petition in Urdu from Haji Abdullah Shah, Gorgati Mahallah, Srinagar, to H.E. the Viceroy, dated 7 August 1916, Foreign and Political Department (Internal B), September 1916, Pros. nos. 192–6, NAI.

[102] Petition from Hakim Maqbool Shah and Muslim Community Kashmir, Srinagar, to the Resident, dated 3 August 1916, OER, F.No. 55/E-3, 1911, JKA.

[103] Ibid.

[104] Copies of Police Reports forwarded by the Home Minister, Jammu and Kashmir State, dated 14 August 1916, OER, F.No. 55/E-3, 1911, JKA.

that no mosque [would] be employed for the use of the state and that all mosques in the state . . . be considered as belonging to Muhammadans, who alone [could] make alterations in accordance with their needs.'[105] This same newspaper further cemented the causal links between religious affiliation and the economic oppression of the Kashmiri Muslims in a later report on the Patthar Masjid. The article cited an eyewitness's account that while 'the Amar Nath festival [was] being held in Kashmir . . . with great pomp and ceremony . . . the fair [was] causing a great deal of hardship and suffering to thousands of poor and voiceless Muhammadans who are impressed on the occasion. They are torn away from their children without the hope of receiving any remuneration, forcibly employed for the convenience of *pujaris* [priests] and made to carry their luggage.'[106] The *Kashmiri Magazine*, edited by Muhammad-ud-din Fauq, a Kashmiri Muslim living in Lahore, made the most effective use of the new concept of the Kashmir state's duty to preserve Muslim historical edifices to then argue for their autonomy. He exposed the explicitly Hindu identity of Dogra rule that allowed it to abnegate its duty towards the monuments of the Muslims. Debating the Patthar Masjid issue, the magazine complained that when, in the course of excavation, a temple, four feet high and three feet broad, had been discovered in Pattan, the archaeological department had taken immediate steps for its protection and repair. The care shown for even 'a diminutive temple' was in sharp contrast with the department's taking 'no steps to preserve the Patthar Mosque, a relic of Mughal rule'.[107] Writing a fortnight earlier, Fauq had suggested that Hindu places of worship were 'daily extended and beautified to please only 5 per cent of the inhabitants of Kashmir.' If 'the religious places of 95 per cent inhabitants of the State' could not be given the same attention, he contended, 'they should at least be restored to the Muhammadans.'[108] Joining in the chorus in the Punjab was the Muslim Kashmiri Conference based in Lahore that had since

[105] *Vakil,* Amritsar, 16 August 1916, *Selections from the Indian Newspapers Published in the Punjab,* p. 691.

[106] *Vakil,* Amritsar, 30 August 1916, *Selections from the Indian Newspapers Published in the Punjab,* pp. 712–13

[107] *Kashmiri Magazine,* Lahore, 14 September 1916, *Selections from the Indian Newspapers Published in the Punjab,* p. 771

[108] *Kashmiri Magazine,* Lahore, 7 September 1916, *Selections from the Indian Newspapers Published in the Punjab,* p. 750.

the early twentieth century served as a forum for expatriate Kashmiris 'to ventilate grievances against the Dogra administration'.[109] In a letter in 1918, it demanded the 'handing over of the Mosque to the Mussalmans of Srinagar,' premising this on the fact that even after the decision of the Dogra durbar to hand the mosque to the archaeological department, it was 'still in the same neglected condition'.[110] The Patthar Masjid had assumed a new significance for the Muslims of Kashmir, both those living in the valley and those outside it.

The project of archaeology had provided an even scale with which to gauge the state's fulfillment of its obligations towards the different communities of its subjects. Muslims in Kashmir increasingly used this unit of measure to strip away the legitimacy of the Dogra state to rule over them. They put forward the condition of their historical monuments as emblematic of the general disabilities they suffered from. From this stepping stone, they leapt to the next and demanded the fulfillment of their rights as a community but made the call from a position of autonomy from the state. To the Patthar Masjid was attached the demand for the restoration to the community of numerous other historical sites of Muslim veneration marking an escalation of the resistance to Dogra rule.[111] Pratap Singh, for one, appeared to have realized that the movement for the restoration of the Patthar Masjid ran deeper than its most obvious outward appearances let on. He remarked that the mosque had been 'in the possession of the state since the time of . . . Maharaja Gulab Singh' and so 'the movement *now* started for its recovery [was] due to ulterior motives and should not be countenanced in any way.' The agitators, he suggested, should 'be given clearly to understand that they have *no rights*.'[112]

[109] Jalal, *Self and Sovereignty*, p. 352.

[110] Letter from the Honorary Secretary, Kashmiri Muslim Conference, Central Standing Committee, Lahore, to the Home Minister, Jammu and Kashmir State, dated 14 June 1918, OER, F.No. 55/E-3, 1911, JKA.

[111] These included the famous mosque of Akhun Mullah Shah built by Dara Shikoh, the Khanqah Sokhta, the Khanqah Bulbulshah, the Malshahi Bagh mosque, the Badshah's dome as well as the Hamam Dara Shikoh and numerous sites claimed as ancient graveyards. OER, F.No.190/P-119, 1915, JKA; *Kashmiri Magazine*, Lahore, 7 September 1916, *Selections from the Indian Newspapers Published in the Punjab*, p. 750; and *Report of the Commission Appointed to Enquire into Grievances and Complaints* (Jammu: Ranbir Government Press, 1932), p. 3.

[112] Order by the Maharaja Pratap Singh, dated 10 October 1922, General Department, F.No. 58/G-240, 1923, JKA. Emphasis mine.

But it was precisely this claim of the superior right of the Muslims to the possession of their neglected religious monuments that was finally acknowledged by the Glancy Commission in 1932. It had been appointed by the British to inquire into Hindu–Muslim riots that broke out in the state in 1931 (discussed in the next chapter). Examining a wide array of economic and political grievances of the various communities in the state believed to have caused the disturbances, the report provided an opportunity for the colonial state to rectify the archaeological excesses of the Dogra state. The commission's report included a sharp criticism of the Kashmir durbar's tendency to privilege Hindus and Hindu claims to shrines. B.J. Glancy wrote:

> The Kashmiri Pandits and Buddhists have laid claim to a large number of buildings which, it is contended, were at one time temples and have now become Muslim places of worship. It is clearly impracticable to uphold claims of this nature. In countries such as Kashmir, where in the past mass conversion has occurred, it is only natural that a number of sacred buildings devoted to the observances of one particular faith should have converted to the use of another religion: where such conversion has taken place and worship is still conducted, restoration to the community representing the original users is obviously out of the question. Nor is it within the bounds of practical politics to hand over the whole of the Shankarachariya (Takht-i-Suleman) and Hari Parbat Hills to the Pandit community: these areas have been extensively built over for a very considerable number of years . . . and it is impossible to recommend the demolition of all houses, grave yards etc. which are at present situated in these localities.[113]

It took a riot to achieve it, but the British did, in the end, put into perspective and place under political restraint the privileging of the principle of antiquity as the moving precept of the archaeological enterprise. Additionally, by recommending the restoration to the Muslim community of practically all the shrines demanded by them, barring those too dilapidated to be safe, the commission acknowledged the validity of Muslim claims staked to these neglected sites of their cultural and religious veneration.

It is interesting to note that among the grievances presented to the Commission, was the Kashmiri Pandit community's unhappiness

[113] *Report of the Commission Appointed to Enquire into Grievances and Complaints*, p. 4.

over the temporary abolition of the state archaeological department.[114]
The reasons for dismantling the department are, unfortunately, not
discussed in the available sources nor is there any clear indication of
when it resumed its functions. However, representatives of the Kashmiri Pandit community protested 'with all the force that [they could]
command . . . against the abolition.' By their own admission, the
'monuments of Hindu religious architecture form[ed] the largest
number of the "protected monuments" of the Department.'[115] If further confirmation were needed of the particular Hindu interests the
archaeological enterprise in Kashmir had served, the Kashmiri Pandits
insisted that, unlike the Muslims, 'the Hindus ha[d] no desire of
seeking the possession of those places of worship . . . under the control
of the Government'.[116]

The years prior to the riots of 1931 and, formally, immediately
after, had seen the emergence of a powerful regional party in Kashmir
called the All Jammu and Kashmir Muslim Conference under the
leadership of Sheikh Mohammed Abdullah. Although this is discussed at greater length in the next chapter, a few points about this party
can be made here. Unlike the earlier self-appointed representatives
drawn from the commercial and landed élite of Srinagar, the Muslim
Conference sought to build a wider base of support among the agricultural and artisan classes of the valley. Its unambiguously anti-Dogra
stand, demanding economic, political and religious rights from the
state, had made the decrepit condition of Muslim shrines in state possession an important symbol of Kashmiri Muslim powerlessness. The
success of their agitation was marked by the fact that the very first issue
to be discussed by the Glancy Commission's report was precisely the
restoration of religious monuments, dealt with under the category
'religious grievances'. The issue of the Patthar Masjid had been a pivot
of the Muslim Conference's political mobilization. In the aftermath
of the events of 1931, the party took more aggressive measures to
reap rewards from the symbolic significance with which the agitation

[114] Ibid.; Sanatan Dharm Youngmen's Association, Kashmir, *Memorandum of
the Kashmiri Pandits on the Terms of Reference of the Grievances Enquiry Commission* (Srinagar, 1931), p. 4.

[115] Sanatan Dharm Youngmen's Association, Kashmir, *Memorandum of the
Kashmiri Pandits*, p. 4.

[116] Ibid., p.3.

around it had imbued the mosque. The shrine also gave the Conference a handle with which to contest the only other section in Kashmiri society with political clout to rival its own, namely religious leaders such as the mirwaiz of the Jama Masjid. Therefore, the Patthar Masjid had an afterlife in the politics of Kashmir even subsequent to the fulfillment by the Glancy Commission of the demand that it be restored to the community as a mosque.

As mentioned earlier, the Dogra government had realized full well the political significance of the agitation around the Patthar Masjid. This perception was reiterated by the fact that in returning the shrine to the Muslim community, as per the Glancy Commission's 'recommendation,' the durbar did so on condition that 'no speeches other than the purely religious be made in the mosque or in the compound attached to it'.[117] However, this was an exceptional stipulation reserved for the Patthar Masjid and was not applied as a proviso for the return of other mosques. As pointed out by the inspector-general of police in Srinagar, counselling against the durbar's policy, the government had never generally condemned the practice of making political speeches at mosques.[118] Refuting the police officer's recommendation, another senior official of the state pointed out that 'the Pathar Masjid ha[d] a great history behind it and [that] it was probably with this history in view that a definite condition was attached to the order of the rendition that the mosque was on no account to be used for political purposes.' He added that there was no reason why 'a general rule or order should govern all mosques and other sacred places recently restored.'[119] Quite evidently then, the Patthar Masjid was a case apart. It provided a mix of religion and politics too potent for the Dogra state, especially since it was a politics that demanded the fulfilment of rights and not a petition for occasional benevolence.

Regardless of the durbar's reservations, by 1933 the Muslim Conference not only went on to raise subscriptions for the construction of a party office in the premises of the mosque but also to create

[117] Notification by the Prime Minister, Jammu and Kashmir, dated 29 October 1931, Political Department, F.No. 373/14-P.S., 1933, JKA.

[118] Confidential letter from the Inspector General of Police, Political Department, F.No. 373/14-P.S., 1933, JKA.

[119] Report by the District Magistrate, dated 8 November 1933, Political Department, F.No. 373/14-P.S., 1933, JKA.

a 'Dar-ul-Fatwa' within it. The Muslim Conference appropriated the right of issuing religious fatwas by employing a religious expert of their own choosing from the region of Poonch and in the face of opposition from government recognized *muftis* (jurisconsults) of Srinagar.[120] To the great worry of both the durbar and the mirwaiz of the Jama Masjid, the Dar-ul-Fatwa organized by the Muslim Conference established branches throughout the valley of Kashmir.[121] The Patthar Masjid agitation indicated a gradual shift in the political leadership of Kashmiri Muslims. The mosque had, after the Glancy recommendations, been made over to the charge of Khwaja Saad-ud-din Shawl as a 'respectable Mohammedan', a representative of the older Srinagar élite, a friend of the mirwaiz of the Jama Masjid and an acceptable figure to the Dogra state. But that the political initiative had changed hands was made patently obvious when Shawl was forced to transfer control over the mosque to the Muslim Conference.[122] The Patthar Masjid had become a potent site for a party seeking political credibility in an arena in which the defense of religious shrines was an efficacious means of protest against a state with its own explicitly religious identity. And the Muslim Conference was determined to extract every capacity of the archaeological enterprise to provide a multitude of new 'old' sites, so to speak, to be recovered and reclaimed.

On 6 February 1932, an astounded governor of Kashmir reported that Sheikh Abdullah had arrived with 'a mob' at the compound of his office and had proceeded to read prayers under a tree claiming that an ancient shrine had been located there. Deaf to protests by the authorities that there were no visible indications of any mosque or shrine, the Muslims, led by Abdullah, declared their intention to read prayers at that spot every Friday and light a lamp every night from then on. A government made more sensitive since the appointment of the Glancy Commission, instituted an investigation into these claims. And sure enough, it was revealed that the tomb of a religious divine had indeed

[120] Letter from the Revenue Minister to Colonel E.J.D. Colvin, Prime Minister, Jammu and Kashmir State, dated 27 June 1933, Political Department, F.nos. 373/14-P.S., 1933, JKA.

[121] Translation of a letter from Mir Waiz Mohammed Yusuf Shah to the Prime Minister, Jammu and Kashmir State, dated 14 June 1933, Political Department, F.No. 373/14-P.S., 1933, JKA.

[122] Note by E.J.D. Colvin, dated 25 October 1933, Political Department, F.No. 373/14-P.S., 1933, JKA.

existed at the site but also that, following a conflagration in 1875, the area had remained deserted. However, the tomb and its location on the premises of the governor's office was mentioned in a relatively recent history written in around 1893 by Haji Ghulam Mohi-ud-din of Saraibal. Evidently, no one had paid much attention to the extinct shrine until the political climate had made it advantageous for the Muslim Conference to do so.[123] Clearly the significance of this performance extended beyond satisfying religious fervour and lay in the deliberate and 'seditious' insult it offered to 'the prestige of the administration'.[124] As the revenue minister saw it, Sheikh Abdullah was animated also by a desire to 'interfere with the religious leadership established on traditional lines' and to subvert the loyalty of 'the riff-raffs'.[125] And in this context few moves could be more audacious than to appropriate the very grounds of the governor's office. Furthermore, as the police reported, this act had 'created a boldness among the people' and stirred up a movement for 'similar action being taken in regard to some other areas such as the Ram Nivas Palace', striking more directly at the Dogra maharajas.[126]

A feature of the post-Glancy period was a markedly more aggressive strategy adopted by Kashmiri Muslims under the leadership of Sheikh Abdullah in relation to their shrines. Muslim control over these was asserted as a chapter in a wider struggle for rights. In 1932, during the opening ceremony of the mosque of Dara Shikoh that had also recently been returned to the Muslim community, a mammoth meeting 'requested' the durbar 'to grant a sufficient amount of money for the necessary repairs of this mosque . . . a monument of past Emperors.' The justification for the demand was that it had 'suffered heavily while in Government possession.'[127] Having secured the autonomy of their

---

[123] Political Department, F.No. 233/299-P.S., 1932, JKA.

[124] Report by the District Magistrate, dated 7 February 1933, Political Department, F.No. 233/299-P.S., 1932, JKA.

[125] Note by the Revenue Minister, dated 15 February 1933, Political Department, F.No. 233/299-P.S., 1932, JKA.

[126] Confidential letter from the Assistant Superintendent of Police to the Senior Superintendent of Police, dated 14 February 1933, Political Department, F.No. 233/299-P.S., 1932, JKA.

[127] Resolutions passed in a meeting of Kashmiri Mosalmans on the occasion of the opening ceremony of Mosque Dara Shikoh, dated 1 July 1932, Political Department, F.No. 503, 1932, JKA.

shrines by ensuring their return to the community, the Muslims of Kashmir went on to require financial contributions from the state, not as patronage but as reparation for past neglect and irresponsibility. This strategy echoed the pattern along which demands in the political, educational and economic realms were also made from the state.

In addition, whereas before 1932 Kashmiri Muslims had demanded the restoration to them of what were clearly mosques and tombs, they now increasingly staked claims to sites disputed between Hindus and Muslims in Kashmir, relying on history and archaeology for validation.[128] Thus, in 1934, the Muslims of a village in the Handwara district (Kashmir) raised a dispute over a spring in the area. The spring had been under the control of Hindus and certain Pandits had received revenue-free grants from the state to conduct worship there. Adjacent to the area there was also a mosque and a graveyard and a tongue of land in between, which both communities had 'traditionally' used to gain access to the spring. In 1932 a group of Muslims took control of this land claiming it belonged to the old mosque and began calling the azan from there.[129] Similarly, a number of Muslims in Srinagar claimed a piece of land where for many years a Hindu ascetic had performed his religious ceremonies, on the grounds that the 'land belonged to some old mosque of theirs'.[130] Instances of Muslims taking a more forceful stance towards shrines contested with Hindus proliferated in the late 1930s and 1940s. This trend appropriated the earlier tactics of the Hindus, using archaeological research, to claim superior rights to certain places of worship. It also represented a growing confidence among Kashmiri Muslims as they widened their struggle against the Dogra state to demand a broad spectrum of economic and political rights.

[128] It is significant, however, that there were several shrines such as Chrar-e-Sharif, the dargah of Maqdoom Sahib, the dargah of Dastgir Sahib at Khanyar (Srinagar) that had never been available for appropriation by any group. Revered by all Kashmiris, they had been the focus of uninterrupted worship and had never been allowed to fall into disrepair. Unfortunately, and possibly due to the lack of controversy surrounding them, they rarely appear in the archives.

[129] Note by E.J.D. Colvin, Prime Minister, Jammu and Kashmir State, dated 20 February 1934, Political Department, F.No. 102.P.S.-15, 1934, JKA.

[130] Confidential Special Diary of the Superintendent of Police, Srinagar, dated 30 April 1934, Political Department, F.No. 184, 1934, JKA.

To conclude, among the most potent ideological tools for voicing protest by the Muslims of Kashmir against a denial of economic, political and religious rights were made available by what would seem on the surface the unlikeliest source: the archaeological project set into motion by the colonial government of India. The result of the unfolding of the archaeological project in Kashmir was the introduction into the political arena of conceptual devices that catalyzed Kashmiri Muslim protest through a powerful intermeshing of religion and the demand for rights.

This was not necessarily the effect sought by the British Indian government, although it was indeed a consequence of its policies. Without denying the deeply transformative effect of colonialism, what is also clear is that colonial manipulation was neither fully planned or deliberate nor entirely successful. The Dogra rulers recast the archaeological project in ways that allowed them to derive their legitimacy through the patronage of Hindu shrines. A growing movement of anti-Dogra Muslim assertion used the archaeological project to appropriate the political vocabulary it made available of the duty of rulers and, conversely the rights of subjects, and to expose the tenuous nature of Dogra legitimacy to rule over a vast majority of its subjects. In ways that would undoubtedly have left Curzon aghast, his pet project had done far more than 'tear the mask off the face of the past.' Acquiring a momentum of its own, it had galvanized a political movement that unmasked the unrepresentative character of the Dogra state in Kashmir.

CHAPTER 5

Political Mobilization in Kashmir
Religious and Regional Identities

I t has been a commonplace when talking of Kashmir and political mobilization in the region to evoke the notion of Kashmiriyat. As with all politically useful vocabulary, the precise definition of the term has remained vague and adaptable, while its value has been kept inflated by summoning up ideas of the uniqueness of the phenomenon and the particular probity of the people it describes. Since the 1930s, the term has increasingly come to be understood as a reflection of a peerless tradition of regional nationalism, standing above petty religious rivalries and founded on the historical survival of what is perceived as a more salient legacy of cultural harmony. However, Kashmiriyat so defined was an idealized 'remembering' of one of several shifting meanings of 'being Kashmiri': it was not only summoned but also circulated in very specific political and historical moments. One such context, beginning roughly around the first decade of the twentieth century and ending with 1947, will be brought into focus in this chapter through an examination of the political practices of Kashmiris in those years.

Until then, as has been seen in this book, the religious nature of the Dogra-Hindu state of Jammu and Kashmir had set into motion a competition channelled along religious lines for the symbolic, political and economic resources of the state among communities also defined religiously. Yet present-day votaries of a 'secular' Indian nationalism would have us believe that this was an aberration of the grander traditions of religious neutrality that were a hallmark of a Kashmiriyat handed down from an ancient past.[1] Sheikh Mohammed

---

[1] See M.J. Akbar, *Kashmir: Behind the Vale*; and Tavleen Singh, *Kashmir: A Tragedy of Errors* (New Delhi: Viking, 1995), both cited in the Introduction, fn. 8. T.N. Madan provides a scholarly exposition on the theme in his *Modern*

Abdullah, a founding member and the most prominent leader of the All Jammu and Kashmir National Conference until his death in 1982, was celebrated as the 'secular' voice of Kashmiri regionalism. For those few in post-1947 Delhi willing to forage a little deeper into the region's culture, Ghulam Ahmad Mahjoor (1887–1952), revered as the 'national poet' of Kashmir, stood out as yet another shining example of Kashmiriyat so defined. These accounts, wishing to see 'secular' India's redemption in Kashmir and in holding on to it, commit the cardinal political mistake of defining the term too precisely and posing a duality between religious affiliation and 'nationalism' untenable in the face of historical evidence This chapter attempts to breach these too-neatly defined lines by demonstrating that the evocation of Kashmiriyat[2] was given currency in Kashmiri politics precisely from a bedrock of religious affiliations. In other words, there were several moments when the political strategy of various groups, whether Kashmiri Pandit organizations or the Kashmiri Muslim-dominated National Conference led by Sheikh Abdullah, or even the lyrics of a Mahjoor, chose to build bridges across religiously defined communities to evoke an 'older tradition' of culturally based regional coexistence. That this conceptualization was not aborted immediately is proof that it was not conjured out of thin air simply for the purposes of political manipulation. However, its success also relied on religious affinities remaining central. Kashmiriyat was imbued with religious notions even if not constrained by 'communally' rigid boundaries. An understanding of the historical context is necessary if neither Kashmiriyat nor religion

---

Myths, Locked Minds, op. cit. Even Prem Nath Bazaz, who was a participant in many of the vital events of Kashmir's history since the 1930s, lends himself to such an Indian 'nationalist analysis', understandable in part because of his own avowedly socialist political leanings and so his incapacity to see worth in any expression of even remotely 'religious' affinities. Bazaz, *The History of the Struggle for Freedom in Kashmir.* As remarked in the Introduction, Sumantra Bose's study, grounded in intensive field research and representing an attempt to provide a deeper understanding of the current crisis in Kashmir, seems among the few that underscores the relevance of religion in the regional identity deployed by popular political groups in Kashmir today. Sumantra Bose, *The Challenge in Kashmir: Democracy, Self-Determination and a Just Peace,* op. cit.

[2] Even though my own research has found no evidence for this actual word being used in the period up to 1947.

are to remain reified and therefore politically empty terms when studying Kashmir. This issue assumes greater urgency given the present-day context when a more selfconsciously religious element has been reinserted into the definition of Kashmiriyat but has been dismissed once more as a betrayal of the 'true' meaning of the term.

Socio-religious Reform Movements: Religious Identity and Political Mobilization

Pratap Singh's reign, by acknowledging, even if under colonial compulsion, the principle of a ruler's obligations had also recognized the rights of subjects. To all intents and purposes this signalled the inauguration of a public space for voicing political grievances. Yet, since this space was not so much an outgrowth of 'natural' trends flowing from the political history of this ruling house, or the recognition of and an attempt to adapt to a local 'national' ferment, but was engendered by colonial pressure and concerns, it was still a very circumscribed realm. Both the Dogra maharaja and, indirectly, the colonial state, made every effort to maintain firm control over it. The colonial state's concern was with preventing the rising nationalisms in British India from spreading into princely India. The imperial government hoped that a maharaja fulfilling his obligations towards his subjects, at the same time as investing the latter with the right to expect such, would be sufficient inoculation against political unrest in British India. Beyond that, the Dogra ruler was encouraged to clip defiance and punish disloyalty directed either towards himself or the colonial government. In this, the maharaja of Jammu and Kashmir executed admirably the role for which he had been rehearsed since the Proclamation of 1858 as a loyal 'breakwater in the storm'. Thus, scenting trouble in 1906–7 when the swadeshi movement was in full swing in Punjab, Pratap Singh, even if jumping the gun a little but commendably, nevertheless, in British estimation, had issued a strongly worded proclamation warning against sedition in the state.[3] At the same time, the foreign minister of the Kashmir durbar, Narayan Das, was ousted from state service on the mere suspicion by the British Resident of his being a 'dangerous Arya Samajist'. His successor Diwan Amar Nath, found to

---

[3] Correspondence regarding political agitation in Kahmir, Foreign Department (Secret-I), Pros. September 1907, nos. 9–39, NAI.

be no more satisfactory as a replacement as he was also believed to sympathize with the agitation in the Punjab, was kept under a watchful eye.[4]

Overt political activity and mobilization through public meetings were prohibited in Jammu and Kashmir until 1932. There was also a ban on the publication of newspapers in the state until the Glancy Commission's report in 1932 had incorporated a recommendation for the freedom of the press. The only sort of 'public' activity allowed was the formation of societies for religious and social reform. And even these carried with them the strict provisoes that they would require prior state sanction for their establishment and the explicit abjuration of any intent to engage in political activity.[5] Taking advantage of even this constricted space conceded by the Kashmir state, there was a proliferation of socio-religious reform organizations beginning with the last decade of the nineteenth century. In 1919, the durbar reported the presence of roughly twenty societies, anjumans and sabhas within the state, representing a variety of particularized interests such as those of the lower castes of Jammu, Rajputs, Dogras, Jammu Brahmans, Sikhs, Thakkars, Kashmiri Pandits and, the category defined most loosely, the Muslims.[6] A list prepared in 1927 reflected an exponential increase in these societies, totalling about one hundred by now and including the numerous branches that the bigger sabhas and anjumans had sprouted in various towns in the state.[7]

The result of this mushrooming of socio-religious reform activities was the creation not of a singular 'public' space but of numerous segregated spaces. These were formally apolitical but further fractured the body of state subjects along religious and also caste-based lines in the

[4] Confidential Note on Kashmir Affairs for 1906–7, by Major Sir Francis Younghusband, Resident in Kashmir, R/1/1/349, CRR, Foreign Department, Secret I, August 1907, Pros. nos. 1–2, IOL.

[5] OER, Political Department, 1921, File no. 66/102-C, JKA; General Department, 1922, File no. 584/P-7, JKA; General Department, 1923, File no. 561/P-50, JKA.

[6] List of Societies, *Anjumans* and *Sabhas* Which Existed in the State on 31 December 1918, OER, Political Department, 1919, File no. 312/7-C, JKA.

[7] Letter from the Inspector-General of Police, Srinagar, to the Public Works Minister, dated 12 November 1927, forwarding a List of Societies, *Anjumans* and *Sabhas,* Political and Quasi-Political, and Religious in Existence in the State on 31 December 1926, General Department, 1928, File no. 264/P-21, JKA.

case of the Hindus. In keeping with a history in which not only the ruler but his subjects as well were identified by their religious affiliations, this was undoubtedly also perceived by the Kashmir government as the safest way to control an emerging public discourse within the state. In these circumstances, any attempt to organize along lines other than the religious and for purposes other than social and religious reform immediately flagged restraint from the durbar. For instance, in 1920 the state government went into a tizzy upon receiving reports of a private meeting held in Srinagar at the home of a prominent Kashmiri Pandit, Vidh Lal Dar, between a 'large number' of Hindus and Muslims. Speaking in the interests of zamindars who, as those present at the meeting felt, were not allowed their fair say in fixing assessment rates of land revenue, what was proposed was the rather mild and unobtrusive remedy of establishing a Zamindari Conference as a platform from which the views of zamindars might be presented to the state authorities. The maharaja instantly reprimanded the governor of Kashmir for not taking steps to prevent even the eventuality of the organization of such a Conference. One might see this either as overreaction on the ruler's part to what was, by any standards, an innocuous intervention or, indeed, as a reaction to a potentially more dangerous trend of representation beyond state-specified spaces of affinity among subjects. As it turned out, whether through the threat of state repression or a petering of interest within the group itself, the Conference proved a 'lifeless organization'.[8] Regardless, a general suspicion was growing in official circles of the Kashmir durbar that socio-religious reform societies were becoming the instruments of political mobilization in the valley. It is interesting that the 1927 List of Societies not only included the words 'political, quasi-political and religious' in its title but also added a new category of information to be gathered on them, namely 'Object, *ostensible and real*'.[9]

That most of the socio-religious reform organizations in the state were covertly engaging in political activity was, therefore, well known to the state. However, as long as these activities flowed along scrupulously regulated channels that prevented unity among a segregated

[8] OER, Political Department, 1920, File no. 196/4-C, JKA.

[9] List of Societies, *Anjumans* and *Sabhas,* Political and Quasi-Political, op. cit. Emphasis mine.

body of subjects, the state was prepared to turn a blind eye. An organization that eventually brought forth the wrath of the Kashmir durbar for its attempts at merging religiously demarcated spaces for public action and more so in an effort at mobilizing for what were unmistakably political goals was the Dogra Sabha. Founded in 1903 under the aegis of the maharaja himself, its affiliates were largely state officials and members of the Dogra élite, each making it a point always to enunciate their loyalty to the person of the ruler and to his throne. Its ranks, included some Kashmiri Pandits and upper-class Jammu Muslims.[10] Yet, although essentially a loyalist organization, the Sabha began to draw the ire and suspicion of the state from the 1920s onwards. In 1926, it held a meeting in Srinagar attended by an audience of about two hundred, including a mix of Dogras, Kashmiri Pandits and a few Muslims. Among the declared objectives of the sabha were not only the creation of 'feelings of loyalty' amongst 'the ryots' towards the ruler but also to bring before the maharaja the legitimate grievances of his 'Hereditary State Subjects'. In line with these lofty goals, the Dogra Sabha aimed to 'unite all the different communities of His Highness's subjects into one organic whole and work in harmony for the progress of the state'. In order to forge this unity, the Dogras of the Sabha agreed to a number of significant concessions including considering a change in the name of the organization since the reference to 'Dogra' struck no chords among Kashmiris.

But the most potent basis for unity within the Sabha lay in the interest shared by the Dogras and the Kashmiri Pandits in persuading the state to redefine the term 'Hereditary State Subject', limiting inclusion within the category to those persons residing in the state since at least the days of Gulab Singh. At the same time, the Sabha voted unanimously in favour of preferential treatment in state service for state subjects so defined (an issue to be discussed at greater length below). However, the fact remained that such broad-based 'scrutiny' of state policy, transgressing the carefully controlled avenues of public discourse separated along religious, caste and even provincial lines, would not be tolerated. Hari Singh was prompt to retaliate and attempted to weaken the organization by reminding the Dogra officials, who were

[10] G.H. Khan, *Freedom Movement in Kashmir, 1931–1940* (New Delhi: Light and Life Publishers, 1980), p. 54.

its leading lights, that government regulations prevented state servants from participating in any political movement.[11] The Dogra Sabha, however, proved unexpectedly resistant to such admonitions and, in November 1929, in a letter addressed to the All India Congress Committee, Lahore, declared itself to be the 'Congress Committee of the Jammu and Kashmir State', providing a common platform for 'Hindu and Mohammaden patriots'. In 1930, therefore, Hari Singh declared the Dogra Sabha dissolved.[12]

For the Hindu rulers of Jammu and Kashmir, a perennial source of concern was the possibility of the mobilization of opinion against them of socially prominent segments of the Kashmiri Muslim population. This was more so since some among them had continued to refer their problems and concerns directly to the viceroy and above the head of the maharaja. One such group (encountered in earlier chapters), was the socially and religiously eminent family of the Naqshbandis of Srinagar, who 'regarded themselves as being in a measure dependants on the favour of the British government'. This, they repeatedly asserted, on the grounds that their stature had been assured by the British in return for services they had rendered the East India Company even before the formation of the state.[13] Thus, as late as 1894, members of the Naqshbandi family continued to solicit audiences with the viceroy himself. Although considered an indecorous breach of protocol, the British never quite refused them the privilege.[14] Couched at one level as purely social calls and an opportunity for the Naqshbandis to reiterate their gratitude and obeisance to the British authorities, their 'real' overlords, at another they served the important purpose of conveying the message of their autonomy from the Kashmir durbar. As an important Sufi family, letting it be known that they had the ear of the British and the viceroy himself would have had important results in enhancing their prestige locally.

---

[11] General Department, 1926, File no. 177/108-G, JKA.

[12] However, having made his point and giving a chastised Dogra Sabha time to cool off and reflect, Hari Singh removed the ban on the Dogra Sabha at his birthday durbar in May 1931. General Department, 1930, File no. 1202/P-17, JKA.

[13] Foreign Department (A-Political E), Pros. October 1882, nos. 28–31, NAI.

[14] Correspondence regarding an interview between His Excellency the Viceroy and Khwajas Habib Shah and Hassan Shah, Nakshbandis of Srinagar, Foreign Department (External B)/Pros. April 1894/ nos. 99–100, NAI.

The Naqshbandis were not the only privileged members of Srinagar Muslim society to play the breach between the dual sovereignty of the paramount power and of the Dogra rulers. In 1886, at least two petitions had been delivered to the Resident, signed by some seventeen or eighteen 'respectable' and landed Kashmiri Muslims—unfortunately not named—and addressed to the viceroy and the Resident. The gist of the petitions was to say that the Muslims of Kashmir had hoped that, with the inauguration of the Residency, there would have been some relief from the 'tyranny and oppression' they had suffered for many years at the hands both of the Dogra state and the Kashmiri Pandits.[15] In 1909, this trend, far from abating, had culminated in yet another memorandum addressed to the viceroy from a group defining themselves more broadly as the 'Representatives of the Kashmiri Mussalmans', certainly members of the Srinagar Muslim élite but unfortunately identified only by illegible seal prints. In their address, they spoke of the hopes of all Kashmiri Muslims, which only the British Resident could guarantee, for 'justice and safety' from a spirit of 'Hindustan for Hindus' that had begun to pervade the Kashmiri Pandits and Punjabi Hindus employed in the state. These 'representatives' made certain broad-based demands relating mostly to an increase in the numbers of Kashmiri Muslims in the state's administration to offset the overwhelming dominance of Hindus. Another cause espoused by them was one that was to assume mounting significance in the politics of the state, namely the question of the education of Kashmiri Muslims. Interestingly, the greatest concern expressed was not simply for the lack of education among Kashmiri Muslims but more for what was deemed its cause: the absence of Kashmiri Muslims among those in charge of education, both as inspectors of schools and as instructors. Muslim teachers, it was argued, were best able to cater to Muslim educational interests.[16] The Dogras were fully conscious of the existence of such a body of 'prominent' Kashmiri Muslims not satisfactorily acquiescent in their hegemony and increasingly inclined

[15] Letter from the Resident in Kashmir to the Secretary to the Government of India in the Foreign Department, dated 13 August 1886, Foreign Department (Secret E)/Pros. October 1886/ nos. 235–300, NAI.

[16] Petition from the Representatives of the Kashmiri Mussalmans Regarding the Employment of Mussalmans in the Kashmir State, Foreign Department (General B); Pros. January 1909, nos. 15/16, NAI.

to mobilize against them in the name of all the Muslims of the valley. The Dogra-Hindu state hoped, therefore, that by giving Muslims permission to form organizations for social and religious reform they would not only be able to co-opt this prominent social segment but also, by providing them a regulated public space within which to build their influence in Kashmiri society, contain their mobilizational activities.

The most active of the Muslim societies formed in the valley was the Anjuman-i-Nusrat-ul-Islam, which, in the Dogra scheme of things, was to function as an institutional expression of the leadership of the mirwaiz of the Jama Masjid in Srinagar. As noted, from the early decades of the twentieth century onwards, and to be played out most dramatically in the 1930s, Kashmiri Muslims were increasingly divided along loyalties owed to one of the two mirwaizes prominent in Srinagar: the mirwaiz of the Jama Masjid or the mirwaiz of Khanqah-i-Mualla (also known as the Shah-i-Hamadan shrine), more broadly representative of the Sufi path.[17] The Dogra rulers noted with interest the evidence of a growing cleavage among Kashmiri Muslims between those adhering to a tradition of Sufism and 'saint worship' and a new element attuned to more orthodox 'Wahabi' doctrines represented by the 'Jama Masjid faction'. Lawrence, the settlement commissioner writing in 1889, had suggested that the sway of the latter Islamic trend was spreading among Kashmiri Muslims. He wrote of the numerous complaints made to him by managers of Sufi shrines and 'others who sp[oke] with authority' in Kashmir that 'Wahhabi doctrines' were being preached and were gaining ground from the early 1880s onwards.[18] Yet, Lawrence had also recorded the dissatisfaction among the more orthodox maulvis with the laxity demonstrated by the valley's Muslims in the performance of their religious duties and in allowing their mosques to fall into disrepair except in 'times of earthquake and cholera [when] the Kashmiri falls to his prayers.'[19] The genuflecting before the more orthodox faction of Islam, represented through its maulvis and mosques, however, was not just an opportunistic hedging of celestial bets, so to speak, by Kashmiri Muslims. Movements to purify Islam in Kashmir, as elsewhere in the Indian subcontinent,

---

[17] For details on khanqah-i-Mu'allah, see fns 78 and 82 in the previous chapter.
[18] Lawrence, *The Valley of Kashmir*, p. 285.
[19] Ibid.

6: 'Preacher and Worshippers at the Wooden Mosque of Shah Hamdan, Srinagar', a Kashmiri Artist, *c.* 1850–60. Add. Or. 1744.

By permission of the British Library.

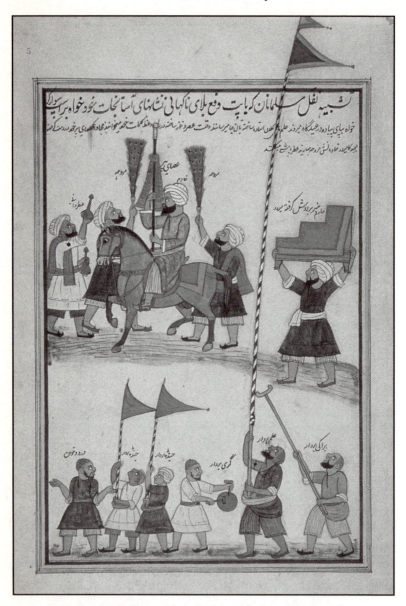

7: 'Muslim Procession "To Ward Off Sudden Misfortune"',
a Kashmiri Artist, *c.* 1850–60. Add. Or. 1664.

By permission of the British Library.

rarely translated into uncompromising onslaughts on strands of religion based on the veneration of saints. Nor indeed is it possible to distinguish a Sufi path of Kashmiri Islam (whether seen in light of a 'folk' or a 'secular-friendly' syncretic version) as entirely separable from a normative and doctrinally-bound Islam in the way in which observers such as Lawrence tended to do.[20]

Therefore, it is hardly surprising that even with the spreading influence of 'Wahabi' ideas, such as was reported at all times, and specifically in times of trouble, the importance of Sufi saints and their powers of intercession were still maintained in Kashmiri Muslim practice. In 1894 Lawrence wrote that during the floods in the Sindh valley in that year, 'marvellous tales were told of the efficiency of the flags of [Sufi] saints which had been set up to arrest the floods' and that the 'people' believed that the 'rice fields of Tulamula and the bridge of Sumbal' were spared by the use of these flags which had been taken from Sufi shrines '*as a last resort*'.[21] Catering to the everyday faith of the valley's believers, Sufi shrines provided remarkably specialized solutions for the dilemmas of most Kashmiris, who believed that 'the saints w[ould] aid if men will call'.[22] While there were saints, serving whom could exempt Muslims from begar, there were others to whom appeals were made for good health, children and success in litigation.[23]

However, even if as a Kashmir-wide phenomenon, the spread of the Wahabi wave was more hyperbole than fact, the Kashmir durbar nevertheless chose to co-opt this more orthodox faction. This was because it was presented with evidence of the growing influence from the 1890s onwards, at least in Srinagar, of Rasul Shah, the mirwaiz of the Jama Masjid, who spearheaded the Wahabi strand. The title of mirwaiz had been used at least since 1901 and the position had gradually become a hereditary one, held by the same family to this day. In 1901, the maharaja's government identified Rasul Shah as the single most useful figure capable of exercising a 'large influence over the

[20] See the excellent monograph by Mohammad Ishaq Khan on the subject. M.I. Khan, *Kashmir's Transition to Islam: the Role of Muslim Rishis* (New Delhi: Manohar, 1994).

[21] Report by Walter Lawrence on the Recent Flood in Kashmir, Foreign Department (External A), Pros. January 1894, nos. 360–2, NAI. Emphasis mine.

[22] Lawrence, *Valley of Kashmir*, p. 286.

[23] Ibid., pp. 288–90.

Muslims of Srinagar with a following of about three quarters of the people.'[24] With the founding in 1899 of the Anjuman-i-Nusrat-ul-Islam, Maulvi Rasul Shah had established a primary school, originally a maktab, that developed into the Islamia High School by 1905.[25] This maktab and the school received patronage from the Dogra maharaja from 1904 onwards through small grants enabling Muslims to receive both religious and secular instruction.[26] The Islamia High School continued to receive active assistance from the Anjuman-i-Nusrat-ul-Islam. The latter was a significant body in Srinagar society representing the interests of a weighty section of the Kashmiri Muslim élite and receiving support and financial assistance from such powerful men as Hassan Shah Naqshbandi, Khwaja Saad-ud-din Shawl, Aziz-ud-Kawoosa and Abdul Samad Qaqru.[27] The Dogra maharaja had thus succeeded in some measure in providing a bait to these eminent members of the Srinagar Muslim élite to participate in an appropriately regulated public arena and to build their social prestige through it. The state also assisted the Anjuman-i-Nusrat-ul-Islam in building up its 'philanthropic' image as a provider for the needs of the Muslim poor. For instance, the unclaimed dead bodies of impoverished Muslims were made over to the anjuman and the amount required for burials was paid by the Kashmir durbar.[28]

The *dastarbandi*[29] ceremonies in 1931 of the new mirwaiz of the Jama Masjid, Maulvi Atiqullah, who succeeded Maulvi Ahmadullah on his death, showed how closely the Anjuman-i-Nusrat-ul-Islam, the office of the mirwaiz of the Jama Masjid and the Muslim élite associated with them, had come to be tied to the maharaja of Kashmir. After the ceremonies, the 'prominent citizens' of Srinagar present entered the Jama Masjid to attend the first sermon of the new mirwaiz,

[24] Letter from the Governor of Kashmir to the Vice President of the State Council, dated 11 March 1901, OER, 1898, File no. 52/L-II, JKA.

[25] U.K. Zutshi, *Emergence of Political Awakening in Kashmir,* p. 165.

[26] Letter from the Judicial Member to the Vice President of the State Council, dated 17 August 1903, and Letter from the Assistant Resident to the Vice President, dated 14 September 1903, OER, 1903, File no. 68/P-57, JKA.

[27] U.K. Zutshi, p. 195.

[28] Letter from the Home Minister to the Chief Minister, dated 23 August 1919, OER, Political Department, 1919, File no. 44, JKA.

[29] Loosely translated as the succession ceremony when a turban is tied on to the new incumbent of any office or position.

at which prayers were offered for Maharaja Hari Singh and the heir-apparent, Karan Singh, and gratitude expressed for 'the favours which have been shown to the survivors of the deceased'. It was also clear that, at least until then, the Jama Masjid mirwaizes had been conscientious about attending the maharaja's durbars and so publicly declaring their association with the Dogra state.[30]

Until 1931, these 'leading Muhammadans' had on critical occasions provided both the maharaja and, through him, the British paramount authority with invaluable support, functioning almost as partners in the dispensation of power of which Kashmir was a part. For instance, upon the outbreak of hostilities with Turkey during World War I, the Resident reported not only on the absence of 'disquiet' in Kashmir but also pointed to the maharaja's capacity to summon 'all the leaders of the Muhammadan community', including the mirwaiz and his other unidentified allies, to express their 'regret at the action of Turkey and their unshaken loyalty to His [Britannic] Majesty's Government' as well as their refusal to see this as a religious war.[31] Thus, the Dogra maharajas had not only gained political points with the British by winning over, as it were, the affiliation of these eminent Kashmiri Muslims but also, very importantly, provided them with an important and legitimized arena in which to actually build their own claims to the leadership of Kashmiri Muslim society. In a spirit of give and take, the petition presented by them to the Resident, for the attention of the viceroy, opened with the expression of their 'hope that . . . [they] may be regarded as properly representing the thoughts of all the Mussalmans of Kashmir and as entitled to speak in their name'.[32]

The Dogra state's sponsorship of the mirwaiz of the Jama Masjid and the élite affiliated with him and his anjuman did not necessarily

[30] Correspondence regarding the death of Mirwaiz Moulvi Ahmadullah and the election of Moulvi Atiqullah as Mirwaiz and President of the Anjuman-i-Nusrat-ul-Islam, General Department, 1931, File no. 58/Mis-18, JKA.

[31] Letter from the Resident in Kashmir, dated 6 November 1914 and Letter from the Resident in Kashmir to the Foreign Secretary to the Government of India, dated 9 November 1914, Foreign and Political Department (Internal B)/ Pros. April 1915/nos. 295–305, NAI.

[32] Address Presented by the Leading Mahomedans of Kashmir to the Resident in Kashmir on 9 November 1914, Foreign and Political Department (Internal B)/ Pros. April 1915/nos. 295–305, NAI.

imply the emergence of a unified public space occupied by the Muslims under their leadership. However, for a time, it served the Kashmir durbar's purpose of keeping in check the Sufi shrine-based orientation of Islam with a far more extensive support base in the valley, although as yet not showing signs of cohesive mobilization. In the early years of the twentieth century the mirwaiz, Rasul Shah, was often heard publicly denouncing the 'worship and deification of saints and other holy personages' from the pulpits of the Jama Masjid.[33] Yet, while in the state's perception Rasul Shah commanded a substantial following among Srinagar's Muslims, it was also aware of the affinity felt by most Kashmiri Muslims for the religious leaders associated with the Sufi shrines of Khanqah-i-Mualla, Hazrat Bal, Chrar-e-Sharif, Dastgir Sahib and Maqdoom Sahib.[34] In fact, as mentioned earlier, the mirwaiz of the Khanqah-i-Mualla (Shah-i-Hamdan shrine) was to emerge as an important and alternative focus for political activity from the late 1920s. This was especially true when Sheikh Mohammed Abdullah, who returned to the valley after his studies at Aligarh Muslim University, chose to hitch his wagon to the Hamadani mirwaiz, seen to lead a more socially broad-based religious constituency, and certainly one less firmly tied to the Dogra state.

In the early decades of the twentieth century the two mirwaizes and their followers were engaged in a vitriolic battle for control over the various mosques and shrines in Srinagar. This rivalry provided the Dogra state with opportunities to intervene in the Muslim public domain, and the capacity also for interfering even with the religious practices of Kashmiri Muslims. The demonstrated incapacity of the two mirwaizes and their followers to come to a peaceful settlement on the issue of who would have first privilege of preaching at which mosque, allowed the Dogra state arbitrarily to divide the mosques of Srinagar into two groups each controlled by one of the parties.[35] Despite this partitioning of the domain of religious shrines, disputes continued to break out among the various factions of Muslims. This enabled the Dogra rulers to brand them as 'troublemakers' and 'disrupters

---

[33] *The Tribune*, 29 November 1904.

[34] Lawrence had mentioned the special reverence in which these shrines were held in Kashmir: *The Valley of Kashmir*, p. 292.

[35] Correspondence regarding the removal of restrictions on preaching in Srinagar during the stay of the Durbar, OER, Political Department, 1910, File no. 176/P-91/Part II, JKA.

of the public peace' and foist further regulation such as a prohibition on preaching unless preceded by a notice of fifteen days.[36] Thus, Pratap Singh could legitimately assert that while 'no interference with the preaching of religious doctrines [wa]s ever intended, but if the preaching ha[d] a tendency which affect[ed] the public peace, it [would be] necessary for keeping law and order that provisions of the law should be strictly enforced.'[37] It also gave the maharaja an opportunity to suggest that the 'factious quarrels and sectarian dissensions' caused by the friction between the mirwaizes went against not only the norms of 'humanity' but significantly against 'the principles of patriotism'.[38] Much to the satisfaction of the Dogra maharaja, the internal bickering among the Srinagar Muslims led them to look to the throne for arbitration. Telegrams poured in from Kashmir's Muslims, either pleading on behalf of the right of one or the other mirwaiz to preach at particular shrines or, on the contrary, urging the durbar to prevent one or the other leader from doing so on specific occasions and at particular sites.[39] Thus, the internal fracture among Srinagar Muslims not only enabled the assertion of greater control over them by the Kashmir durbar but also prevented the emergence of any unified leadership capable of mobilizing Kashmiri Muslims that might have threatened either the maharaja or the Hindus of the state.

Muslim-owned newspapers in the Punjab had been quick to comment on the very limited nature of the political leadership provided by these members of the Kashmiri Muslim élite to the general body of their poorer co-religionists in the state. As noted in the last chapter, in October 1912, the *Zamindar* of Lahore had excoriated the spiritual leaders and well-to-do Muslims of Kashmir not only for preventing

[36] Ibid., OER, Political Department, 1910, File no. 200/N-19/C, JKA.

[37] Letter from the Maharaja to the Prime Minister, dated 20 June 1910, OER, Political Department, 1910, File no. 176/P-91, JKA.

[38] Speech by the Maharaja before a gathering of Muslims of all shades of opinion, OER, Political Department, 1910, File no. 144/P-91, JKA.

[39] Application of certain Muslims regarding the preaching at Maqdoom Sahib by Rasul Shah in contravention of orders, OER, Political Department, 1902, File no. 47/L-157, JKA; Petition from some Kashmiri Muslims asking the Maharaja to prevent Khwaja Samad Joo Qaqru from preaching at Makhdoom Sahib and vilifying the Hamdani Mirwaiz, OER, Political Department, 1913, File no. 235/C-10, JKA; Application from certain Mohammadens of Srinagar requesting the Government to withhold the permission granted to Mirwaiz to preach at Khanyar, OER, Political Department, 1920, File no. 212/41-C, JKA.

their community from receiving education but also for stopping their grievances being brought before the durbar.[40] Earlier, in September 1911, the *Observer* of Lahore had provided a forum for the expression of the discontent of the 'Muhammadan subjects' of Kashmir through an open letter addressed to the maharaja and the Resident in Kashmir. The letter had also lamented the absence of any influential Muslim willing to represent Kashmiri Muslim interests in the state and 'to reproduce the photo of [their] condition' before the ruler.[41]

Among the earliest organizations for social and religious reform active in Jammu and Kashmir state had been the Arya Samaj founded in 1892. With four branches in the state, its activities had remained largely confined to Jammu for most of its existence where it focused on proselytizing among the lower castes, the Meghs and Doms.[42] However, while its reach within Jammu and Kashmiri society was limited with few successes in its goals of conversion from among Muslims, widow remarriage or even fighting the caste system,[43] the Arya Samaj nevertheless made its impact felt in quite a different domain. Drawing its widest support and membership from among the Punjabi Hindus who had settled in the state and were employed either as officials of the state or as traders,[44] the Arya Samaj kept the political and religious temperature running high in the state on two fronts. On the one hand, the Samajis took to criticizing openly other religious traditions such as Islam in their public meetings[45] and, on the other, their

---

[40] *Zamindar*, Lahore, 8 October 1912, *Selections from the Native Newspapers Published in the Punjab*, pp. 850–1.

[41] L/R/5/192, 'Selections from the Native Newspapers Published in the Punjab', 1911, pp. 975–6, IOL.

[42] Letter from Captain Trench, Assistant Resident in Kashmir, to Rai Sahib Diwan Amar Nath, Chief Minister to His Highness, dated 16 September 1910, OER, Political Department, 1910, File no. 215, JKA.

[43] G.H. Khan, *Freedom Movement in Kashmir*, pp. 50–3.

[44] Fortnightly Report for the Second Half of October 1917, Foreign Department (Political B)/Pros. November 1917/no. 7, NAI; Demi-official letter from the Governor of Kashmir to the Home Minister to His Highness, dated 9 April 1921, OER, Political Department, 1921, File no. 157/C-11, JKA.

[45] Confidential Report from the Assistant Superintendent of Police to the Superintendent of Police, dated 8 April 1921, OER, Political Department, 1921, File no. 157/C-11, JKA.

shuddhi[46] activities brought them increasingly into confrontation with the Muslims of the valley, heightening religious consciousness among them and prompting an effort at internal unity.[47] Thus in 1923, on the occasion of the Juma-al-Vida, when nearly 20,000 Muslims had gathered at the Jama Masjid in Srinagar for their prayers, the mirwaiz talked of the dissension caused by the Arya Samajis who, he suggested with no small degree of exaggeration, were even digging up the dead for the purposes of converting them from Islam. He urged the Muslims to unite in order to combat the 'Arya threat'. The district magistrate in Srinagar further noted that the Samajis and Muslims continued to deliver lectures against each other and for and against shuddhi, constantly causing commotion in the 'general public'. This threat to the public peace further strengthened the repressive hands of the Dogra government, which decreed as a result that no public speech was to be delivered without first obtaining the permission of the senior magistrate of the locality.[48] Even earlier, in 1910, a group of Punjabi Hindus, had written to the maharaja expressing their fears that the Kashmiri Muslims were preparing to plunder the Hindus as soon as the durbar had moved to its winter capital in Jammu. They requested the maharaja not to leave Srinagar or, if that were impossible, then asked that 'certain defensive measures . . . be adopted for the protection of the Hindu people'. The maharaja obliged by instructing the chief minister to take such precautionary measures as may be required in 'the best interests of the people inhabiting' the state.[49] While these religious tensions provided the Kashmir durbar with an excuse to keep a firm rein on the public activities of its subjects, the anti-shuddhi Kashmiri Muslim activists did him another favour. They effectively

[46] Literally purification through the re-conversion of adherents of other faiths such as Islam back to Hinduism.

[47] OER, Political Department, 1923-24, File no. I-85, JKA; OER, Political Department, 1924, File no. J-66, JKA.

[48] Memorandum submitted by the Foreign Member of the State Council for submission to His Highness the Maharaja Sahib Bahadur, General Department, 1924, File no. 740/P-12, JKA.

[49] Application of Ram Chand, Amar Nath, Jewan Singh, Daya Ram Lala, etc. to the Maharaja, dated 18 September 1910, and Maharaja Pratap Singh's Confidential Memorandum to the Chief Minister, OER, Political Department, 1910, File no. 258, JKA.

fought the maharaja's own religious battles for him since he, as a Sanatan Dharmi Hindu,[50] had little sympathy with some of the religious ideas propagated by the Arya Samaj such as their condemnation of idol worship and the caste system.

The other front on which the Arya Samaj's activities had a significant impact was in catalyzing Kashmiri Pandit activities in the domain of reform and in galvanizing them in defence of their political and economic interests. As late as 1872, the Kashmiri Pandits seemed thoroughly uninterested in the idea of social reform within their community. In that year, Pandit Sheonarain, a member of the Kashmiri Pandit community long settled in Awadh (in British India), had visited the valley with a view to establishing closer ties between the émigré Pandits and those in the 'mother country'. To this end, he mooted the idea, heartily approved of by Ranbir Singh and his chief minister Wazir Punnu, of founding an 'association for mutual support and mutual correspondence' which would also 'awaken' Pandit interest in social reform. At this point, this proposal simply aroused the suspicion of the Kashmiri Pandit community who viewed this as a back-handed attempt at attacking their regionally specific religious customs. The émigré Pandits had, over the years, sought to fit themselves into their new adoptive social environments and did so by clinging to their Brahman status, claiming in fact greater purity than even the Brahmans of Hindustan. This competition with the Hindustani Brahmans had simultaneously led them to espouse some of the latter's practices, such as stricter vegetarianism and greater discrimination in consuming food cooked by Muslims, than had been usual in Kashmir. Eventually, 're-formed' in the plains of Hindustan, many Pandits domiciled there turned around to criticize their brethren in Kashmir as being ignorant and remiss in maintaining the purity of their status by mingling too freely with the Muslims.[51]

However, the reaction of the Pandits of the valley to Sheonarain's

[50] The Sanatan Dharma translates loosely as the 'original' or 'pure' religion which, with its Brahmanical priesthood, caste system and religious rituals, had become the target of 'reformist' movements such as the Arya Samaj.

[51] Report on Cashmere for 1871 by the Officer on Special Duty, Foreign Department (Political A), April 1872, nos. 37–40, NAI. See also Henny Sender, *The Kashmiri Pandits: A Study of Cultural Choice in North India* (Delhi: Oxford University Press, 1988).

project reflected not merely a defense of their 'religion'. It also represented a closing of ranks against a potential threat to their administrative and economic dominance in the state from a group that had, since its exodus to Punjab and Awadh, done equally well in state service, in business and in the new professions and whose members might now apply to the Dogra government for employment. That this fear was grounded in some reality was borne out by the fact that one of the senior-most posts on the State Council formed in 1889 was held by Suraj Koul, a Kashmiri Pandit but from Lahore. At any rate and for the moment, Sheonarain gave up his attempts in view of the animosity he encountered from a community which, until recently, had performed a religious ceremony associated with death rites for those Pandits who had chosen to leave the valley.[52]

By 1931, however, there would be a remarkable change of heart and perceptions when the Pandits of Kashmir would look beyond their mountain walls to evoke 'a community both here and outside the State', linking itself up with even the Indian National Congress leader, Pandit Motilal Nehru.[53] The Kashmiri Pandit émigrés in British India were then written about, not as deserters or potential rivals, but as the unwitting victims of Muslim fanaticism in the valley's past. The aim was to call to mind parallels with a present in which the Muslim majority was once again flexing its muscles to deprive the Kashmiri Pandit community of its legitimate rights. But that was 1931 and several steps too far into the story.

An earlier group of rivals, threatening the administrative dominance of the Kashmiri Pandits from around the last decade of the nineteenth century, had been the large numbers of Punjabis imported by the Dogra state to man the higher rungs of the state's administration. The turning point for the Kashmiri Pandits can be dated to 1889, when the newly instituted State Council had changed the court language from Persian to Urdu and simultaneously framed rules for holding competitive examinations for appointment to government service.[54]

[52] Report on Cashmere for 1871 by the Officer on Special Duty, op.cit.

[53] *Memorial Presented by the Sanatan Dharm Youngmen's Association to H.H. the Maharaja Bahadur,* dated 24 October 1931 (Srinagar: Sanatan Dharm Youngmen's Association, 1931), p. 3.

[54] OER, Political Department, 1891, File no. 24, JKA; OER, Political Department, 1907, File no. 33, JKA.

These changes were prompted by the desire for modernization and greater rationalization of the princely state's administration, a demand made increasingly by the paramount colonial power concerned with turning the princely states into more 'representative' regimes (discussed in Chapter Three). The cumulative effect of these measures was that the Kashmiri Pandits were increasingly put out of the running for the most prestigious ranks of the administration. Having invested in their literacy in Persian for centuries in order to maintain their hold on power through state employment, they suddenly found the rug pulled from under their feet since few of them were fluent in Urdu. Nor, educationally speaking, were Kashmir's Pandits equipped with the skills which 'modern' instruction in British India had provided to an increasing number of Indians trained specifically for civil service. Suddenly deemed unqualified, the Kashmiri Pandits saw most of the plum jobs in the state going to large numbers of Punjabis deputed to the state from British India and bringing with them their own cohorts of relatives to fill vacancies.[55] And with the special concessions made for the Dogras in Service[56] and education,[57] this threatened to leave the Pandits with little more than control over the lower echelons of the bureaucracy.

This was a particularly harsh strike at a community that, especially for its Karkun members, had regarded government service as the sole guarantee for its social and economic survival. In the words of an illustrious member, P.N. Bazaz, the Pandit 'from his very birth . . . [wa]s trained for "service". Mothers bless[ed] their sons, *purohits* their *jajmans*, and all elders their young folk, that they m[ight] get jobs [in

[55] Letter from McMahon to Talbot, dated 8 July 1897, Foreign Department (Secret-E)/Pros. February 1898/nos. 183–286, NAI; Bazaz, *The History of the Struggle for Freedom in Kashmir*, p. 136.

[56] Bazaz, *The History of the Struggle for Freedom in Kashmir*, p. 146. As early as in 1894, Pratap Singh had talked of his projections of how the Dogra Rajputs 'as in former times, will look to service as their natural destiny'. OER, Political Department, 1894, File no. 67, JKA.

[57] In 1922, at the annual meeting of the Kashmir University Mahasabha held in Lahore under the presidentship of the maharaja of Kashmir, the latter ordered that Rajput students who wished to study at either the Prince of Wales College in Jammu or the Sri Pratap Singh College in Srinagar be exempted from the payment of monthly fees. The justification offered for the concession was that they

government] and promotions.'[58] The widespread Pandit perception of government employment was, and is to this day, that while for other communities it was merely a step towards greater political leverage, for the Pandit it determined his very being.[59] This frame of mind was conditioned largely by the history of the community and its memory preserved collectively by Kashmiri Pandits. As they remember it, their survival as a community was due in large measure to their indispensability to the administrative machinery of the various rulers of the valley. A much reviled figure in the Pandit rendering of history was Sultan Sikandar (*r.*1389–1413), also known as *but-shikan* (the iconoclast), who, living up to his sobriquet, persecuted the Hindus of Kashmir to such unbearable limits that he caused the emigration of large numbers to the plains of Hindustan. His son, and polar opposite, Sultan Zain-ul-Abidin (*r.*1420–70), also known as *bud-shah* (the great king), faced with a debilitated administration, reversed his father's policies of religious intolerance as much out of his own ethical predilections as out of a sense of political expediency. The demonstrated need for Kashmiri Pandits as an invaluable body of highly literate people to man his administration prompted him to reinstate their political influence as well as their religious privileges.[60] For a community that had retained a sharp sense of having survived the worst of Muslim tyrannies, it seemed especially galling that it was with a Hindu ruler in power that the tantalizing prize of high office was slipping out of their grasp.

Not only were Punjabi Hindus receiving the premium of employment, but also societies formed to represent and guard their interests were beneficiaries of the maharaja's patronage. One such organization was the Hindu Sahayak Sabha founded in 1906 with the object of helping the Punjabi Hindus of the state 'in time of need'. By 1908, the sabha had expanded its activities to providing proper cremation and funerary rites for the unclaimed dead bodies of Hindus. Rejecting a suggestion by the then chief minister, Diwan Amar Nath, that this task

---

belonged to the 'ruling race'. Memorandum by the Member for Education, dated 20 February 1923, General Department, 1923, File no. 1611/E-26, JKA.

[58] Bazaz, *Inside Kashmir*, p. 283.

[59] Ibid., p. 284.

[60] Sender, *The Kashmiri Pandits*, pp. 14, 17–18, 20.

be placed in the hands of the police department or the Srinagar Municipality, the maharaja sanctioned not only the disbursal of funds to the sabha for the purpose, but also offered any executive assistance they might need from the state.[61] By 1917, the Hindu Sahayak Sabha was also tapping into the symbolic religious benefits to be gained from the patronage of one of the most important pilgrimage centres of the state, the cave shrine of Amarnath. The sabha provided accommodation for the large numbers of Hindus who participated in the annual pilgrimage, roughly half of whom were Punjabis by the early decades of the twentieth century. In return for these 'philanthropic' deeds, it was rewarded with a substantial land grant from the state for the construction of a permanent office in Srinagar, despite the opposition of the Kashmiri Pandits living in the neighbourhood.[62]

For the astute Kashmiri Pandit there were two lessons to be learned: that it was good to be Punjabi, of course, but even more importantly that it was necessary for them to begin organizing to protect their religious, economic and political interests. In reaching this conclusion the Kashmiri Pandits were prompted not only by the visible advantages derived by the Hindu Sahayak Sabha but also by that other Punjabi-Hindu-dominated socio-religious reform movement, the Arya Samaj. While there is little evidence of direct confrontation between the Kashmiri Pandits and the Hindu Sahayak Sabha, their relationship with the Arya Samaj, on the other hand, was fraught with tension. The strained relations between the two can be attributed not only to the fact that the Arya Samaj was largely manned by the Punjabi Hindu officials of the state, the immediate rivals of Kashmiri Pandits for power, but also to religious disagreements. Like the Dogra rulers, the Kashmiri Pandits as Sanatan Dharmis had little sympathy for the Samaj's reformist propaganda against 'idol-worship', excessive expenditure on rituals, or against the validity of any religious text other than the Vedas. However, the Kashmiri Pandits also realized that the only effective way to prevent the Arya Samaj from gaining ground in

[61] Correspondence on the Subject of the Disposal of Dead Bodies by the Hindu Sahayak Sabha, OER, Political Department, 1911, File no. 42/M-203, JKA; OER, Political Department, 1919, File no. 44, JKA.

[62] Correspondence Regarding the Grant of Land Situated in Maisuma, Srinagar, in Favour of the Hindu Sahayak Sabha, OER, Political Department, 1917, File no. B-75/48, JKA.

their community was to organize for social reform and regeneration themselves. In 1910, one strand of Kashmiri Pandits chose not to beat but join them, albeit indirectly by forming a separate organization called the Arya Kumar Sabha functioning within the wider Arya Samaj movement.[63] While it endorsed the social reform ideals of the Samaj, such as the abolition of child marriage, encouragement of widow re-marriage and cutting back expenditure on rituals, the Arya Kumar Sabha was still based on Sanatanist principles. Nevertheless, the Arya Kumar Sabha never quite caught on in Kashmir and few Pandits join-ed its ranks. [64]

A much more vigorous challenge to the Arya Samaj came from the Sanatan Dharma Sabha of Srinagar founded in 1893.[65] As its name suggests, the ostensible reason for its foundation was the spreading of the Sanatan Dharma and its defense against the activities of Arya Samajis. Led by various fairly conservative members of the Kashmiri Pandit community such as Hargopal Kaul and Pandit Amar Nath Kak, [66] the society also had a clear reformist agenda, seeking to fortify the community's defences and regenerate it for the purposes of re-gaining its diminished prestige. Among the reforms advocated by the Dharma Sabha was the lowering of expenses on marriage by, for instance, cutting down or entirely abandoning the costly consump-tion of meat.[67] Another concern common to the array of Pandit orga-nizations was the education of women and the Sanatan Dharma Sabha played a pioneering role in this respect, establishing the first school for Hindu girls at Srinagar.[68] Concerned with their lag in modern educa-tion that threatened to marginalize the Kashmiri Pandits in the matter

[63] OER, Political Department, 1918, File no. 262/77-C, JKA.

[64] G.H. Khan, 'Early Socio-Religious Reform Movements in Kashmir', in Mohammad Yasin and A. Qaiyum Rafiqi (eds), *History of the Freedom Struggle in Jammu and Kashmir* (New Delhi: Light and Life Publishers, 1980), pp. 90–1.

[65] List of Societies, *Anjumans* and *Sabhas* which existed in the State on the 31st December 1918, OER, Political Department, 1919, File no. 312/7-C, JKA.

[66] *Census of India*, Jammu and Kashmir, 1901, p. 24.

[67] U.K. Zutshi, p. 198. Anyone who has witnessed a Kashmiri *wazwan* or feast at marriages in which sometimes an average of twenty-eight meat preparations are served knows how expensive the ceremony can be.

[68] P.N. Bazaz, *Daughters of the Vitasta* (New Delhi: Pamposh, 1959), pp. 217–18.

of government employment, in 1906, the Dharma Sabha also established the Pratap Hindu College, later known as the Sri Pratap College.[69]

The issue of widow remarriage first actively advocated by Hargopal Kaul, on behalf of the Dharma Sabha, had a stormy history. Though winning a few supporters from 1924 onwards, and managing to celebrate half a dozen such marriages in 1929 and 1930, advocates of widow remarriage were more often than not 'jeered at, ridiculed and pelted'.[70] Finally, an attempt was made to persuade the maharaja to legalize widow remarriage in the state. The opinions of all those with authority in the Hindu community were elicited through a meeting convened in Srinagar in 1931 under the auspices of a district official. In the end, their efforts came to nothing as the state authorities, choosing to rely on the opposition of the more conservative section of the Dharma Sabha led by Pandit Amar Nath Kak, disbanded the meeting on the grounds that any decision would have to await the Dharma Sabha's verdict.[71] The outcome of this aborted attempt at such far-reaching reform was that a younger element marked itself out with goals of more radical change and formed their own societies. One such society was the Fraternity Society founded in 1930 under the leadership of Prem Nath Bazaz. Nevertheless, its buoyantly idealistic objectives had limited success in the face of opposition from the conservative faction. But the Fraternity Society was reborn as the Sanatan Dharma Youngmen's Association, also known as the Yuvak Sabha,[72] this time becoming the most active representative of Kashmiri Pandit interests confronting the Kashmiri Muslims and their agitation for rights in 1931.

In the social reform movements among Kashmiri Pandits, change was linked to religion rather than to appeals of its inherent 'rationality'. This was partly a reflection of the predominance of the conservative element, but it was resorted to also to facilitate reform in that it lent the movement legitimacy in a state in which religion was still the pre-eminent marker of social identity. Yet, on the other hand, as was seen in the attempt to legalize widow remarriage, it also eventually circumscribed the capacity for change by applying breaks on reform that

[69] U.K. Zutshi, p. 199.

[70] Bazaz, *Daughters of the Vitasta*, pp. 235–6.

[71] Ibid., pp. 236–40.

[72] Ibid., pp. 240, 241, 249.

might go too far and make the Pandits appear less than perfectly Hindu. The appeal to religion on matters that did not necessarily require religious justification was also a factor of the heightened defence of religion that characterized the atmosphere in public discourses in Kashmir in the early decades of the twentieth century. It was also a result of the nature of the state where access to resources were controlled by a very Hindu maharaja.

The shambles in which the meeting to solicit Hindu opinion on the issue of widow remarriage ended, quite as much as attempts at reforms in the first place, had one salutary effect. For the first time, the meeting had brought together on a single platform not only a wide spectrum of Hindu opinion but also a collective body of Kashmiri Pandits. Additionally, the effort common to all Pandit reformist organizations was the creation of a certain uniformity of practice and so establishing greater unity within Kashmiri Pandit society. The resulting sense of solidarity, divisions between the conservative and radical elements notwithstanding, inspired the popular twentieth century Kashmiri Pandit poet Zinda Kaul to write his first lyrical poem entitled 'Unity and Sympathy' and to recite it at a Dharma Sabha meeting in 1896.[73] It is significant that this poem, unlike his verses composed after 1931— such as 'Ferryman, Lead Me and My Countrymen,'[74] referred not to Hindu–Muslim unity in Kashmir but specifically to an emerging sense of pride in Kashmiri Pandit cohesion. The awareness of a Kashmiri Pandit community, defined by certain common religious practices and a shared sense of the urgency of restoring their position—particularly in the domain of government employment—bound them closely together in politically critical ways for the future.

'Kashmir for Kashmiris': The Kashmiri Pandits and Regional Identity

As with almost every other sense of community solidarity, that of the Pandits was also partly forged and hastened by confrontation with an external element. From the late nineteenth century onwards this stimulus was provided by the threat posed to their leverage within Kashmir by the Punjabi Hindu community. Mobilizing against them

[73] U.K. Zutshi, p. 199.

[74] Zinda Kaul, 'Ferryman, Lead Me and My Countrymen', in A.N. Raina, *Zinda Kaul* (New Delhi: Sahitya Akademi, 1974), pp. 37–8.

was part of the agenda of almost every Kashmiri Pandit reformist organization. Thus, the Sanatan Dharma Sabha had published a pamphlet that criticized not only the Arya Samaj's reformist activities but attacked also its overwhelmingly Punjabi Hindu constituency. The Arya Samaj attempted to have the Kashmir durbar ban the pamphlet. It took special exception to the Dharma Sabha's call for a 'Kashmir for Kashmiris' coupled with the demand for 'the exclusion of Punjabis and other non-Kashmiris . . . from State appointments and the sole employment of Kashmiri Hindus'.[75] The Yuvak Sabha also traced its origins in a confrontation with Punjabi Hindus, growing out of a body of Pandits who had grouped together to fight a law suit against some Punjabi Hindus occupying land belonging to the temple of Shival in Srinagar.[76]

By 1921, the Kashmiri Pandits, equipped in greater numbers with the modern education provided by the Christian Mission School and the Sri Pratap College, still found avenues to employment in the higher rungs of administration barred to them. They conducted their contests with the Punjabis in new arenas such as those provided by the British Indian press. In that year, Shankar Lal Kaul, a Pandit writing under the pseudonym of 'Kashmiricus' published a scathing indictment of the Dogra state's recruitment policy in the *United India and Indian States*. He suggested that

> Kashmiris are treated as strangers in their own house. In their own country their status is nil. A post of rupees 40 falls vacant in some office . . . ninety to one an outsider is brought to fill it up—and the state officials who indulge in this luxury have not . . . good sense enough to bring at least as good a man from outside to fill up the post, as could be available in Kashmir . . . a good-for-nothing outsider almost illiterate—but whose qualification is a communal or geographical alliance with some powerful official in the state—is given a post to which a Kashmiri graduate may aspire . . . The latest civil and military lists of the state presents the miserable spectacle of 5 per cent Kashmiri Hindus, 1 per cent Kashmiri Mussulmans—and less than 7 per cent of the rest of the state subjects— and by state subjects we mean the children of the soil of Jammu and Kashmir—whatever the state authorities may mean by it . . . The state has

[75] Letter from J. Manners, Resident in Kashmir, to J.B. Wood, dated 1 September 1917, Home Department (Political)/Pros. September 1917/no. 6, NAI.
[76] G.H. Khan, *Freedom Movement in Kashmir*, pp. 57–8.

established two colleges and . . . every year more and more students pour into them—and what are their prospects? . . . The state has encouraged them to be ambitious . . . diverted them from and unfitted them for pursuing humbler occupations—in short, the end is—it has ruined them.[77]

In its struggles against the dominance of Punjabi Hindus the Kashmiri Pandit community had strategically broken new ground for mobilization, speaking not just for Kashmiri Hindus but also for Kashmiris more generally and for state subjects. To further their community goals they were not past forging connections, in more senses than one, with Kashmiri Muslims. In August 1922 notices were posted in Srinagar over the signature of Sarwar Nand, a Kashmiri Pandit, and Mohammed Malik, a Kashmiri Muslim, dissuading Kashmiri boys from attending a performance given by a bioscope company at Hazuri Bagh. The reason given was that 'Punjabi boys were present in that area'. Subsequently a counter notice was distributed 'on behalf' of Kashmiri Muslims saying that the Pandits had falsely appended the signature of a Muslim on the previous notice. The British Resident reported that there were was 'considerable minor bickering of this sort between the Kashmiri Pandits and Punjabi communities'.[78] One objective of these attempts at fashioning a broader alliance, also evident in the Kashmiri Pandits and the Dogra Sabha working together in the mid-1920s, was to have the definition of the term 'Hereditary State Subject' altered to exclude encroachment on state employment by 'outsiders'.

In 1899, the growing demand that priority be given to state subjects in state employment had produced only a hollow attempt to redress the situation. It took the form of vague instructions issued in the same year by the viceroy that *mulkis* (natives) be given preference in state employment.[79] Quite evidently, this pitiful resolution would not satisfy increasingly determined groups in the state since, by evading

[77] Press cutting of an article titled 'Miserable Kashmir' published in *United India and Indian States*, Madras, dated Thursday, 22 September 1921, in OER, Political Department, 1921, File no. 73/97-C, JKA.

[78] R/1/1/1411, CRR (Political Department), Letter from C.J. Windham, Resident, dated 16 August 1922, IOL.

[79] Letter from Talbot, Resident in Kashmir, to Cunningham, Secretary in the Foreign Department, Foreign Department (Secret E)/Pros. February 1898/nos. 183–286, NAI.

any clear definition of a state subject, the status of a mulki devolved on anyone who cared to make the claim.[80] The clamour against 'outsiders' only grew in the following years, and continued pressure yielded yet another fairly meaningless attempt at definition in 1912, in which the ownership of land was deemed the defining criterion.[81] This new designation included all 'persons who ha[d] tendered a duly executed Rayat Nama and ha[d] acquired immovable property within the state territories' as well as all persons who had been living in the state for at least twenty years. While the privileged entry of subjects so defined in state service was acknowledged, exceptions were also made for state servants (and their descendants) who 'though not state subject[s], ha[d] not less than 10 years [of] approved service in the State.' In effect, the dominance of Punjabis was left securely in place since most of them had lived in the state for at least twenty years, if not longer. The unsatisfactory nature of the concession of 1912 was highlighted by yet another Kashmiri Pandit writing under the pseudonym Satis Superque in 1921 in the *United India and Indian States*. He suggested that over the preceding decades

> sites and plots have been acquired by outsiders who have humoured our benign Highness into condescension, by men who have either possessed influence with the maharaja, or have held some high and responsible positions in the state. A few months or years' stay has given them hereditary rights of a state subject to freely acquire lands whenever and wherever they liked. Ex-ministers who have some half a century back been in the state have come forward to assert their rights and secure some immovable property.

Pointing to the glaring deficiency of the 1912 definition, the writer suggested that a truly fair delineation of the term 'state subject' would encompass only persons able to prove 'hereditary residence' in the state for at least five generations. It could not include those others who had 'secured this title by presenting a mere rayatnamah, or acquired the rights by mere contract—serving in the state.'[82]

[80] Bazaz, *The History of the Struggle for Freedom in Kashmir*, p. 135.

[81] 'Report of the Committee to Define the Term "State Subject" ', Political Department, 1935, File no. 199/RR-18, JKA.

[82] Press cutting of an article titled 'The New Era in Kashmir', published in *United India and Indian States*, Madras, dated Thursday, 22 September 1921 in OER, Political Department, 1921, File no. 73/97-C, JKA.

In 1927, these various moves having failed to satisfy either an increasingly vocal Kashmiri Pandit community or the Dogra Sabha, Hari Singh instituted yet another definition. According to it 'all persons born and residing in the state before the commencement of the reign of Maharaja Gulab Singh and also all persons who settled therein before the commencement of 1885 and have since been permanently residing in the country' were now considered state subjects. Simultaneously, Hari Singh decreed that no person who did not fit the bill would be permitted either employment in state services or the right to purchase agricultural land in the state.[83] At this point the Dogra Sabha, presumably satisfied with the fresh concessions, withdrew from this particular arena of debate.

For the Kashmiri Pandits, however, while the threat of the Punjabi official had been mitigated considerably, they were now forced to turn their attention to a new and even more potent rival. The Kashmiri Muslims, vastly outnumbering both the Punjabi Hindus and the Pandits, had begun to mobilize for their own rights and from a standpoint as legitimate as that of the Kashmiri Pandits in their being equally 'sons of the soil'. While the Pandits had tactically included, at least implicitly, the interests of Kashmiri Muslims when making regionally based demands for a proper definition of the term 'state subject', they were eventually confronted with the logical extension of their strategy. As state subjects the Kashmiri Muslims were as entitled to consideration from the Kashmir durbar as were the Pandits. But Pandit privileges were decidedly shakier when faced with Muslim demands for special concessions to overcome their educational 'backwardness' and for representation in the state services in proportion to their numbers. Forming only 5 per cent of the population of the valley against the 95 per cent of Muslims, the regional solidarity they had waxed so eloquently on only recently began to sour a little.

Representing Kashmiri Muslim Interests: Regional or Religious Identity?

That the discrepant interests of the Kashmiri Pandits and Muslims, belying the regional cohesion claimed by the former, had not manifested themselves sooner was because the Muslims entered the fray of the state's politics considerably later than the Pandits. Aside from a

---

[83] 'Report of the Committee to Define the Term "State Subject"'.

lack of internal unity (when compared with the older self-conscious efforts at constructing solidarity among the Pandits) Kashmiri Muslims were also concerned to correct their lag in education prior to any active participation in politics.[84] The Kashmiri Pandits were well in advance of the Muslims in taking to modern education. Therefore, the efforts of the former at mobilizing in favour of preferential treatment for state subjects in government employment had no resonance in what was, at best, a meagrely educated Muslim community. Yet, the year 1907 marked a decisive shift when a group of 'Representatives of Kashmiri Mussulmans' spoke out on behalf of Kashmiri Muslims. They were as concerned with marking their own social leadership in Kashmir as they were with the plight of their co-religionists in the valley. They brought to public notice the lack of Muslim representation in the state administration and suggested that only provision of adequate education would correct this situation. At the same time their memorandum pressed the point that the 'backwardness' of Muslims was caused by Hindu officers who neglected Muslim interests and Hindu teachers who wished to keep the Muslims illiterate.[85] From this point on, the Kashmiri Muslim 'representatives' concentrated on demands from the state for increased inputs into the education of their co-religionists and the induction of larger numbers of Muslims into the state structure. And these demands were made as the rights due to an under-represented majority.[86]

Support for this increasingly assertive posture adopted by Kashmiri Muslims also came from outside the state. In 1909, the All-India Mohammedan Educational Conference meeting in Rangoon appealed to the maharaja of Kashmir that since Muslims formed a clear majority of his subjects, the number of Muslim teachers and school inspectors should be increased and additional scholarships should be made available to Muslim students.[87] Also speaking from outside the

[84] Bazaz, *The History of the Struggle for Freedom in Kashmir*, p. 136.

[85] Memorial presented by the Representatives of the Kashmiri Mussalmans to Sir Louis Dane, Secretary in the Foreign Department, Foreign Department (Internal A)/Pros. February 1907/nos. 163–4, NAI.

[86] Petition from the Representatives of the Kashmiri Mussalmans Regarding the Employment of Mussalmans in the Kashmir State, Foreign Department (General B)/Pros. January 1909/nos. 15/16, NAI.

[87] OER, Political Department, 1911, File no. 70/P-37, JKA.

state terrritory, the Muslim Kashmiri Conference of Lahore made appeals on behalf of Kashmiri Muslims' rights to educational advancement and representation in the state. In that year, the conference drew the maharaja's attention to the resolutions of the All India Mohammedan Educational Conference and requested that he act upon them. At its annual session in 1912, the Muslim Kashmiri Conference suggested that the Kashmir durbar employ 'Musalmans from the Punjab in the state service if competent Musalmans in the State' could not be found. The response of the maharaja was that the new definition of 'state subjects' instituted in 1912 obliged him to reserve administrative employment for the latter. Since this had not prevented the employment of Punjabi Hindu officials, the ruler's justification was regarded as a clear instance of the discrimination practised in Kashmir against Muslims.[88]

This point appeared to be confirmed in a speech made by Pratap Singh at a prize distribution ceremony in Jammu. He suggested that he had not only 'provided equal opportunities for all classes of his subjects' but in fact gone further to furnish 'special facilities' for Muslims. Therefore, he concluded that Muslims had no one but themselves to blame for their educational backwardness. Their deficiency in the matter was only evidence that they did not particularly value either education or state service, probably finding themselves more drawn to other vocations.[89] This statement, demonstrating the utter incomprehension of and reckless disregard by the durbar of Kashmiri Muslim concerns, pushed segments of the Srinagar élite led by the two mirwaizes, Hassan Shah Naqshbandi, Saad-ud-din Shawl and others, to step up the pressure on the state. In 1924, on the occasion of the visit to Kashmir by the viceroy, Lord Reading, they presented him with a memorial demanding, besides more government jobs and better educational facilities for Muslims, ownership rights for the peasantry, the abolition of begar and the restoration of all mosques under the control of the durbar. This memorandum represented a widening in the nature of demands made by the Srinagar Muslim élite, seeking now to emerge as leaders of a broader segment of Muslims. Hari Singh responded with severe repression of the memorialists.[90]

[88] OER, Political Department, 1912, File no. 254/P-127, JKA.

[89] U.K. Zutshi, p. 222.

[90] Bazaz, *The History of the Struggle for Freedom in Kashmir*, pp. 137–8.

In an effort to contain what was turning into a dangerous political trend of outspokenness among Kashmiri Muslims, Hari Singh adopted a policy that attempted to conciliate educated Muslim opinion, if somewhat ambiguously. After the enactment of the definition of a 'Hereditary State Subject' in 1927, the durbar had announced the grant of twelve new scholarships to eleven Hindus and one Muslim. Confronted with vociferous resentment from Muslim memorialists in both Jammu and Kashmir, the maharaja announced the award of additional scholarships to ensure an even distribution between Hindus and Muslims.[91] Contemporaries such as Prem Nath Bazaz have suggested further that the memorialists from Jammu were secretly promised that, from that point forward, Muslims alone would fill 50 per cent of vacancies in the state service. In 1930, a notice had been issued by the Srinagar Municipality inviting applications for certain posts and specifying that only Muslim candidates would be considered. However, strident Kashmiri Pandit protest that the state was engaging in 'communalism' forced the immediate withdrawal of the notice.[92]

Nevertheless, the entitlement of Kashmiri Muslims to a parity of rights with other classes of subjects seemed finally to have gained some recognition from the Kashmir durbar. This represented an acknowledgement not merely of their large numbers but also of the principle that the state was duty-bound to redress their disadvantages as a community long kept in a backward condition. Another significant outcome of these assorted petitioning activities was that in the late 1920s the Kashmiri Pandits were becoming aware of the competition they would have to contend with from the more numerous and increasingly self-assured Kashmiri Muslims. Their own sense of a religiously-informed community identity and interests, in defence of which they had mobilized only recently, did not prevent them from dubbing as 'communal' a parallel movement among Kashmiri Muslims. Replicating the Indian National Congress's rhetoric, Kashmiri Pandits pitted the 'communalism' of the Muslims against what they described as their own more genuinely 'national' struggles. They offered as proof their exertions in obtaining a redefinition of the term 'Hereditary State Subject' and in being the first to raise 'the cry of Kashmir for

[91] His Highness' Government, Jammu and Kashmir, *Evidence Recorded in Public by the Srinagar Riots Enquiry Committee*, 1931.
[92] U.K. Zutshi, pp. 224–5.

Kashmiris'.[93] What stood out starkly was the disingenuousness of the Pandits in equating their particularized interests with those of all Kashmiris, and generalizing their efforts to defend them into a region-wide, or as they insisted, a 'national' struggle. Confronted for the first time with an assertive Muslim population mobilizing for a share of the same pie, the comfortable adherence by the Pandits to a common regional cause evaporated and they began to speak increasingly in the language of an endangered religious minority.

This was the broader context in the 1930s when a small group of young Muslims, recently educated in various British Indian universities, began to participate actively in the politics of the valley. Prominent among them was Sheikh Mohammed Abdullah who had earned his degree at Aligarh Muslim University. Disappointed by the very limited changes instituted in the recruitment rules for the civil service and finding few opportunities to accommodate their newly earned educational qualifications, these men began to meet at the Muslim Reading Room in Srinagar. They gradually coalesced into the Reading Room Party. Faced with the durbar's refusal to reserve jobs for Muslims if they could not 'earn' them through equal competition with other communities, they inaugurated in 1930 an extensive propaganda campaign against the durbar and against the Kashmiri Pandits who had taken once again to active protest.[94]

The Kashmiri Pandits were concerned not only with the militant posture adopted by Sheikh Abdullah and his colleagues but also with a renewed threat of unemployment for members of their own community. In April 1930, the Kashmir Government Retrenchment Committee had submitted its report to the durbar. It had recommended a reduction of 1050 men from the menial staff and 250 from the clerical staff. The report was given effect to promptly and all state subjects above 53 years of age and non-state subjects above 50 were prematurely pensioned off.[95] This was bound to affect adversely the educated section of Kashmiri society, especially the Pandits, who

---

[93] *Memorial Presented by the Sanatan Dharm Youngmen's Association on Behalf of Kashmiri Pandits to His Highness the Maharaja Bahadur of Jammu and Kashmir,* dated Srinagar, 24 October 1931 (Srinagar: The Kashmir Mercantile Press, 1931), p. 3.

[94] Bazaz, *The History of the Struggle for Freedom in Kashmir,* pp. 148–9.

[95] *Tribune,* Thursday, 1 May 1930, p. 12.

already felt that the numbers of their unemployed was worryingly large. More so when this was combined with announcements only a month earlier that the amount allotted in the government's budget for state scholarships granted exclusively to Muslims had been doubled.[96] Even the tenuous assertion of a set of regional interests by the Kashmiri Pandits was now definitely fading and was practically extinguished on 13 July 1931, when a group of Muslims led an attack on Hindus in Srinagar. The result was a withdrawing into religious boundaries both by Kashmiri Muslims and Pandits, each accusing the other of engaging in self-seeking politics.

Of Lions, Goats, Ahmediyas and Ahrars: Intra-Muslim Rivalry in Kashmir

The date 13 July 1931 is considered by several scholars to mark the inauguration of the 'freedom struggle' waged by Kashmiris against Dogra rule.[97] Neither the events of that day in Srinagar nor the death toll of twenty-two demonstrators and one policeman seem remarkable when compared to contemporaneous developments in British India. However, the significance of the date drew from the fact that it was the first time that a gathering of Kashmiri Muslims openly challenged the authority of the maharaja and his government.

By mid-1931 rumours had been spreading about the maharaja's officials deliberately mistreating Muslims and Islam in Jammu. The report that elicited the most vituperative reaction was of a Hindu police constable who had prevented a Muslim subordinate from saying his prayers and had followed this insult up with the injury of throwing the latter's copy of the Quran to the ground. Later investigation found this incident to have been grossly exaggerated, although not entirely without foundation. It brought to a head a gathering discontent born out of a number of factors other than the purely religious among Muslims in the state,[98] and, by the time news of the constable's actions reached Srinagar, the stage was set for the momentous events of the following days. On 25 June, Abdul Qadir, the

[96] *Tribune*, Wednesday, 5 February 1930, p. 4.

[97] Bazaz, *The History of the Struggle for Freedom in Kashmir*, pp. 154–5; Bamzai, *History of Kashmir*, p. 657; U.K. Zutshi, p. 228.

[98] R/1/1/2064, CRR (Political Department), Fortnightly reports on the internal situation in the Kashmir State for 1931, IOL.

Pathan servant of a European vacationing in Kashmir, made an inflammatory speech at a meeting in a Srinagar mosque condemning the Dogra maharaja and 'inciting his hearers to kill Hindus and burn their temples'.[99] He was promptly arrested for this. A general impression created by accounts of subsequent events was of an unprovoked attack led by Srinagar Muslims against unwitting Hindus. However, the Kashmiri Pandits and other Hindus, shaken by the expression of such hostile sentiments as those of Qadir, had disseminated their own set of rumours. One such, spreading like wildfire and indicating the fear felt by a 'minority' of possibly losing ground in the state to a Muslim 'majority', was that the Dogra ruler was about to permit cow slaughter.[100] Segments of both the Hindu and Muslim populations in Kashmir were raising their defenses and the situation was moving inexorably towards a confrontation.

On 13 July when Abdul Qadir was to be tried at the Central Jail in Srinagar, a crowd had attempted to enter the jail to protest his prosecution. In retaliation, the police fired into the gathering that then scattered and went on a rampage in Srinagar city. In Maharajgunj, a quarter of Srinagar inhabited almost exclusively by Kashmiri Pandits and Punjabi Hindu traders, 'crowds of Mohammadan hooligans' attacked shops, looted large quantities of goods and 'committed indiscriminate assaults'.[101] The Resident, however, acknowledged that 'there had . . . recently [been] much discussion among Mohammadans [in Kashmir] about their grievances against the comparatively small Hindu community . . . which, as *a result of a mistaken policy of many years standing, ha[d] been allowed to monopolize most of the appointments in the State.*'[102] Despite admitting evidence of a growing resentment and debate among the Muslims in Kashmir, the Resident still confessed that 'no one [had] for a moment suspected than [*sic*] any danger was to be feared in the city of Srinagar'.[103] Evidently taken by

[99] R/1/1/2064, CRR (Political Department), Resident's Fortnightly Report for 1 July 1931, IOL.

[100] R/1/1/2064, CRR (Political Department), Maharaja Hari Singh's Message, dated 9 July 1931, IOL.

[101] R/1/1/2064, CRR (Political Department), From the Resident in Kashmir dated 17 July 1931, IOL.

[102] Ibid. Emphasis mine.

[103] Ibid.

surprise by the overt 'activism' of Kashmiri Muslims, the maharaja's government devised makeshift and quick fix solutions. Relying on the tested strategy of his predecessor, Hari Singh 'received a deputation of all the leading Muslims of the city' with a view to removing their apprehensions. Loyalist groups of Muslims meeting with the ruler included a deputation of Muslim jagirdars from Muzeffarabad who, on 31 July, assured him of their 'unfaltering loyalty'. However, as the Resident suggested, the greatest difficulty the maharaja would have to face came not from the small Kashmiri Muslim élite but from the public disapproval of his policies freely expressed in British India and particularly in the Punjab.[104]

The events of July 1931 had catapulted a number of new actors on the political stage of Kashmir, each seeking to capitalize on the momentum of Muslim discontent unleashed through these incidents. A younger generation of Muslim politicians led by Sheikh Mohammed Abdullah and aiming at broader social bases of mobilization was pitted against the older and more socially exclusive élite leadership of the Jama Masjid mirwaiz, Saad-ud-din Shawl and others. These Kashmiris were joined in their competition for the leadership of Muslims in the valley by two rival sets of interests from the Punjab represented by the Ahmediyas and the Ahrars. By mid-August 1931, the Resident was already reporting on dissatisfaction among the Kashmiri Muslims being fuelled by letters from Muslim organizations from outside the state urging them to keep up their agitation. Under such prompting, Kashmiri Muslims led by Sheikh Abdullah had refused to meet with the maharaja on 6 August 1931, aiming to 'procrastinate' until 14 August which had been declared 'Kashmir Day' throughout 'Muhammedan centres in British India' by the Kashmir Committee formed only a week after the killings of 13 July.[105] This was an early instance of the reliance Sheikh Abdullah had begun to place on the Ahmediyas, who were prominent in the Kashmir Committee, in his struggles against not only the Dogra-Hindu state but also against the Kashmiri Muslim élite led by the then Mirwaiz-i-Jama Masjid, Yusuf Shah. The Kashmir

---

[104] R/1/1/2064, CRR (Political Department). From the Resident in Kashmir, dated 3 August 1931, IOL.

[105] R/1/1/2064, CRR (Political Department), From the Resident in Kashmir, dated 17 August 1931, IOL.

Committee had also enjoyed the support of large numbers of Kashmiri Muslims settled in the Punjab.

Some words first about the dilemmas of Kashmir politics spilling over into the much more perplexing fray of British Indian politics, especially in the Punjab. The connections between Kashmir and Punjab were not new, particularly in the context of the Dogra search for legitimacy from Lahore, as argued earlier on in this work. Taking advantage of these older ties, Pratap Singh himself had opened lines of communication with sections of the Hindu-owned press in Punjab, as well as Bengal, in an effort to muster support for himself in the years between 1889 and 1905 when he had been deprived of his governing powers. As the preceding chapters have shown, the Punjab press, whether owned by Hindus or Muslims, had never ceased to communicate their views on Kashmir affairs and thereby foment a public debate in the major cities of Punjab. In the absence of a Kashmir-based press, prohibited by the Dogra rulers until 1932, newspapers from Punjab had consistently filtered into the valley, carrying with them their editorializing opinions on the situation in Kashmir.[106]

In the aftermath of the events of July 1931, Hari Singh decided to rewire contacts between Kashmir, Punjab and the rest of British India. With a view both to ascertaining the reactions of and influencing prominent British Indian figures, he turned to Sir Tej Bahadur Sapru, the Liberal politician from the Punjab but of Kashmiri Pandit extraction. In a letter dated 6 September 1931 he informed Sapru that he was 'glad to know that Mr Gandhi and Pandit Malaviya [a right-wing Congress leader] were interested in the happenings in Kashmir.' He asked further that 'his thanks, kind regards and best wishes' be conveyed to them as well as his indebtedness to Mr Moonje, a leader of right-wing Hindu militant politics who would (as he mysteriously suggested) 'know how to assist'. Hari Singh added in his communication an assertion of the reliance he placed both on Sapru and Colonel Haksar,

[106] The British Resident in Kashmir had himself commented on how he believed that the 'situation' in Kashmir in July 1931 had been considerably exacerbated by the censorship of especially Muslim owned newspapers in the valley as well as the prohibition on Muslim leaders from India entering the state. The implication probably being that suppression gave greater force to the news and opinions carried by both. R/1/1/2064, CRR (Political Department), Report from the Resident, dated 19 June 1931, IOL.

another prominent figure in British India of Kashmiri Pandit extraction, 'for doing whatever [wa]s necessary . . . in connection with this *frivolous* agitation.'[107] If the Dogra rulers themselves kept the borders of public opinion between their state and British India porous, they could scarcely claim surprise when diverse groups of Muslims from Punjab in turn reacted to and sought to influence developments within Jammu and Kashmir.

Prominent Punjabi Muslim leaders had demonstrated political interest in the grievances of their co-religionists in Kashmir as early as 1892. As mentioned earlier, their concern was partly institutionalized in the formation of the All-India Muslim Kashmiri Conference in 1911 in Lahore. This organization became more actively involved in Kashmiri affairs after 1924,[108] in reaction to the harsh treatment by the maharaja of the Kashmiri Muslim delegation to Lord Reading in that year.[109] In July 1931, the Conference had been reconstituted as the All-India Kashmir Committee in Punjab under the presidentship of Bashir-ud-din Mahmud Ahmad, the Khalifa (Caliph or leader) of the Ahmediya community based in Qadian. Among its members was Sir Muhammad Iqbal, the Kashmiri-born poet and philosopher.

At the same time, Kashmir began to emerge at the centre of the politics of yet another Punjab-based group known as the Majlis-i-Ahrar-i-Islam (henceforth referred to as the Ahrars).[110] Led among others by Saiyid Ataullah Shah Bokhari, the Ahrars were composed of anti-British urban Muslims and reformist members of the *ulama* with links to the Indian National Congress. The plight of Kashmiri Muslims under a Hindu ruler supported by the colonial government became the focal point of their propaganda. However, the most pressing political concern for the Ahrars was to stem the activities of the Ahmediyas both in Kashmir and in the Punjab itself. Their animosity

---

[107] Maharaja Hari Singh to Sir Tej Bahadur Sapru, 'Sapru Papers', Series III, File S, cited in Barbara N. Ramusack, 'Exotic Imports or Home-grown Riots: The Muslim Agitations in Kashmir in the Early 1930s', Unpublished Paper Presented at the Third Punjab Studies Conference, University of Pennsylvania, 7 May 1971.

[108] Spencer Lavan, *The Ahmadiyah Movement* (Delhi: Manohar, 1974), pp. 148–50.

[109] *Tribune,* 27 August 1931, p. 7.

[110] For a fuller discussion of the politics of the Ahmediyas, Ahrars and Sir Mohammad Iqbal, see Jalal, *Self and Sovereignty.*

towards Mirza Ghulam Ahmed, the founder of the Ahmediya movement, and his followers was rooted in critical doctrinal differences. The most galling aspect of Ahmediya beliefs to the Ahrars and
many other Muslims was that they seemed to challenge the finality of
Muhammad's Prophethood.[111] Kashmir occupied a special place for
the Ahmediyas too in that they believed that the messiah Christ was
buried in Srinagar at Roza Bal.[112] They funded significant missionary
and educational work both in Kashmir and in Punjab.[113] Of course,
the grand prize for which both the Ahmediyas and the Ahrars were in
competition was Muslim support in Punjab itself. However, the Kashmiri Muslims had become symbolic of the oppression Muslims, more
generally, suffered and would continue to suffer under British rule.

On 12 July 1931, the Ahrars demanded an independent investigation into the condition of Muslims in Kashmir.[114] On 24 July 1931,
the All-India Kashmir Committee called for an enquiry by the Government of India into the incident of 13 July in Srinagar, determined
the observance of 14 August as 'Kashmir Day', and went so far as to
suggest a review by the British parliament of the 1846 Amritsar
treaty.[115] By the end of August the Ahrars decided to infiltrate Jammu
territory with *jathas* (bands) of supporters.[116] A frenzy of action and
reaction over Kashmir had begun between the Ahrars and the Ahmediyas. The Kashmir durbar could have neutralized both the Ahmediyas
and Ahrars by the simple expedient of closing the borders. What made
both strains of Punjabi Muslim interference in Kashmir at this time so
much more effective was that they had gained sympathetic adherents
within the state. While Jammu's Muslim cultivators had welcomed
the Ahrar jathas, the Ahmediyas and Sheikh Abdullah were locked into
their own mutually supportive alliance.

[111] David Gilmartin, *Empire and Islam: Punjab and the Making of Pakistan*
(Berkeley: University of California Press, 1988), pp. 96–7.

[112] A shrine in good repair exists to this day at Roza Bal in Srinagar and contains
a grave of such extensive length as to convince most Kashmiris that only a tall
'Westerner' could be buried within. Personal communication from a Muslim
attendant of the shrine, Srinagar, July 1997.

[113] Spencer Lavan, *The Ahmadiyah Movement*, p. 146.

[114] *Tribune*, 14 July 1931, p. 8.

[115] *Tribune*, 29 July 1931, p. 8.

[116] *Tribune*, 29 August 1931, p. 9, and 4 September 1931, p. 8.

In Jammu province, the mobilizational activities of the Ahrar *jathas* provoked months of violent 'communal' rioting that racked the tehsils of Mirpur, Rajouri, Seri and Kotli, between 1931 and 1934. Largely a rural revolt, Muslim cultivators directed their wrath against Hindu revenue officials, landowners and moneylenders and engaged in no-revenue campaigns.[117] In reaction, the state took the 'unfortunate' decision in January 1932 of extracting revenue forcibly in Mirpur tehsil by sending out its collectors under armed escort.[118] From there, the rural revolt spread with remarkable speed and attacks were made on the state's revenue collectors, Hindu shopowners, moneylender-owned shops and the Sikh population of the state. The situation grew too difficult for the maharaja's government to handle on its own and so the state was compelled to call in British troops.[119]

Ahrar agitation in the state had converged with a series of grievances felt by the largely Muslim cultivators of Jammu province. The revolt had been preceded by a period of propaganda carried on in mosques against Hindus and the state administration, 'these being represented as identical'.[120] The greatest ire of the Jammu cultivators was directed against their urban and rural Hindu creditors, who were accused of dispossessing them of their lands at a time of agricultural depression when they were unable to repay their debts.[121] Instances of the transfer of lands were particularly evident in the very same areas racked by rioting such as Mirpur and Kotli. Most of the land was acquired by Hindu *sahukars* (moneylenders or traders), some by larger landowners and the rest by officials, some of whom were not even resident in the state.[122] Hindu moneylenders, the cultivators felt, were favoured by the local courts in money suits and in the execution of money decrees

---

[117] R/1/1/2223, CRR (Political Department), Fortnightly Reports on the Internal situation in Kashmir during 1932, From the Resident, dated 18 January 1932, IOL.

[118] R/1/1/2245, CRR (Political Department), Extract from a demi-official letter from C.V. Salusbury, Officer on Special Duty, dated 5 February 1932, IOL.

[119] Bazaz, *History of the Struggle for Freedom*, p. 159.

[120] R/1/1/2279 (1), CRR, Report by C.V. Salusbury on the Revenue Administration of the Mirpur Tahsil, IOL.

[121] Ibid.

[122] Note by the Settlement Commissioner, Jammu and Kashmir state, dated 1 April 1915, OER, 1912, File no. 273/ H-79, JKA

inspite of the Agriculturists Relief Regulation.[123] In areas where some Muslims were known to be moneylenders, their houses too were looted so proving that the strained financial relations between agriculturists and moneylenders was one of the main causes of the disturbances.[124]

There were several other factors that exacerbated the position of cultivators, predominantly Muslim in Jammu province. Many of them had relied heavily on supplementing their incomes with wages earned outside the state. Since 1931, owing to the suspension of large projects in British India, such as the canal works in neighbouring Punjab and general financial depression, these sources of income had shrunk considerably and increased the burden of the revenue demand of the state. Mirpur tehsil's villagers had also supplied a large quota of troops to the British Indian army during World War I,[125] and many of them found themselves unemployed in the 1920s. At the same time, a keen land hunger had developed over the preceding decade in Mirpur specifically, and Jammu province more generally, owing to the competition among Hindu 'capitalists' and from among retired soldiers for the acquisition of cultivable tracts. As a consequence the price of land was inflated out of proportion to any increase in agricultural prices that had in fact registered a fall since the onset of the Depression.[126] The state had carelessly read the increase in land prices as an indicator of growing prosperity and in 1930 raised the already unbearable land tax by 14.4 per cent in several of the southern tehsils of Jammu.[127]

The riots in Jammu had the effect of stoking the fire of Hindu–Muslim antagonism throughout the state. In Kashmir, however, after the incidents of July 1931, there were no riots on the scale of those

[123] R/1/1/2279 (1), CRR, Report by C.V. Salusbury on the Revenue Administration of the Mirpur Tahsil, IOL.

[124] R/1/1/2279 (1), Demi-official letter from Lieutenant E.J.D. Colvin, Prime Minister, Jammu and Kashmir State, to C. Latimer, Resident, dated 30 June 1932, IOL.

[125] R/1/1/2279 (1), CRR, Report by C.V. Salusbury on the Revenue Administration of the Mirpur Tahsil, IOL.

[126] Ibid.

[127] Note by Pandit Anant Ram, Director Land Records, dated 4 January 1932, Political Department, 1931, File no. 385/R-G, 41, JKA.

witnessed in Jammu. And no commonality of interests emerged between the Muslims of the valley with those of Jammu. Muslims in the two provinces shared few social bonds as the Jammu Muslims had closer 'caste', marriage and economic ties with Punjab.[128] In fact Prem Nath Bazaz confirms a 'provincial prejudice' underlying relations between the Muslims of the two areas. They differed in 'race, language and culture' and ordinarily, 'when the atmosphere [was] not surcharged with any communal bitterness', this was made emphatically apparent. 'The Muslims of the two provinces d[id] not like each other and they frankly express[ed] it.'[129] Whether grounded in fact or not, the Kashmiri Muslims were convinced that their co-religionists of Jammu hogged the best jobs in government.[130] The state army was at least one arena of the state in which the Jammu Muslims found employment whereas all Kashmiris were debarred from it. All the same, through the decade of the 1930s and the 1940s, Muslim political leaders from the two regions sometimes forged alliances with each other, sometimes parted ways, but almost always chose to ride on each other's shoulders.

If there was no unity of response by the Muslims of the Jammu and Kashmir provinces, such cohesion was also lacking among the major political figures within Kashmir. As we know already, periodic clashes over religious precedence and territory between the two mirwaizes had been common fare in Srinagar. This sustained trace of hostility manifested itself also in doctrinal disagreements over the validity or otherwise of the Sufi doctrines that held sway among Kashmiri Muslims. But in July 1924, open 'warfare' began when Ahmadullah, the Hamadani mirwaiz, invited the Ahmediyas to address the Muslims of Srinagar from the Khanqah-i-Mualla.[131] The Jama Masjid mirwaiz, divided with the Hamadani imam in doctrine but sharing the confusingly similar name of Ahmadullah Shah, 'excommunicated' his rival. The Ahmediyas appeared to have gained a foothold in sections of

---

[128] *Census of India* (Jammu and Kashmir), 1931, part I, pp. 103–4, 107.

[129] Bazaz, *Inside Kashmir*, pp. 262–3.

[130] Ibid.

[131] Ian Copland, 'The Adullah Factor: Kashmiri Muslims and the Crisis of 1947' in D.A. Low (ed.), *The Political Inheritance of Pakistan* (London: Macmillan, 1991), p. 225..

Kashmiri Muslim sympathies, such as those of the Hamadani mirwaiz, and later Sheikh Abdullah, by creating the impression, denied vociferously by the British, that they had the ear of the powerful in the colonial establishment.

After the July 1931 'riots', Sheikh Mohammed Abdullah openly took sides with the Hamadani mirwaiz. To a certain degree this was a result of prompting from the Ahmediyas, with whom the Sheikh allegedly had links going back to his youth.[132] Members of the Reading Room Party and the Youngmen's Muslim Association that Sheikh Abdullah had helped found were said to have attended the annual session of the All India Muslim Kashmiri Conference in 1931.[133] This bit of circumstantial evidence led both the Jama Masjid mirwaiz and the British to allege that Sheikh Abdullah himself was an Ahmedi or a Mirzai (the follower of Mirza Ghulam Ahmed, the founder of the Ahmedi sect). The British themselves later denied this. However, whether a Mirzai or not, Sheikh Abdullah used both the All India Kashmir Committee and the Hamadani mirwaiz to build up his political stature. Of course, as mentioned earlier, the broader social appeal of a Sufi-based worship among Kashmiris, doctrinally supported by the Hamadani mirwaiz, held its own attractions for a politician-on-the-rise.[134]

The links forged between Sheikh Abdullah and the Hamadani mirwaiz were strengthened also by the Kashmiri Pandits choosing to side with Mohammed Yusuf Shah, who had succeeded his father in 1931 as the Mirwaiz-i-Jama Masjid. By 1932, there was evidence that some of the Kashmiri Pandits had joined in the fray of the intra-Muslim rivalry over the right to preach raging in Srinagar. Members of the Kashmiri Pandit community backed the mirwaiz Mohammed Yusuf whom, it was said, they 'respect[ed] and support[ed]' whereas 'all of the . . . community heartily hate[d] S.M. Abdulla and all his works.' So much so that certain Kashmiri Pandits, posing as the Mirwaiz-i-

[132] Satish Vaid, *Sheikh Abdullah Then and Now* (Delhi: Maulik Sahitya Prakashan, 1968), pp. 1–2, 20; Joseph Korbel, *Danger in Kashmir* (Princeton: Princeton University Press, 1954), p. 17.

[133] *Tribune*, 26 August 1931, p. 5, and 27 August 1931, p. 7.

[134] Sheikh Abdullah, *Flames of the Chinar* (New Delhi: Oxford University Press, 1993), pp. 28, 40, 149–50.

Jama Masjid's Muslim pleader Assad Ullah, were drafting petitions on his behalf arguing his right to preach at particular mosques in Srinagar.[135] It is highly unlikely that this support was born out of any religious sympathy felt by the Kashmiri Pandits towards the mirwaiz. Mohammed Yusuf represented not only the most potent foil to a trend of popular Muslim self-assertion represented by Sheikh Mohammed Abdullah, but also a force more sympathetic to the Dogra Raj which had protected Pandit interests.

However, Yusuf Shah had begun to demonstrate resentment at the durbar's attempt at putting down the 'trouble-making' Muslims. When the governor of Kashmir forbade him from preaching at one of the smaller mosques of Srinagar, the Jama Masjid mirwaiz interpreted this as an instance of 'His Highness's government *sacrificing loyal Muslims to factious agitators.*'[136] By 1933, the district magistrate in Srinagar was warning the durbar about a shift in the strategy of the mirwaiz, Mohammed Yusuf, who, he suggested, was espousing a new anti-government stance and 'openly spreading disaffection'. As the district magistrate reported, 'beginning . . . his new movement', the mirwaiz poured abuse on the durbar's ministers in public meetings.[137] In October 1933, Mohammed Yusuf had marked the inauguration of this new attitude in a speech he delivered before a gathering of a few thousand Muslims at the Jama Masjid in Srinagar. He urged his audience that 'it was wrong to think that religion was different from politics, as the service of the community and religion were one and the same thing.'[138]

But a common posture of opposition to the durbar did not in any way mean a mitigation in the rivalry between the mirwaiz of the Jama Masjid on the one hand and the Hamadani mirwaiz supported by

[135] Note from Mr B. Lawther, Inspector General of Police, Kashmir, to Kanwar Hira Singh, Political Secretary to the Government of Jammu and Kashmir, dated 25 August 1932, Political Department, 1932, File no. 138/P.S. 252, JKA.

[136] R/1/1/2223, CRR (Political Department), Fortnightly reports on the internal situation in Kashmir during 1932, report dated 30 July 1932, IOL. Emphasis mine.

[137] Note from the District Magistrate, Srinagar, to Col. E.J.D. Colvin, Prime Minister of H.H.'s Government, dated 18 October 1933, Political Department, 1933, File no. 44, JKA.

[138] Copy of a speech delivered by Mirwaiz Mohammed Yusuf on 6 October 1933, Inspector C.I.D.'s Daily Diary, dated 7 October 1933, Political Department, 1933, File no. 33, JKA.

Abdullah on the other. If anything, the competition grew more violent through the decades of the 1930s and the 1940s, as both groups vied with each other for the support of the Kashmiri Muslim community. The methods employed in the rivalry were often plainly undignified. Sticks, stones and even *kangris*[139] were hurled at each other by the two sides, in a battle between the lions (since his supporters called Abdullah the Lion of Kashmir) and the goats (in reference to the beards of the mullahs).

To the greater indignation of Yusuf Shah, Sheikh Abdullah had himself taken to preaching at the various mosques of the city,[140] and had diverted to himself offerings from Kashmiri Muslims that had formerly been given to the Mirwaiz-i-Jama Masjid.[141] As discussed in the preceding chapter, Sheikh Abdullah had claimed the Patthar Masjid as his preserve, from which base he sought to establish an alternative religious authority by appropriating the right to issue fatwas through his own appointed muftis. In the 1930s the contest between the lions and goats was extended to the control of a new set of shrines such as the mosque at Hazrat Bal, which housed a hair of Prophet Muhammad. Considered a most sacred site in Srinagar, the rivalry between the two Muslim factions provided yet another occasion for the Dogra state to intervene in the Muslim religious domain by issuing an order prohibiting either party from preaching there.[142] However, over the following decades Sheikh Abdullah's party established a distinct ascendancy over its rivals at Hazrat Bal.[143] Shrines such as Hazrat Bal were important to control for an emerging politician

[139] R/1/1/2064, CRR (Political Department), Fortnightly Reports on the internal situation in Kashmir during 1931, report dated 3 January 1932, IOL. A kangri is an earthen vessel filled with burning coal and held close to the body as a way to keep warm in the cold winters of Kashmir.

[140] R/1/1/2223, CRR (Political Department), Fortnightly reports on the internal situation in Kashmir during 1932, report dated 1 September 1932, IOL.

[141] R/1/1/2223, CRR (Political Department), Fortnightly reports on the internal situation in Kashmir during 1932, report dated 18 July 1932, IOL.

[142] R/1/1/2337, CRR (Political Department), Fortnightly reports on the political situation in the Kashmir state for the year 1933, report dated 18 July 1933, IOL.

[143] Muhammad Ishaq Khan, 'The Significance of the Dargah of Hazratbal in the Socio-Religious and Political Life of Kashmiri Muslims', in Christian W. Troll (ed.), *Muslim Shrines in India* (Delhi: Oxford University Press, 1992), pp. 172–88.

because they drew in the allegiance of large numbers of Muslims from the valley. The six annual fairs and regular Friday congregations held there provided occasions for social contact between urban and rural Muslims when both spiritual and material needs were satisfied.[144]This explains the acute need felt by both parties to control such important symbols of the cultural and religious affinities of Kashmiri Muslims.

However, Sheikh Abdullah did more than just 'preach' politics from the pulpits of various mosques and directed considerable energy towards dominating these platforms. He managed to undercut the élitist and, by his own recent assessment, 'loyalist' Jama Masjid mirwaiz to draw popular support primarily by tapping into a multitude of grievances suffered by Kashmir's Muslims. His reputation, spreading steadily since the events of July 1931, registered a leap every time he was arrested by the Kashmir durbar since jail-going had become a badge of honour among nationalists throughout the Indian subcontinent. In a remarkable turn-about of trends, by September 1931, Abdullah's popularity had grown to such proportions that the British were worried about the effect events in Kashmir might have on the communal situation in India, especially in Punjab. Consequently, they put pressure on the durbar to form a body that would look into and remedy the more obvious Muslim grievances. As a result, on 20 October 1931, the maharaja announced the appointment of a commission of enquiry headed by Bertrand J. Glancy, a senior member of the Indian Political Service.

The Glancy Commission invited submissions from all segments of the state's society. Importantly, the commission had not invited complaints from individuals but from representatives of the only recognized entities in the state; its various religious communities. Sheikh Abdullah appeared to be everywhere and speaking for every class of Kashmiri Muslims in the months when the commission was gathering evidence. Two important recommendations made were to allow the formation of political parties and the publication of newspapers in the state. Sheikh Abdullah capitalized on the first by founding the All Jammu and Kashmir Muslim Conference in October 1932, and used this organization to reinforce the wide social base of support in the valley that he had begun to garner through his representative activities in presenting testimony before the Glancy Commission.

[144] Ibid., p. 180.

In Srinagar, the food control policy of the Dogras had been breaking down gradually since the summer of 1931, when the rice crop was 'scantier than usual' as a result of floods and the ravaging effects of a crop disease called rai. In conditions of shortage, the poorer segments of the city's population had been finding it increasingly difficult to obtain their staple at a rate they could afford. In the countryside, the zamindars were unwilling to relinquish their limited harvests, wishing to hold on to as much of it as possible for themselves. This caused prices to take a dramatic turn upwards further aggravating the problem in Srinagar. In 1932, though, the harvest was better and this, in combination with the durbar's decision to import rice from British India, signalled a sudden downswing in prices. While useful for the urban sector, this spelt disaster for the cultivators.[145] Therefore, between 1931 and 1932, both the Srinagar poor and the agriculturists of the valley had cause for discontent and Sheikh Abdullah and his Muslim Conference found fertile ground for mobilization against the status quo.

The trade depression beginning in 1929 had already provided an undertow of discontent throughout the valley. A large population in Srinagar was dependent on the different handicraft industries such as shawl- and carpet-weaving, silk, papier mâché and silver works.[146] The depression produced adverse conditions for trade and consequently for the artisans. The prices of shawls, an industry which had already been dealt a blow in the 1870s, fell further[147] and not only were petty shopkeepers hit hard but large numbers of shawl embroiderers and papier mâché workers lost their jobs.[148] Labour unrest in the silk factory in Srinagar, brewing on and off since 1924, provided Abdullah with another constituency of supporters. In a lengthy report, presented in 1932, he elaborated on the problems faced by the Kashmiri Muslims in the context of the collapse of the silk trade.[149] Abdullah suggested that bringing in profits of 'lakhs of rupees' to the Kashmir

---

[145] R/1/1/2223, CRR (Political Department), Fortnightly reports on the internal situation in Kashmir during 1932, report dated 4 July 1932, IOL.

[146] *Census of India* (Jammu and Kashmir), 1931, part 1, pp. 36, 216.

[147] Ibid., p. 216.

[148] Bamzai, *A History of Kashmir*, p. 649.

[149] Note by Sheikh Abdullah, President of the All Jammu and Kashmir Muslim Conference, on the Present Management of the Sericulture Department, Political Department, 1932, File no. 216/P.S. 250, JKA.

durbar, the silk industry provided employment to about 51,000 families in one capacity or another. These included an urban population of weavers and reelers and a rural body of mulberry tree and silk-worm rearers. The industry was converted into a government monopoly in the late nineteenth century and its management entrusted to a handful of Europeans and a much larger body of Kashmiri Pandits. Abdullah alleged that the silk factory in Srinagar had been tottering to a breakdown in recent years owing only partly to the trade depression and mostly to the irresponsibility of its managers. He suggested that the condition of the already impoverished workers was made worse by the high-handedness and lack of sympathy with which the Pandit managerial staff treated them. The latter were accused of embezzlement; withholding the pay of labourers to ensure a captive workforce; the expulsion of large numbers of others rendering them jobless in the harsh years of the depression; the non-payment of pensions to others. Encouraged by Sheikh Abdullah, the workers at the silk factory adopted combative postures against the Pandit managers, and indirectly against the government, which owned the factory and so was ultimately responsible.[150] Considering the large numbers employed by the silk industry, Abdullah was carving himself an impressive political niche.

Conditions in the countryside of Kashmir were no better than in its cities. As discussed in Chapter Three, a body of landless labourers had emerged through the decades after Lawrence's settlement; begar continued to ensure that the Kashmiri cultivator had no control over his own labour; agrarian indebtedness was on the rise; the zamindar continued to be crushed by a heavy revenue demand and illegal cesses continued to be extracted by a revenue department still dominated by the Kashmiri Pandits. Through the 1930s and the 1940s Sheikh Abdullah and his colleagues, Mirza Afzal Beg and Bakhshi Ghulam Mohammed, seemed to be indefatigable, listening to the complaints of zamindars, drawing up petitions on their behalf and turning the Muslim Conference into the single most powerful representative voice of the Kashmiri Muslims. Demands made by Abdullah on behalf of

[150] C.I.D. Diary for 29 May 1936, Political Department, 1932, File no. 216/ P.S. 250, JKA.

Kashmir's cultivators were for responsible government, a reduction in the land revenue by 50 per cent, and correction of the usurious rates at which money was lent. Espousing socialist symbols and rhetoric, Abdullah even devised a flag for his party, not too subtly coloured red and imprinted with a plough.[151] And considering the broad religious lines followed by economic deprivation in the valley, class and religious community melted as easily into one another as did anti-'capitalist' and anti-Hindu rhetoric. As the mirwaiz Yusuf Shah had also suggested, there was no distinction between religion and politics in a state in which privileged access to the resources of a Hindu state had kept the vast majority of its Muslim subjects on its periphery. Mobilizing for the rights of the poorest Kashmiri Muslims would unavoidably have to take into account the 'discrimination . . . made between two people in a Government where favouritism [wa]s evident in the [most] trifling matters.'[152] Through 1932 and 1933, the Muslim Conference led by Abdullah used the newly sanctioned press in Kashmir to conduct propaganda against the dominance of Kashmiri Pandits in the countryside. The language used was sometimes immoderate and always uncompromising in its condemnation of the latter community. Suggestions were made that the 'Kashmiri Pandit [wa]s by nature an enemy of the Muslims' and that there were 'as many kinds of Pandits as [there were] snakes' with the difference that the bite of a snake would not prove fatal.[153] In 1933, in a speech delivered by Abdullah in the small Kashmiri town of Tragapura, he suggested that the task of the Muslim Conference and the Muslims of the valley was to 'turn out [the] Hindus, who from times past [had] been giving [the Muslims] trouble' and exhorted the crowd to 'take revenge'.[154]

[151] R/1/1/3492, CRR (Political Department), Fortnightly reports on the political situation in Kashmir state for 1940 (July to December), report for the first half of October 1940, IOL.

[152] Statements received from the Muslims of Kashmir by the Glancy Commission through S.M. Abdullah, Political Department, 1932, File no. 23/22-P.I., JKA.

[153] Publication in the *Tarjuman* of articles against the Kashmiri Pandits, Political Department, 1933, File no. 249/PP-10, JKA.

[154] Delivery of a seditious speech by Sheikh Mohammed Abdullah, Political Department, 1933, File no. 31, JKA.

Constructing Kashmiriyat: Religion and Rights

However, from these early days of unconstrained criticism of the Hindu state and particularly its Pandit allies, Sheikh Abdullah's political rhetoric took a new turn roughly around the mid-1930s. One of the recommendations of the Glancy Commission had been for the formation of a franchise commission to draw up a scheme of representative government in the state. A legislative assembly, with very limited powers and none to appoint ministers (which remained the prerogative of the maharaja) was brought into being by a Constitution in 1934. Known as the Praja Sabha, this seventy-five seat legislative assembly was made up of 33 elected, 12 official and 30 nominated members. The principle of separate electorates with reserved seats had been implemented and of the 33 elected seats, 21 were reserved for Muslims, 10 for Hindus and two for Sikhs. The franchise was, however, limited to men paying at least Rs 20 a year in land revenue or grazing taxes, thereby effectively leaving out large numbers of the poor among whom the Muslim Conference had been mobilizing.[155] The official and nominated members still formed a majority on the Praja Sabha and, as Abdullah saw it, in order to counter this imbalance it was critical for the Muslims to win the support of the Hindu and Sikh elected members.[156] This led Abdullah and the Muslim conference to tone down some of the anti-Hindu oratory. The 'secular' vocabulary of the Indian National Congress was sought to be approximated by an increasing use of the language of rights. However, a key distinction that remained in the political rhetoric of Abdullah from that of Nehru was the refusal of the former to distinguish between religion and rights. Congress nationalists of the Nehruvian strand had denied the validity of a defense of rights unless argued from a secular position. What Kashmir had shown was that the denial of the rights of the majority was deeply rooted in the religious nature of the state that presided over them.

After 1934, the Muslim Conference took two key political decisions. The first was to seek a rapprochement with those members of

[155] Some estimates suggest an electorate comprising only 3 per cent of the total adult population. Lamb, *Kashmir: A Disputed Legacy*, p. 92.

[156] Notes on the interview of S.M. Abdullah with Sir Barjor Dalal, Chief Justice, Jammu and Kashmir state, dated 24 March 1934, Political Department, 1934, File no. 6/A-8, JKA.

the Kashmiri Pandit community who might concede that the Muslims of the valley had been politically and economically marginalized and, from that basis, work together on a strategy of regional mobilization against the Dogra state. Early in 1935, Sheikh Abdullah and Prem Nath Bazaz, the left-leaning Pandit, jointly started an Urdu newspaper called the *Hamdard* as a 'standard-bearer of democracy and unity of all Kashmiris without any consideration of caste or creed.'[157] Little support came from the vast majority of Pandits. The second critical decision taken by the Muslim Conference came in June 1939, when it changed its name to the All Jammu and Kashmir National Conference (henceforth the National Conference). Addressing the Muslim Conference several months earlier in March 1938, Abdullah had suggested that 'like [the Muslims] the majority of the Hindus and the Sikhs in the state ha[d] immensely suffered at the hands of the irresponsible [Dogra] government'. He urged the members of the party to 'end communalism by ceasing to think in terms of Muslims and non-Muslims when discussing [their] political problems . . . and open [the] doors to all such Hindus and Sikhs, who . . . believe[d] in the freedom of their country from the shackles of an irresponsible rule.'[158] Even then Abdullah made no concessions on the rights claimed by the Muslims of Kashmir as Muslims. Speaking in Baramulla in 1939 his invitation to the Pandits to join the 'national movement' was subtly qualified by the 'dubious' assurance 'that they would get safeguards according to the sacrifices they [had] made.'[159] Predictably, once again few Kashmiri Pandits were willing to flock to the side of the National Conference.

The comfortable dominance of the Kashmiri Pandits in the state had been truly shaken for the first time after the publication of the Glancy Commission's report. The enquiry and its conclusions seemed to have conceded the Kashmiri Muslim contention of their unfair neglect and biased exclusion from the representative institutions of a state in which they formed a majority. The British insistence and at least an apparent desire on the part of the maharaja's government to correct the situation led Kashmiri Pandits to speak increasingly in the

[157] Bazaz, *Struggle for Freedom*, p. 166.

[158] Ibid., p. 168.

[159] R/1/1/3398, CRR (Political Department), Fortnightly reports on the political situation in Kashmir state for the year 1939, report for the first half of March 1939, IOL.

language of an endangered minority. A handbill entitled 'Agitation Zindabad' (Long Live the Agitation) was circulated among the Pandits in Srinagar immediately after the maharaja passed orders to implement the Glancy Commission's recommendations in 1932. In a bizarre allusion to Napoleon, it exhorted the Pandits to 'produce [his] spirit [and] show to the world that though [they] were small in number [they] were so intelligent that heavens too whirl before [them].'[160]

A battle over claiming minority status as a way to bargain for special privileges ensued in Kashmiri politics in the post-Glancy period. For the Kashmiri Pandits their small numbers made their claim an obvious one. Yet, Kashmiri Muslims led by Sheikh Mohammed Abdullah asserted that they too occupied the position of a minority within the state, clearly not on the basis of their numbers but certainly in the treatment they had received at the hands of a Hindu-dominated establishment. The definition of minority status both by the Kashmiri Pandits and Muslims was rooted in religious affiliation. However, what distinguished the politics of the Kashmiri Pandits from those of the Muslims of the valley were the approaches the two adopted to remedy the disadvantages of their respective 'minority' standing. The handbill mentioned above reminded the Kashmiri Pandits that 'the British tremble[d] at Jawahir's name'.[161] That Jawaharlal Nehru was a Kashmiri Pandit (albeit from a family that had emigrated to British India centuries earlier) was convenient. The strategy increasingly embraced by the Kashmiri Pandits was to appeal more broadly to the Hindus of British India,[162] where they did form a numerical majority, to balance their position seen to be in jeopardy within the state. Pandit Kashyap Bandhu, a leading member of the Kashmiri Pandit organization of the Sanatan Dharm Youngmen's Association, had written in January 1932 to the Hindu Sabha in the British Indian city of Patna (Bihar). He suggested that it was evident from the manner in which the Glancy Commission was 'injuring the Hindu religion' that it was determined to 'root out Hinduism from the country' in order to 'please the Muslims'. Bandhu appealed to the Hindu Sabha to 'raise [its]

---

[160] R/1/1/2223, CRR, Translation of a handbill titled 'Agitation Zindabad', IOL.

[161] Ibid.

[162] R/1/1/2223, CRR, Fortnightly reports on the internal situation in Kashmir during 1932. From the Resident, dated 1932, IOL.

voice' and to 'stir the Hindu world . . . so that they may protest against the [Glancy] Commission's actions.'[163] In 1936, Pandits such as Jia Lal Kilam were even advocating forging a broader Hindu alliance with their erstwhile rivals, the Punjabis resident in the state.[164]

In an ironic reversal of roles, it was the Kashmiri Muslims represented by Abdullah who were now flying the flag of a regional nationalism. For instance, the National Conference told the Kashmiri Pandits that if they wished for the introduction of the Devanagari script in addition to the Perso-Arabic in Kashmir, the Muslims would not object, except that as 'nationalists they ought to have only one script'.[165] However, both the intransigence of the Kashmiri Pandits and the ground reality of Muslim disadvantages led to an insistence on the inseparability of religion from a concept of rights before a genuinely 'national community' could be forged in Kashmir. The thinking of Prem Nath Bazaz, among the few Kashmiri Pandits to support the National Conference between 1934 and 1947, reflected such a concession. He wrote that the 'progress and prosperity of Kashmiri Pandits [wa]s synonymous with the complete political, social and economic freedom of Kashmir and the liberation of the Muslim masses.' The vast majority of the Pandits, however, supporting the Hindu Yuvak Sabha continued 'to oppose the *legitimate* aspirations of the Muslims'.[166]

The demand for a parity of religious rights by Muslims expressed since the last decade of the nineteenth century was revived with verve by Sheikh Mohammed Abdullah in the late 1930s at the same time as it was placed within a regional setting. In 1937, Abdullah began a speech by ventriloquizing for Nature bemoaning the fate of Kashmir, and went on to list a series of Kashmiri Muslim grievances. Kashmiri Muslims at their most rebellious were reinserting themselves into *their* landscape. Thus spoke Abdullah:

[163] R/1/1/2262 (1), CRR, English translation of a letter from Kashyap Bandhu to Jagat Narain Lal of the Hindu Sabha (Patna), dated 25 January 1932, IOL.

[164] C.I.D. Diary for May 1936, Political Department, 1932, File no. 216/P.S. 250, JKA.

[165] R/1/1/3789, CRR (Political Department), Fortnightly reports on the political situation in Kashmir state for the year 1942, report for the first half of May 1942, IOL.

[166] Prem Nath Bazaz, *Struggle for Freedom,* pp. 161–2. Emphasis mine.

You have no leisure to hear my talk of woe.
Silence is my speech, 'speechless is my tongue.'
The Tulip, Narcissus and the Rose
Have taken up a few leaves of the pages
Of my tale of woe and blood.
They lie scattered over the orchard.[167]

The woes of the Kashmiris that Abdullah wished to call attention to
were those born out of their position as powerless Muslims in a Hindu
state. Asking his audience to disregard his record as a 'past master in
the game of exciting feelings', he suggested that they think of the more
important question of whether they could 'live in the state as Muslims
or [whether they would have to] eschew Islam.'[168]

The Muslim community, he argued, though visible in terms of
their large numbers had, otherwise, disappeared before the 'sister community' of the Hindus who assumed 'that [since] the ruler was a
Hindu and the state was Hindu', the 'Hindu Dharam (religion) would
naturally prevail'.[169] Abdullah demanded the 'grant of *perfect religious
liberty*', insisting that Hindus would no longer be allowed to think of
them as 'mere sheep and goats and not as Muslims'.[170] He went further
to warn that the Dogra maharaja could continue to rule only when he
satisfied the demands of 'the subjects', identified now as Muslims,
particularly as Hari Singh had stated upon his accession that his own
'religion [was] justice'. Sheikh Abdullah, however, in making his
protest against a denial of religious rights was careful to tie it into an
argument also about a denial of economic rights. In lamenting the
penalties incurred by Kashmiri Muslims for cow slaughter, he spoke
of their inability to afford the luxury of 'oxen become useless' when
they were too old to conduct agricultural work. He also alluded to the
cultivators' difficulty in paying the grazing tax when they did not have
enough to feed themselves.[171] While the cow was sacred to 'them'
(Hindus), it was not to 'us' (Muslims) and so there was no reason why

[167] Speech delivered by Sheikh Mohammed Abdullah in Jammu, dated
10 April 1937, Political Department, 1937, File no. 131/Sp-13, JKA. No author-
ship for the verse is indicated.
[168] Ibid.
[169] Ibid.
[170] Ibid. Emphasis mine.
[171] Ibid.

the Muslims should take a back seat in their own land. Abdullah emphasized that the Muslims wished 'the Hindus to have their rights' but only so long as the Muslims had their own. The Hindus would have to understand that no governance in Kashmir could be possible 'without their [Muslim] consent' and a satisfaction of their demands.[172] The 'us' and the 'them' of the Muslims and the Hindus, and an equality of their rights, had to be accepted before coexistence would be possible in Kashmir.

The acuity of religiously based discrimination in the state of Jammu and Kashmir was never lost even when the National Conference muted its most strident criticisms of it. In 1942 Sheikh Abdullah, when campaigning in the rural areas, advised zamindars not to surrender foodgrains to the revenue department if it used violence but instead to distribute it among the poor. Few of the agriculturists in Kashmir would have been in any doubt about the community identity of the revenue officials being resisted. Similarly, the allusions to the Kashmiri Pandits were transparent when Sheikh Abdullah addressed labourers at the silk factory in Srinagar and pointed to 'the capitalist . . . [who] always wanted to suck the blood of labourers'.[173] Or when the Kashmir durbar was criticized for shielding the urban powerful through its food control policy while not providing similar protection in the rural areas against food scarcity.[174] The reward for these obviously populist appeals was that, by 1942, the National Conference was said to enjoy the support of 75 per cent of Srinagar's Muslims and Abdullah's party was considered the best organized and supported in the valley.[175]

The last years of the princely state of Jammu and Kashmir saw a number of dramatic developments that pushed the National Conference to make some politically visible efforts at bridging the divide

[172] Ibid.

[173] R/1/1/3789, CRR (Political Department), Fortnightly reports on the political situation in Kashmir state for the year 1942, report for the second half of May 1942, IOL.

[174] R/1/1/3638, CRR (Political Department), Fortnightly reports on the political situation in Kashmir state for 1941, report for second half of May 1941, IOL

[175] R/1/1/3789, CRR (Political Department), Fortnightly reports on the political situation in Kashmir state for the year 1942, report for the first half of November 1942, IOL.

between Kashmiri Pandits and Muslims. Two important parties from British India, the Muslim League and the Indian National Congress, had begun to make forays into the politics of Kashmir. In 1943, the Mirwaiz-i-Jama Masjid and a breakaway faction of the National Conference, still calling itself the Muslim Conference and dominated by urban Jammu Muslims, began to manifest distinctly pro-Pakistan tendencies.[176] As a way to compensate for their increasing marginalization in Kashmir *vis-à-vis* Abdullah's National Conference, they looked to the Muslim League and Mohammad Ali Jinnah for their political salvation. And when the latter visited Kashmir in 1944, he received a rousing welcome from these groups (and a corresponding rebuff from the National Conference).[177]

The Indian National Congress drew its equally limited support from two different segments of Kashmiri society. First of all, a much-publicized 'friendship' between Sheikh Abdullah and Jawaharlal Nehru beginning in 1938, when they first met, was apparently the basis of a political alliance.[178] Abdullah needed the Indian National Congress, especially its wing organized to support the subjects of princely India and known as the State People's Party, to strengthen the National Conference's hand *vis-à-vis* the Dogra state in the context of an impending decolonization. In turn, Nehru, whether one emphasizes his sentimental attachment to the valley of his ancestors or not, chose to see in Abdullah another pietist of secular politics in his own image at the same time as he was politically mindful of the National Conference's popularity in Kashmir.[179] Second, large numbers of Kashmiri Pandits also veered towards supporting the Congress. As Bazaz notes, in doing so they 'were not prompted by any burning desire for freedom or even by the wish to secularize state politics'. Instead they helped 'the cause of Indian nationalism . . . [because], despite the statements of the Congress leaders to the contrary, [it] was becoming another name for Hindu nationalism.'[180] Association with the Indian

[176] R/1/1/3924, CRR (Political Department), Fortnightly reports on the political situation in Kashmir state for the year 1943, report for the period ending 31 March 1943, IOL.

[177] Bamzai, p. 667.

[178] This was a friendship that had distinctly soured by 1953.

[179] Alastair Lamb, pp. 95–6.

[180] Bazaz, *Struggle for Freedom*, pp. 174–5.

National Congress, therefore, cloaked in 'secularism' two different positions, both of which were in fact grounded in clearly religious sensibilities. In fact, the Congress had, through its history, hardly ever conducted a scrupulous card check: so long as members spoke from its own pulpit, 'communalism' was 'nationalism'.[181]

On 12 May 1946, the Cabinet Mission sent to India declared that when the British left India, its paramountcy would lapse and the rights of princely states would return to them. This announcement of an imminently independent Dogra state of Jammu and Kashmir sent Abdullah into a flurry of political alliance-making. He was keen to consolidate as wide a popular base as possible to pre-empt a continuation of Dogra 'autocracy' after the British departure. On 20 May Abdullah launched his 'Quit Kashmir' movement, declaring the Amritsar treaty of 1846 a sale deed and so asking the Dogras to leave.[182] Adopting an anti-Dogra stance, the National Conference sought, now more than ever, to rally the support of the Kashmiri Pandits in a 'national' struggle for freedom. In an impassioned speech, Abdullah suggested to them that 'those Hindus who . . . [believed] that Dogra rule should remain, should . . . [not] forget that . . . Kashmiris [were treated] as a bought up race *without distinction of religion*.'[183] While significant numbers of Pandits responded to the call of the 'Kashmir Gandhi', they did so with caution and the realization that 'his efforts in due course would transfer all political power into the hands of the state Muslims.'[184] Discrepant interests continued to vitiate efforts at bridge-building.

Unfortunately, I was unable to find much archival material for the years 1946 and 1947, so it is not possible to say much more about the relations and negotiations between the Kashmiri Pandits and the Abdullah-led National Conference. However, an examination of the first major economic reforms proposed and enacted by Sheikh Abdullah between 1948 and 1953 provide indications of the compulsions to

[181] See Jalal, 'Exploding Communalism', op. cit.

[182] *The Hindustan Times*, 24 May 1946, Press cuttings on the Quit Kashmir Movement, Department of Information, Srinagar.

[183] *Daily Herald*, 26 May 1946, Press cuttings on the Quit Kashmir Movement, Department of Information, Srinagar. Emphasis mine.

[184] *Eastern Times*, 30 May 1946, Press cuttings on the Quit Kashmir Movement, Department of Information, Srinagar.

conciliate a variety of special interests within Kashmiri society, including Pandit concerns, under which Abdullah had to operate while still asserting the importance of redressing Muslim grievances. It must be asserted right away that, typical of government-sponsored land reforms, those in Kashmir were never enacted fully to the letter or oftentimes indeed even close to it. Insofar as they were enacted, however, all saving clauses and politically expedient compromises notwithstanding, they proceeded from the New Economic Plan formulated by the National Conference in 1944 and elaborated in its manifesto known as 'New Kashmir'. Perhaps the three most significant goals enunciated in it, geared to the interests of Kashmiri agriculturists, were the abolition of landlordism, land to the tiller, and co-operative association. The new state took its first concrete steps towards agrarian reform in 1948 with the abolition of jagir, *muafi* and mukarrari grants. In that same year it also took measures postponing the realization of all debts for twelve months and protecting tenants from arbitrary eviction without court procedure. Moreover, 6250 acres of khalsa (state-owned) land were distributed free of cost to landless labourers.[185] These were followed by the Distressed Debtors' Relief Act of 1950 seeking to alleviate agrarian indebtedness and creating Debt Conciliation Boards. Debts were considered fully met upon evidence of payment of the principal and 50 per cent as interest.[186] Also in 1950, the state enacted its most publicized land reform measure known as the Big Estates Abolition Act. This legislation set a maximum limit of 22¾ acres on the holdings of landowners. Proprietors could, however, retain orchards, grass farms, and fuel and fodder reserves beyond this ceiling and would have full freedom to choose which acres of their holdings they would keep for these purposes. Land in excess of this amount was transferred in ownership right to the tiller without compensation to the original owner.[187]

However, corruption in the National Conference machinery mitigated the harsher aspects of the reforms for the big landowners. The

[185] Land Reforms Officer, Jammu and Kashmir State, *Land Reforms* (Srinagar: 1952), p. 6.

[186] Michael Brecher, *The Struggle for Kashmir* (New York: Oxford University Press, 1953), p. 159.

[187] *Report of the Land Compensation Committee Appointed by the Jammu and Kashmir State Constituent Assembly, 1951–52* (Jammu: 1952), p. 18.

commonest way, typical also of land reforms enacted in the rest of India, to evade resumptions was by breaking up joint families, thereby entitling each adult male to the limit of 22¾ acres.[188] The dilution of the radical promises made in 1944 was intended to ensure political and social stability in the countryside. Although not all Kashmiri Pandits were by any means wealthy landowners, nor the only members of the landed élite, large landholdings were certainly common among them.[189] It is said that over 30 per cent of the land in the valley belonged to them prior to the reforms, much of which had been obtained at the time of the first settlement of the 1880s. An equally large proportion was obtained through purchase after 1934, when proprietary rights were granted to Kashmiri cultivators following the agitation of 1931–2.[190] Considering that the Pandits comprised approximately 5 per cent of the Kashmiri population, their control of over 30 per cent of the land speaks for significantly large holdings. However, Pandits did not resist the abolition of big landed estates quite as shrilly as did their Dogra counterparts.[191] To a certain degree this can be attributed to the flaws in implementation referred to above. Yet, these loopholes would have worked to the advantage of Dogra landowners too. Here a crucial distinguishing factor may have come into play in the valley. This had to do with the provision of the Act that exempted orchards from appropriation, and thus paved the way for big landholders to escape the ceiling by converting cereal acreage into orchards.[192] The returns from orchards, especially from apple orchards, tended to be much greater than from the cultivation of foodgrains.[193] So by retaining their orchards as well as converting some of their cereal acreages, the bigger landlords of Kashmir, whose ranks included Pandits, reversed some of their losses by entering into the highly profitable world of horticultural

---

[188] Robert I. Crane (ed.), *Area Handbook on Jammu and Kashmir State* (Chicago: University of Chicago Press, 1956) p. 361.

[189] This is evident from the survey of a village in Anantnag district conducted by T.N. Madan, 'Religious Ideology', op. cit., p. 29.

[190] Bazaz, *Struggle for Freedom*, p. 545.

[191] Kashmir Information Bureau, 'Jammu—An Objective Analysis' (1952), p. 6.

[192] Nisar Ali, *Agricultural Development and Income Distribution* (New Delhi: Rima Publishing House, 1985), p. 5.

[193] Ibid., p. 212.

exports. Once again, while the beneficiaries of this exemption were by no means only the Pandits or indeed all the Pandits, there were certainly prominent elements among them who were given an important stake in supporting the new state.

However, an arena in which the National Conference made conspicuous concessions to Pandit privileges was in administrative employment. Their primary vocation, especially of the Karkuns, being employment in government service, 10 per cent of the state jobs were reserved for Pandits.[194] While it is true that a much larger proportion of 50 per cent was reserved for Muslims, the smaller numbers of the Pandits made this an impressively generous allowance. Indeed the Pandits were getting much more than their proportion of the population entitled them to and, through the liberality of the National Conference, were said to be better represented in state service than they had ever been before.[195]

This period was also the heyday of the articulation of the notion of Kashmiriyat by the National Conference. Among the first goals that Sheikh Abdullah's government set for itself was to involve all Kashmiris in a 'nation-building' programme.[196] The use of those particular words is interesting in that they suggest a fresh enterprise. Selected cultural fragments from an imagined past were collected to construct a Kashmiriyat that would draw in both the Pandits and the Muslims. This was evident, for instance, in the periodization adopted by Sheikh Abdullah and his associates in their recounting of the history of the valley. Their reconstruction of the 'biography' of Kashmir moved not from periods of Hindu to Muslim to Sikh rulers but from an age of Kashmiri rule, through a long interregnum of 'foreign' dominance beginning with the Mughals in 1586, before the end of Dogra hegemony marked a triumphant return to rule by Kashmiris. Day after day, and week after week, Kashmiris were told that they had been 'slaves' of alien rulers for more than five hundred years until their final liberation after 1947.[197] This espousal of a 'secular' ideology, read through

[194] *Gajendragadkar Commission Report* (1953), p. 57.

[195] Prem Nath Bazaz, *Kashmir in Crucible* (New Delhi: Pamposh Publications, 1967), p. 194.

[196] Information Bureau, *Jammu and Kashmir (1947–50): An Account of the Activities of the First Three Years of Sheikh Abdullah's Government* (Jammu: Ranbir Government Press, 1951), p. 21.

[197] Inder Malhotra, 'The Separatists', *Seminar*, no. 58, 1964, p. 30.

a secularly written history, was intended also as a way to keep at bay a centre in Delhi that had begun to encroach upon Kashmiri 'autonomy' increasingly in the early 1950s. The homogenizing Indian nation's version of accommodating difference had become synonymous with the command issued to alternative identities that they erase themselves. An excessive display of Muslim-ness among Kashmiris would provide Delhi's politicians with the excuse to intervene in order to defend the integrity of secular nationalist India.

But, as has been argued in the preceding sections, a Kashmiri regional identity was embraced through political and economic compromise between religiously defined communities. The votaries of Kashmiriyat never lost sight of their religious affinities, nor were these deemed incompatible with a regionally shared culture. The poetry of Mahjoor shows how the bridges of conciliation were built:

> Who is the friend and who the foe of your (native land)?
> Let you among yourselves thoughtfully make out.
> The kind and stock of all Kashmiris is one;
> Let you mix milk and sugar once again.
> Hindus will keep the helm and Muslims ply the oars;
> Let you together row (ashore) the boat of this country.[198]

Intended to invoke as well as eulogize Kashmiri regional unity, the degree to which an awareness of Hindu and Muslim differences remains embedded in these lines is arresting. One might add here that although Mahjoor almost certainly did not mean it in this light, equally striking in the sharing of tasks he describes is that while the Pandits controlled the boat the Muslims performed the labour of rowing it. This has been the dilemma of Kashmir in the twentieth century. It is remarkable how often it was when Kashmiri Pandit privileges were protected that the health of a secular Kashmiri 'nationalism' was deemed good and its future safe. To a certain extent what is involved in this equation is nothing more or less than an acknowledgement of the necessity of allaying minority fears in the interests of building a secure nation. However, as argued earlier, while the Pandits are indeed numerically a minority in Kashmir, for the most part their small numbers rarely interfered with their access to power. The tenuousness of forging a regional unity out of what was primarily a

---

[198] Ghulam Ahmad Mahjoor, cited in Bazaz, *Struggle for Freedom*, p. 296.

strategy of accommodating and conciliating privilege has become more than amply evident today.

Beginning in 1989, large numbers of Kashmiris, tired of waiting for both the government in Delhi and 'their own' in the valley to redress their grievances, took to the path of militancy. What was remarkable was the speed with which and the scale on which there was an exodus of Kashmiri Pandits from the valley, some undoubtedly forced, others engineered, while the majority were 'voluntarily' undertaken.[199] According to one estimation, of a population of 140,000 Pandits approximately 100,000 moved to Jammu, Delhi and other parts of India after 1990.[200] While many of them survive hopelessly in inadequate camps, for others the process of rehabilitation has been less difficult (although the uprooting from their native land has undoubtedly affected all of them). In the course of this mass migration, Kashmiri Pandits have recalled memories of the persecutions of Sultan Sikandar, when large numbers of the community left the valley for other parts of India. Of course the two conditions are not analogous. Sultan Sikandar may indeed have persecuted the Kashmiri Pandits, but he did so from a position of power. The present insurgency, however, represents the protest of the powerless in the valley. And the rhetoric of most Kashmiris has in fact echoed the language of the National Conference when it was at the height of its popularity. For instance, the Jammu and Kashmir Liberation Front, probably still the group enjoying the widest support in Kashmir, has asked repeatedly for the return of the Kashmiri Pandit community to the valley in order to give Kashmiriyat and the call for independence made on that basis its 'true meaning'. At the same time it has also refused to concede an inch on the demand that the plight of the Kashmiris, most of whom happen to be Muslims but certainly include Pandits, needs addressing first. Pandits who have shared a similar experience of marginalization have continued to allude to a tradition of peaceful coexistence, manifested in the willingness of Muslims 'to die for' the protection of Pandits.[201]

For the rest, however, a paring down of their power and influence

---

[199] One has to be cautious in assessing the degree of voluntariness in decisions made from a position of insecurity and the threat, even if only potential, of the loss of life and property.

[200] Sumantra Bose, p. 71.

[201] Ibid., p. 77.

has led them to echo the accusations frequently voiced by their forbears in the earlier decades of the twentieth century: of 'communalism' and 'fundamentalism' among Kashmiri Muslims destroying a long heritage of a secularly conceptualized Kashmiriyat and, increasingly, also of attempting to wreck the integrity of the Indian nation. Receiving moral and political support from right-wing Hindu parties in India, these Pandits are deemed the greater secularists and nationalists, while the Kashmiri Muslims, whose demands have remained for a greater degree of self-rule and sensitivity to their material needs, have been condemned out of hand as religious 'fundamentalists' and, as such, traitors. Forgetting all too easily the intimate links between region, religion and rights in Kashmir, secularism has become, to paraphrase the words of Mohammad Ali Jinnah, the play of conjurers.

Conclusion

Azadi (Freedom)

Let us all offer thanks,
For Freedom has come to us;
It is after ages that she has beamed
Her radiance on us.

In western climes Freedom comes
With a shower of light and grace,
But dry, sterile thunder is all
She has for our own soil.

Poverty and starvation,
Repression and lawlessness,
It is with these happy blessings
That she has come to us.

Freedom, being of heavenly birth,
Cannot move from door to door;
You will find her camping in the homes
Of a chosen few alone.

. . . There is mourning in every house;
But in sequestered bowers
Our rulers, like bridegrooms,
Are in dalliance with Freedom.

—Ghulam Ahmad Mahjoor[1]

Today the majority of Kashmir's Muslims largely believe that they are scarcely better off than they were through 101 years of Dogra rule. The personalized sovereignty of the Dogra-Hindu monarchy and the paramount British power buttressing it disappeared in

[1] Ghulam Ahmad Mahjoor, *The Best of Mahjoor* (Srinagar: Jammu and Kashmir Academy of Art, Culture and Languages, 1989), p. 107.

1947. Yet, the redress of their economic, political, cultural and religious grievances eluded them even as the Kashmiris gained their 'freedom' in that year. Mahjoor's disappointment was shared by large numbers of his fellow Kashmiris. As he saw it, the freedom long anticipated by them was watered down to mean that while a privileged few reaped its benefits, the rest remained mired in 'poverty and starvation'. Implicit in his verses is an ire directed not only against the Indian state to which the Dogra maharaja had acceded on 26 October 1947, but also against the valley's own 'rulers'. In 1944, Sheikh Abdullah had won the support and affection of Kashmiri Muslims by promising a redistribution of wealth in the valley of so radical a nature as to inaugurate a new era of plenty. Yet when his reforms were actually implemented in the early 1950s the immunities of the highest echelons of Kashmir's society remained firmly in place. A small number of Muslims made gains while the need to cajole the Kashmiri Pandits into supporting the new 'nation' retained for them their niches of power both in the state's administration and in the land. Although Mahjoor died in 1952, it was already evident that the social and economic inequities of the past had survived and would continue in the new age of freedom.

Another pledge not redeemed was that made on behalf of the Indian nation by Jawaharlal Nehru in November 1947 to consult, through a referendum, the wishes of the Kashmiri people on the state's accession to the Indian union. When this failed to materialize, Abdullah's advocacy of independence for Kashmir from the Indian and Pakistani states alike led to his being thrown behind bars by Nehru's government in 1953. He was in and out of jail until 1972 and remained out of power until 1975 while Congress Party-led governments in Delhi made their separate arrangements with successors handpicked by them. For over three decades, in return for their endorsement of Kashmir's accession, these selected politicians received the most generous grants-in-aid disbursed by the Indian centre to any state. The ritual of elections was performed regularly enough, yet as most Kashmiris assert today, except for those held in 1977 and 1983 not one of them was fair and free from manipulation. The unrepresentative leaders they threw up funnelled Delhi's monetary boons into strengthening their own limited patronage networks rather than in alleviating the plight of the people they were meant to serve. In this way they appeared to parody

Dogra rule rather than mark a break from it. However, this is not to overemphasize continuity. The language of 'constitutional rule', even if honoured more in the breach than in the observance, certainly created a greater awareness of rights, such as the right to vote, to assemble and to free speech. This was in evidence among Kashmiris in the elections of 1983 and the insistence upon their enactment was in marked contrast to the very different situation prevailing in 1953.[2] It is not possible in these concluding pages to review over half a century of history. Other works have addressed the many salient and critical issues that must also be borne in mind for their role in transforming the history of the state since 1947—such as the nature and the timing of integration against the background of the tribal invasion; the complex character of the National Conference, which was simultaneously a vehicle of popular anti-monarchical aspirations and a non-sectarian formation as well as a body dominated by a key group of Kashmiri Muslims; that while its accommodative character may have been evident in 1947–52 and again in 1977–83, strong centralizing tendencies within the Conference and the rise of a new generation that did not identify with the symbols of 1931 and after made the situation more than explosive by the end of the 1980s. Yet, even granting these critical transformations, the compromised nature of a freedom handed down from above rather than negotiated from below had remained as palpably clear to most Kashmiris as it had to Mahjoor. Reaching their threshold of tolerance in 1989, Kashmir's Muslims have taken to violence and militancy to demand a fulfilment of rights they feel they have long been denied.

The language of religion in which their demands for rights are made has given the Indian nation, espousing a secularist credo, the ideological handle it needs to delegitimize and repress the popularly backed insurgency. However, this is clearly a misconceived reading of the problem. Under the Dogra rulers, as much as today, the protest of Kashmiri Muslims represents not so much a defence of Islam but of the rights of a community defined as Muslims by ruling hierarchies minded to dole out patronage along religious lines. The nexus between region, religion and rights in Kashmir was formed without reference (or deference) to the rhetoric of an Indian 'secularism' founded on a necessary notional irreconcilability between religion and nation. This

---

[2] M.J. Akbar, *India: The Siege Within* (New York: Viking, 1985)

owed, not least, to the fact that Kashmiris had been subjects of a princely state technically outside the purview of direct colonial interference and so also of anti-colonial Indian nationalist appropriation and definition. Without denying the significance of Islam as faith, the preceding chapters have argued that the religious sensibility enmeshed in the political assertion of Kashmiri Muslims is explained by the nature of the state of which they were subjects between 1846 and 1947.

Having said this, however, it is clearly not sufficient to explain the religious idiom in which Kashmiris increasingly registered their protest by merely recognizing, as many studies do, that the Dogra rulers were Hindus while preponderant numbers of their Kashmiri subjects were Muslims. South Asia has, historically, been more than familiar with such divergences in the religious affiliations of rulers from those they ruled. As has been contended in this book, the critical difference lay both in the changes registered in the terms of sovereignty accompanying the incorporation of the Dogra state into the imperial framework as well as the new arenas from which the Dogras were encouraged to derive their legitimacy to rule. The creation of the state of Jammu and Kashmir in 1846 flowed from the geo-political and strategic considerations of the English East India Company in the critical northwestern frontier of its expanding Indian dominion. These led it to patch together territories formerly separate and part of diverse hierarchies of sovereignties and place them under the control of Gulab Singh. This manner of conjuring the new state had made the transfer of Kashmir particularly perplexing for the East India Company. Unlike his 'home-base' in Jammu, Gulab Singh had no prior history of rule in the valley and so, by 1846, when the state was created, no opportunity to fit himself into the older hierarchies of power either within Kashmir or those that tied Kashmir to the wider world of the subcontinent. However, in the interest of maintaining a stable polity in this sensitive frontier region, the East India Company resolved this potentially vexing dilemma by strengthening the hands of their Dogra ally and by assisting him to vacate power from all subordinate levels in Kashmir. At the same time, the British also vested a territorially finite and a lesser form of their own monolithic sovereignty in the person of the Dogra ruler.

In the process, the Dogra maharajas were far from turned into abject and powerless creatures of their imperial masters. Indeed, Dirks's argument for a hollowing of Indian crowns under colonial rule is entirely belied by the evidence of the Dogra rulers of Jammu and Kashmir. The present book has shown that the alteration in the political topography of India under colonial rule helped the Dogras to secure their hold on power in ways unparalleled in pre-colonial India, even apart from the external guarantee of imperial protection they enjoyed. Expunging the right to wage war and make peace from the domain of princely India certainly circumscribed the field of political operation and the sovereignty previously enjoyed by Indian rulers, subordinating it to the paramount British power. Yet it also secured both their internal position and the external boundaries of their sovereignties. Allegiances of subjects within territorially delimited states were now owed solely to their own rulers (even if indirectly also owed to the paramount British power) and were no longer open to negotiation by Indian political rivals both within and outside their state. These adjustments in the terms of sovereignty had monumental consequences for the relations between the rulers and the ruled. The hollowing of the crown to accommodate colonial paramountcy saw a corresponding bulging of princely sovereignty based on a wide array of religious tropes. Therefore, it was under colonial rule that the Dogras were able to inaugurate a Hindu sovereignty, a political form enabling an unprecedented degree of control by a ruler over the domain of Hindu religion and religious patronage.

Contrariwise, what was good for the Dogra rulers was not necessarily so for their Kashmiri Muslim subjects. With the forcible surrendering of power by all subordinate levels of Kashmiri society to the person of the Dogra maharaja, Muslims found themselves gradually unrepresented and unprotected in an exercise of domination without legitimacy. Gulab Singh's policy had specifically targeted Kashmiri Muslim power-holders and was coupled with a concerted effort, on the other hand, to co-opt the Hindu minority of Kashmir, the Pandits. Their indispensability to the administrative machinery of the Dogras had protected the Kashmiri Pandits who converted their immunities into the acquisition of landed wealth and political power. Although a few Muslims also retained their privileged economic status in the valley, they represented an insignificant minority and functioned within social and political spaces firmly controlled by the Dogra rulers.

It would be wrong to assume that Kashmiri Muslims were left out of the power-sharing arrangements of the Dogra state simply because they were Muslims. I have tried to show that this marginalization became possible only because Kashmiri Muslims became decidedly peripheral to the sources from which the Dogras, encouraged by their British overlords, derived legitimacy for their sovereignty. For their rule to function unsupported by the majority of their subjects, the Dogra rulers required reinforcement from an external source of power. The British provided such support from the moment of the foundation of the state. Yet the colonial government was also concerned to ensure that the arbitrary feat of creating a new state be accompanied by some legitimizing devices. The legitimacy of the Dogra sovereigns placed over the valley was sought from arenas that had little relevance for the vast majority of the people their rule encompassed. Very significantly, their mandate to rule was derived extra-territorially from their association with the Rajputs, or subsequently by expanding their being Rajputs to emphasizing their Hindu-ness. The Dogras acquired, at least in some perspectives, a veneer of acceptability since both sets of correlation extricated them from the recentness of their rulerships and placed them in the ranks of India's most ancient sovereigns; in nineteenth-century colonial sociology, being 'traditional' rulers also made them 'natural' leaders. While the Kashmiri Pandits were invited to transfer their loyalty to their new rulers in this context, these sources of legitimacy, emphatically, made no reference to and had no resonance among Kashmiri Muslims.

Both the colonial government's own pursuit of legitimacy and that of the Dogras allowed the latter to preside over the transformation of Jammu and Kashmir from a state ruled by a Hindu into a Hindu state. Pre-colonial aspirants to political power, whether Hindu, Muslim or Sikh, had been forced to acknowledge their inability to subject to political control the domain of religion in which shrines and religious orders had a multitude of sponsors straddling territorial frontiers. The assertion of political power required outmanoeuvring other rivals in the patronage of all shrines, regardless of religious affiliation.

By the second half of the nineteenth century, however, the overlapping arrangements of both polities and the arenas of religious patronage were irrevocably dismantled. Once again, this was both related to and facilitated by the colonial insistence on the territorially restricted nature of the sovereignty of India's princes. The Dogra rulers capitalized on this to modify fundamentally the relationship between religion, religious patronage and territory. The politics of faith was integral, even central, to their quest for legitimacy and their hold on power. An intricate framework was fashioned in which a religious centre in Jammu corresponded to a political centre and the sway of the Dogras, both as rulers and as the leading sponsors of the Hindu religion, extended to the frontiers of the state. Such firm control over a territorialized Hindu religious arena was unprecedented in Indian history. As a result, the fluidity and politically competitive nature of pre-colonial patterns of patronage that had ensured a measure of deference to the Muslim religious and cultural domain in Kashmir suddenly disappeared.

The central contention of my book, then, is that it was the declining relevance of Kashmir's Muslim subjects to the Dogra state's search for legitimacy that left overwhelming numbers of them in the most abject state of helplessness. That they had no effectively powerful voice until the 1930s to protest this marginalization only compounded the problem. Access to the state's resources, symbolic, political, economic and cultural, was selectively restricted to its Hindu subjects. It seems hardly surprising, then, that a consciousness of religiously-based neglect would play a pivotal part in what was, above all, a mobilization by Kashmiri Muslims for material and cultural rights denied to them. No small role was played by the colonial state in underwriting the sovereignty of the Dogra rulers while encouraging them to derive their legitimacy from arenas that bypassed the most numerous segment of their subjects in the valley.

However, in exploring the profound changes wrought by colonialism, I do not suggest a colonial agenda that was either entirely deliberate or beyond manipulation by any of the colonized. Attempts by the paramount power to provide legitimacy to the Dogra rulers had unanticipated effects which drew the British even more deeply into the affairs of Jammu and Kashmir. It is also true that colonial intervention in Indian society, whether in directly controlled territories or indirectly ruled princely states, was not a static and unchanging phenomenon. As the preceding chapters have shown, there were several identifiable shifts in the articulation of the sovereignty and the legitimacy of the Dogra state. The first was provided at the very foundation of the state of Jammu and Kashmir, when sovereignty was simply transferred to a new ruler and accompanied, as an afterthought, by the correlation of the Dogras with the Rajputs. The second historical shift was provided in the aftermath of the rebellion of 1857, when a general scheme of 'strengthening an Indian aristocracy that would buttress British rule' was implemented by the imperial state.[3] A third shift was highlighted by a transformation in colonial policy towards the state of Jammu and Kashmir in evidence by the closing decades of the nineteenth century. By this time, the mutually opposed interests of the Hindu state and the Kashmiri Muslims had begun to make for an extremely volatile political situation in which mobilization for economic, political and cultural interests was ever-ready to erupt into religious conflagration. This, coupled with a more global manifestation of impatience with dynasts incapable of playing a more representative role to stem the incoming tide of popular nationalisms, encouraged the colonial state to rein in the Dogra rulers, as also other Indian princes. By placing upon them the burden of acknowledging the 'obligations' they owed to their subjects, the British gave simultaneous currency to the notion that subjects could, conversely, expect the fulfilment of certain rights.

These dual conceptual concessions signalled the inauguration of a public space for voicing political and economic grievances. However, what emerged were numerous spaces segregated along lines of religion, sect and caste. The continued separation of the body of Kashmiri subjects along religious lines, within the context of a language of obligations and rights, was not necessarily the effect sought by the colonial state in the late nineteenth and early twentieth centuries, although it was indeed the consequence of their earlier policies. However, studies that see the colonial state as the exclusive agent in the history of India fail to recognize the very real capacity of a variety of Indians, and certainly of princely actors, for reinterpreting imperial projects to suit their own political compulsions.

Notwithstanding colonial intervention to rein in their Dogra allies and attempts to remake them into rulers more representative of their subjects, irrespective of religion, by 1931, the valley was in the grip of a full-blown political movement of resistance against the Dogra maharaja that invoked the notion of Kashmiriyat. Erroneously identified as a secular conceptualization of regionalism, this identity relied on building bridges, at particular historical moments, across religiously defined communities to evoke a tradition of culturally

---

[3] Bernard Cohn, 'Representing Authority in Victorian India', op. cit.

based regional coexistence. Yet this notion of cultural harmony was predicated on the requisite condition of protecting Kashmiri Pandit privileges and a consequent subsumption of the interests of the majority Muslims. Any attempt to change the balance resulted, and has continued to do so, in a withdrawing into hostile religious perimeters by the Hindus and mutual accusations of engaging in 'communal' politics by the Pandits and Muslims of Kashmir.

This book has emphasized the need to come to terms with both the complexity of the uses made of religion by Kashmiri Muslims and the challenges this has posed to Indian secularism. This is indispensable in order to make sense of the Kashmiri past and its present: the ground was broken more than a hundred years ago for a regional people to register their protest in a religious idiom. Instances of the religious basis of national or regional identities are not peculiar to South Asia. By contrast in the view of one strand of anti-colonial Indian national ideology which rose to dominance at the moment state power was captured, religion was theoretically castigated as a false, because a politically divisive, creed. Yet, paradoxically post-1947 Indian secular nationalism has played no small role in keeping alive a sense of the regional and religious particularity of Kashmir, at the same time as it has worked towards effacing it. In 1947, at the moment of independence and also the partition of the subcontinent along religious lines, India claimed Muslim majority Kashmir as its prize; a vindication of its secular credentials and a repudiation of Muslim Pakistan's 'communal' politics. In the rhetoric accompanying this incorporation, the Indian nation valorized its achievement precisely by stressing the Muslim nature of Kashmir and Kashmiris. The accrediting of an Islamic identity to the Kashmiris was related to yet another purpose they were to serve in the secular nation-state. They were the nation's security blanket with which to reassure an even more critical constituency in the aftermath of the traumas of partition: the Muslim minority that had remained in India either by choice or by force of circumstance. However, the thrust of nationalist rhetoric has moved gradually towards erasing Muslim-ness, especially since, in light of the new militant mood of Kashmiri self-assertion, it can no longer remain safely part of a secularist state's project of a controlled ascription of religious identities.

For their part, while Kashmiri Muslims have resisted appropriation by 'secular' nationalist ideologies since 1947, they have similarly defied assimilation within an Islamic rhetoric that fails to recognize their regional specificities. Without conceding an inch in their own adherence to Islam, at the moment of the partition of India most Kashmiri Muslims voted clearly (and the vast majority continue to do so today) against the Pakistan option. The reference to religion in the political mobilization of Kashmiris has been, for the most part, free from markers generically or stereotypically associated with a process of Islamicization. Thus, barring a few relatively marginal militant groups active in current day Kashmir, few in Kashmir have ever demanded the application of the Sharia' (Islamic law) or the veiling of women.

It was the tendency of the Kashmiri Pandits to turn to India, with its comfortable Hindu majority, when in trouble in Kashmir that earned for them the honour of being secular nationalists. That they merely demanded protection of religiously conceptualized interests is obfuscated by an Indian nation that has not acknowledged the tenuous nature of its own secular credentials. In contrast, the Kashmiri Muslims' demands for a similar protection of rights, denied to them as a religious community by both a Hindu Dogra and a 'secular' Indian state, has been all too easily misread as engaging in an illegitimate politics of religious fundamentalism. This duality in nationalist treatment is born, in the ultimate analysis, of the fact that Kashmiri Muslims have, by and large, chosen to tread a path all their own and certainly one that leads them neither to Delhi nor to Islamabad. Above all, the clamour by Kashmir's Muslims is for a legitimate government. It is the helplessness in which they were placed first by their Dogra rulers and then by Indian politicians, each neglecting to negotiate their legitimacy with the popular constituency of Kashmir, that has provoked a militant response. This will have to be recognized if freedom is ever to come to Kashmir, to use Mahjoor's words, 'with a shower of light and grace' based on a change of heart and minds in the subcontinent.

Glossary

anjuman	association or society
Ankut	harvest festival
arti	a hymn sung as an invocation to a deity at the end of worship
assami	lawful holder of cultivable land
azan	Muslim call to prayer
bakal	petty retailer who also functioned as a money-lender; also called a wani
bakaya	arrears in revenue
Bakr-Eid	also called Eid-ul-Adha; the 'festival of the sacrifice' celebrated as a commemoration of the Prophet Abraham's willingness to sacrifice his son upon Allah's command; on this occasion many Muslims sacrifice animals
bands	minstrels; also known as bhaggats
Basant	spring festival
begar	forced labour usually unpaid or very nominally remunerated
bhaggats	minstrels; also known as bands
brahman	the first in rank in the Hindu social hierarchy; priests are drawn from this caste category
buher	sing. buhur; an endogamous group among Kashmiri Hindus; usually employed as grocers and confectioners
chak	a block of land demarcated for revenue purposes
chakdar	tenure-holder of unreclaimed land
chakladars	contractors for land revenue
chela	disciple

crore	ten million
daftar-i-diwani	revenue department
Dar-ul-Islam	abode of Islam; a dominion in which Islam can be publicly practised
Dar-ul-Fatwa	department of juristic rulings; an institution that promulgated fatawa (sing. fatwa) in reply to legal questions
devanagari	the script in which modern Sanskrit and certain other Indian languages are written
dharmadhikari	a religious functionary
dharmarth	religious charity
Diwali	the festival of lights marking the return of Rama, the Hindu deity and eponymous hero of the epic the *Ramayana*, to his capital city of Ayodhya from his exile
durbar/darbar	royal audience, audience hall or court; the government of a princely state
Dussehra	the ten-day-long festival celebrating the victory of Rama, the Hindu deity and eponymous hero of the epic the *Ramayana*, over the demon-king Ravana
fatwa	in Islamic law, an opinion given by an appropriate authority in a Muslim religious congregation
Gadadhar	the 'mace-bearer'; another appellation of the Hindu deity Hanuman
gaddi	cushion on which an Indian ruler sits; throne
galwans	horse-keeper; horse-trader
garbha-griha	the sanctum sanctorum of a Hindu temple
gor	derived from the Sanskrit guru; refers to one of the endogamous groups of Kashmiri Pandits also known as the Bhasha Bhatta; many of them performed priestly functions
Granth	the revered text of the Sikhs, which contains the writings and teachings of their Gurus
guru	a teacher or spiritual guide; also the title of the founders of the Sikh religion, the Sikhs recognizing a hierarchy of ten Gurus

hakim-i-ala	governor
hanudi	land grants to Hindus on easy terms of revenue assessment
Hanuman	the Hindu monkey God who assisted Rama in his battle with the demon-king Ravana; he is revered as the ideal devotee of God
imam	leader of prayers; for Shias, male descendants of the Prophet
jagir	the right to the assessed land tax in an area given in lieu of salary or as a reward for service
jagirdar	the holder of a jagir
jajman/yajnaman	chief sacrificer; patron
jama masjid	a mosque at which Friday congregational prayers are held
jatha	bands of supporters
jati	sub-caste by occupation into which Hindus are born
Juma-al-Vida	the last Friday of the month of Ramadan
kangri	a portable brazier
karkhanadar	owner of a manufactory or workshop
karkun	civil servant; one of the endogamous groups among the Kashmiri Pandits, usually employed in secular occupations
khalsa	'pure'; the Sikh army; also, in revenue terms, refers to crown lands
khanqah	a Sufi hospice
khillat	robe of honour
lakh	one hundred thousand
Lori	a winter festival when bonfires are lit at night and to the accompaniment of dance and music
mahanta	Hindu temple priest
mahatmya	sacred texts that narrate the myths and legends of important Hindu deities, praise the deity's pilgrimage centre and prescribe the rituals to be observed there
maktab	Quranic school, usually attached to a mosque

masjid	mosque
maulvi	Muslim religious leader
mian	an appellation of respect; among the Dogras, reserved for an endogamous sub-group into which the rulers had traditionally married
miras	inheritance; a hereditary right to occupy cultivable land recognized by the village community
mirwaiz	a religious leader whose position as leader of prayers or chief preacher had become hereditary; in the period studied by this book, there were two mirwaizes in Srinagar
mofussil	rural hinterland
muafi	revenue-free assignment of land
muezzin	the person who calls Muslims to prayer five times a day from a mosque
mufti	a person learned in the Quran, the Hadith and in Islamic law
Muharram	the first month of the Islamic calendar; during the first ten days of this month Muslims, and especially Shias, commemmorate the martyrdom of Imam Hussain at the Battle of Karbala (680 AD)
mukarrari	land assignment on easy terms of revenue assessment
mulki	of the country; native
mullah	Muslim religious leader
mutwallis	managers of Muslim shrines
nagas	serpent deities
nangar	artisan
nazar/nazrana	gift or offering to a political superior or to a holy person, usually in gold coin
padshah	emperor
panth	Sikh brotherhood or community
pargana	lowest unit of administration consisting of several villages and corresponding to a district
pashm/pashmina	under-fur of goats used to make Kashmiri shawls

patwari	village accountant
peshkash	tribute
pirzada	literally a descendant of a Pir (saint), hence also a custodian of a shrine and a Muslim religious figure
purohita	Hindu priest
raja	king, ruler; under colonial rule the title 'Maharaja' was usually reserved for the rulers of the bigger states such as Kashmir, Mysore, or those of Rajputana
rajgi	dominion of a raja; rulership
rajyabhisheka	coronation; anointment
Rama	the hero of one of the two major epic poems of ancient India, the *Ramayana*, revered as a deity by Hindus as an incarnation of Vishnu
rasum	customary perquisites; used specifically here to refer to unofficial perquisites not sanctioned by the state
Rishi	an order of Sufi mystics local to Kashmir
sadhu	wandering ascetic; religious mendicant
sahukar	money-lender
samaj	society
sanatan dharma	the 'original' or 'pure' religion; Hinduism as practised by the Dogra maharajas and others which, with its brahmanical priesthood, idols, caste system and elaborate rituals, came under attack from reform-minded groups such as the Arya Samaj
sanyasi	Hindu ascetic
sarkar	government; also an honorific used for a political superior
shagird	pupil; also used to refer to a weaver in Kashmir
shaivite	a follower of the Hindu God Shiva
shakta	Hindu sect centred on the worship of the female principle of divine power (shakti)
shali	unwinnowed rice
sharia	moral injunctions that form Islamic law

Shia	the minority faction in Islam who broke away over the question of the inheritance of the spiritual authority of the Prophet Muhammad; they reject the succession of the first four Caliphs and support that of Ali, the Prophet's son-in-law, and his descendants
Shiva	Hindu God of procreation and destruction
shivala	high-domed temple usually dedicated to the worship of Shiva
shuddhi	purification through reconversion to Hinduism
Sikh	the follower of an Indian religion founded in the fifteenth century in Punjab by the teacher Guru Nanak
singhara	water chestnut
stupa	structure containing relics of the Buddha or others revered by the Buddhists; a funerary mound to the Buddha's memory
Sufi	Muslim mystic
Sunni	the majority of the followers of Islam and dominant in India; they accept the succession of the first four Caliphs and the principle of consensus in determining the selection of the successors to the Prophet Muhammad
tehsil	a revenue subdivision including several parganas
tehsildar	officer in charge of a tehsil
thakurdwara	a temple dedicated to Vaishnavite worship
tirtha	sacred centre; place of pilgrimage
tush/shahtush	under-fur of the Tibetan antelope used to make extremely fine Kashmiri shawls
ulama	learned individuals (singular form *alim*) specializing in the Quran and Islamic law
Vaishnavite	a follower of the God Vishnu
Vishnu	Hindu God of preservation; among his incarnations are Rama and Krishna
wani	petty retailer who also functioned as a moneylender; also called a bakal

wazarat	the jurisdiction of a wazir (minister)
wazir	minister
yajnaman/jajman	chief sacrificer; patron
zamindar	literally 'landholder', the individual responsible for collecting and passing on to the government its revenue claim; used in Kashmir also to refer to cultivators
zat	subdivision among Muslims denoting birth into a common common clan group or referring to a hereditary occupation
zer-i-niaz	land grants on easy terms of revenue assessment
ziarat	a pilgrimage; a shrine built at the grave site of a Sufi saint
zillallah	the shadow of God; a title used by some Muslim sovereigns

Bibliography

I. Manuscript Sources

1) National Archives of India, New Delhi

(a) Foreign Department Records
(b) Foreign and Political Department Records
(c) Home Department Records
(d) Patriotic Poetry Banned by the Raj

2) Jammu and Kashmir State Archives, Jammu Repository

(a) Old English Records
(b) Political Department Records
(c) General Department Records
(d) His Highness Maharaja Pratap Singh's Private Records

3) India Office Records and Library, London

1. Colonial Government Records

(a) Crown Representative's Records, Political Department, R/1/1
(b) Crown Representative's Residency Records, R/2
(c) Punjab Foreign Proceedings
(d) Punjab Government, Department of Revenue and Agriculture also listed in some years as Agriculture, Revenue and Commerce Department.

2. Private Papers

(a) Mss.Eur.F.157 Bailey Collection
(b) Mss.Eur.G.91 L.B. Bowring's Memoir
(c) Mss.Eur.F.85 Henry Lawrence Collection, Arthur Broome's Letters To and From Sir Henry Lawrence, dated 1846
(d) Mss.Eur.D.974 Hugh Rees James Papers
(e) Mss.Eur.A,129 Journals of Edward Moffat, 1858–77
(f) Mss.Eur.B.369, Vol. 5, Journals of T. Machell, Travels in Hindoostan, The Punjab, Scinde and Kashmir, 1855–56
(g) Mss.Eur.A.129, Journals of John Edward Moffat, 1858–77

(h) Mss.Eur.F.143, Walter Roper Lawrence Collection
(i) Mss.Eur.F.231/26 Lyveden Collection
(j) Mss.Eur.F.86/166 Temple Collection
(k) Mss.Eur.B.133, Ralph Young, Journal of a Trip to Kashmir, 1867

4) British Library, London

(a) B.L. MS 40, 129, Broadfoot Papers
(b) Mss 30, 786, British Library, Elliot Papers, Bahadur Singh, Yadgar-i Bahaduri

II. Printed Sources

1) Official Publications

(a) ASSESSMENT REPORTS

Rai Bahadur Lala Narsing Dass, *Assessment Report of the Sri Pratapsinghpura Tahsil of the Shahr-i-khas District in Kashmir,* 1902.

Pindi Dass, *Assessment Report of the 97 Villages of the Old Nagam Tahsil,* 1904.

Ram Dhan, *Assessment Report of Sri Pratapsinghpura Tahsil, 1920.*

J.L. Kaye, *Assessment Report and Report on Assignments of Land Revenue, Tahsil Uri, District Muzaffarabad,* 1898.

Pandit Man Mohan Nath Koul, *Assessment Report of the Karnah Tahsil of the Mozaffarabad District,* 1901.

Walter Lawrence, *Assessment Report of the Lal Tehsil.*

———, *Assessment Report of the Ullar Vihu Tehsil in Kashmir,* 1891.

Pandit Prem Nath, *Assessment Report of the Muzaffarabad Tahsil of Muzaffarabad District,* 1936.

———, *Assessment Report of the Anantnag Tahsil of the Anantnag District,* 1922.

———, *Assessment Report of the Awantipura Tahsil of the Anantnag District,* 1920.

Pandit Anant Ram, *Assessment Report of the Kulgam Tehsil of Anantnag District,* 1922.

H.L. Rivett, *Assessment Report on the Mian Jagir Villages Situated in Kashmir Proper,* 1897. Also, J.L. Kaye's Preliminary Report on Rivett's report.

———, *Assessment Report of the Muzaffarabad Tahsil of Muzaffarabad District,* 1899.

———, *Assessment Report of the Uri Tahsil of the Muzaffarabad District,* 1898.

Sardar Hari Singh, *Assessment Report of the Jasmergarh Tehsil of the Kathua District of the Jammu Province,* 1924.

Sardar Thakur Singh, *Assessment Report of the Handwara Tahsil of the Northern Wazarat of the Kashmir Valley*, 1922.

Babu R.C. Singha, *Assessment Report of the Baramulla Tahsil*, 1905.

———, *Assessment Report of the Uttarmachipura Tahsil in Kashmir*, 1905.

(b) LAW REPORTS

All India Reporter, selected years
Punjab Law Reporter
The Jammu and Kashmir Law Reports
Jammu and Kashmir High Court Rulings, S. 1979–1991 (AD 1922–1934), Anand Mohan Suri (ed.)
Kashmir Law Journal
Laws of Jammu and Kashmir: Being a Collection of all the Enactments...in Force in Jammu and Kashmir State, 2 vols, Jammu: Ranbir Government Press, 1941.

(c) OTHER OFFICIAL REPORTS

Administration Reports, Jammu and Kashmir, 1911 to 1944/45, IOL, V/10
Ain-i-Dharmarth (Regulation for the Dharmarth Trust), Jammu, Ranbir Press, 1884.

Annual Report of the Archaeological Survey of India, Frontier Circle, for 1908–9.

Diwan Bahadur Amar Nath, *Administration Report of the Jammu and Kashmir State*, 1912–1913.

Beg, Mirza Afzal, *On the Way to Golden Harvests, Agricultural Reforms*, Jammu: Government of Jammu and Kashmir, 1950.

Census of India, (Jammu and Kashmir), Reports for 1901, 1911, 1921 and 1931.

Chatterji, J.C., *The Kashmir Series of Texts and Studies; Being a Prospectus of the Publications of the Archaeological Department of the Jammu and Kashmir State*, Srinagar, 1911.

———, *A Report of the Archaeological and Research Department, Jammu and Kashmir, for the Sambat years 1960–62*, Jammu: Ranbir Prakash Press, 1909.

Dogra, Sant Ram, *Code of Tribal Custom*, 1917.

Gajendragadkar Commission Report, 1953.

Glancy, B.J., *Report of the Commission Appointed Under the Orders of His Highness the Maharaja Bahadur, dated 12th November 1931, to Enquire into Grievances and Complaints*, Jammu: Ranbir Government Press, 1932.

Government of Jammu and Kashmir, *Jagirs, Muafis and Mukarraris*, Srinagar, February 1956.

His Highness' Government, Jammu and Kashmir, *Evidence Recorded in Public by the Srinagar Riots Enquiry Committee,* 1931.

His Highness' Government, Jammu and Kashmir, *Orders on the Recommendations Contained in the Glancy Commission's Report,* in the *Jammu and Kashmir Government Gazette,*18 April 1932.

Jammu and Kashmir State Information Bureau, *Jammu and Kashmir (1947–50): An Account of the Activities of the First Three Years of Sheikh Abdullah's Government,* 1951.

———, *A Report of the Archaeological and Research Department, Jammu and Kashmir, for the Sambat years 1960–62,* Jammu, 1909.

Jammu and Kashmir State Land Reforms Officer, *Land Reforms,* Srinagar, 1952.

Jammu and Kashmir State Ministry of Information and Broadcasting, *Five Years,* New Delhi, 1953.

Kak, R.C., *Memoirs of the Archaeological Survey of Kashmir, No. 1, Antiquities of Marev-Wadwan,* Archaeological Survey of Kashmir, 1924.

Report of the Committee to Define the Term 'State Subject', Jammu, 1928.

Report of the Constitutional Reforms Conference, Jammu, 1932.

Report of the Land Compensation Committee Appointed by the Jammu and Kashmir State Constituent Assembly, 1951–52, Jammu: 1952.

2) Other Printed Sources

Cunningham, Alexander, *Description of the Temples of Kashmir,* 1848.

Memorandum of the Kashmiri Pandits on the Terms of Reference of the Grievances Enquiry Commission Appointed by His Highness the Maharaja, Srinagar 1931.

Memorial Presented by the Sanatan Dharm Youngmen's Association on Behalf of Kashmiri Pandits to His Highness the Maharaja Bahadur of Jammu and Kashmir, dated Srinagar, 24th October 1931, Srinagar: 1931.

Sanatan Dharma Young Men's Association, *Kashmir Hindus and the Recent Disturbances,* Srinagar,1931.

H.H. Maharajah Pratap Singh, *Diary of an Inspection Tour to the Gilgit Road,* Lahore, 1893.

3) Newspapers and Press Reports

The Tribune

Press Cuttings on the Quit Kashmir Movement, Department of Information, Srinagar.

Selections From Native Newspapers Published in the Punjab, series available at the India Office Library and Records, London. L/R/5.

Selections From the Vernacular Newspapers Published in the Punjab, N.W. Provinces, Oudh, and the Central Provinces, series available at the India Office Library and Records, London. L/R/5.

Selections From Vernacular Newspapers Published in the Punjab, series available at the National Archives of India, New Delhi.

III. Unpublished Dissertations and Papers

Khatoon, Zohra, 'Shrines of the Pirs at Jammu', M.Phil. dissertation, University of Jammu, 1981.

Ramusack, Barbara N., 'Exotic Imports or Home-grown Riots: The Muslim Agitations in Kashmir in the Early 1930s', Paper Presented at the Third Punjab Studies Conference, University of Pennsylvania, 7 May 1971.

Zutshi, Chitralekha, 'Community, State, and the Nation: Regional Patriotism and Religious Identities in the Kashmir Valley, *c.* 1880–1953', Ph.D. dissertation, Tufts University, 2000.

IV. Published Books and Articles

A. URDU

Anjuman Nusrat-ul-Islam, *Sir Syed Kashmir, Hazrat Mirwaiz Maulana Rasul Shah Sahib: Bani Anjuman Nusrat-ul-Islam Srinagar Ke Satanven Yomi Vasal Pe Ek Mukhtasar Tawaruf*, Srinagar, not dated.

Fauq, Mohammad-ud-din, *Shabab-e-Kashmir*, Srinagar: Gulshan Publishers, repr. 1993.

———, *Taarikh-e-Kashmir*, Srinagar: Chinar Publishing House, first published 1910, repr. 1992.

Hassan Khuihami, *Tazkirat-e-Auliya-e-Kashmir*, Srinagar: Ghulam Mohammed Noor Mohammed, repr. 1989.

Hussain, Khan Bahadur Sheikh Muhammad Maqbool, *Halat-e-Masjid-e-Jama*, Srinagar: Kashmir Pratab Steam Press, 1916.

Kaul, Har Gopal, *Guldasta-e-Kashmir*, Lahore: Farsi Ayra Press, 1883.

Maqbool, Master Mohammed, *Ner-i-Azm: Sir Syed Kashmir*, Srinagar, not dated.

Saifuddin, Mirza, *Khulastah-ul-Tawarikh*, translation from Persian by Mirza Kamal-ud-din Shaida, Srinagar: Gulshan Publishers, repr. 1984.

Zafar, Sayyadah Ashraf, *Saiyyid Mir Ali Hamadani*, Srinagar: Gulshan Publishers, 1991.

B. ENGLISH

Abdullah, Sheikh, *Flames of the Chinar*, New Delhi: Oxford University Press, 1993.

Aitchison, C.U., *A Collection of Treaties, Engagements and Sunnuds Relating to India and Neighbouring Countries,* vol. 6, Calcutta: Foreign Office Press, 1876.

Akbar, M.J., *The Siege Within,* New York: Viking, 1985.

———, *Kashmir: Behind the Vale,* New Delhi: Viking, 1991.

Alam, Muzaffar, *The Crisis of Empire in Mughal North India: Awadh and the Punjab, 1707–1748,* Delhi: Oxford University Press, 1986.

Ali, Nisar, *Agricultural Development and Income Distribution,* New Delhi: Rima, 1985.

Ali, Shahamat, *The Sikhs and Afghans,* London: John Murray, 1847.

Anand, Mulk Raj, 'The Pictorial Situation in Pahari Painting', *Marg,* 1968, no. 4.

Anderson, Benedict, *Imagined Communities: Reflections on the Origin and Spread of Nationalism,* London: Verso, 1991.

Arbuthnot, James, *A Trip to Kashmir,* Jammu: Vinod Publishers, repr. 1992.

Archer, W.G., *Indian Paintings From the Punjab Hills,* 2 vols., Delhi: Oxford University Press, 1973.

———, *Paintings of the Sikhs,* London: H.M.S.O., 1966.

Aynsley, Mrs. J.C. Murray, *Our Visit to Hindostan, Kashmir and Ladakh,* London: William H. Allen, 1879.

Badehra, Ganeshdas, *Rajdarshini,* Tr. Sukhdev Singh Charak, Jammu: Jay Kay Book House, 1991.

Baden-Powell, B.H., *The Land Systems of British India,* 3 vols., Delhi: Oriental Publishers, repr. 1974.

Bamzai, P.N.K., *Culture and Political History of Kashmir,* 3 vols., New Delhi: M.D. Publications, 1994.

———, *A History of Kashmir,* Delhi: Metropolitan, 1962.

———, *Socio-Economic History of Kashmir, 1846–1925,* New Delhi: Metropolitan, 1987.

Barton, Sir William, *The Princes of India,* New Delhi: Cosmo, repr. 1983.

Bayly, C.A., *Indian Society and the Making of the British Empire,* Cambridge: Cambridge University Press, 1993.

———, *Empire and Information: Intelligence Gathering and Social Communication in India,* Cambridge: Cambridge University Press, 1996.

———, *Origins of Nationality in South Asia,* New Delhi: Oxford University Press, 1998.

———, 'The Pre-history of "Communalism"? Religious Conflict in India, 1700-1860', *Modern Asian Studies,* 19, 2 (1985), 177–203.

Bazaz, Prem Nath, *Daughters of the Vitasta,* New Delhi: Pamposh, 1959.

———, *Inside Kashmir,* Srinagar: The Kashmir Publishing Company, 1941.

————, *The History of the Struggle for Freedom in Kashmir*, Karachi: National Book Foundation, 1976.

Biscoe, C.E. Tyndale, *Kashmir in Sunlight and Shade*, New Delhi: Mittal, first published 1921, repr. 1995.

Bose, Sugata and Jalal, Ayesha, *Modern South Asia: History, Culture, Political Economy*, Delhi: Oxford University Press and London: Routledge, 1988.

Bose, Sugata, *Agrarian Bengal: Economy, Social Structure and Politics, 1919–1947*, Cambridge: Cambridge University Press, 1986

Bose, Sumantra, *The Challenge in Kashmir: Democracy, Self Determination and a Just Peace*, New Delhi and London: Sage and Thousand Oaks, 1997.

Brecher, Michael, *The Struggle for Kashmir*, New York: Oxford University Press, 1953.

Brinckman, Arthur, 'The Wrongs of Cashmere', in S.N. Gadru (ed.), *Kashmir Papers*, Srinagar: Free-Thought Literature, 1973.

Brittlebank, Kate, *Tipu Sultan's Search for Legitimacy: Islam and Kingship in a Hindu Domain*, Delhi: Oxford University Press, 1997.

Bruce, Hon. Mrs. C.G., *Peeps at Many Lands: Kashmir*, London: A&C Black, 1915.

Buhler, George, 'Detailed Report of a Tour in Search of Sanskrit MSS made in Kashmir, Rajputana, and Central India', *Journal of the Bombay Branch of the Royal Asiatic Society of Great Britain and Ireland* (Extra Number), vol. XII, no. 34, 1877.

Cannadine, David, *Aspects of Aristocracy: Grandeur and Decline in Modern Britain*, New Haven and London: Yale University Press, 1994.

————, *The Decline, Revival and Fall of the British Aristocracy*, New Haven and London: Yale University Press, 1990.

————, *Ornamentalism: How the British Saw Their Empire*, Oxford: Oxford University Press, 2001.

Chakrabarti, Dilip K., *A History of Indian Archaeology*, New Delhi: Munshiram Manoharlal, 1988.

Charak, Sukhdev Singh, *Life and Times of Maharaja Ranbir Singh*, Jammu: Jay Kay Book House, 1985.

————, *A Short History of Jammu Raj*, Pathankot and Jammu: Ajaya Prakashan, 1985

Chatterjee, Partha, *Nationalist Thought and the Colonial World: A Derivative Discourse*, Minneapolis: University of Minnesota Press, 1993.

————, *The Nation and Its Fragments: Colonial and Postcolonial Histories*, Princeton: Princeton University Press, 1993.

————, *Texts of Power: Emerging Disciplines in Colonial Bengal*, Minneapolis and London: University of Minnesota Press, 1995.

Cohn, Bernard S., *Colonialism and Its Forms of Knowledge: The British in India*, Princeton: Princeton University Press, 1996.

———, 'Representing Authority in Victorian India', in E. Hobsbawm and T. Ranger (eds), *The Invention of Tradition*, Cambridge: Cambridge University Press, 1989.

Cole, H.H., *Illustrations of Ancient Buildings in Kashmir*, London: W.H. Allen & Co., 1869.

Colley, Linda, *Britons: Forging the Nation, 1707–1837*, New Haven and London: Yale University Press, 1992.

Copland, Ian, 'The Abdullah Factor: Kashmiri Muslims and the Crisis of 1947' in D.A. Low (ed.), *The Political Inheritance of Pakistan*, London: Macmillan, 1991.

———, 'Islam and Political Mobilization in Kashmir, 1931–34' in *Pacific Affairs*, 54, 2 (Summer 1981), 228–59.

———, *The Princes of India in the Endgame of Empire, 1917–1947*, Cambridge: Cambridge University Press, 1997.

Crane, Robert I. (ed.), *Area Handbook on Jammu and Kashmir State*, Chicago: University of Chicago Press, 1956.

Cunningham, J.D., *A History of the Sikhs*, Calcutta: Bangabasi Press, 1904.

Dass, Diwan Jarmani, *Maharaja: Lives and Loves and Intrigues of Indian Princes*, Delhi: Hind Pocket Books, 1970.

Dhar, Somnath, *Tales of Kashmir,* New Delhi: Anmol Publishers, 1992.

Digby, William, *Condemned Unheard: The Government of India and H.H. the Maharaja of Kashmir*, New Delhi: Asian Educational Services, first published 1890, repr. 1994.

Dirks, Nicholas B., *The Hollow Crown: Ethnohistory of an Indian Kingdom*, Ann Arbor: University of Michigan Press, 1996.

Drew, Frederic, *The Jummoo and Kashmir Territories*, Delhi: Oriental Publishers, repr. 1971.

Edwardes, Emma, *Memorials of the Life and Letters of Major-General Sir Herbert B. Edwardes*, 2 vols, London: Kegan, Paul, Trench and Company, 1886.

Edwardes, Herbert Benjamin and Merivale, Herman, *Life of Sir Henry Lawrence*, London: Smith, Elder and Company, 1873.

Fergusson, James, *Archaeology in India With Especial Reference to the Work of Babu Rajendralal Mitra*, New Delhi: K.B. Publications, repr. 1974.

Fisher, Michael H., *Indirect Rule in India: Residents and the Residency System, 1764–1858*, Delhi: Oxford University Press, 1998.

Forster, George, *A Journey From Bengal to England,* 2 vols., Patiala: Punjab Languages Department, first published 1808, repr. 1970.

French, J.C., *Himalayan Art,* Delhi: Neeraj Publishing House, first published 1931, repr. 1983.

Galwan, Ghulam Rassul, *Servant of Sahibs,* London: Simpkin, Marshall, Hamilton, 1923.

Ganguly, Sumit, *The Crisis in Kashmir: Portents of War, Hopes of Peace,* Washington, DC and Cambridge: Woodrow Wilson Centre Press and Cambridge University Press, 1997.

Gauba, Khalid Latif, *His Highness: Or the Pathology of Princes,* Ludhiana: Kalyani Publishers, 1971.

Gellner, Ernest, *Nations and Nationalism,* Ithaca: Cornell University Press, 1992.

Gilmartin, David, *Empire and Islam: Punjab and the Making of Pakistan,* Berkeley: University of California Press, 1988.

Gilmour, David, *Curzon,* London: John Murray, 1994.

Girdlestone, Charles, *Memorandum on Cashmere and Some Adjacent Countries,* Calcutta: Foreign Department Press, 1874.

Goswamy, B.N., 'Pahari Painting: the Family as Basis of Style', *Marg,* 1968, XXI, no. 4, pp. 17–62.

Goswamy, Karuna, *The Glory of the Great Goddess: An Illustrated Manuscript from the Alice Boner Collection in the Museum Rietberg Zurich,* Zurich: Museum Rietberg, 1989.

———, *Kashmiri Painting: Assimilation and Diffusion: Production and Patronage,* New Delhi: Aryan Books International, 1998.

Grierson, G.A., *Linguistic Survey of India,* 11 vols, Delhi: Motilal Banarsidass, 1967–8.

Griffin, Lepel H., *Punjab Chiefs,* Lahore: C.F. Massey, 1890.

———, *Rulers of India: Ranjit Singh,* Oxford: Clarendon Press, 1892.

Hangloo, R.L., *Agrarian System of Kashmir, 1846–1889,* New Delhi: Commonwealth Publishers, 1995.

Hardinge, C., *Viscount Hardinge,* Oxford: Oxford University Press, 1891.

Hardy, Peter, 'The Growth of Authority Over a Conquered Elite: The Early Delhi Sultanate as a Possible Case Study', in J.F. Richards (ed.), *Kingship and Authority in South Asia,* Madison: University of Wisconsin-Madison South Asia Publication Series, no. 3, 1978.

———, *The Muslims of British India,* Cambridge: Cambridge University Press, 1972.

Hervey, Mrs., *The Adventures of a Lady in Tartary, Tibet, China, and Kashmir,* 3 vols., London: Hope & Co., 1853.

Hobsbawm, E.J., *Nations and Nationalism Since 1780,* Cambridge: Cambridge University Press, 1991.

Hodson, George H., (ed.), *Hodson of Hodson's Horses*, 2 vols, London: Kegan, Paul, Trench and Co., 1886.

Honigberger, John Martin, *Thirty Five Years in the East*, London: H. Bailiere, 1852.

Hugel, Baron Charles, *Travels in Kashmir and the Punjab*, London: John Petheram, 1845.

Hussain, Hakim Imtiyaz, *Muslim Laws and Customs*, Srinagar: Srinagar Law Journal Publication, 1989.

Hussain, Syed Tassadaque, *Customary Law and the Indian Constitution*, New Delhi: 1987.

Hutchison, J. and J. Ph. Vogel, *History of the Punjab Hill States*, 2 vols., Simla: Department of Languages and Culture, 1982.

Huttenback, Robert A., 'Gulab Singh and the Creation of the Dogra State of Jammu, Kashmir and Ladakh', *Journal of Asian Studies*, 20 (1961), 477–88.

———, 'Kashmir as an Imperial Factor During the Reign of Gulab Singh', *Journal of Asian History*, 1, (1968), 77–108.

Ince, John, *The Kashmir Handbook*, Calcutta: Wyman Brothers, 1867.

Inden, Ronald, 'Ritual Authority and Cyclic Time in Hindu Kingship', in J.F. Richards (ed.), *Kingship and Authority in South Asia*, Madison: University of Wisconsin-Madison South Asia Publication Series, No. 3, 1978.

Jacquemont, Victor, *Letters From India*, 2 vols., London: Edward Churton, 1834.

Jagmohan, *My Frozen Turbulence in Kashmir*, New Delhi: Allied Publishers, 1991.

Jalal, Ayesha, *Democracy and Authoritarianism in South Asia*, Cambridge: Cambridge University Press, 1995.

———, 'Exploding Communalism: The Politics of Muslim Identity in South Asia' in S. Bose and A. Jalal (eds), *Nationalism, Democracy and Development: State and Politics in India*, Delhi: Oxford University Press, 1997.

———, *Self and Sovereignty: Identity Formation in South Asian Islam Since 1850*, New Delhi: Oxford University Press, 2001.

Jeffrey, Robin (ed.), *People, Princes and Paramount Power*, Delhi: Oxford University Press, 1978.

Johnson, Paul, *The Birth of the Modern: World Society, 1815–1830*, New York: Harper Collins, 1991.

Journals and Diaries of the Assistants to the Agent to the Governor-General, North-West Frontier and Resident at Lahore, 1846–49, Allahabad: Pioneer Press, 1911.

Kalhana, *Rajatarangini,* Tr. M. Aurel Stein, 2 vols, Delhi: Motilal Banarsidass, 1961.

Kaul, Gwash Lal, *Kashmir Then and Now,* Srinagar: Chronicle, 1967.

Khan, G.H., 'Early Socio-Religious Reform Movements in Kashmir', in Mohammad Yasin and A. Qaiyum Rafiqi (eds.), *History of the Freedom Struggle in Jammu and Kashmir,* New Delhi: Light and Life Publishers, 1980.

————, *Freedom Movement in Kashmir, 1931–40,* Delhi: Light and Life Publishers, 1980.

Khan, Muhammad Ishaq, *Experiencing Islam,* New Delhi: Sterling Publishers, 1997

————, *History of Srinagar, 1846–1947, A Study in Socio-Cultural Change,* Srinagar: Aamir Publications, 1978.

————, *Kashmir's Transition to Islam: The Role of Muslim Rishis,* Manohar: New Delhi, 1994.

————, 'The Significance of the Dargah of Hazratbal in the Socio-Religious and Political Life of Kashmiri Muslims' in Christian W. Troll, *Muslim Shrines in India,* Delhi: Oxford University Press, 1992.

Knowles, Rev. J. Hinton, *A Dictionary of Kashmiri Proverbs and Sayings,* New Delhi: Asian Educational Services, first published 1885, repr. 1985.

————, *Kashmiri Folktales,* Srinagar: Gulshan Publishers, repr. 1996.

Korbel, Joseph, *Danger in Kashmir,* Princeton: Princeton University Press, 1954.

Koul, Pandit Anand, *Archaeological Remains of Kashmir,* Srinagar: The Kashmir Bookshop, 1935 (?).

————, *Geography of the Jammu and Kashmir State,* no bibliographic information available.

Lahore Political Diaries, vol. 6, Allahabad: Pioneer Press, 1915.

Lal, Lala Ganeshi, *Siyahat-i-Kashmir,* tr. Vidya Sagar Suri, Chandigarh: Punjab Itihas Prakashan, 1976.

Lamb, Alastair, *Kashmir: A Disputed Legacy, 1846–1990,* Hertingfordbury: Roxford Books, 1991.

Latif, Muhammad, *History of the Punjab,* Calcutta: Central Press, 1891.

Lavan, Spencer, *The Ahmadiyah Movement,* Delhi: Manohar, 1974.

Lawrence, Walter, *Provincial Gazetteers of Jammu and Kashmir,* New Delhi: Rima Publishing House, repr. 1985.

————, *The Valley of Kashmir,* Srinagar: Chinar Publishing House, repr. 1992.

Leach, Linda York, *Mughal and Other Indian Paintings,* 2 vols., London: Scorpion Cavendish, 1995.

Lee-Warner, William, *The Native States of India*, Delhi: Tulsi, repr. 1979.

————, *The Protected Princes of India*, London: Macmillan, 1894.

Lord, John, *The Maharajas*, London: Hutchinson, 1972.

Ludden, David (ed.), *Making India Hindu*, New Delhi: Oxford University Press, 1996.

Losty, Jeremiah P., *The Art of the Book in India*, London: The British Library Reference Division, 1982.

Madan, T.N., *Modern Myths, Locked Minds*, Delhi: Oxford University Press, 1997.

————, 'Religious Ideology and Social Structure: The Hindus and Muslims of Kashmir', in Imtiaz Ahmad (ed.), *Ritual and Religion Among Muslims in India*, New Delhi: Manohar, 1984.

Madhok, Balraj, *Kashmir: Centre of New Alignments*, New Delhi: Deepak, 1963.

Mahjoor, Ghulam Ahmad, *The Best of Mahjoor*, Srinagar: J&K Academy of Art, Culture and Languages, 1989.

Malhotra, Inder, 'The Separatists', *Seminar*, no. 58, 1964.

Menon, Dilip M., *Caste, Nationalism and Communism in South India: Malabar 1900–1948*, Cambridge: Cambridge University Press, 1994.

Metcalf, Thomas R., *Ideologies of the Raj*, Cambridge: Cambridge University Press, 1995.

Napier, W., *The Life and Opinions of General Sir Charles Napier*, 4 vols, London: John   Murray, 1857.

Neve, Arthur, *Thirty Years in Kashmir*, London: Edward Arnold, 1913.

Neve, Ernest F., *Things Seen in Kashmir*, Jammu: Jay Kay Book House, repr. 1993.

Nund Rishi, *Unity in Diversity* (The Poetry of Hazrat Sheikh Nur-ud-din), tr. B.N. Parimoo, Srinagar: J & K Academy of Art, Culture and Languages, 1984.

O'Hanlon, Rosalind, 'Maratha History as Polemic: Low Caste Ideology and Political Debate in Late Nineteenth-Century Western India', *Modern Asian Studies*, 17, 1 (1983), pp. 1–33.

Osborne, The Hon. William G., *The Court and Camp of Runjeet Singh*, Karachi: Oxford University Press, first published 1840, repr. 1973.

Pandit, M. Amin (ed.), *Alamdar-i-Kashmir: Standard-Bearer, Patron-Saint of Kashmir*, Srinagar: Gulshan Publishers, 1997.

Panikkar, K.M., *The Founding of the Kashmir State: A Biography of Maharajah Gulab Singh*, London: George Allen and Unwin, 1930, reprinted 1953.

Pearson, Hesketh, *The Hero of Delhi*, London: Collins, 1939.

Political Diaries of the Agent to the Governor-General, North West Frontier and Resident at Lahore, Allahabad: Pioneer Press, 1909.

Puri, Balraj, *Kashmir Towards Insurgency*, New Delhi: Orient Longman, 1995.

Raina, A.N., *Zinda Kaul*, New Delhi: Sahitya Akademi, 1974.

Ram, Diwan Kirpa, *Gulabnama*, tr. Sukhdev Singh Charak, New Delhi: Light and Life, 1977.

Ramusack, Barbara N., *The Princes of India in the Twilight of Empire*, Columbus: Ohio State University Press, 1978.

Robinson, Francis, *Separatism Among Indian Muslims: The Politics of the United Provinces' Muslims, 1860–1923*, Cambridge: Cambridge University Press, 1974.

Sender, Henny, *The Kashmiri Pandits: A Study of Cultural Choice in North India*, Delhi: Oxford University Press, 1988.

Seth, Mira, *Dogra Wall Paintings in Jammu and Kashmir*, Delhi: Oxford University Press, 1987.

Sever, Adrian, (ed.), *Documents and Speeches of the Indian Princely States*, 2 vols, Delhi: B.R. Publishing Corporation, 1985.

Sharma, D.C., *Documentation on Kashmir*, Jammu: Jay Kay Book House, 1985.

———, *Kashmir Under the Sikhs*, Delhi: Seema Publications, 1983.

Sharma, Shiv Chander, *Antiquities, History, Culture and Shrines of Jammu*, Jammu: Vinod, 1997.

Singh, Bawa Satinder, *The Jammu Fox, A Biography of Maharaja Gulab Singh of Kashmir, 1792–1857*, New Delhi: Heritage Publishers, 1988.

Singh, Chetan, *Region and Empire: Panjab in the Seventeenth Century*, Delhi: Oxford University Press, 1991.

Singh, Karan, *Autobiography, 1931–1967*, Delhi: Oxford India Paperbacks, 1989.

Singh, Tavleen, *Kashmir: A Tragedy of Errors*, New Delhi: Viking, 1995.

Smyth, Major G. Carmichael, *A History of the Reigning Family of Lahore, with Some Account of the Jummoo Rajahs, Their Seik Soldiers and their Sirdars*, Lahore: Government of West Pakistan, repr. 1961.

Stern, Robert W., *The Cat and the Lion: Jaipur State in the British Raj*, Leiden: E.J. Brill, 1988

Stokes, Eric, *The Peasant and the Raj: Studies in Agrarian Society and Peasant Rebellion in Colonial India*, Cambridge: Cambridge University Press, 1980.

Suri, Sohan Lal, *Umdat-ul-Tawarikh*, Daftars III and IV, tr. Vidya Sagar Suri, Delhi: S. Chand, 1961.

Temple, Richard C., *Journals Kept in Hyderabad, Kashmir, Sikkim and Nepal*, 2 vols, London: W.H. Allen & Co., 1887.

Thomas, Raju, (ed.), *Perspectives on Kashmir: The Roots of Conflict in South Asia*, Boulder: Westview, 1992.

Thorp, Robert, *Cashmere Misgovernment*, Calcutta: Wyman Brothers, 1868.

Titley, Norah M., *Miniatures From Persian Manuscripts*, London: British Museum Publications, 1977.

Torrens, Lieut. Col. Henry, *Travels in Ladakh, Tartary and Kashmir*, London: Saunders, Otley and Co., 1862.

Trotter, Lionel James, *Life of Hodson of Hodson's Horses*, London: William Blackwood and Sons, 1901.

Vaid, Satish, *Sheikh Abdullah Then and Now*, Delhi: Maulik Sahitya Prakashan, 1968.

Veer, Peter van der, *Religious Nationalism: Hindus and Muslims in India*, Berkeley: University of California Press, 1994.

Vigne, Godfrey Thomas, *A Personal Narrative of a Visit to Ghuzni, Kabul and Afghanistan*, London: George, Routledge, and Co., 1843.

————, *Travels in Kashmir, Ladak, Iskardo*, 2 vols, New Delhi: Sagar Publications, first published 1842, repr. 1981.

Wakefield, W, *The Happy Valley*, London: Sampson Low, Marston, Searle and Rivington, 1879.

Wangu, Madhu Bazaz, 'Hermeneutics of a Kashmiri Mahatmya', in Jeffrey R. Timm (ed.), *Texts in Context*, Albany: State University of New York Press, 1992.

Wheeler, James Talboys, *The History of the Imperial Assemblage at Delhi*, London: Longmans, Green, Reader & Dyer, 1877.

Wilson, H.H., *The Hindu History of Kashmir*, Calcutta: Susil Gupta, repr. 1960.

Winichakul, Thongchai, *Siam Mapped: A History of the Geo-Body of a Nation*, Honolulu: University of Hawai Press, 1994.

Wink, Andre, *Land and Sovereignty in India: Agrarian Society and Politics under the Eighteenth Century Maratha Swarajya*, Cambridge: Cambridge University Press, 1986.

Younghusband, Francis, *Kashmir,* Srinagar: Gulshan Publishers, first published 1908, repr. 1996.

Zutshi, Chitralekha, *Languages of Belonging: Islam, Regional Identity, and the Making of Kashmir*, Delhi: Permanent Black, 2004.

Zutshi, U.K., *Emergence of Political Awakening in Kashmir*, Delhi: Manohar, 1986.

Index

Abbott, Captain J., 32, 112
  Abbott line, 112
Abdali, Ahmed Shah, 22
Abdullah, Sheikh Mohammed
  agrarian mobilization, 271, 272–3
  attends Muslim Kashmiri
    Conference, 267
  challenging Jama Masjid Mirwaiz
    and Muslim elite, 218, 260,
    268–70
  economic reforms after 1947,
    281–4
  establishes ascendancy at Hazrat
    Bal, 269–70
  establishes broad base of support
    among Muslims, 270–3
  and labour unrest, 271–2
  political mobilization around
    religious shrines, 218–22,
    268–70
  New Kashmir, 282, 289
  and Quit Kashmir movement, 281
  represented as spokesman for
    secular Kashmiriyat, 224–5
  statements against Kashmiri
    Pandits, 273
    tones down, 274
  supported by Ahmediyas, 260,
    263, 267
  supports Hamadani mirwaiz, 238,
    267
Afghan wars, 135, 142
Afghanistan, 11, 21, 25, 142
Afghans, 4, 22, 23, 27, 61, 78,
  103

agrarian reforms after 1947, 281–4
agrarian system of Kashmir
  agrarian indebtedness, 169–73,
    272
  Albion Bannerji on the position of
    the cultivators, 173–4
  bakaya, 172
  begar, 154–6, 173
  chakdari system, 156–9
  dharmarth villages, 155–6
  dustbardari, 173
  fate of lands vacated temporarily
    during the famine, 157, 166
  food control system, 152–3, 271
  lambardars, 164–5, 172
  maharaja as owner of all land,
    149–5
  methods used by Kashmiri Pandits
    to increase land holdings,
    157–60, 166–7
  mirasdars v assamis, 165–7
  moneylenders, 169, 170–1
  Pirzadas and lighter assessments,
    152
  position of Muslim jagirdars,
    162–4
  pressure on land, 171–3
  privileges of Dogra mians, 160–2
  privileges of Kashmiri Pandits,
    148–9, 150–1, 152, 153–5,
    166–8
  Ranbir Singh's settlement of 1880,
    166
  revenue department, 150
  speculators in revenue, 151–2

Hazrat Bal, 53, 103, 209, 238
  ascendancy of Sheikh Abdullah at,
    269–70
  repair of by Nawab of Dacca, 200
Hereditary State Subject, 251–3
Hervey, Mrs
  uses begar, 65
  offers to buy a Kashmiri girl, 66
Hindu religious orders
  control of under Ranbir Singh,
    117, 119
  patronage by kings, 106
  power of *vis-à-vis* political patrons,
    107–9
  territorially overlapping nature of,
    108–9
Hindu Sahayak Sabha, 170, 245–6
Hira Singh, 24, 25
Honigberger, John Martin, 96
Hugel, Baron Charles, 69

Imperial Assemblage
  celebrating Victoria as Empress of
    India, 87
  and construction of 'religious
    princes', 88–90
  and expression of colonial
    sociology, 88–9, 92–3
  freezing relations between princes,
    110
  and marking aftermath of 1857,
    87–8
  and representation of Dogra rulers,
    90–2
incorporation, 45–7
Iqbal, Muhammad, 18, 20, 262
Imam-ud-din, Sheikh, 51, 99
  revolt of, 51, 54
Indian National Congress,
  and Kashmir after independence,
    289
  and Kashmiri Pandits, 280–1

  and Sheikh Abdullah, 280
insurgency in Kashmir, 286, 290
Iraqi, Shams-ud-din, 39
izad boli system, 152

Jacquemont, Victor, 3, 23
jagirdars, 23*n*16
  abolition of jagirs in 1948, 282
  Bamba jagirdars, 163–4
  Dogra mians in Kashmir, 160–2
  loyal to the Dogras in 1931, 260
  position of after Lawrence's
    settlement, 168–9
  pre-colonial rights of, 47
  profusion of in Kashmir, 61
  Sikh-appointed in Jammu and
    Kashmir, 29–30, 33, 50–1,
    53–5
Jama Masjid, Srinagar
  Gulab Singh's treatment of, 102
  Pratap Singh contributes to repairs
    of, 209
  Ranbir Singh funds repairs of, 201
  repair by Muslims as assertion of
    community leadership, 209–10
  See also mosques
James, Hugh Rees, 59, 64, 102, 103,
    104
Jammu and Kashmir Liberation
    Front, 286
Jammu and Kashmir state
  British traders demand right to
    buy property in, 133–4
  founding of, 4, 15, 18, 25–34
  juridical definition of subjects,
    176–8
  links with the Punjab
    intermeshing political
      networks, 28–35, 98–9, 261
    intermeshing religious
      networks, 31–2, 76–7, 94,
      99, 111

reorganization of archaeological
department, 196–7
separation of subjects along lines
of religion, 175–8, 226
speaks in the name of state
subjects, 140
Sri Pratap Jammu and Kashmir
Laws (Consolidation) Act, 177
warns against anti-British sedition
in the state, 226
princely India
British construction of as traditional and religious India,
82–6, 87, 88–90, 93
British lobby demanding withdrawal of protection for, 131,
133–4
British requirement for greater
representativeness, 129–32,
226
and colonial India, 10, 11–14
double-allegiance of subjects of,
56–7
forms of address to be used, 110
and Indian nationalism, 132,
226–7
indirect rule, 13–14
and the obligations of rulers, 16,
226, 295
perceptions of in the aftermath of
the 1857 rebellion, 82, 132
ranked precedence among rulers
in, 110–11
subjects of territorially demarcated, 112–13
territorial delimitation of sovereignty in, 111–13
as traditional rulers, 15
war and removing the right to
wage it, 110, 292
Prinsep, James, 185
proclamation of 1858, 10, 192, 226

and religion in British India, 82,
84
and religion in princely India, 82,
83–7, 93, 114
Pudukkottai, 11*n*23, 12, 13, 90*n*27
Pulhalun, shrine at, 52
Punjab
Kashmiri immigrants in, 41, 157,
216
links with Jammu region
festivals, 76
linguistic, 76
painting, 73–6, 77–8
religious, 76–7
newspapers of
criticism of Kashmiri Muslim
leadership, 239–40
criticism of Kashmir state,
141–2, 174, 200–1,
213–16, 261
political parties in the Punjab
involved with Kashmir
Kashmir Committee, 260, 262
Muslim Kashmiri Conference,
215–16, 255, 262
See also Ahmediyas *and* Ahrars,
See also Jammu and Kashmir
state *under* links with
Punjab
See also Sikh kingdom
Punjab hill states, 68
British efforts to separate from the
Sikhs, 67, 68–73, 78–9
cultural continuum within, 73–6
Punnu, Wazir, 151, 161, 163, 242
Purmandal, 76, 94
claimed as Dogra preserve, 109
competing patrons at, 105–7
Dogras cut off Sikh patronage at,
109
Gulab Singh's patronage at, 106
particular sacredness of, 107